Profiting from the World's Economic Crisis

Profiting from the World's Economic Crisis

Finding Investment Opportunities by Tracking Global Market Trends

Bud Conrad

WILEY

John Wiley & Sons, Inc.

Published by John Wiley & Sons, Inc., Hoboken, New Jersey.
Published simultaneously in Canada.

For general information on our other products and services or for technical support, please contact our Customer Care Department within the United States at (800) 762-2974, outside the United States at (317) 572-3993 or fax (317) 572-4002.

Wiley also publishes its books in a variety of electronic formats. Some content that appears in print may not be available in electronic books. For more information about Wiley products, visit our Web site at www.wiley.com.

Library of Congress Cataloging-in-Publication Data:

Conrad, Bud.
  Profiting from the world's economic crisis : finding investment opportunities by tracking global market trends / Bud Conrad.
        p.   cm.
    Includes index.
    ISBN 978-0-470-46035-1 (cloth)
  1. Financial crises–United States.   2. United States–Economic conditions–21st century.
3. United States–Economic policy–2009-   I. Title.
    HB3722.C686 2010
    330.973–dc22

                                                                        2009051050

Printed in the United States of America

10   9   8   7   6   5   4   3   2

To my children Darlene Friedley and Daniel Conrad.

Contents

Acknowledgments

F irst and foremost, I wish to thank my friend and mentor, David
Galland, who encouraged me to develop my ideas in publishing
newsletters for Casey Research. He has honored me by calling
our work a partnership. While I tend to think in arcane economic
and engineering channels, he is able to bring material to a much more
understandable level for the public. The chapters of this book are more
valuable as they are made more understandable by his contribution in
forming the final written page. I encourage readers to check out our
offerings and extensive ongoing free material at www.caseyresearch.com.

I also want to thank Doug Casey who liked my charts at one of the
big conferences and brought me into his then expanding organization
of newsletters and financial services. Olivier Garret, CEO, gave me
encouragement when needed. I can't say enough for the hardworking
professional and support people around the globe of our organization.

I want to especially thank many readers of my articles and people
who have heard my talks and debated the scenarios to bolster the important conclusion about where our system is going. Ruth Mills, crash-
integrated these many interconnected and supportive analyses into this
cohesive explanation of our economic system, and without her support

the book wouldn't have come together. I was helped greatly in the early stages of editing by Richard Scheck, and one complicated chapter by Doug Hornig who also provided encouragement.

I also want to thank family and friends including my daughter Darlene Friedley who hasn't seen much of me for a year, and my son Daniel Conrad who took time from his challenging responsibilities at Google to mentor me and build the basic structures of the book with a white-board. Also, thanks to my significant other who encouraged me regularly, Phoebe Newlove. Bruce Janigian gave me early advice and Bob Dickey encouraged me as he has for most of my lifetime.

Introduction

The global financial collapse will affect all your investments, and you need protection.

That, in a nutshell, is what this book is about. This book will help you understand the forces behind the global financial collapse, how our government leaders helped create this new reality, and how you can comprehend the current market forces so you can make better investment decisions beyond the recommendations of traditional Wall Street advisors.

This book explains the big-picture forces that will drive paper currencies to ruin. The train is already on the track, steaming toward a bridge that is out, and the U.S. dollar—which has been the bedrock of the world's currencies—is the train that will crash into the canyon of no confidence in our lifetime.

My goal in this book is to explain how this catastrophe will unfold, as it destroys wealth around the world for those who believe their governments when they say that the situation is "at a bottom" or "showing green shoots of recovery." *Believing such comforting lies will lead to destruction of your personal wealth.*

In contrast, understanding and protecting yourself with reasonable measures will lead you to financial survival. Being ahead of the curve, and armed with the insights of this book, can lead to big personal profits. Here's why you need to read this book:

- To understand why inflation is coming!
- To learn how to identify the best investment sectors—and why this is more important than simply picking individual stocks.
- To understand how we got here, to see where we are going, and to invest wisely.
- To see how a system model, that emphasizes the cycles caused by feedback, gives better predictions than steady-state equilibrium models used by economists.
- To learn how to review charts and know where data can be found for predicting the big trends and making investments.
- To understand how the historical experiences of the Great Depression, Japan after 1990, and Germany confirm the parallels and differences to today's crisis.
- And to get my reasons for investment recommendations for today: gold, oil, higher interest rates, energy, food.

■ ■ ■

As an economist with both an MBA from Harvard and a bachelor's degree in electrical engineering from Yale, and as a successful investor for 25 years, I've written this book by drawing on all aspects of my experience, education, and work. That includes my work as Chief Economist for Casey Research, which has produced valuable research and more than a dozen newsletters for investors for 30 years (including *The Casey Report, Casey's Energy Opportunities, Casey's Gold and Resource Report*, and *Casey's International Speculator*—see www.caseyresearch.com for details on these and to avail yourself of the free information there including my favorite, the *Daily Dispatch*).

I emphasize *data* to confirm the realities, and I am specific about what to look at, so you can accurately measure what is driving our economy. I've used my investment experience to develop models that you can use to predict specific measures to make successful investments. Because I have such a different approach, I was able to predict the current crisis back in 2006. And at the beginning of 2009 I predicted that gold would go to $1,150; that crude oil, then trading at $45, would go to $80; and that the 10-year Treasury would go from 2.2 percent to 4 percent—all of which happened—along with a number of other economic measures like the budget and trade deficit.

■   ■   ■

The key to the future is really quite simple: Paper money is a CON-fidence game that will end with your cash being worth only the paper it is printed on. This is the book's fundamental thesis: that the paper dollar will collapse in my lifetime, eventually requiring the issuance of a new currency. The financial collapse we are now experiencing is far from over. It will become the largest financial crisis the United States has ever faced. Because the United States is at the center of the world economy, this crisis is affecting all nations. The imbalances are so big that there is no way to return to stability through normal means.

But a simpleminded, long-term projection is not adequate in the short term, because the swings up and down are big, and they get in the way of a straight slide to the bottom. It can be seen that governments, central banks, sophisticated investors, and psychology all take their turn at affecting the shorter-term ups and downs. All these need to be dealt with, and I offer a framework to interpret the world events as we ride this roller coaster of short-term fluctuations toward the longer-term destruction of the dollar itself.

The paper money systems of the world are not based on any promise of convertibility to any tangible commodity, like gold. Yet they have been used to define the value of everything we buy and sell. Without the limitation of redemption (in gold), governments can create wealth for themselves by paying new money to their special-interest supporters. When they do so, they decrease the wealth of others. Printing money does not change the value of the planet and the things in it. But the *claims* on those things change, and those who control the bigger share of those resources do change.

Even casual observers know that something is up, and their discom-fort is justified. They know they aren't getting anything from the bailout of big banks by government, and they wonder who is benefiting. My analysis shows how large the bailouts have become and how this will affect all of us in the years ahead. I anticipated the huge government bailouts because I understood that the recession from overleveraged mortgages would be very damaging, and I could see how politicians would be predisposed to appease their powerful financial supporters from Wall Street.

However, this book doesn't focus *only* on the simple direction of complete paper money collapse. I provide both the big picture of what's happening to our economy, *and* I drill down to the details of what is important and how to analyze particular sectors. Most people think of investments only in terms of stocks and bonds, but this is short-sighted; you also need to consider and weigh the benefits of investing in commodities, real estate, currencies, and interest rates. Obviously, there are a lot of relationships, but when you see how the big forces of government spending, dollar collapse, and inflation all interconnect, then the related collection of investment recommendations becomes a clear picture that is simple to understand.

To help you understand the interrelations of the financial landscape, and to explain just how extremely stressed the economic positions of the world have become, I've created hundreds of charts and graphs to prove my points throughout the book. I created these charts to show you what is *really* going on in the financial markets around the world, and how that will affect your future. I provide a model for whether the stock market is overvalued or undervalued, and I give criteria for selecting gold mining stocks. I provide a model for trading grains that is unique.

My approach is different from the traditional theoretical economic models because I explain why markets go to such cyclic extremes. My explanation confirms what traders already understand: Markets are dynamic, follow trends, form bubbles, and collapse. The point is that markets are normally continually moving through cycles just like a pendulum, and are not in equilibrium, which is the basis of most economic models. Economists allow for shocks as if they were some surprise, but they miss the point that the economic pendulum is normally swinging back and forth and is not static. This difference is at the heart of understanding how the system works. I've used my electrical engineering training to look at the relationships and include the feedback of self-reinforcing systems that move in vicious and virtuous cycles.

Making the big decisions is what this book is about. It can help you identify the correct investments to have in your portfolio. Many investors just want to know what the best stock to buy today is, and Wall Street pundits give out that advice daily. But stock picking is really a small part of overall investing success. The bigger returns are made from being in the right market at the right time. I like being specific, so Figure I-1 shows just how wildly successful an investor could have been making the right decisions only once for each of the past four decades:

- Suppose you had invested in one ounce of gold, costing only $35, in 1970.
- Then, suppose you had used your profits to buy Japanese stocks during the 1980s.
- Then, suppose you had invested those proceeds in the NASDAQ during the 1990s.
- Finally, suppose you had used those proceeds to invest again in gold.

As you can see from Figure I.1, if you had made the above decisions during the last four decades, that single initial investment of $35 would have grown to more than $166,000. That was with no leverage and only four trades. Certainly, no one actually met that goal, because Figure I-1 was developed in hindsight. For comparison, if you had invested the $35 in the S&P 500, you would only have $457. You would have done a

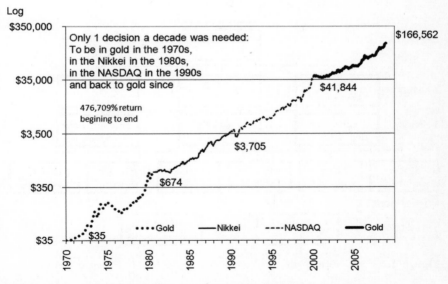

Figure I.1   How to Turn $35 into $166,000+, from 1970 to 2009

little better hanging on to gold, which is now more than $1,000. The point is to emphasize the value of knowing the right sectors for focus for the times presented. And that is my goal for this book: to help you understand these big-picture cycles, so *you* can capture those profits.

As the value of paper currencies decrease over time, *your investments need to get in front of that inevitability* by avoiding long-term holdings denominated in currencies, like bonds or annuities. Instead, I recommend that you hold physical assets like agricultural products, energy, or gold. (Alternatively, for example, you can profit by being in debt in dollars that you pay back after they have lost purchasing power.) Why, when, and how are the subjects of the rest of this book.

How This Book Is Organized

Figure I-2 is a roadmap of the interconnected chapters of this book. I've divided the book into five parts as listed on the left side. Chapters are identified in boxes with the number following the name.

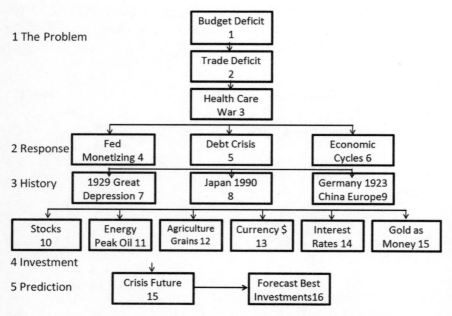

Figure I.2   Structure of the Book *Profiting from the World's Economic Crisis*

The arrows give the logical flow of the intellectual thread through the chapters. For example: the budget deficits lead to the trade deficit, and health care and war expand government expenditures to the point of requiring big responses from the Federal Reserve. You may be tempted to jump to the concluding chapters to see how to invest, but that shortcut would miss understanding how the foundational forces and historical perspectives lead to those conclusions. Instead of reading the last chapter as if just eating one meal, I recommend learning how the system works to provides guidance for investment decisions, so you will be able to feed yourself for a lifetime.

Part One takes a fresh look at the major problems that led to the current global financial crisis in three chapters on our federal budget deficit; the trade deficit; and the costs of health care, Social Security, and the military. Projections confirm how intractable the deficits will become.

Part Two describes how the Federal Reserve is responding and how it will have to accommodate even more because of the expanding problems laid out in Part One in order to keep the government running. Chapters 4 to 6 look at how the Fed is, essentially, just printing money; how this crisis is fundamentally a debt crisis; and how all aspects of our economy interrelate with each other in a systematic view.

Part Three provides historical perspective for confirmation of the interpretation of where our system may be headed. Chapters 7 to 9 search for lessons we can learn from parallel events. First, we'll look at how the current financial crisis really compares to the Great Depression. Then we'll look at what our current crisis has in common with how Japan's bubble burst in 1990. Finally, we'll look at the extreme currency collapse, primarily in Germany, but also in other countries.

Part Four covers investment opportunities, in stocks, energy, food, the dollar itself, interest rates, and gold. You can read these chapters in any sequence, but I'll give you a preview of my short-term preference: it's gold.

Finally, Part Five provides two chapters that use the ideas of the book to provide a forecast of financial predictions for the next decade, and predict how I think the investments will perform in 2010.

■   ■   ■

The journey of this book is as much a "Show You How" as it is an "Explanation of Why." Join with me as I navigate through the dangerous waters of complex economic systems to bring to you a clear vision of how the ship will sail over these rough seas. If we have the bearing right, we will know how to follow the inevitable, to protect ourselves, and to reach the safe harbor of exceptional profits.

The key recognition that I hope this book can bring to both casual observers and more intensely curious analytical investigators is that the overall economic system is in such serious crisis that individuals (that means *you*) must *actively pursue protection from what will be the demise of the dollar* as we have known it for the last 200 years.

The conclusion of this book identifies how the major forces that are driving financial collapse can be used to recommend future investments. You will see how the ongoing structural shifts that are already in place will wipe out the purchasing power of trillions of paper dollars from unsuspecting participants who do not understand the dollar collapse that is coming in the decades ahead.

Read and grow rich!

Part One

ECONOMIC FORCES

P arts One and Two of this book lay the foundation that will be used for making investment recommendations in Part Four. The budget deficit, the trade deficit, and the underlying problems of our health care, military costs, and interest costs, all combine to build the serious imbalances that will drive our future.

All of these items are so interrelated that it is almost difficult to put one before the other, but I start (in Chapter 1) with what I believe is the most fundamental—namely the federal government budget deficit. It is the budget deficits that will affect the dollar the most. Chapter 2, on the trade deficit, explains how interrelated foreign investment is to our government debt. Chapter 3 describes health care, Social Security, and the military, which are the biggest items that are causing the problems of the budget deficit. Because they are so insurmountable, you see how extremely problematic is the hand that has been dealt our leaders, and you will be able to conclude where the argument about inflation versus deflation has to go.

This is pretty heavy reading, but it will be worth your effort, because it will position your outlook for decades to come.

Chapter 1

The Budget Deficit
Drives the Growth
of All Debt

The goal of this book is to provide you with the tools to invest wisely and protect yourself against the mismanagement of our monetary systems by our government. Our money is produced by our government, so understanding how government deficits are the root of money creation puts you a step ahead in understanding where the value of our money is likely to go. This chapter explains how our government spends money, collects the taxes, and more important, makes up the difference by creating new money when big deficits arise.

To put this in perspective, I begin by looking at the largest aggregate of the world quantity of money as identified by the International Monetary Fund (IMF), called Total Reserves plus Gold at Market, and I compare that against industrial production in Figure 1.1. It shows how

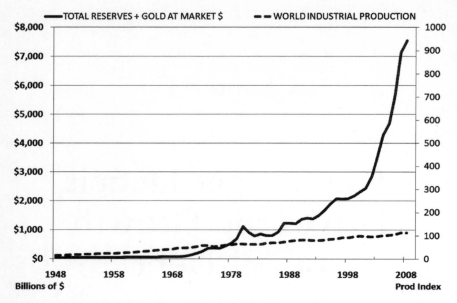

Figure 1.1   Money Has Grown Much More Than Industrial Production

the creation of paper money by all the central banks in the world has grown much more rapidly than industrial production. What that means in the long run is that the paper money will decrease in its purchasing power as the governments produce more and more paper.

Figure 1.2 shows the result of dividing the quantity of money by the amount of industrial production. If money were growing at the same rate as production, the ratio would be a straight line across the graph. It's no surprise that governments have been printing much more money than we have been producing goods, but it is informative to notice that the increase in quantity of paper money in the world dramatically increased after the United States went off the gold standard and stopped trading gold for dollars after 1971.

There was a time when money was based on a measure of gold or silver, but that is not so today. Today, money is debt. For confirmation of that, consider that the dollars held in your wallet are called Federal Reserve Notes and are officially a liability on the Fed's balance sheet.

Those Federal Reserve Notes were issued against the assets of the Fed, which until recently has mostly comprised federal government

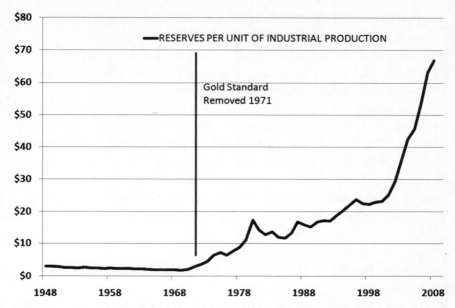

Figure 1.2 Money (World Reserves) Divided by Production Is 20 Times 1970 Level

debt—namely Treasuries and an historical artifact of a pittance of gold. Of late, much of those Treasuries have been replaced by toxic paper purchased as part of the broader bailout.

In this chapter, my purpose is to pick apart the components of U.S. government debt in such a way that by the time you're finished reading, you'll be in the top 1 percent of Americans in understanding the depth of the crisis we are now facing. I start with the debt issued by the central government because this is the central driver for creating new money. Government debt is called Treasuries, or more specifically T-bills, Treasury Notes, and Treasury Bonds, depending on the length of the term, and it is basically the result of government borrowing when it spends more than it collects in taxes.

The increase in government debt allows the increase in household and business spending, which leads to the growth in personal and international debt. It is the continual growth of our debt that has gotten us to the place of overleverage, which will now unwind with many difficulties.

It is correct to think of government debt as the mother of all debt because it starts the whole bubble process by first creating the money and liquidity that allows the private sector to spend and get into more debt. Ultimately, it is the combined debt of the government that weighs on the intrinsic value of the currency it is denominated in.

If you find this concept a bit confusing, don't worry: These days, most people, including economists, do not have a clear idea what money really is. The lack of any clear understanding of what a dollar is (or therefore what it's worth) stacks the deck in favor of those in control of the currency. Simply, breaking away from a gold standard (or any tangible link for that matter) set the table for the world's biggest confidence game—a game that is growing bolder with each passing day.

The Budget Reflects the State of the Nation

Every year, the president and Congress go through an elaborate budget process to decide how much the government will spend and tax. The Congressional Budget Office (CBO) analyzes the president's proposal and gives its own estimate of its financial impact. Figure 1.3 shows the CBO's long-term estimates for the ratio of government debt to the size of the economy. The government's own projections show a clear trend for huge government budget deficits and ever-increasing levels of outstanding debt.

This projection into the future reflects the "alternative fiscal scenario" representing what is likely to occur if today's fiscal policies continue. This projection is based on a reasonable set of assumptions and does not include any of the many big proposals now being floated, including universal medical care and "cap-and-trade" (i.e., the U.S. government's proposal to control pollution by requiring CO_2 polluters to put a limit on their emissions—to "cap" them—in exchange for rights that they can trade in the open market).

Figure 1.4 takes a closer look at the actual deficit and how fast it has been growing, and this chart should raise alarms all by itself. As of November 2009, the difference between tax receipts and government outlays for the last 12 months was $1.5 trillion. That is approaching four times the largest previous budget deficit.

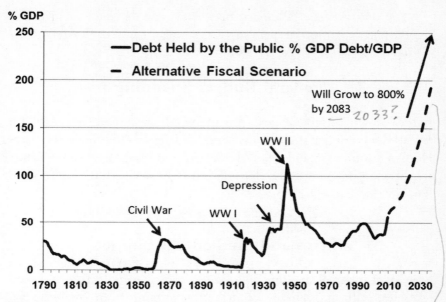

Figure 1.3   The U.S. Government Debt Will Explode over the Next Two
Decades to 800% of GDP
SOURCE: Congressional Budget Office: The Long-Term Budget Outlook, June 2009.

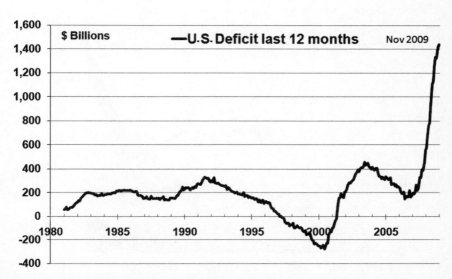

Figure 1.4   The Actual U.S. Deficit Is at a Record $1.5 Trillion
SOURCE: U.S. Treasury.

The deficit is the difference between spending outlays and tax receipts. The expansion of spending is the bigger cause of the deficit.

Federal Budget Spending

A breakdown of federal government spending, shown in Figure 1.5, reveals the two biggest sectors as national defense and human resources. Human resources includes Social Security and Medicare, both of which are growing dramatically. Defense has also grown with the invasions of Iraq and Afghanistan.

Taxes and the Federal Budget

Individual income taxes are the biggest source of federal government revenues, with another big contribution coming from Medicare and

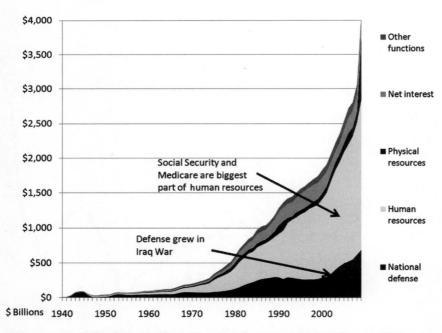

Figure 1.5   Federal Budget Spending Reaches Toward $4 Trillion in 2009
SOURCE: Midsession Review OMB, August 2009.

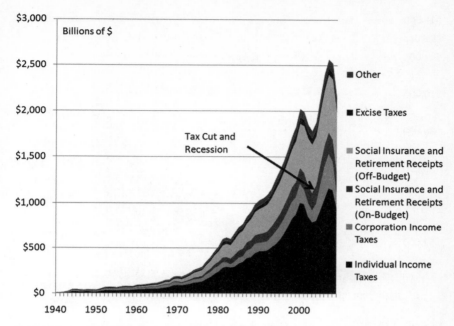

Figure 1.6   Tax Receipts Reached Only $2.1 Trillion
SOURCE: Midsession Review OMB, August 2009.

Social Security-related taxes. Importantly, total tax revenues of $2.2 trillion fall well short of the government's almost $4 trillion annual budget, as shown in Figure 1.6.

For the federal government to spend more than it taxes, it has to borrow the difference. The mechanics are that the Treasury sells interest-bearing T-bills, notes, and bonds. The buyers of those Treasury instruments are in effect lending the government the money needed for current spending priorities, in exchange for a yield to be paid over time.

Federal Budget Borrowing

Figure 1.7 describes who is lending money to the U.S. government so that it can continue its large-spending programs, which are bigger than the taxes. If we understand who are the sources of the money, we can better understand whether the government can continue these huge

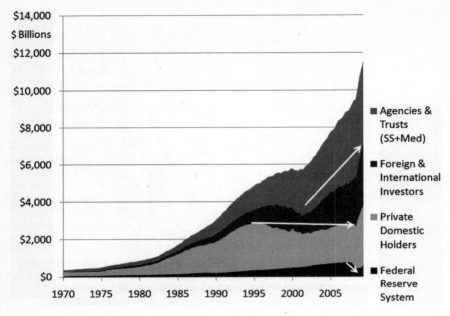

Figure 1.7   Buyers of U.S. Government Debt: Agencies and Trusts, Foreigners, Private Domestic, Fed

deficits if some of these parties can't step up to the plate, as they have in the past.

Let's take a closer look at each group shown in Figure 1.7.

- **Private Domestic Buyers:** The American public are major purchasers of Treasuries. During World War II, it was considered patriotic to buy government bonds to support the war effort. Today, these purchases are driven more by risk aversion and the desire to earn a "safe" yield.
- **Foreign and International Investors:** In the 1990s, a new dynamic emerged, as foreign and international investors became a major new purchasing force for U.S. government debt. As a result, increases in government spending were no longer reliant on U.S. households making the decision to set aside savings in order to buy Treasuries. As you can see in Figure 1.5 on federal government spending, when the government was offered cheap money in seeming endless quantities—money that originated from a

The Budget Deficit Drives the Growth of All Debt   11

consumption-mad U.S. public and recycled through the foreign suppliers back to the Treasury—it began spending with both hands.

- **The Federal Reserve System:** The Fed is another regular buyer of U.S. government debt. Although this is traditionally small in comparison to the other sources of funding, the Fed's Treasury purchases are disproportionately important because those purchases expand the nation's money supply. It is notable that the Fed was a seller of Treasuries in 2008, a result of essentially swapping its "good" Treasuries for hundreds of billions of dollars worth of suspect mortgage-backed and other asset-backed paper from troubled financial institutions.

- **Agencies and Trusts:** Finally, Figure 1.7 shows how agencies and trusts are a large component of government debt, although this debt is materially different in that it reflects debt owed to the government itself. This category arose based on the government's contention that a reserve should be accumulated to cover the Social Security and Medicare obligations assumed for the large group of retiring baby boomers.

Agencies and Trusts Explained

To meet this demographic challenge, the necessary accounting entities were established and regulations put into place to collect the funds to build these reserves. These reserves are considered obligations of the government, owed to the government, to be tapped as necessary to provide the considerable—and eventually overwhelming—entitlements due under Social Security and Medicare.

The problem is that the funds supposedly being set aside for retirees are not there! Sure, the trust funds are there, but the money is already spent on a wide variety of programs, from defense to paying interest on the government's many debts. I repeat: *There is no money in them.* At this point, the accounting entities hold nothing more than nonmarketable securities that are correctly viewed as Treasury bills that can't be sold to anybody. The money collected for Social Security and other programs is put in the trust funds where the surplus after paying retirees' current benefits is used to buy the government debt. That is the portion of Figure 1.7 identified as Agencies and Trusts. The Social Security Trust surplus decreases the amount of the deficit and the amount borrowed from the public.

Ahead of the onslaught of the retirement payouts, these trusts have built up funds in excess of their immediate spending requirements. That will change as the large wave of baby boomers reach retirement and begin to draw down these accounts in earnest—at which point the government will find itself faced with yet another huge demand on funds it doesn't have.

The Total Public Debt of the government is $12.5 trillion. Not including these Trust Funds leaves the amount of Federal Debt Held by the Public at about $7.5 trillion. When the government runs a deficit of $1.5 trillion, that is added to the Debt Held by the public. If the Trust Funds grow, that is added to the Total Public debt.

How Will the Deficits Be Funded?

It's clearly important to understand how the future deficits will be funded. Having just examined the primary buyers of the Treasury instruments, I can now attempt to project which of these buyers are able and likely to step up their purchases in order to provide the fuel for the government's planned ramp-up in deficit spending.

The President's Office of Management and Budget (OMB) has provided an estimate of the size of federal government debt out to 2013 (see Figure 1.8). Let's take a look at each of the four components of this chart:

- **U.S. Private Domestic Holders:** In my analysis, I assume that U.S. private domestic holders can probably increase their holdings moderately now that households are consuming less and saving more, and financial institutions have money to invest in Treasury paper.
- **Foreign and International Investors:** Important foreign holders, notably the Chinese, Japanese, Russians, and Indians (among others), have openly announced their decision to cut back on further purchases and their existing holdings of U.S. government debt. Further, the source of funds previously allocated to their purchases—trade surpluses—have fallen sharply with the recession. As a consequence,

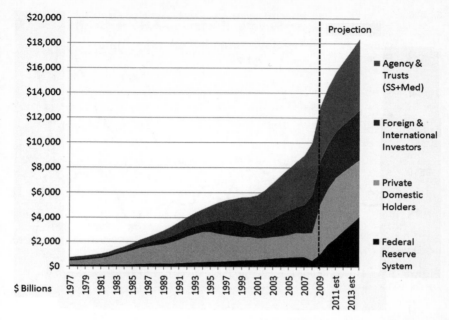

Figure 1.8 How the Total Federal Government Debt Will Grow with the Help of the Fed
Source: Office of Management Budget and author's estimate of Fed portion.

going forward, foreign buying is unlikely to increase, and it will likely shrink.

- **Agency and Trusts:** These are really not a part of the equation at this point, but they reflect programs on "auto-pilot" and are quickly headed to the point where they will negatively impact the deficits, rather than helping to alleviate them.
- **The Federal Reserve:** Adding this all together (and I am being conservative in my assumptions), there are simply not enough buyers to cover the accelerating federal deficits. That leaves the lender of last resort—the Federal Reserve—as the only remaining candidate to satisfy the government's massive funding needs. There is no viable alternative. The likely effect of that massive new money creation is reflected in projection to the right of the dashed line in Figure 1.8.

The federal government is not the only borrower in our credit markets. Typically, households and businesses (which make up the private

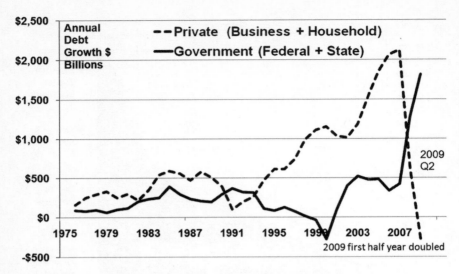

Figure 1.9 Government Borrowing Takes Over from Private Borrowing
SOURCE: Fed Reserve Z.1.

sector) borrow more than the government. But in this serious recession, borrowing by the private sector has collapsed. The largest part of private borrowing was for mortgages for housing, and we all know the many reasons for the collapse of mortgage lending. Businesses have also cut their credit demands. In a sense, this is fortunate for the federal government: As the private sector stopped borrowing from the credit markets, the federal government is able to borrow more than ever before and still able to do so at modest rates because the other demands for credit dropped so dramatically. Part of the reason that the federal deficit has been able to expand is that the private sector borrowing has collapsed in the credit crisis, as shown in Figure 1.9.

History Puts the Credit Crisis in Perspective

Using a log scale, the huge changes at the higher levels of spending and taxing are less pronounced and seem more possible, as shown in Figure 1.10. The spikes for the World Wars spending were huge. Those wars had immediate causes and a specific ending. The financial drain did not linger.

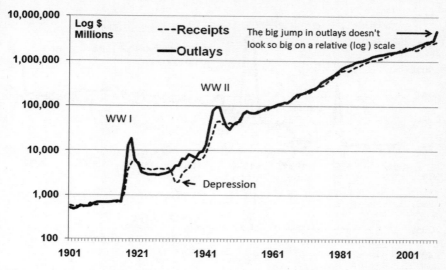

Figure 1.10   How Federal Government Spending and Taxing Increased during the Last Century

In this big picture, it is not so obvious that the receipts (taxes) dropped to half during the Depression, from around $4 billion to $2 billion. We are experiencing a tax receipt drop of 15 percent in 2009, but the government is not projecting anything like what happened during the Depression.

Dividing the measures by GDP gives a relative base to see just how big a $2 trillion budget deficit is in relation to the size of the economy (see Figure 1.11).

The accumulated government deficit as a ratio to GDP jumped during the World Wars and is climbing again very rapidly. Currently, the outstanding cumulative total deficit is a mind-numbing $12.5 trillion.

Historical Projections Have Underestimated Deficits

As unpleasant as it is to look just over the horizon at the unsupportable deficits, if history is any guide, then the level of unpleasantness is probably

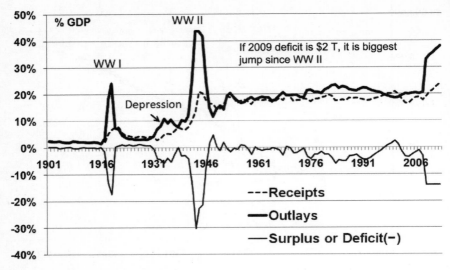

Figure 1.11 Federal Outlays and the Deficit Jumped in World Wars—Just Like They're Doing Now

significantly understated. Supporting that point, see Figure 1.12, which shows historical deficit projections.

Figure 1.12 shows the historical projections for U.S. surpluses/deficits, year by year, starting in 2001. For example, the highest line in Figure 1.12 shows the estimate calculated in 2001 for future-year surpluses. As you can see, the forecast expected only increasing surpluses from 2001 through 2011. Stating the obvious, that projection was wildly off the mark—as were the longer-term projections developed in every subsequent year, through 2008. And in 2009, the deficit of $1.4 trillion is a scale of deficit not remotely contemplated as recently as the 2008 projection.

With this dismal historical record, I'm extremely skeptical about the 2010 forecasts that have deficits rebounding significantly in 2011 and beyond, if for no other reason than that, absent some unforeseeable event, it's irrational to assume that the government's budgetary imbalances will improve as dramatically as indicated by those improving deficits. Instead, it is far more likely that the economy will remain under stress for some years to come, at the same time that new programs are implemented that *increase*, not decrease, government spending.

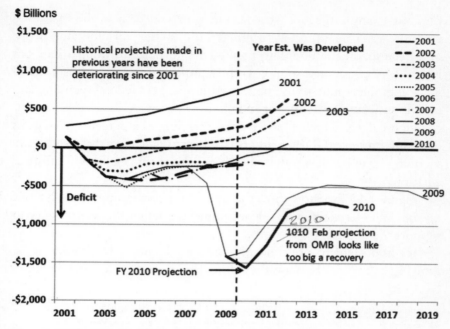

Figure 1.12   U.S. Deficit Projections Became Worse Each Year
Source: CBO, OMB.

One possible savings could be a reduction in direct stimulus spending. But looking closely at the $787 billion stimulus program passed in 2009, you can see that most of it will actually be spent in 2010 rather than in 2009. The health care programs being debated are estimated to cost a trillion dollars over the coming decade. Renewable energy, education, and new bailout programs are likely. And if interest rates jump, as I very much expect they will, the government's already massive interest costs will also jump.

My conclusion is that the actual deficits will be considerably worse than projected.

The Components of Government Spending

At the beginning of this chapter, I presented a chart prepared by the Congressional Budget Office (CBO) showing the long-term projections for federal spending, out to the year 2030 (refer back to Figure 1.3).

Of course, any projection that far out is certain to miss the mark and therefore can't be expected to reflect how things will ultimately work out. Even so, the methodology used by the purportedly nonpartisan staff is generally considered sound, so their projections can serve as a useful starting point to understanding the components of federal spending and the intransigent nature of that spending.

Figure 1.13, which shows federal spending as a percentage of gross domestic product (GDP), is important because it shows that health care spending grows at levels that absorb too much of our overall effort as a nation.

Figure 1.13 also shows how the second-biggest component—interest on the debt—is affected by the accumulating deficit that is necessary to support the medical projections.

It's important to note that the lines on Figure 1.13 should *not* be growing over time, because they show the percentage of spending as a

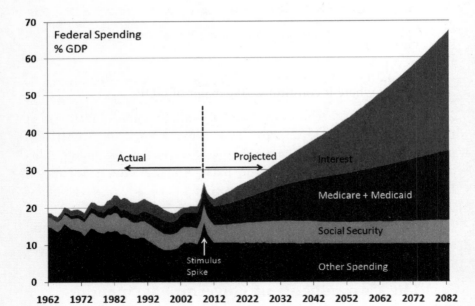

Figure 1.13   Health Care Spending and Interest on Debt Are Increasing to Levels that Our Government Can't Support
SOURCE: Congressional Budget Office, The Long-Term Budget Outlook, June 2009 Alternative Fiscal Scenario.

fraction of the output of the country. If things were stable, all these lines should be *flat,* not increasing.

As an aside, I expect the GDP to grow more slowly than the CBO anticipates, the result being that this ratio of expense to GDP will look even less favorable.

In the longer term, the interest rate is assumed to be around 5 percent. With government deficits so large and projected to get larger, that interest rate could easily grow to 10 percent, which would mean that the current projection is far too optimistic.

In time, as credit eventually unfreezes, a resurgence in private sector borrowing will only add to the pressure for higher rates. If confidence is lost in the dollar, interest rates will rise to compensate for loss in purchasing power of the currency.

The problem with higher interest rates is the compounding effect, where interest has to be paid on funds previously borrowed to pay the interest on prior borrowing. It creates a self-destructive spiral. In fact, the scenario we are now looking at is analogous to that which historically has resulted in runaway inflation of the sort experienced in many Latin American countries over the last 40 years.

The long-term chart shown in Figure 1.13 contains the central message: There is absolutely no way government spending can increase to the point where it constitutes 70 percent of GDP.

In other words, the current trajectory just can't happen. Something very important will break well before we get there. Figure 1.13 gives me confidence in saying that government will likely be limited in its expansion by a collapsing dollar, and that many government expenditures will be less than estimated because they will be based on depreciating dollars. Furthermore, the pathway of debt and deficit will be changed by the inflation that decreases the value of outstanding debt.

Government Is Taking over More and More of Our Economy

Although many Americans (including myself) are growing tired of America's never-ending bailouts, it is important to brace yourself because there are a lot more on the way. The following sections describe a few of the bailouts we will be seeing that will add to the government problems and that haven't gotten much media coverage.

State Government Bailouts

State budget troubles are worsening. States have already begun drawing down reserves, and the remaining reserves are not sufficient to weather a significant economic downturn. Also, many states have no reserves and never fully recovered from the fiscal crisis in the early part of the 2000s.

The vast majority of states cannot run a deficit or borrow to cover their operating expenditures. As a result, states must close budget shortfalls by either drawing on reserves, cutting expenditures, or raising taxes. These budget cuts often are more severe in the second year of a state fiscal crisis, after reserves have been largely depleted. The federal government will eventually be forced to step in and offer states some form of assistance to prevent economic collapses and humanitarian disasters. This means another bailout.

Unemployment Bailout

State-funded trusts, which pay unemployment benefits, are running out of money. The federal government has increased these funding problems through its repeated extensions of unemployment benefits, with the total run of the benefits now being extended to 99 weeks in states with over 8 percent unemployment. Because it is likely there will be more layoffs, shortfalls in unemployment funding are going to come faster and be bigger than most anyone expects. In response to these shortfalls, Congress will loan the states whatever is necessary to keep unemployment benefits coming, even if they have to print every last dollar. After propping up financial institutions and indirectly paying their executives billions of dollars, they now have (politically speaking) no choice.

The Pension Benefit Guaranty Corporation (PBGC) Bailout

PBGC is an agency established by Congress to insure participants in defined-benefit pension plans against losing their pension in the case of their employer going under. Nearly 44 million Americans in more than 29,000 private-sector plans are protected by PBGC, and some 1.3 million workers are already covered by plans that have been taken over by the agency. Although the PBGC is financed from insurance premiums collected from companies and the assets it assumes from failed pension plans, it is widely presumed that the federal government would bail out PBGC if it became unable to meet its obligations for retirees.

There are several reasons to expect that PBGC might need such a bailout:

1. PBGC is underfunded by $22 billion to September 2009.
2. PBGC underfunding by sponsors with distress criteria totaled $168 billion in 2009, up from $47 billion in 2008.
3. The economic downturn and financial market meltdown will likely cause PBGC to take over many private pension plans, and most of these will be severely underfunded.
4. The agency's board decided to move a large share of the portfolio out of safe assets (such as Treasury bonds) and into riskier assets (such as stocks).

So depending on how underfunded the pension plans it takes over next are, and how badly its investment portfolio does, it is possible the PBGC will require a federal bailout.

Housing Bailouts

Because a recovery from our downward spiral is unlikely until the housing markets stabilize, there is a good possibility that we will see another, bigger federal housing bailout as Congress continues to try to jump-start the economy. Most commentators misunderstand the true moral hazard of bailouts. Although bailouts might have an adverse effect on the future actions of individuals and businesses by encouraging risk taking, the real problem is their effects on future actions of the government. Specifically, each bailout makes it harder to say "no" to the next bailout. This pressure to fund future bailouts is made far worse if those receiving bailout money are truly undeserving. After all, if the government is going to give $45 billion to Citigroup (one of the banks responsible for our current mess) and insure $306 billion of its riskiest assets, then how can it say "no" to bailing out the state of California (for example) or South Carolina?

This "me, too" phenomenon will get much worse after the treasury market collapses, and the Fed starts monetizing the treasuries that were sold to fund the current bailouts. If the Fed printed money to bail out the banks, why shouldn't it print *more* money to fund unemployment benefits? Politically speaking, you can't bail out the irresponsible and then let the responsible sink, which means Congress isn't going to be saying "no" to a lot of the bailout requests. Unfortunately, these bailouts will become increasingly meaningless because, when you bail out everyone, you bail out no one, as you destroy your currency.

The experiment now being conducted couldn't have been done when dollars were redeemable for gold, because there would be a collar on the expansion of debt.

The current spending to bail out the financial problems is much bigger than what was done in the Depression, and the consequences look to be a terrible drain on the rest of the economy that has to foot the bill. A relatively small group of failing banks is receiving immense sums.

The dollar can't weather this big an assault, and the foreigners that own too much U.S. government debt (that now pays essentially zero interest) are not going to like how things evolve from here. This looks like a disaster in the making, and I don't say that lightly. Monetary meltdowns have occurred too many times, in too many countries, to discount that possibility here in the United States.

How Government Debt Compares to Inflation in Other Countries

A primary reason to spend time understanding the government's massive debt, is that it can lead us to a better understanding of how big the inflation might result from the Fed's large-scale monetization of that debt.

I took data from a study of previous financial crises by Laeven and Valencia and selected those that became currency crises. Figure 1.14 compares the outstanding debt of those countries to their inflation at the inception of their crisis.

The variability is huge, but the current Debt-to-GDP of the United States puts our country right in the middle of this group of countries: around 50 percent and growing. (I'm using debt held by the public rather than total public debt to be consistent with the rest of the study. The difference is described previously in this chapter.) The United States has

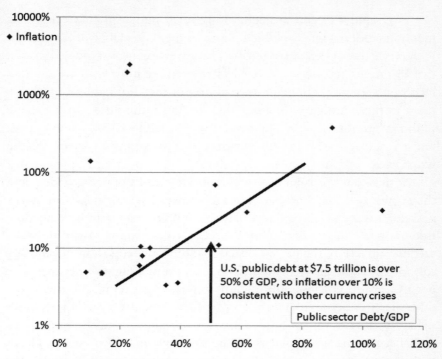

Figure 1.14   The Federal Debt/GDP Level Suggests Inflation Could Be
Much Higher
SOURCE: Laeven and Valencia (2008) IMF Study.

many strengths not enjoyed by many of the crisis countries, most notably
in the worldwide acceptance of the dollar as a basis for other currencies.
But that particular advantage could become a double-edged sword if
the U.S. dollar were to collapse and lose its international standing. Even
so, the dots of the potential inflation that might follow the kind of
deficit we have incurred suggest that a much higher rate, perhaps above
10 percent, would not be unusual at some distant future.

Conclusion

The purpose of this chapter has been to confirm the huge and growing
federal government budget deficits, deficits that appear set to persist and
to worsen until the point where the system breaks.

The rapid rise and projected long-term budget deficit cannot be met by traditional buyers, which increases the importance of the Federal Reserve as the lender of last resort. The government and the Fed protest that this monetization won't occur, but I can see no way to avoid it—at least not without a complete turnaround in the very nature of government in this country, with a redefining of both the scale and the scope of the institution. That is a best case I will be happy to see come to pass, but it remains unlikely at this writing, and so we must prepare for the worst case.

At this point, broader measures of money have stopped growing, and the economy is flat. There are fewer borrowers, as households and business don't want to take on new debt and lending standards have become more restrictive as wary banks remain risk averse. In this environment of credit contraction, the price of assets that rely on credit (housing and autos, for example) are declining. As the economy's sluggish performance persists, profits collapse, jobs disappear, and wages remain stagnant. Industrial commodities that were overhyped by speculators and index funds fell at the start of the collapse. Thus, for the short term, there is serious global economic slowdown as bad debts are wound down and this leads to deflation. But the deficits have planted seeds of future inflation that will be difficult to manage.

What is money? Money in these United States is an abstraction, but it is an abstraction based on debt. And with steep increases in debt now in the cards, the dilutive effect on the purchasing power of the underlying currency is a certainty.

The conclusion is that the federal government is spending far more than we can afford, and the best projection from the government itself says that this deficit will continue to extremes that will hurt our currency. Even without all the details presented here, it should be obvious that government officials and their close buddies the bankers all benefit when the government creates new money for themselves, and that the taxpayer and outsiders are left with the bill. The incentives are lined up: Who wants to vote for a congressman who raises taxes? For those in power, there is everything to be gained by spending more, and little incentive to return to balanced budgets. So the system is fundamentally flawed in such a way that it is unlikely to be repaired until another serious crisis forces some action.

As the government has created more debt, it also creates more money for spending, and some of that spending has spilled over into buying foreign goods. Our trade deficit accumulates and becomes our country's debt to the world. The next chapter explains how big our international debt has become and how that foreign debt has been recycled back to support our government domestic debt. It is important to see how these are all related and driving toward the same conclusion: monetary difficulties ahead.

Chapter 2

The Trade Deficit and U.S. Dependency on Foreign Investments

A rising largely from a huge trade deficit, the United States depends on the world for its growth and investment capital. This huge trade deficit constitutes a dangerous situation for the value of the dollar because foreigners now hold $11 trillion of investments that are not under the direct control of our monetary authorities. If they decide to cash them, these countries and individuals would create havoc by causing the value of the dollar to fall. Surprisingly, the system has continued for decades, to the benefit of both the United States and our trading partners.

In this chapter, I show how large these trade flows have become and how they affect our markets. I also identify the sources for data that you can use to track the changes in these trade flows to see when investment opportunities arise. I conclude with the expected direction of events from these big-picture forces.

The United States Is the Largest Debtor

No country has ever amassed this large of a trade deficit. U.S trade deficits arise from buying foreign goods in greater amounts than foreigners buy of our products. We now buy $2 billion more foreign goods and services than we sell every day! The yearly total was $700 billion. The two biggest sources were importing energy (oil) and manufactured goods. We depend on imports for two-thirds of our oil. The United States uses a quarter of the oil produced in the world while we constitute 5 percent of the population. We are in even worse shape in measuring our oil reserves because we hold only 2 percent of world total. The need for imports of oil will be with us for many years. And because the cost of labor in Asia is only 10 percent of our own, even a big shift in currency valuation would have little effect on their competitive advantage. Therefore, our trade deficit will be with us for a long time.

Manufacturing in the United States became uncompetitive when Asia set up its factories to provide low-cost products to the world. U.S. companies aided in the hollowing out of our manufacturing by actively seeking foreign producers, while investing in and setting up factories off shore. Today, almost all clothing, electronics, and popular consumer items are made by foreign labor. One industry after another has moved to offshoring production, which has led to the collapse of manufacturing jobs across our nation.

This competition, often referred to as globalization, is behind the collapse of the Big Three automakers. Congress' pathetic attempts to bail out this once-prominent industry are mired in impossible wage and benefit expectations that mean bailouts are only wasting money in the rat hole of an unworkable business model.

The contrast between the trade deficit of the United States and all the nations of the Earth is obvious in Figure 2.1.

The danger in trade deficits comes not just from an individual year's shortfall but from the *accumulation* of the annual deficits. The result for the United States is that we owe foreigners $7 trillion, and we're adding more than a half trillion each year, as shown in Figure 2.2.

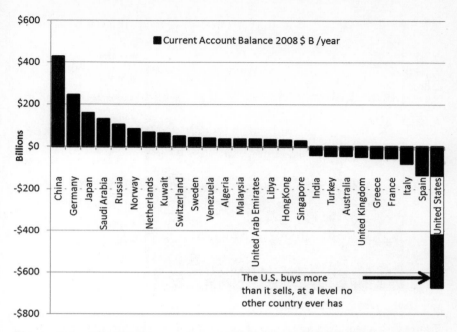

Figure 2.1   The U.S. Current Account Deficit is the World's Biggest
Source: CIA Factbook.

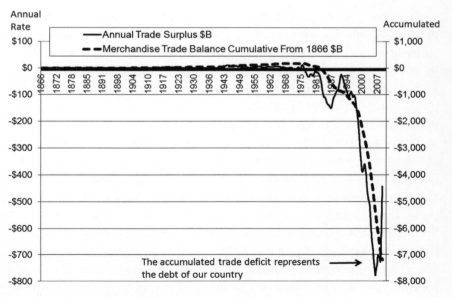

Figure 2.2   U.S. Trade Balance Accumulated to $7 Trillion

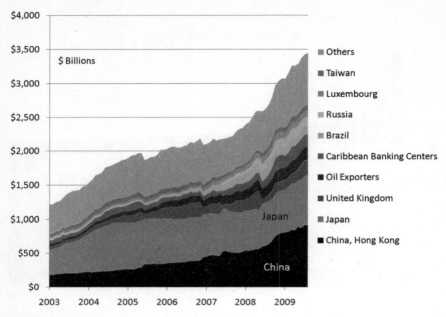

Figure 2.3   Our Trading Partners Hold Half Our Government Debt
Source: U.S. Treasury TIC.

Figure 2.3 shows the biggest holders of U.S. Treasuries to give an indication of the countries that have a stronger world competitive position and whose currencies might appreciate against the dollar. The holdings by foreigners of U.S. Treasuries has grown to the amazing number of $3.5 trillion. It is essentially the band of Treasuries identified in Figure 1.7 as Foreign and International Investors. From a purely investment point of view, such large holdings, particularly by China and Japan, could be thought of as risky for them. It is even more risky for us, as they could change their minds about being relatively passive investors, even threatening positions in the political arena. These large holdings have come about from their selling so many goods to us. The surprising thing about these Treasury holdings is how the total has continued to grow for as long as it has. It is pretty clear that with half our government debt held by foreigners, it becomes important that we accommodate them in developing our own monetary policy. To this end, previous Secretary Henry Paulson traveled many times to China, and one of Secretary Geithner's first trips was also there.

Here's how Shen Jianguang, economist at one of China's largest investment banks, the China International Capital Corp., sees our precarious situation: "The U.S. Treasury Secretary is trying to convince other countries, including China and Japan, to buy its government bonds. This is the first time a developed country needs help from developing countries to ride out its crisis."* For the United States to depend on China for its financial security is a surprising turn of events from just a few decades ago when so many in Asia were still in poverty. The implications of these big imbalances will affect our politics and relations in the decades ahead.

The Connections between the Trade Deficit and the U.S. Economy

The trade deficit is not only an isolated economic measure, but something that is intimately connected to the rest of the economy, most notably the budget deficit. Figure 2.4 shows the government deficit and the trade deficit as feeding on each other.

When the federal government spends more than it taxes, the budget deficit puts more money in the hands of the public than it would have from just the earnings from wages and profits. The public is now set up to spend more, and part of that spending is on imported goods. The shelves of Wal-Mart are lined with competitively priced goods from

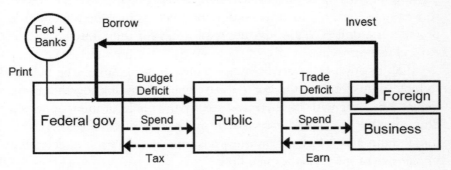

Figure 2.4   The Budget Deficit Gives the Public the Money for the Trade Deficit

*Bloomberg, November 3, 2008: www.bloomberg.com/apps/news?pid=20601087&sid=akUo9OCJA 3PI&refer=home.

China. When Chinese manufacturers are paid in dollars, they take them to the Chinese central bank, exchange them for Chinese yuan, and pay their workers and suppliers. The Chinese authorities then reinvest their dollars in the United States in safe Treasuries issued by the U.S. government. The foreigners are recycling the trade surplus to support the U.S. government in its big deficits.

The trade deficit is just the start of an interconnected series of events that feeds back to the United States. To see the full impact, we have to look at the first step—sending money to foreigners in massive quantities. What foreigners do with their big stashes of dollars affects us. Their investment decisions for the big accumulating balances will affect the value of the dollar.

So far, a surprisingly positive feedback loop of mutually supportive actions has been set up. Foreigners have taken the dollars and reinvested them in the debt of the United States. We have a huge government budget deficit that needs to borrow great amounts of money to pay for government programs. Because foreigners have a big supply of investment funds, they have been investing them back into our government deficit, keeping taxes low, while we funded two wars. Homeowners have been borrowing big amounts against their houses, and with the big supply of foreign investment, that was easy to do.

The supportive relationship is that foreigners have been buying our Treasuries and mortgage securities, which continues to keep funding the growing debt of the United States. Figure 2.4 shows this interrelationship in more detail. The most important aspect is that the trade deficit provides the dollars as a ready supply of funds for the United States to expand its borrowing.

If all that is a bit overwhelming to absorb, it just might be helpful to look more closely at the various components that link together using Figure 2.5. Bear with me here and follow the circle of interconnected flows around the central arrows that link all the items together. Figures 2.6 through 2.12 confirm these relationships, showing in detail the similar size of the related capital flows.

Let's take a closer look at how the various links of consumer spending were supported by the trade deficit and foreigners reinvesting in the United States. The importance is to see the many interrelated parts and to realize how important all of them are in defining our most recent bubble. The easiest way to describe the links is to think of how they

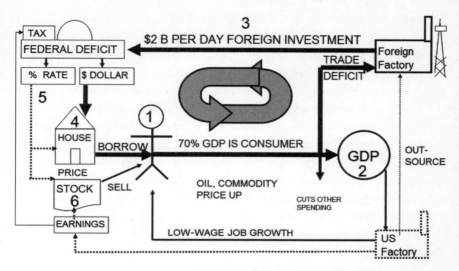

Figure 2.5   U.S. Consumer Supports the U.S. and World Economy by Borrowing

supported each other up to 2007. The explanation for Figure 2.5 follows the numbers around the loop:

1. Consumer spending amounts to about 70 percent of what is added together to become our GDP. Other components are the government, business investment, and trade.
2. The GDP is about $14 trillion a year. Consumers have enjoyed easy access to credit from borrowing against their homes. They were able to maintain and expand their lifestyles by borrowing, which constitutes living on credit. They have been buying imported goods such as Toyotas and flat-panel TVs, building the $700 billion of trade deficit annually.
3. Foreigners have bought Treasuries and mortgage debt at the same rate of about $2 billion per day.
4. The ready availability of funds provided a base for mortgage borrowing and kept rates on borrowing low.
5. Foreign investment also keeps the dollar itself funded as the demand for dollar-denominated investment is kept high. Because rates are kept low, borrowing is affordable, and that keeps the demand for homes high, which was inflating housing prices. This led to Home Equity Lines of Credit being extended, bringing more credit, which

led homeowners to spend even more. It was a positive feedback loop that supported itself because as more foreign investment supported housing, government deficits, and the dollar; consumers were able to purchase more foreign goods.

6. Another supporting link comes from low interest rates, which caused stocks to rise. The returns demanded by stock market investors become less when banks and bonds pay less interest, so the competitive returns on stocks can be lower, pushing their price (i.e., the P/E multiple) higher. As rates fall, companies can afford to borrow to expand; as their cost of borrowing drops, this cuts operating costs and boosts profits. A rising stock market makes the consumer feel wealthy and more confident about spending on those TV screens.

The result is a positive spinning cycle where the economy appears strong and consumer confidence runs high.

This loop came to a crashing halt in 2007. I had anticipated that foreigners would become wary of holding so many dollars and would slow their investments. But it was instead the bloated-housing borrowers who found themselves under water, unable to meet payments once their low teaser mortgage rates reset at higher levels. That led to defaulting, which started the big chain that has shaken the foundations of our financial structure. Figures 2.6 and 2.7 document the close relationship of the measures identified around the loop. Figure 2.6 shows how foreign investment into the United States follows along with the trade deficit.

The very close relationship confirms the loop described in Figure 2.5. Foreign holdings of a country's debt are often thought of as a potentially dangerous situation. But in this case, because foreigners have turned around and continued to increase their purchases of our government debt, they have facilitated our government's big budget deficits. As long as foreigners continue to buy our government debt, it can be thought of as a hidden support. There is no guarantee that the government deficit will be purchased by foreigners. If foreigners weren't buying those investments, households would need to set aside savings to provide the funds.

Figure 2.7 also confirms the similar relationship between the size of the federal deficit and the amount of Treasuries bought by foreigners. The similar shape of the curves is obvious, and the most important conclusion is that from 1996 through 2006, almost all the new government

Figure 2.6   Trade Deficit and Foreign Investment Move Together

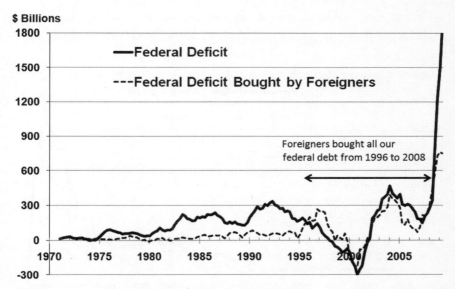

Figure 2.7   The Entire Federal Deficit Was Purchased by Foreigners from 1996 to 2008

SOURCE: Federal Reserve.

debt issued by the U.S. federal government was bought by foreigners. It meant that U.S. households did not have to save to fund the U.S. deficits; foreigners did the heavy lifting for us, keeping rates low and the economy bubbling and spending.

The Connection between Home Mortgages and the Trade Deficit

When you connect all the pieces together, you can see that much of the funding for the housing bubble was supported by foreign investment. Figure 2.8 shows the rise in mortgage borrowing corresponding to the rise in the trade deficit. It is safe to say the foreigners funded our housing bubble. This relationship is obvious in the circular diagram, but the relationship is not usually tracked by economists. Both grew during the years of the housing bubble, but just recently dropped, with the drop in new mortgages being more severe. Because mortgage borrowing is slowing, it is a given that consumer spending will be slowing as we continue the worldwide recession. Because GDP is fed by consumers, I had no trouble in predicting the economy would be slowing; and

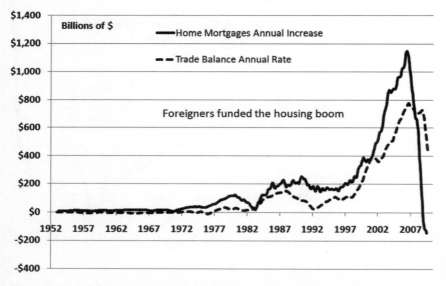

Figure 2.8 The Correlation between Mortgage Borrowing and the Trade Deficit

because consumers buy from abroad, exporters are finding they have overcapacity for the world market for their goods. In other words, we are a connected planet (via globalization), and the actions of these key measures have generated worldwide recession.

Figure 2.8 also confirms the feedback loop of Figure 2.5. This would be just a surprising coincidence if you didn't understand how all these items around the loop work together. I don't think homebuyers knew that their foreign goods purchases were indirectly funding their home mortgages.

Consumers have been spending and not saving. The biggest reason for low saving has been the growth in borrowing, especially against houses. The problem for the U.S. economy is that savings is one of the pools of money to supply the debt markets. Because foreigners have funded our borrowing, we have not needed household savings. If foreigners slow their investment, there will be a serious credit shortage. Conceivably, consumers could become a source of funds for this debt, but to do so their spending would have to slow. Now that the credit crisis has caused consumers to slow their spending and borrowing, they are starting to save more. Saving means less spending, and that means slowing economic growth as seen in Figure 2.9. Going forward, the

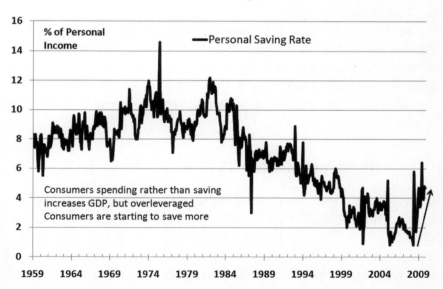

Figure 2.9   How U.S. Consumer Saving Has Decreased Since 1959: U.S. Consumers Spend All They Earn

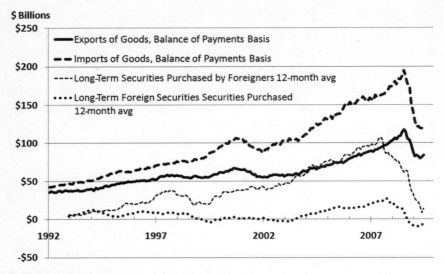

Figure 2.10   Both U.S. Trade and Investment in the United States Have Dropped in Crisis

tapped-out consumer is in no position to take on the big and growing government debt. Taken together, the U.S. economy is likely to slow for a long time as the debt bubble unwinds, with foreigners in control of a big chunk of our debt.

In the current crisis, the amount of trade has been falling for both exports and imports. Also, the crossborder investments in long-term securities have dropped in both directions. As evident in Figure 2.10, these measures are confirming a bigger slowing of economic activity internationally than has been recorded in previous normal business cycle slow periods.

Implications of a Falling Trade Deficit

We're entering into a new era of the world economy as trade has collapsed. The U.S. trade deficit is falling, meaning we are not importing as much. That comes from our slowing economy and from the lower price of oil. It's notable that the trade deficit has dropped from a rate of $750 billion to $400 billion. Figure 2.11 shows the investment into the United States and the trade balance, with both declining.

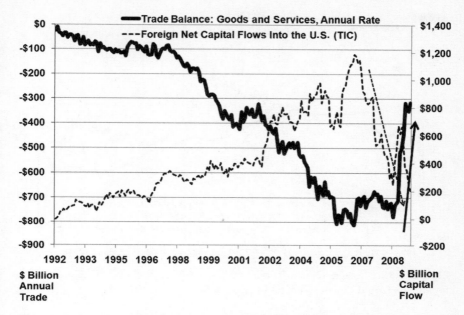

Figure 2.11   U.S. Trade Balance Declines with Foreign Investment Decline
SOURCE: Treasury, TIC Federal Reserve.

A smaller foreign trade surplus means foreigners have fewer dollars available to reinvest in the United States. Foreigners accumulate dollars for investing in the United States from the sale of goods to us. Given the record budget deficits that need to be financed, falling foreign investment couldn't come at a worse time: It indicates significant pressure on interest rates, because if they were not buying our debt, we would have to raise rates to attract more buyers.

Among the consequences is that U.S. corporations and citizens will increasingly be called on to fund the U.S. government deficit. That means consumers will be spending less, and it also means that our economy will not be growing.

Trade Deficits and Government Budget Deficits

For years, the trade deficit has been bigger than the budget deficit, providing foreigners with a cushion of dollars with which they could

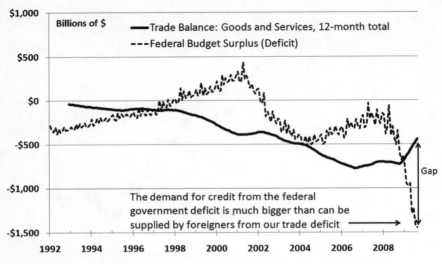

Figure 2.12   Federal Deficit Remained Smaller Than the Trade Deficit so Foreigners Could Finance Federal Budget Deficit, until 2009

then reinvest in U.S. government Treasuries, thereby supporting the U.S. government deficit.

In Figure 2.12 (which may take a bit of looking at before you understand it), you can see that the trade deficit (solid line) is now falling well short of providing the funds necessary to cover the budget deficit (dashed line), and a large gap has opened between the two. This is a sea change in terms of providing coverage for the government's spending. Simply, the skyrocketing federal government budget deficit cannot be accommodated by foreigners.

This means other sources for government borrowing will have to be developed. Enticing additional purchasers of Treasuries will require raising rates.

The Effects of the Trade Deficit

The trade deficit is usually described as manageable because foreigners are reinvesting with us. But the danger is enhanced because of the structural dislocation from outsourcing and the reduction of our productive capacity. As U.S. factories are closed in favor of cheap foreign labor, U.S.

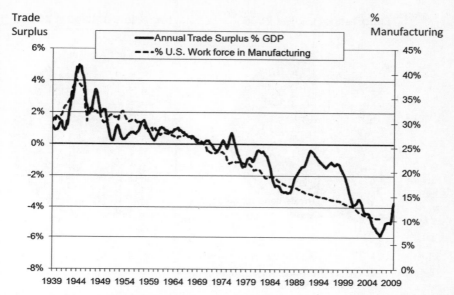

Figure 2.13 How U.S. Manufacturing Jobs Were Lost as the U.S. Imported More Goods, 1939–2004

manufacturing jobs are lost. Figure 2.13 shows that this is a long-term trend that started after World War II.

Trade expansion has been supported by multinational corporations and government programs like NAFTA and the World Trade Organization over many years. Chinese workers earn only a few dollars a day, whereas American workers expect $20 an hour. Although Washington may impose a few trade barriers to curry political favor, the cost differences are so large that traditional manufacturing jobs are never going to return to U.S. shores. It is unlikely that the employment situation will improve very fast in the years ahead. My key point is that all these pieces are interrelated. For example, if the trade deficits were eliminated by edict, that might give new job opportunities to U.S. workers; but that would also dry up a huge source of credit for funding the government deficits. It could mean higher interest rates for borrowers.

Our interconnected world is complex, which is why Figure 2.5 helps illustrate the interrelationships.

Another consequence of our borrowing so much abroad is that we are affecting the availability of international capital. Figure 2.14 shows

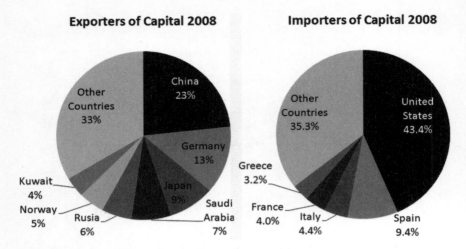

Figure 2.14   The United States Imports More Capital Than Any Other Country with China the Biggest Supplier
SOURCE: Bank of International Settlements.

that the United States consumes 43 percent of the international capital. In 2008 and 2009, the big suppliers of world capital were the big Asian exporters led by China and Japan, and also the oil exporters.

If foreigners became reluctant to invest in the United States, there would be serious problems of less capital to keep interest rates low and to support the dollar.

In the first half of the last century, the United States had a trade surplus. Over time, however, competitors moved onto the world stage, and we have been buying more and more, so that the accumulated surplus has gone away, and we now owe a debt to the world. Figure 2.15 sums up the trade flows since 1866: It shows that as a ratio of GDP, the United States has gone from being a lender to being the biggest debtor to the world. The negative position is an obligation to foreigners, and a potential problem for the dollar.

As the United States has been borrowing to finance its foreign purchases, foreigners have been acting like a financing arm by loaning us the money to buy their goods. This cycling of debt appears to be a wonderful balancing act, and as long as it keeps going, why should we worry? Of course, there is no such thing as a free lunch. The accumulated trade deficit is like selling off U.S. assets because we are giving foreigners dollars that they can spend on our assets. So how big is that foreign

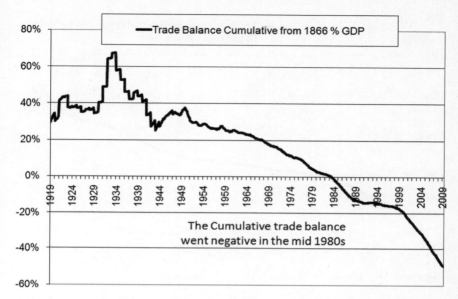

Figure 2.15   How the United States Went From Biggest Lender to Biggest Borrower: The Accumulated Trade balance became Negative in the 1980s

position? By taking the accumulated foreign trade deficit and dividing it by the tangible assets of the United States, we get an indication of just how much of our assets we have pledged to foreigners, while we live high on the hog with current consumption.

The result is shown in Figure 2.16: We have done the equivalent of selling off almost 20 percent of our tangible assets! In essence, the United States has bought more than it produces for enough years that foreigners have a very big claim on our country's assets. This data on tangible assets comes from the Federal Reserve's Z.1 report on the wealth of the nation, for both households and businesses. Real estate is the biggest item of tangible assets.

Foreign investment in the United States has grown to $11 trillion, as shown in Figure 2.17. The words "loan" and "investment" become synonymous in this context, as that is what foreigners do when they buy a Treasury bill. But this situation is now at such an extreme that there is no way the United States could stop everything it is doing and just decide to pay off all that foreign debt. The GDP of the United States for the year is only $14 trillion, so to pay back $10 trillion, we would have

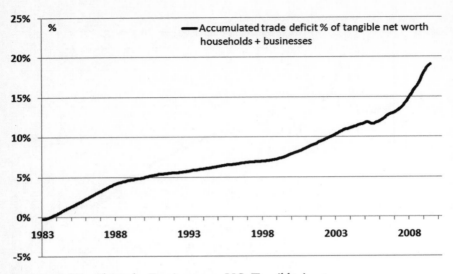

Figure 2.16 Claims by Foreigners on U.S. Tangible Assets

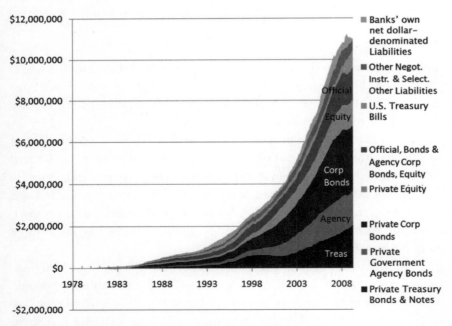

Figure 2.17 Holdings by Foreigners of U.S. Assets
Source: Treasury TIC Data.

to give to foreigners everything we produce, for two-thirds of a year. That isn't going to happen.

I believe we are *never* going to pay off these accumulated deficits. We can't—at least not with dollars that aren't worth anything like what they buy today. Therein lies the deadly embrace of this strange relationship, where the world's biggest and most powerful country is sitting on the biggest international debt in history. We are not in the driver's seat regarding the future of how this will unwind.

Trade Imbalances Hurt the Dollar Status and Set Up Foreign Investors

The amazing size of this trade imbalance could not have developed under the system that was in place during the last credit crisis of the 1930s. International accounts were settled in gold. If a country ran out of gold or access to gold, it would find its currency revalued, which would prevent it from running up such a deficit.

A long-term problem is that the debt accrues interest even if it just sits there, even when it is not expanded with new trade deficits. It is easy to see that the consequences of the trade deficit will be with us for a long time.

Governments with large accumulated trade surpluses have created Sovereign Wealth Funds (SWF) to manage their trillions. Table 2.1 shows the size and country of a number of these. They control an

Table 2.1   Sovereign Wealth Funds Are Big Players

Country	Assets ($M)	Country	Assets ($M)
Abu Dhabi	1,300,000	United States (Alaska)	40,100
Singapore	330,000	Libya	40,000
Norway	315,000	Brunei	30,000
Saudi Arabia	300,000	South Korea	20,000
Kuwait	250,000	Malaysia	18,300
China	200,000	Kazakhstan	17,800
Russia	158,000	Canada	16,600
Singapore	115,000	Taiwan	15,000
Australia	61,500	Iran	12,900
Qatar	50,000		
		TOTAL	$3,079,500

amazing amount of money that is primarily dollars for investment. They can affect markets because of their size. Even more important, they are beholden not only to the best investments based on returns; they will be acting as political arms of the sovereign states. They are important to the markets, and their policies and action need watching.

The United States has survived such a large accumulated deficit with comparatively little damage because it enjoys the status of being the currency that most other foreign central banks use to back the issue of their currency. The usage has given the dollar special status, called the Reserve Currency. An advantage of being the Reserve Currency is that our international debt is denominated in dollars. We can print up dollars to pay off our debt.

During the 1998 Asian crisis, many overindebted countries found that they lacked dollars to pay off their debt. Most of their debt was denominated in dollars. As their currency fell, the amount of debt they owed in their own currency rose.

The parallel of our situation to that of Asia a decade ago is ominous. Many of those Asian countries had healthy economies that fell apart in weeks once foreigners lost confidence in their ability to pay off debt. They had competitive manufacturing capabilities with trained workforces. That strength no longer exists in the United States. Asian currencies collapsed when foreign investors lost confidence in the ability of the debtor nations to pay down their obligations. When the lenders balked at rolling their loans forward, the loss of confidence proceeded into a collapse in a few months.

The Asian Crisis of 1997 to 1998 started in Thailand and rolled across South Korea, Malaysia, and Indonesia, eventually requiring debt rescheduling and IMF bailouts. Those countries owed debt in dollars that they could not print.

The special position of the dollar as reserve currency came about after World War II when the United States was the only world economy left standing. In agreements at the 1944 Bretton Woods (NH) conference, the world decided to let the United States exchange gold for dollars at $35 per ounce and then have all other countries set their exchange rate against the dollar. The dollar was "as good as gold."

The dollar was set free from that restraint in 1971 when Nixon slammed the door on further requests for gold. The world central banks did not really have a good alternative, and they continued to maintain dollars as their biggest reserve holding. It was as much from continuing the precedent as from confidence in the U.S. system that the dollar continued as Reserve Currency.

The U.S. dollar is not the only currency, however. Flawed as they are, other currencies have been increasingly used in international transactions. The Bank of International Settlements keeps track of cross-border External Positions. The amount of dollars used is growing, but the share of the total is declining from 70 percent in 1983 to 20 percent in 2007, as shown in Figure 2.18. The specific numbers are less important than to recognize that the dollar is not the only currency for world transactions, and that its Reserve status is eroding as confidence declines in our policies that allowed deficits to grow so big.

A significant countervailing force to dollar weakness is that most currencies in the rest of the world have their own internal weaknesses. For example, Japan has too much debt, and the euro has many divergent government fiscal policies. All these currencies are fiat, based on nothing but flimflam promises of faith. The important caveat is that although it is easy to see flaws in the dollar, all paper currencies contain seeds of debasement. All of the world's paper currencies are vulnerable to losing value.

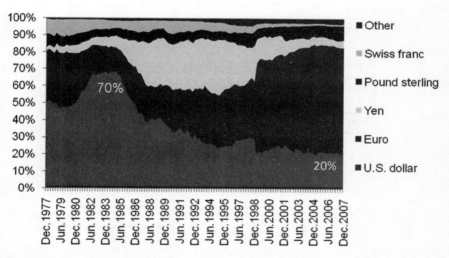

Figure 2.18   Reporting Banks' Cross-Border External Positions

Connecting the Trade Deficit, Budget Deficit, and the Fed

Figure 2.19 shows the bigger picture connections beyond the trade deficit and related foreign investment. I add the expansion of the money creation by the government and Federal Reserve. The key addition is that the federal government deficits are a form of money creation. The federal government can issue Treasuries to borrow money from the public to expand its spending beyond its tax collections.

That new source to cover budget deficits will be the Federal Reserve, which will print money to fill the void. Much more will be said about this problem in Chapter 4 on the Federal Reserve, but the important lead-in to why the Fed actions will become more important is that our dependence on foreigners is about to become inadequate to the spendthrift actions of our government. There are likely to be some dismal consequences from these big government deficits.

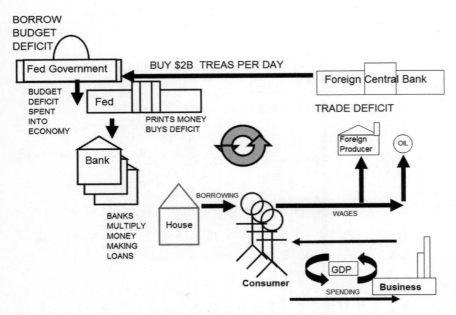

Figure 2.19   The U.S. Trade Deficit Feeds Our Budget Deficit and the Fed Feeds the Money Supply

The mercantilist export model is for Asia to provide goods to the West but with a twist that they loan us the money to buy their goods. Debt can't expand forever, even if it is from the producers. The system is now recognizing this limitation.

The West has come to the worst slowing since World War II, and the effect is spreading to Japan and China who have reached overcapacity and lending limits. This decline in the global economy is beyond a typical recession. Asia is still looking to continue its export-led economy. China is keeping its currency down, and Japan is talking of ways to support U.S. consumers. The fear is that this debt-laden symbiotic international embrace is starting to blow up. The West is saddled with unpayable debt and a weakening economy. Will we be forced to sell more assets to foreigners in retribution for living too high on the hog? Or will the East find that the pile of paper assets they took in trade for goods blows up in their face and turns out to be worthless?

Some of both will occur, but I would not want to be an SWF holding a trillion of the U.S. promises. Asia's central banks have U.S. paper assets of $4 trillion. The value of such assets will come into question the day they all try to sell them. They will be paid only in depreciated purchasing power dollars—if at all!

A forward policy shift on the part of the exporters to consume at home is likely to take years to put in place. China is starting, with a $585 billion stimulus program at home. The money for such domestic spending could come from selling off the Treasuries it has purchased. That could drive U.S. interest rates higher. If Asia is able to expand its markets at home, Asian consumers will compete with Westerners for their output, possibly pushing prices higher. If foreigners slow their buying of U.S. debt, U.S. rates will rise and the dollar will weaken.

If foreigners got upset with the policies of the U.S. government, they could buy up assets like farmland and commodities to get rid of their dollar holdings. But if they did, prices of everything would jump, thereby decreasing the purchasing power of their dollars. The situation is that foreigners have been careful to stay within the bounds of recycling their dollars through big, nonspecific investments like Treasuries.

If one country tried to get out ahead of the others, they would wind up with more of the pie before the disaster spread. But the results would be so bad for everybody that no country has carried through on such plans. In fact, Asian countries have been supporting their workers by backing the dollar, which then helps their exports.

Sources to Watch

I want to warn you that the following section is much more detailed than a casual reader may want to tackle. I go into much more depth because I believe that the foreigners hold the matches to ignite the fire of dollar destruction that has been set by the Federal government budget deficits. I watch these measures of foreign investment very closely using the tools and analysis that are partly of my own invention. While it is important, it is complex enough that you might want to skip to the section on custody accounts at the Fed.

Details of the foreign flows give us insight as to whether the delicate balance may be coming unglued so we can be ready to make investment decisions.

There are two sources of regular government reporting that you can access to see the international flows and closely watch the trade crisis develop:

1. Treasury International Capital (TIC) System
2. Custody accounts at the Federal Reserve

Let's take a closer look at each.

Treasury International Capital System

The more comprehensive of the two sources is the monthly report from the Treasury called the Treasury International Capital (TIC) System (www.ustreas.gov/tic/index.html). We want to know if foreigners are continuing to invest in the United States by summing all the cross-border flows. We do this by combining the various forms of foreign investments in the United States in the form of Treasuries, Agencies (Fannie and Freddie), Corporate Bonds, and Equities and further subtract out the changes in U.S. investments abroad to get a picture in total of cross-border flows. The usual picture is that foreigners are buying the $2 billion a day to keep our economy afloat and to keep their exports flowing.

Figures 2.20 through 2.28 show in more detail the composition of the particular flows, along with my interpretation.

Foreign Purchases of U.S. Assets Slows

Cross-border flows of capital investments of all kinds have dramatically fallen off. The big picture, as reported in the U.S. TIC System's most comprehensive measure of cross-border money flows, shows a decline in the 12-month sum through October 2009, as presented in Figure 2.20.

The annual sum peaked in August 2006 at just under $1.2 trillion. That number collapsed to less than zero by September 2009. The 12-month sum gives a better indication of the situation than does the latest monthly data because numbers jump around.

Figures 2.21 to 2.28 break down this over all international flow so we can see the subcomponents to get a better understanding of the kinds of flows and therefore how foreigners are investing. A big component of investing flows is investments in long-term securities. By mid 2009, this had also dropped to zero. Figure 2.21 has the similar configuration to the big total of Figure 2.20, as it is a big part of that total.

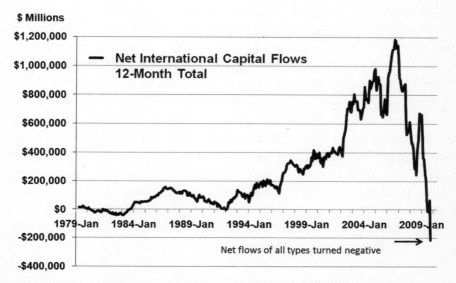

Figure 2.20   Foreign Investment Flows into the United States Turned Negative in 2009

SOURCE: U.S. Treasury TIC Report, www.ustreas.gov/tic/ticpress.shtm#1.

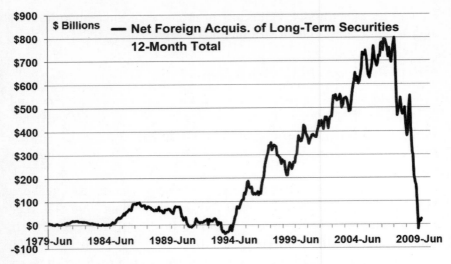

Figure 2.21   Foreigners Stopped Buying Long–Term Securities
SOURCE: U.S. Treasury TIC Report, www.ustreas.gov/tic/ticpress.shtm#1.

The composition of investments has shifted. The world has been moving away from riskier assets toward Treasuries and government-supported Agency debt. Foreigners can buy our equities, our corporate bonds, Agency debt as issued by our Government Sponsored Enterprises like Fannie and Freddie, as well as the safer government Treasury issues. Obviously, the equities investments offer potentially better returns, but also higher risk. Similarly, corporate bonds include the risk of the success of the corporation. To get an idea of how much risk foreigners are willing to take, we look at which segments are expanding. Agency debt was most commonly backed by real estate, and issued under the auspices of Fannie or Freddie, with only an implied support from the Federal government. Since the government has taken over these agencies, the debt carries an even bigger implied guarantee by the government. So I've grouped them with the treasuries in looking at what foreigners are buying. The big picture of Figure 2.20 shows overall investment dropping close to zero, but the investment into treasuries and agencies has been rising as shown in Figure 2.22.

An even closer look into the investment by foreigners into just U.S. government Treasury debt shows a dramatic shift from long-term paper of over one-year duration to shorter-term T-bills (see Figure 2.23).

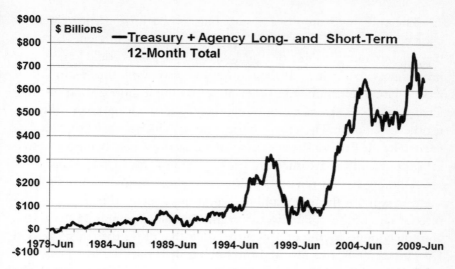

Figure 2.22   Foreigners Continue to Buy Treasuries, T-bills, and Agencies
SOURCE: Treasury TIC data.

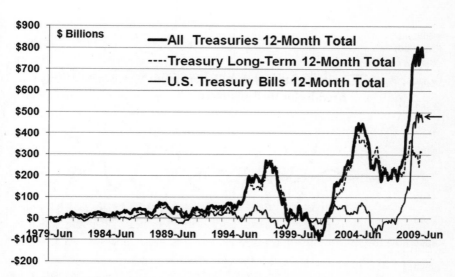

Figure 2.23   Foreign Purchases of T-bills Jumped as the Credit Crisis
Accelerated in 2008
SOURCE: Treasury TIC data.

The shift to 3-month Treasury bills as the investment vehicle of choice (shown in Figure 2.23) is probably due to foreigners fearing that higher interest rates on the longer-term paper could cause their investments to decline. Perhaps investors also want the flexibility of redeploying their money in other places within a short period of time. That could come from a lack of confidence in the long-term prospects for the U.S. dollar. Then there is some good evidence that excess dollars created by the Federal Reserve in swap transactions were being reinvested in short-term U.S. Treasuries to provide support for U.S. markets.

As foreigners turned to the most liquid short-term Treasuries to give them maximum flexibility and the safest investment, the effects on the interest rate of those T-bills was very noticeable. Figure 2.24 shows the absolutely huge buying of 3-month T-bills that drove the rate to zero in December 2008. I've inverted the buying shown in the black line and left-hand scale so that it lines up with the drop in interest rates of the other line. We usually think of Fed actions as being the driving force of short-term interest rates. And yes, the Fed cut its target to a range from

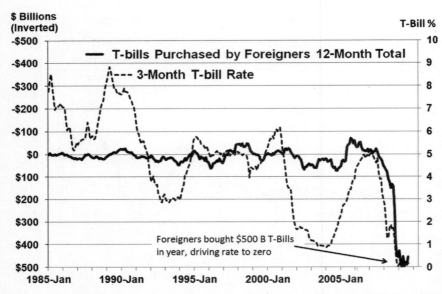

Figure 2.24 How Foreign Purchases of U.S. T-bills Helped Drive Rates to 0% by 2009
SOURCE: Treasury TIC Data.

25 points to zero. But the market was already trading at that level. The driver was the foreigners who lost confidence in riskier investments. Our economic commentators have not recognized the importance of the force of foreign investments enough.

The investments of choice, away from the less secure and into government-supported debt, and away from the longer term, suggest that foreigners' appetite for U.S. investment is less robust.

There have been times recently when foreigners did cause panic in our markets. I show some examples of cracks in foreign confidence that coincide with major shifts in our own markets. Figure 2.25 shows foreign, long-term net investment into the United States. Buried in the irregular movements are two months when foreign investment hit the proverbial fan. Foreigners became spooked in August 2007 and again in August 2008. They are shown in the downward spikes for those months.

These were key dates. The first was when the Fed recognized that it had a very big problem, cut rates, and announced a whole new approach to managing the economy. Most call August 2007 the recognition of how serious the credit crisis actually was. The stock market peak was still two months away, but the credit markets knew there were problems afoot. Prior to that time, Ben Bernanke and Hank Paulson were saying that the problem was "contained." I would claim that the real panic set

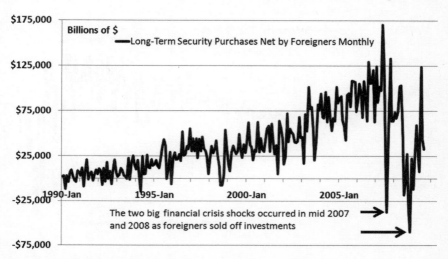

Figure 2.25   Foreign Investment Withdrawal Caused Two Crises in U.S.
SOURCE: Treasury TIC data.

in when foreigners sold off some of their holdings. The big Fed actions brought some stability. Then again, in 2008, a similar spike down sell-off brought new fears. Immediately thereafter, Fannie and Freddie had to be, in effect, nationalized.

The biggest drop by foreigners in 2008 was in buying the debt of Fannie and Freddie (see Figure 2.26). Fannie and Freddie provide the guarantees and much of the money for mortgage debt. Agency debt is issued by Government Sponsored Entities (GSE), and the biggest and well-known of these are Fannie and Freddie. Paulson had lobbied Congress for authority to step in with $200 billion to backstop them if problems might arise. He hid behind the idea that if he provided the threat of having the authority to bailout the GSEs, with what he called a "bazooka," there would not be a run on the bank. Foreigners called that bluff in the summer of 2008, and over the weekend, Paulson put them both in conservatorship. Basically, the government takeover was forced by foreigners losing confidence and selling their Agency holdings. They are still selling.

Foreigners have also lost confidence in the safety of investing in corporate bonds, as shown in Figure 2.27.

Foreigners have also slowed their purchase of U.S. equities. The monthly volatility makes the data hard to see, so here I smooth the data

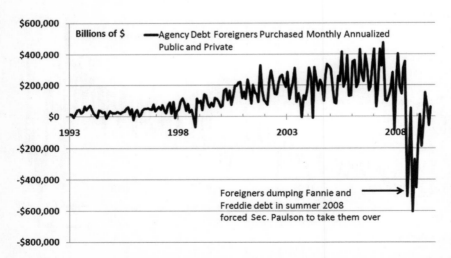

Figure 2.26 Foreigners Selling off Record Amounts of Agency Debt in 2008 Brought Fannie and Freddie Collapse
SOURCE: Treasury TIC data.

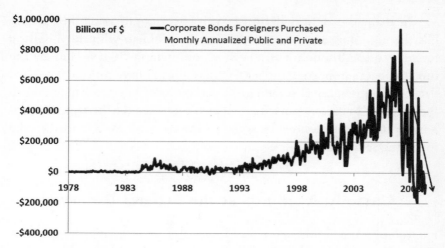

Figure 2.27   Foreigners Stopped Buying Corporate Debt in 2008
SOURCE: Treasury TIC data.

by adding the last 12 months together. We can confirm that foreigners are an important contributor to U.S. stocks by overlying the price of stocks, as shown in Figure 2.28. The relationship is obvious: Foreigners are one of the drivers of the market, and their investments move with the price of stocks.

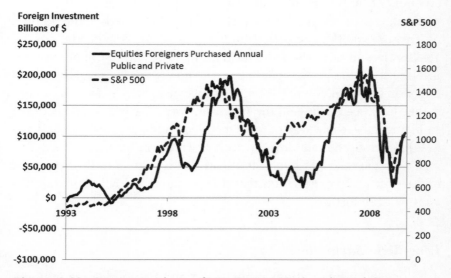

Figure 2.28   Foreign Purchases of U.S. Equities Track with Stock Prices
SOURCE: Treasury TIC data, S&P.

To make the right investments, it is necessary to watch key players like the big foreign investors. But there is a problem with the TIC data for investors. Although it is relatively comprehensive, it is late: By the time the data is reported, the market may already have moved. The TIC data is comprehensive, showing the structure of what is happening in the markets, but it is reported about two months after the fact. There is a more up-to-date source for some of the data that is described in the following section.

Custody Accounts at the Federal Reserve

I developed the following analysis over the years as my personal indicator for watching the pressure on interest rates by foreigners. The indicator is valuable for trading as it is current and published weekly. It is an early warning of what foreign official investors are doing. It is the custody accounts at the Federal Reserve. The Fed acts like a broker for foreign central banks who buy government debt. It is published on Thursday afternoons in the H.4.1 report, (www.federalreserve.gov/releases/h41).

It has only two categories: the amounts of Treasuries and of Agencies bought by foreign officials, which means by foreign central banks. The value is to see the trends early. Figure 2.29 overlays the amount of Treasuries being bought by foreign central banks with the rate on 10-year Treasuries to show the relationship. The amount of purchases is inverted so that as more is purchased, the line moves down. The general direction has been down as foreigners have been buying Treasuries even as they have been selling off the Agencies, corporate bonds, and equities. In Figure 2.29, there was an important lead of bigger foreign purchases in 2008 before the rate dropped to 2.2 percent in December. We have seen a rise on the right side of the chart that is current to the beginning of 2010. It is my expectation that foreign purchases will slow and that rates will rise further.

Long-Term Implications

The long-term implications of the direction of the dollar are ominous in that foreigners have stacked up too big a pile of dollar holdings that

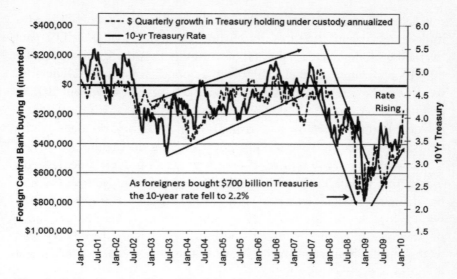

Figure 2.29   Foreign Central Bank Buying U.S. Treasuries Moves Opposite Rates
SOURCE: Federal Reserve H.4.1 Custody.

they would rather divest. They know they can't just drop their holdings on the market because that would precipitate a crisis. They are moving to safety by selling off riskier types of assets, and are buying short-term T-bills even with interest at effectively zero. They left a pretty big wake in their shift, forcing Fannie and Freddie into receivership and adding to the sell-off in stocks in late 2008.

The preceding detailed analysis of the Treasury TIC and the Fed Custody data are basic fundamental tools that give us early warning about where financial markets are going. They can be monitored from the data on their web sites, and they give us early warnings about the important forces of other countries' actions on the investments into the United States.

What Will Be the Effect of the Increasing Trade and Budget Deficits?

The imbalances discussed in these first two chapters are already so big that we can already see how these fundamental forces will affect where our economy is headed in the decade ahead. The increasingly negative budget deficit and trade deficit are shown together in Figure 2.30 and overlaid with the decreasing value of the dollar over the last few decades.

Recognizing the huge imbalances is only the first step. We need to see where these will lead. The question is what the government will do and how markets will handle the situation. The easiest path is to neglect the dollar and let it fall in purchasing power. That way, the debt can be paid off in depreciated dollars. The government is the biggest debtor and is also in charge of the actions to keep it strong or to let it slide. It seems logical that it will let the dollar slide. Dollar-enforcing actions (such as balancing the budget by raising taxes) would curtail consumer spending, would slow the foreign build-up of debt, with the added consequence of slowing the economy and losing jobs, which would probably lead to tossing the politicians out of office at the next election. That is not going to happen!

Going forward, the risk of a big collapse remains. The short-term benefits of foreigners recycling their trade dollars into the United States may not last if they fear that their dollar investments are a diminishing asset. If they were to actively divest, it is pretty clear that there is nobody

Figure 2.30   The Dollar Weakens with the Budget and Trade Deficits
SOURCE: Federal Reserve Bank of St. Louis.

to sell their holdings to that would be big enough to buy all the assets they own. Their only opportunity would be to buy physical assets like U.S. real estate or world-traded products. In that case, the U.S. dollar would suffer big inflation. That might not be so bad for debtors who would be paying off their debts with diminished dollars. But it bankrupts dollar holders, and destroys consumers' ability to purchase foreign goods. It is bad for households to have their dollars evaporate.

A big inflation would be damaging to most businesses, as the foundation of trust in the basic measure would be eroded. It is from such events that complete currency collapse is possible. The problem for the United States is that so much of the decision-making power about international trade debt is in the hands of foreigners because they hold the dollars. The U.S. investor will have to be nimble to find ways to avoid losses. The trade deficit will damage the long-term value of the dollar.

Conclusion

The United States has accumulated the biggest trade deficit of any country in history. This happened under a scheme where the dollar had no redeemability in gold, so there was no requirement to get back to balance. Foreigners supported the deficit as it fueled their exports.

This process supported the big government deficits and fueled credit availability for housing expansion, while keeping interest rates low and the dollar higher, as foreign investment added liquidity and demand for dollars.

The United States has done the equivalent of selling off a quarter of its tangible assets and decimated its domestic manufacturing, while maintaining a high-growth lifestyle. This is now beginning to break down. If foreigners lose their trust in their dollar-denominated holdings, there will be a run on the dollar because there will not be any big investors willing to hold the depreciating asset. The Reserve Currency status will be replaced by other currencies and physical assets. The dollar will decline in purchasing power in the decade ahead, and it could crash if there is an escalating loss of confidence. There are just too many dollars in the world.

The world trading imbalances and the large foreign investments have created partners locked in a precarious imbalance. The outcomes will include currency revaluation and economic trade wars. Volatility in the short term will mask the direction of the damage that has been done to the financial world that has been based on the dollar since World War II. The question to ask on a regular basis is whether the confidence, particularly of foreigners, can be maintained in the currency that is the foundation of profligate spending on a worldwide basis.

The investment implication is that it is unsafe to hold dollars; therefore, alternatives such as gold, energy, and food commodities are likely to do far better than traditional U.S. stocks and bonds. Shorting the dollar, finding foreign investments, getting money out of the country, and shorting interest rates all fit the long-term scenario for those seeking a profitable investing strategy. These are described in more detail in later chapters, but before we get to the investment recommendations, we need to confirm that the damaging deficits will be with us for a long time by examining how big our medicare, Social Security and and war funding costs are going to be.

Chapter 3

The Big Costs of Health Care, Social Security, and the Military

The big government deficits drive the serious economic dislocations that our financial system faces, as described in Chapter 1.
Because of the importance and difficulty of dealing with the
biggest components, I expand on them in this chapter. The reason to
do so is to emphasize how difficult it will be to try to return to a more
balanced budget even if it becomes more widely recognized how problematic the big deficits are. So let's journey together to look inside the
biggest segments of government spending to see how serious the damage
to our financial stability can become.

Health Care and Social Security Costs

The biggest and most complicated segment of our federal government spending is the money spent for social services. Most is for the elderly, under the title of Medicare. With all the many things we do in this country, it was a surprise to me that medical services are the single biggest sector of our economy.

I found out firsthand how expensive medical care can be when I recently spent one day in the hospital for surgery after I fell off my bicycle and broke my arm. The official bill for just this one-day hospital stay was $100,000. That may seem high, but the total costs were even higher when you consider this twist: That $100,000 did not even include the cost of the surgeon; it did not include the cost of the anesthesiologist; it did not include the cost of nursing; it did not include the cost of x-rays, postoperation care, physical therapy, the hospital emergency room three days earlier, or a whole slew of other extremely highly priced services.

Figures 3.1 to 3.8 show how large the expanding health care and Social Security costs have become. The heated debate swirling around Washington looking for new programs is not concentrating on the costs. Politicians claim that there will be ways to cut costs at the same time as extending health care insurance to the 40 million of our citizens who have no coverage. The debate is important with trillions of dollars at stake. My view is that adding millions of new people to the system will come with much more costs than are now estimated.

Given all that, the CBO analysis presents a situation of excessive government spending that clearly requires major adjustments. Figure 3.1 shows how Medicare costs are expected to jump to more than double the fraction of GDP that they are today. There are two drivers of the increase. The first is the well-known demographic retirement of baby boomers all at once; the population of old people is going to dramatically increase. But the second is almost as big: Medical costs themselves are rising as new procedures are invented to keep us alive longer. The combination is—to use the overused word—unsustainable.

The result of this long-term demographic bubble is that projections for the Social Security and Medicare requirements explode as a fraction of GDP. See Figure 3.2 for the government's own prediction of

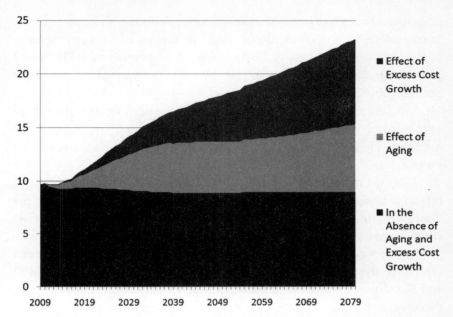

Figure 3.1   Medicare Costs Will Rise from Both Aging and New Medical Procedures
SOURCE: Longterm Budget Outlook, supplemental data.

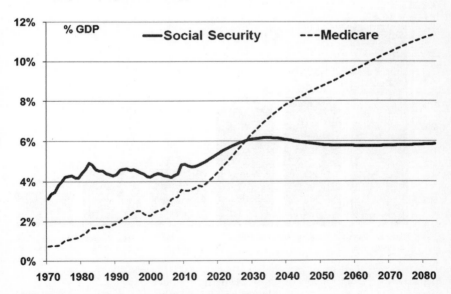

Figure 3.2   Medicare Will Bankrupt the Country
SOURCE: A summary of the 2009 Annual Reports of Social Security and Medicare Boards of Trustees.

how these two programs will take over our economy. The situation is much worse for the medical portion than for Social Security because of the increase in expenses. The combined 17 percent of GDP Social Security and Medicare expenditure by the government in 2083 will not happen.

Medical care has become astronomically expensive: It is 16.5 percent of GDP, which dwarfs 10.5 percent for housing and 9.6 percent for food. Figure 3.3 shows the relative size of the big sectors of our economy.

The cost of health care in the United States is almost double that of other industrialized countries, as shown in Figure 3.4. Major statistics for the big-picture quality of health, such as life span and infant mortality, are not any better in the United States.

The federal government has greatly expanded its spending on health care since the inception of Medicare in 1962, both as a share of GDP and as a share of government spending (see Figure 3.5). Health care as a percentage of GDP was only .05 percent in 1962 and has steadily grown to 6 percent, with every indication of growing more.

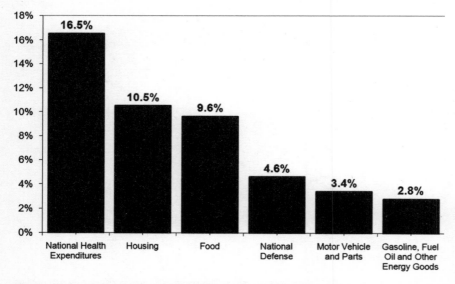

Figure 3.3 Components of Gross Domestic Product
SOURCE: Bureau of Economic Analysis (2006), Centers for Medicare and Medicaid Services (2006), Blue Cross Blue Shield Association, 2007 Medical Cost Reference Guide.

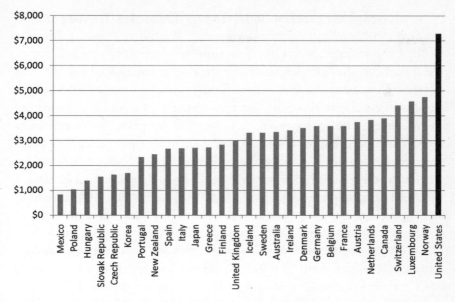

Figure 3.4   Health Care Cost Per Capita in the United States Is Double
Other Countries

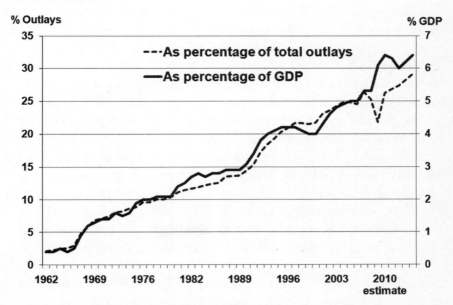

Figure 3.5   Federal Budget for Health Care Grew from 2% in 1962 to 25%
Today of Outlays
SOURCE: Office of Management and Budget.

Social Security Will Drag Deficits Lower

With the slowdown in tax receipts from fewer people earning wages, the income to the Social Security funds is declining. Social Security has been running a surplus that helped defray other government costs. The surpluses are about to be replaced by demands for funds that exceed the revenues. The Congressional Budget Office produced an update of the situation in August 2009. It reports that the percentage of GDP that will be required to make the projected Social Security retirement payments will be around 6 percent (see Figure 3.2). But that is funded by Social Security taxes of only around 3 to 5 percent of GDP revenues, leaving the balance (ongoing deficit) at between 1 to 3 percent.

As percentages, these numbers sound small figures and do not appear like a significant danger but this deficit could become several hundred billion dollars per year. The bigger retirement problem is the medical costs that are continually escalating. To see how big the yearly expenses might become, I multiplied the percent balance by the projected GDP to get a dollar figure. This is partly understating how the scenario will unfold by using 2009 dollars as the measure, so potential inflation for the dollar is not included. The result is that there will be big spending on Social Security in the baby-boomer retirement years ahead, as calculated for Figure 3.6.

The root cause for the big jump in medical expense is not based on government policies but that so many workers will be retiring together. There was a big jump in births right after World War II when soldiers came home and people felt more secure about their future. The Social Security system has never been a funded retirement program, where money was saved up by workers for their eventual retirement. Although that makes sense, that's not the way it works. Instead, as we all know, existing workers contribute a portion of their pay as they work, and those funds are immediately paid out to retirees. So the ability to support the retirees is based on the ability to tax the current workers. There are several problems that make the situation worse, with the most important being that life spans have increased dramatically. Calculating the number of workers providing retirement benefits for the number of retirees then becomes an important measure of the size of taxes that would be expected to be provided by the government.

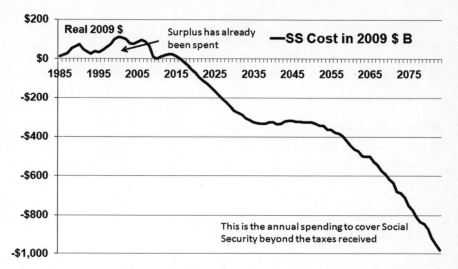

Figure 3.6   Social Security Will Drag Deficits Lower Once Trust Fund Surplus Is Exhausted

SOURCE: CBO's Long-Term Projections for Social Security: 2009 Update August 2009; www.cbo .gov/ftpdocs/104xx/doc10457/08-07-SocialSecurity_Update.pdf.

When the Social Security system was created by Roosevelt during the depths of the Depression, there were something like 15 workers for each retired person. Currently, that number is five workers per retiree. The problem is that it is heading to only two-plus workers for each retiree. One might expect that a retired person requires as much to live on as a working person does, once you add the high cost of end-of-life medical care into the total: after all, a retired person needs fewer trips to a ski slope, but his medical care escalates dramatically with sophisticated medical procedures. There is no way that each worker would give up a third of his or her income to support the retired person. (See Figure 3.7.)

Social Security payments and Medicare coverage for the next 75 years have been calculated to cost $60 trillion discounted to today. Different government studies come to slightly different numbers that range around that level. We don't have the means to pay that big an obligation out of normal tax revenues, which are in the $2 trillion range per year for the entire federal government.

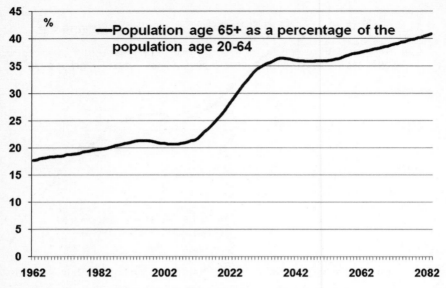

Figure 3.7   There Won't Be Enough Workers to Fund the Baby Boomers' Retirement

Defense Spending Is Continuing to Grow

Another component of the federal deficit is the requirement for defense. Defense outlays jumped dramatically during the Bush administration to pay for the Afghanistan and Iraq wars. Much of the costs of the wars are incurred after the actual hostilities have ceased. Programs for veterans who've lost limbs and lost their ability to earn income are expensive. Rebuilding destroyed materials and rebuilding the nation's defenses are expensive. While ongoing supplementary requests make it appear that the war is only costing $200 billion a year, a more comprehensive analysis done by Nobel Prize laureate Joseph Stieglitz estimated the total cost at $3 trillion.

When I asked him if he was getting arguments that this figure was too high, he said, to the contrary, that the estimates were conservative. The Congressional Budget Office presented three estimates that ranged from $2.6 trillion to $4.5 trillion for the wars (see Figure 3.8). The United States was able to fund these in an indirect sense by borrowing from foreigners.

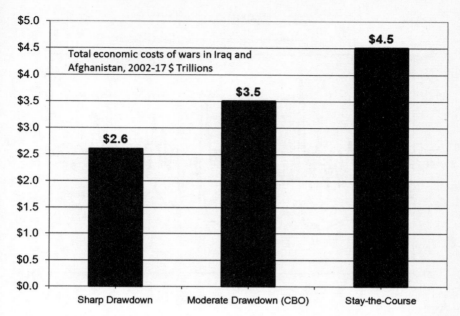

Figure 3.8   Total Economic Costs of Iraq and Afghanistan Wars
SOURCE: CBO.

The United States spends as much on its military as the whole rest of the world. It is a big burden on our society in terms of cost. It gave us a tremendous edge in world negotiating power as we have troops stationed across the globe in some 600 installations and 100 countries. But it's pretty clear that this kind of expense is more than we can afford.

Wars tend to be associated with large government deficits and the result tends to be inflationary. History confirms that result in the inflation seen around major wars going back to 1812 and the Civil War. Those previous inflationary bouts occurred even though the government mostly kept the dollar officially pegged to gold. That meant that during the conflict prices rose, but on the cessation of hostilities, prices dropped back as debts were paid and confidence in the system was regained. We no longer have that restraint on government spending (see Figure 3.9).

And of course the reason behind the higher inflation is the big government spending required to finance wars. Figure 3.10 shows the calculation of federal debt based on the size of the increase in debt

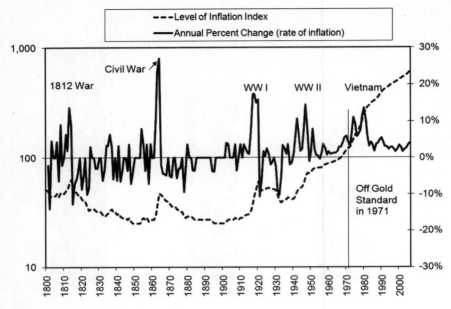

Figure 3.9   Wars Bring Government Spending Which Brings Inflation
SOURCE: Minneapolis Fed.

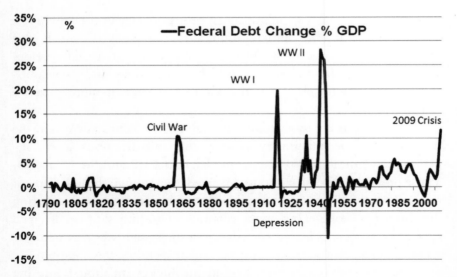

Figure 3.10   Federal Debt Jumped in Wars

divided by the GDP. (This is different from the rate of change of the ratio of debt to GDP.)

The concern about expanding our obligations is not just about the past administration. Admiral Michael Mullen, the highest-ranking U.S. military commander, said the situation in Afghanistan is deteriorating. General Stanley McCrystal obtained approval from President Obama to escalate the troops another 30,000 in Afghanistan. That will bring the total to 100,000, and it means we will be there for several more years. Contractors will double that number and since the cost per person is about $1 million, we are looking at a $200 billion per-year cost. Somewhere in my distant memory, this seems to rhyme with our disastrous experience of Vietnam. Despite widespread public dissatisfaction, that war and the spending went on for years. If history is a guide, I expect our military costs to continue at an elevated level also for a long period. Regardless of my political opinion, the economic consequences of continued military spending will continue to drain our resources and ensure that we live with a budget deficit for a long time.

Conclusion

The point of going into all these details about the difficulties of supporting the huge baby boomer retirement cohort and the ongoing military disturbances around the planet is not just to provide political opinion about what supposedly "they" should do; it is also to provide a roadmap of just how serious these financial demands are on our future budget outlook. My goal is to warn you so that you are not lulled into comfort by politicians regularly promising they will "cut the deficit in half by the year 20XX." It is not the kind of situation that can be fixed with a stroke of a politician's pen. And because it is so difficult, I expect it will be the markets that dictate back to our nation that they are not willing to continually support our spendthrift ways.

Even though it is indirect, foreigners have been subsidizing our government debt and thus subsidizing our foreign interventions. The time is not far off when they will dictate to us how much they will support our policies. Wen Jiabao, China's premier, said this at a news conference: "Most importantly, we hope the United States will keep an appropriate size to its deficit so that there will be basic stability in the

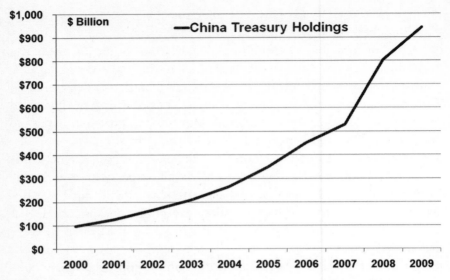

Figure 3.11 China and Hong Kong Have Acquired $1 Trillion of Treasuries Mostly Since 2000

exchange rate, and that is conducive to stability and the recovery of the global economy."[1]

China can speak with authority as it holds almost $1 trillion of Treasuries as shown in Figure 3.11.

The most likely outcome in the decades of Baby Boom retirement ahead is that the government's inability to tax the ongoing population at the level expected by the retirees will mean that the deficit will explode and lead to debasement of the dollar. The important thrust of all this economic analysis is to warn you that the problems are too big for ordinary fixes, so you need to *protect yourself.*

When government spending is too big to be met by taxes, deficits explode. The answer to meeting that deficit is the subject of the next chapter on the Federal Reserve, which has the mission of creating our money. How it does this is crucially linked to how big these deficits become.

---

[1] Yahoo! Finance, November 9, 2009. China's Premier Warns Obama to Get America's Deficit to an "Appropriate Size" http://finance.yahoo.com/tech-ticker/article/368426/Chinas-Premier-Warns-Obama -to-Get-Americas-Deficit-to-an-Appropriate-Size."

Part Two

FINANCIAL CRISIS RESPONSE

Part Two analyzes how the Federal Reserve will have to respond to the budget deficit to keep the government running. Chapter 4 begins by detailing how the Federal Reserve, along with our banking system, creates money. In some sense, the Federal Reserve is a pawn of the government's deficits. The Fed has to react by doing what it can to manage the situation.

In Chapter 5, on the importance of debt in predicting our economy, I dig inside the parameters of the debt market to break out who the borrowers and lenders are. This crisis is at root a debt crisis, and the extreme growth of debt has distorted the balances in ways we have never seen before. The details show how the government's borrowing will distort markets and affect the Fed.

Chapter 6 provides a new way of looking at how all these factors of our economy interrelate. By adding the feedback loops and time factors, you can see how cycles swing beyond equilibrium to much bigger extremes, on a repeated basis. The fundamental underlying structure is dynamic. This gives rise to a "virtuous cycle" or a "vicious cycle." The description is complex because our whole economic system is so big, but reading these explanations is worthwhile because they will help you understand the structure better than most formally trained economists.

Although this section is definitely theoretical, the implications are very real for all of us, and we are experiencing the results just now. Putting together how the cycles work, and how seriously imbalanced our debt situation has become, is the bedrock against which we can evaluate our investment plans.

Chapter 4

The Federal Reserve Prints Our Money (Stop the Presses!)

W e have come to a critical juncture in the United States where the budget deficits are so big as to overwhelm our ordinary sources of borrowing money. The answer to making ends meet is so obvious as to seem impossible: The Federal Reserve, as owner of our currency, can print up new money, diluting the purchasing power of all the rest of the currency, to fill the void. This process is as simple as I just explained it, but it's quite a bit more complex when reviewing the details and the process of all the parties. This chapter lays out that detail for those who want to watch and understand the structure.

The process seems clouded in mystery, almost as if a screen has been purposely stretched over the inner workings, so that we are left thinking that the leaders who are running the machinery of our financial system have special powers to control the nation's economic systems, wreaking havoc or bringing blessings. It's really not that mysterious, and once you understand the games that are being played, you will be able to see a few steps ahead what is likely to unfold in our plot of the economic shifts in the coming decade.

What Is the Fed? A Private Profiteer or a Government Agency?

Everybody knows the Federal Reserve is extremely important, and the financial press looks for every clue to determine what Fed Chairman Ben Bernanke's next step will be to manipulate our money system.

The institution carries far more reverence than it deserves. Former Fed Chairman Alan Greenspan has been called the maestro and the second most powerful man in the western world. Bernanke, the current chairman, hasn't quite captured the aura of the wizard, but his actions are certainly impacting our financial system. It's important to understand the responsibilities and the now-expanding actions of this almost 100-year-old institution as it usurps even greater power to control our financial future.

It may be hard to imagine that our country did just fine when we had no central bank. We had no central bank for a half century before the inauguration of the Federal Reserve by an act of Congress on the night before Christmas, 1913 when no one was watching. We see their imprint today on our paper dollars. Dollar bills are officially identified as Federal Reserve Notes because they are issued by the Federal Reserve, fashioned something like a note to borrow. The Federal Reserve issues the Federal Reserve Notes as a liability on its balance sheet, which is held against assets that were composed mostly of treasuries of the federal government.

The Federal Reserve, in its initial days, held gold as backing for the currency. It still holds title to 262 million ounces of gold, which at today's price (at the time of this writing) of $1,000 an ounce is a substantial $262 billion.

The official duties of the Federal Reserve (as described by its own document www.federalreserve.gov/pf/pdf/pf_1.pdf) fall into four general areas:

1. Conducting the nation's monetary policy by influencing the monetary and credit conditions in the economy in pursuit of maximum employment, stable prices, and moderate long-term interest rates.
2. Supervising and regulating banking institutions to ensure the safety and soundness of the nation's banking and financial system and to protect the credit rights of consumers.
3. Maintaining the stability of the financial system and containing systemic risk that may arise in financial markets.
4. Providing financial services to depository institutions, the U.S. government, and foreign official institutions, including playing a major role in operating the nation's payments system.

We watch the Federal Reserve's influence on the markets primarily through its setting of the short-term overnight interest rate on money loaned between banks. This Fed funds rate becomes an indicator for setting many other rates. The rate is set by operations in the open market through its Federal Open Market Committee (FOMC). The committee meets about every six weeks to decide whether to raise or lower this key interest rate, and with much fanfare, the FMOC publicizes its current target.

The actual rate can be different from the target, but the Federal Reserve will intervene to drive the rate higher or lower to achieve its announced target. A decade ago, the Federal Reserve didn't even announce what its target was, hiding behind the screen so that market participants would have to assess from the Federal Reserve actions what the Fed's policy target rate was. We now sit at the unusual situation of the Federal Reserve having lowered its interest rate to an official range of between 0 percent and a quarter of a percent, with the idea that low rates should help stimulate the economy, allow for loans to be provided at relatively low rates so that businesses and consumers will borrow to spend, and generally expand economic growth. The rate has never been lower.

The United States banking system has been called a Fractional Reserve System because the regular commercial banks (which create our personal checking accounts and give us mortgages for our houses) are required to keep only a fraction of their deposits on reserve at the Federal Reserve to back up their deposits. The rest they can loan out to make profits.

In the original design of the system, the fraction of deposits required to be placed with the Federal Reserve—called the reserve requirement—was an important policy tool to expand and contract the ability of banks to make new loans and thereby multiply the amount of credit and deposits throughout the system. The reserve requirement percentage has been decreased, and the kind of funds against which reserves are required then also decreased, so that currently we are in a situation where there is in effect almost *no* requirement for banks to have reserves at the Fed. Although the requirement structurally exists, the dollar amounts are so small as to have little effect on the operations of banks. Basically, commercial banks run into other limitations (such as their capital adequacy) before they are limited as to how much they can loan out. Consequently, since this policy tool is no longer effective it is rarely discussed.

The legal structure of the Federal Reserve is often debated as to whether it is a private entity with independence from the federal government or if it is really a branch of the financial operations of the federal government. There are 12 branches of the Federal Reserve Bank scattered across the regions of the country, and the board of governors operates out of Washington, DC.

Key leaders and presidents are appointed by the President and confirmed by Congress. Legally, the Federal Reserve exists as an independent corporation whose shares are owned by commercial banks which are members of the Federal Reserve System. Mainly, that means there are shares held by the large banks of the country. These shares pay a modest dividend, but in comparison to other flows, the influence of the shareholders is nonexistent.

While the legal structure exists for independence, the reality is that the Federal Reserve is very much at the center of the policymaking activities of the federal government by coordination with the Treasury. There should be no mistake that *the Federal Reserve is not an independent entity.* It is a branch of the policymaking and implementation aspects of our financial system as directed in coordination with the federal government.

Their other main constituents are the commercial banks of the United States, which they are charged with supporting and regulating. The investment banks (which deal with issuing corporate shares) were not directly regulated by the Federal Reserve, but in the financial crisis of 2008–09 almost all investment banks of any size converted themselves into bank holding companies. That structure allows investment banking and commercial banking to coexist under the same corporate structure, so that there are virtually no important investment banks that are beyond the reach of Federal Reserve regulation. The investment banks converted to give them access to the rescue funds available to banks regulated by the Fed.

The important point of this discussion of bank regulation is to notice that the Federal Reserve acts to support the banking system in its primary role as the banker's bank, to ensure the strength and viability of all banks in the United States. So the Fed has a separate loyalty to the banks.

Who Benefits from the Fed?

The dictum "Follow the money!" involves determining for whom the Federal Reserve works. Most people don't realize that *the Fed is a private corporation that made a profit of about $45 billion last year.* It holds something like $700 billion of government Treasuries on its books that pay interest of around 4 percent, or $28 billion of income. In any normal corporation, those profits would be distributed to the shareholders. But for the Federal Reserve, profits are freely contributed back to the Treasury of the U.S. government! In essence, they turn in their profits to contribute to keeping the federal deficit a little lower. The chairman and governors are appointed by the president and approved by Congress, so it's pretty clear that the Fed is in bed with the federal government.

It's also pretty clear that the Federal Reserve, on a day-to-day basis, does everything it can to support, bail out, and only loosely regulate its shareholders—namely, the big banks. The origins of the Federal Reserve, which was concocted by big bankers in a secret meeting on Jekyll Island off the coast of Georgia, indicate its founding mission of supporting the bankers.

It is my conclusion that the Federal Reserve acts as a handmaiden for the banks and also the policy tool for the federal government. The role of leadership requires balancing the conflicting goals of its different constituents. Notice who is not represented: the general public!

The Federal Reserve's responsibilities are officially assigned two somewhat conflicting objectives:

1. To support the dollars that it issues, in such a way that they maintain their value
2. To support the growth of the overall economy

The conflict arises between the obvious balancing act of supporting the dollar by keeping interest rates high and, on the reverse side, supporting the economy by keeping interest rates low, thereby making loans easier to obtain. The problem, of course, with low interest rates and expanding debt is that the combination can lead to inflation, which decreases the purchasing power of the dollar. So the two goals are in conflict. The Fed has to navigate to what it believes is a happy medium.

How Is the Fed Affecting Our Investment Horizon?

All these structural mechanics are merely outlines of what the Federal Reserve has been defined to be. The real crux of the matter for investment analysis is for us to interpret what the Fed policymakers are *doing* and how big an impact this can have on the economy.

This provides opportunities for investment from interpreting what will be the future financial outcome, most importantly for the interest rates and the value of the dollar.

The first and most obvious of the extreme actions the Federal Reserve took to respond to the Credit Crisis of 2007–2008 was to cut the overnight interest rate to almost 0 percent. That means that banks can borrow at practically no cost. When they make loans, the profits that come from the spread between their borrowing and their lending cost can now be quite large. By this measure, it's a wonderful time to be a bank.

On the other hand, all the existing banks now sit with the problem that many of their loans made in previous and more optimistic times are now falling into delinquency and some fraction will disappear in default, costing the banks hundreds of billions. That is why there are such huge bailouts to keep these institutions alive.

It would seem to me that just putting these institutions out of business and starting new banks would have given us a much cleaner result, with much less cost to the taxpayers. Our policymakers (especially Hank Paulson, who had been chairman of investment bank Goldman Sachs, and Ben Bernanke) made the policy decision to use government money (your tax dollars) to bail out overleveraged and deceptive financial institutions. Their argument was that these banks were somehow necessary for the rest of the economy and thus were too big to allow to fail. The bailout programs have reached unimaginable proportions, now counted in the trillions of dollars. The new Treasury Secretary Timothy Geithner is following in the same footsteps.

The Fed Is Out of Control

In the hundred-year history of the Fed, there has never been anything even close to the kind of egregious expansion of the Federal Reserve balance sheet we are currently seeing. A major policy action of the Federal Reserve has been to debase its existing balance sheet. Prior to 2007, the Federal Reserve balance sheet contained nearly riskless federal government debt issues of the Treasury in the form of Treasury bonds, Treasury bills, and Treasury notes.

Figure 4.1 shows the incredible growth of toxic waste that has been piled into the assets of the Federal Reserve, doubling its entire balance sheet in the process.

As you can see, in the first year of this crisis, the Federal Reserve bought up many strange forms of cats and dogs, and they paid for the mangy creatures by selling off their much more stable T-bills, T-bonds, and T-notes. Put simply, in the first round of this crisis (in 2007), the Fed

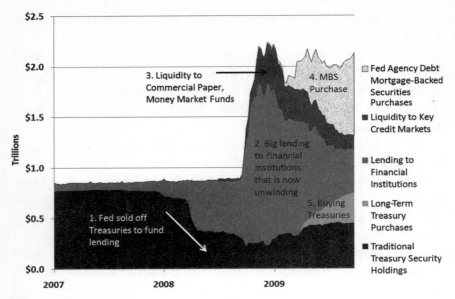

Figure 4.1   Federal Reserve Credit Easing Policies
SOURCE: Federal Reserve.

sold off the family jewels to fund the early bailouts, rather than printing up money, thereby keeping inflation in check.

But by the second round (in 2008)—where the total of the graph in Figure 4.1 spikes much higher, from $1 trillion to $2 trillion—the Federal Reserve threw all caution to the wind and began printing money in earnest. Nothing like this has ever been done before in the entire history of the Federal Reserve. The Fed did it with many different kinds of newly invented programs:

- The Fed bought toxic-waste assets from the banks.
- It accepted as collateral toxic waste against loans to the banks.
- It intervened in specific markets, such as the commercial paper and money market funds.

The Fed has certainly benefited participants in the specific markets where it has poured money into the system. But it has done this at great risk to the dollar, because it has created money that will flow through the banking system in an inflationary way when the economy recovers.

To evaluate the effects of the various programs, I have combined them into categories. Figure 4.1 shows the five steps the Federal Reserve took; here's what each step illustrates:

1. The Fed delayed major introduction of programs as it worked out how serious the situation had become and what its legal authorities were. The first step was to provide significant direct funding to particular financial institutions, and to fund that by selling off its holdings of government Treasuries. The total money supply was not changed, so inflationary forces were modest.

2. By the second half of 2008, after the collapse of Lehman Brothers in August, the Federal Reserve became aggressive in bailing out financial institutions. The big jump in the assets occurred at this time.

3. At the same time, new liquidity was provided to specific markets that had pretty much shut down, as lenders became fearful of getting their money back. Normally, such a big increase in money would be inflationary, but banks have not been making new loans, so the effects are small so far.

4. As panic receded, the Federal Reserve was able to pull back much of its lending to financial institutions, and it used those proceeds to develop two new programs to purchase mortgage-backed securities and Federal Agency debt, with the clear objective of supporting the housing market and indirectly the banking institutions involved in mortgage operations. Interest rates for mortgages have come down. The purchases are huge, with a promised program of $1.25 trillion for mortgage-backed securities (MBSs) and $200 billion for Agency debt.

5. The Federal Reserve also embarked on a program to buy $300 billion of federal government Treasuries. From one view, this is simply restoring some of the previously sold-off Treasuries on the Fed's balance sheet. From another view, it's dangerous for the Federal Reserve to buy up federal government debt because it is this very process that nets out to printing money for the federal government to spend through its deficits, and it is a signal for eventual inflation.

So the Federal Reserve came to the rescue somewhat belatedly but with programs that can potentially be damaging to the dollar. The problem is that the Federal Reserve now has all kinds of questionable assets on its books that could be very difficult to sell if it were to try to exit its big easing programs. The Federal Reserve has been secretive, defying lawsuits and opposing even basic government auditing. It won't explain the details of who obtained what support and the actual value of the assets on its books. Foreigners are asking questions, and the most likely interpretation is that if the Federal Reserve can act so precipitously, then the long-term purchasing power of the dollar is very much in question. This kind of monetary expansion has almost always led to significant price inflation in the following periods.

How Did the Fed Pay for Its Big Expansion?

Of course, as on every balance sheet, liabilities must match assets. In the case of the Fed, it's important to understand the changes in the nature of its liabilities as they spiked higher along with assets. How that was accomplished can help us understand much about the economic environment we are now in, so let's take a look at Figure 4.2.

Historically, the Federal Reserve's main purpose was to issue paper dollar currency. That's what the bottom chunk in Figure 4.2 identifies. As you can see, currency has grown only modestly in the whole time of this graph of 2007–2009. The only important liability that the Fed had on its balance sheet until mid-2008 was the currency. All that changed as the credit crisis became a panic.

What is clearly far from normal is that the Federal Reserve has invented deposits out of thin air to buy up all those toxic assets from the banks. The Federal Reserve invents a deposit at the Federal Reserve in the name of the institution from which it buys Treasuries, MBS (or toxic assets). It then winds up with the assets, and the institution now has an account to spend as it wishes. That provides banks and other financial institutions with a lot of cash to keep on deposit at the Federal Reserve. Normally, such deposits would be drawn down and invested in other loans that would pay interest. Until 2009, no interest was paid on the deposits at the Federal Reserve. But now, with the Federal Reserve paying interest, the banks have not drawn down these excess reserves, and they are still sitting at the Federal Reserve.

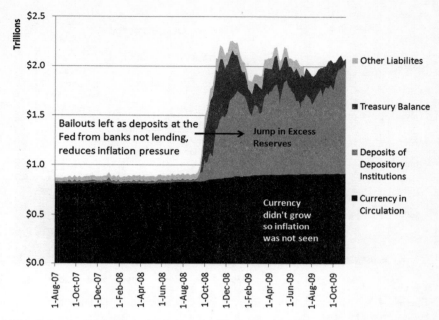

Figure 4.2   Federal Reserve Liabilities Grew from Deposits
SOURCE: Federal Reserve.

The monetary base is defined as currency in circulation plus the reserves at the Fed. The total is what the Fed is supposed to be able to control. The longer-term picture, shown in Figure 4.3, shows how unprecedented the current expansion has become.

If banks acted in a manner consistent with history, they would loan those deposits, helping to expand business and otherwise generate economic activity. But in the current unprecedented situation, the banks are not interested in taking on new risks, and many traditional customers find they are already overleveraged and don't want to take on additional borrowing. In short, despite having plenty of deposits, banks don't want to lend, and borrowers don't want to borrow; so new lending has pretty much dried up. There was the big jump in deposits in mid-2008, and there is a worrisome increase just starting again at the end of 2009.

As a consequence, these huge balances owned by the banks just sit on deposit at the Federal Reserve. That's important, because it has helped keep the inflationary pressure from the Federal Reserve's actions in check. That would not have been the case had the banks withdrawn

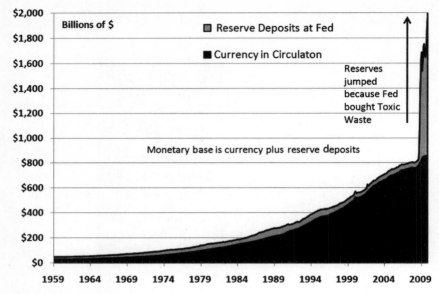

Figure 4.3   Monetary Base Jumped Like Never Before from Bailouts
SOURCE: Federal Reserve.

the deposits from the Fed to make new loans, thereby multiplying the lending and borrowing throughout the banking system.

The more inclusive measures of our money supply include deposits at banks, and they have not grown in the dramatic way that the monetary base has grown. Figure 4.4 shows increases in the monetary measures, but nothing like the extreme rate of the monetary base. So at this juncture, we are not seeing the downstream effects of large inflationary pressure.

What might get the banks lending again? Logically, the appearance of tangible green shoots, but not the overhyped green dye that is being sprayed over the dead roots that abound in today's economy. But it's also entirely plausible that an activist administration and Congress will decide to forcefully encourage the banks to lend, either through dictate or by unleashing a new wave of loan guarantees that offer the banks all the upside, with little or no downside, if the loans go bad.

An important measure of whether the Fed's bailouts are working is to monitor whether banks are expanding their lending. It's important because it's the basis of the administration's goal to "get capital markets working again." Figure 4.5 shows how banks are trying to reinflate the bubble, but it's not working; the banks are still not making new loans.

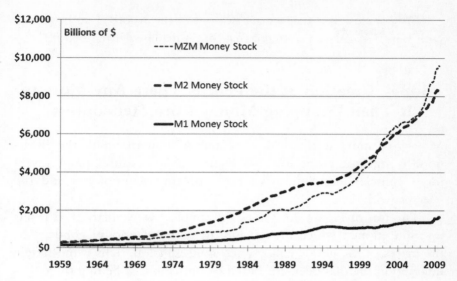

Figure 4.4   Money Is Growing, but Not Like the Monetary Base
SOURCE: Federal Reserve.

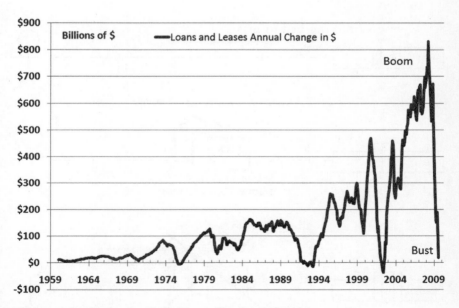

Figure 4.5   Banks Cut Back Loans, Despite Fed Easing
SOURCE: Federal Reserve.

My conclusion is that we are not out of the woods. I do not agree with Ben Bernanke's assessment that things may be getting better.

Money Creation at the Fed: Is There Any More to It Than Dropping Money from Helicopters?

Money creation at the Fed is central to understanding the likelihood of inflation going forward. Figure 4.6 shows three progressively more complex descriptions of how the important players and the systems work.

The top of Figure 4.6 shows the simplest view: If the Fed prints up more money, which then chases the same quantity of goods, then the prices of the goods will rise, creating inflation. This is the simple description that has been attributed to Bernanke for getting the economy going and making sure prices don't fall. Bernanke is famous for repeating Milton Friedman's suggestion that the Fed could drop money from helicopters to ensure that there was enough money so that prices

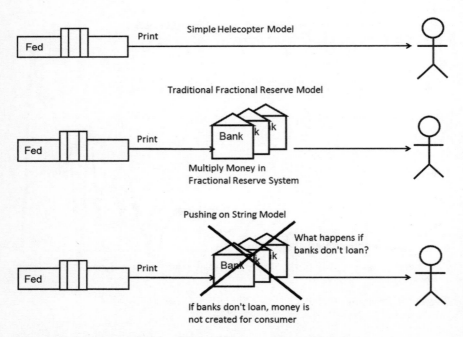

Figure 4.6   Three Models of Federal Reserve Money Creation

wouldn't fall. The first line in Figure 4.6 describes that process in an overly simple fashion.

But it is really much more complicated than just having the Fed print up some dollars. Whether we have money in a checking account or paper dollars in our hand, we think of both of them as money. The decision to have paper dollars is a convenience for consumers and businesses. If a lot of people want to have extra dollars in their pocket around Christmas, they can go to their banks and exchange their check for paper dollars. The Federal Reserve makes sure that the banks can drive up their Brink's truck to exchange their demand deposits that were just described for paper dollars.

The official name for our paper dollars is Federal Reserve Notes. Exchanging paper for checking account money doesn't affect the consumer's ability to spend, so the measure of money supply that is most commonly used is the sum of paper money and demand deposits at banks. That is often called "narrow money supply," and the Fed reports it every week with the name "M1."

The creation of demand deposits, however, is extremely important because there are more of them than paper dollars. The simplest way to create them is for a person to deposit Federal Reserve Notes into their checking account.

How the Fed Really Creates Money

The root way new money is created by the Fed is for the Fed to purchase an asset from the open market, like from a bank, of something like a group of Treasury bonds. To do so, it creates out of thin air a deposit at the Federal Reserve, which is in the name of the bank for the price of the Treasuries it purchased. It is this creation of the deposit out of thin air that is called "printing money." Notice that there was no paper dollars involved at this stage. To complete the cycle, a bank could draw down its deposit at the Fed, just as you or I would write a check to pay a bill. The commercial banks' deposits at the Fed are called reserve deposits.

Banks Create More Money than the Federal Reserve

But now the fun of our system gets more complex. It is the banks that create much more deposits than the Federal Reserve makes of paper money plus reserve deposits at the Fed. This happens by the magic of the money multiplier, where the new money "printed" by the Fed is multiplied through the commercial banks into many times the original deposit.

That happens by the commercial bank loaning out the money it gets, say from selling a Treasury bond to the Fed. The complex part of the system is that the borrower typically buys something (for example, a house) from a person who now deposits that money into another bank. That other bank then has new money to make a new loan. This process could theoretically go on forever, but the structure of the U.S. money and banking system is that the Federal Reserve requires all banks to keep a fraction of deposits called the "reserve requirement" on the books of the Federal Reserve. That requirement is nominally 10 percent, but as we shall see, it is actually much less in practice.

With the first bank only able to loan out 90 percent of the new deposit, the second bank can only lend out 90 percent of the 90 percent of its new deposit, and the process eventually converges on a maximum creation of new deposits that is 10 times the original new deposit. Thus, in the example just described, the banks create 10 times as much money as the Fed does. It is through this process of lending and relending slightly smaller amounts multiple times that the banks are responsible for the majority of new credit (i.e., money) created, not the Fed. The Fed simply starts the process with its high-powered money. The details are elaborate, but the big-picture view is that it is easy to create credit, which acts as money.

A multiplication of the money is included in the second model of the money creation system, shown in the middle of Figure 4.6.

There's More Money Created by Non-Banks

New loan funds come from not just our banks, but also from insurance companies, government-sponsored enterprises (GSE), money market funds, and many other institutions that create credit. So a key part of understanding the supply of credit is recognizing that the availability of funds (from all the different parts of our financial sector) goes beyond just the banks. Asset-backed securities (ABS) are suppliers of credit, as are Ginnie Mae and Fannie Mae loans, which have much the same function as bank loans. Traditional economics books describe only the banking system, and the money measures (which are published as M1, M2, M3) are measures of the deposits (on the liabilities side of the balance sheet) of only bank ledgers, so they ignore the credit creation of these other institutions.

Any GSE- or ABS-issuing entity can participate in facilitating credit, where they take in money to be loaned out. They are sometimes called "non-bank banks," because they are not regulated like banks, but they borrow and lend like banks except they don't take deposits. Thus, the amount of credit that can be created is larger than what is measured by the deposits of traditional banks and is reported by the Fed as M1 and M2. These non-bank institutions have no reserve requirement and have no Federal Deposit Insurance.

As an example of a newer kind of money, Figure 4.7 shows how rapidly money market funds have grown. They were invented in the 1970s as a way to provide higher interest rates than the regular banking system was allowed to pay on checking accounts. Now, our brokers

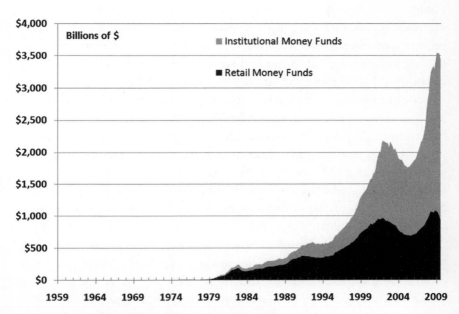

Figure 4.7 Money Market Funds are Bigger than M1
SOURCE: Federal Reserve.

offer them to us so easily that we don't think about what category of money they represent. Figure 4.7 shows that institutional money funds and retail money funds added together are $3.5 trillion. The traditional narrow measure of money, M1, which is a combination of currency, normal demand deposits (checking accounts) and a few smaller items like traveler's checks, is only half as much at $1.7 trillion.

I think the less-well-informed also skip over the complexity of our physical paper money. How much paper money in our pockets gets printed is just the decision of all of us as to whether we want cash in dollar bills or in our checking account. The physical printing to meet that preference is different from the Fed and commercial banks inventing deposits out of thin air. M1 adds together demand deposits of $440 billion and paper Federal Reserve Notes of $859 billion, and a few cats and dogs like travelers checks, for a total of $1,655 billion. The effect on the system's ability to expand through multiplying deposits is different for paper cash, as it can't be loaned and reloaned.

The next complexity is that there are plenty of sources of immediately available transactions accounts that are not formal checking accounts. One way that developed was the ability of banks to "sweep" demand deposits into savings accounts overnight. Because the reserve requirement on savings accounts is zero, the banks were able to avoid leaving cash on deposit at the Fed earning no interest. These made the measure M1 understate the amount of money available for transactions. The newer measure, called Money of Zero Maturity (MZM), at $9,550 billion, attempts to count up the funds that can immediately be used to buy things (as opposed to savings accounts, which have a term). MZM is much bigger than M1. (And bigger than M2.) It is calculated by starting with the M2, adding institutional money funds, and subtracting small denominated-time deposits. It gets more complicated as you peel back the covers of the definitions of money because there is no good definition that is clear.

And that problem is based on the fact that there is no redeemable value for any of the measures for money, except the confidence that others will trade real things for the money. At root, the whole scheme is a CONfidence game, or at least based on the confidence that the dollars will continue to buy things. That arose out of historical convention from when dollars were convertible to gold before 1971. Now dollars are not convertible to anything officially, but of course they are convertible to everything at whatever the conventional mass psychology of the value of money says they are worth. The Fed, as part of the government, can create money for itself and the government to spend, and the banks can loan money that they create to collect interest and make gains. The commercial banking system creates far more of the money in the form of newly invented deposits for loans than does the Fed. So there is plenty of reason for the owners of this system to keep it going. If they overuse the creation, they create bubbles and diminish the purchasing power of the money they are creating. So there is some limit on their dilution of the money pool. But since they get the first use and all the benefit, the incentives are to continue to create more money while talking of being "vigilant" and having an "exit strategy" to keep the image of money having value from being damaged at its source. I think it is all a sham, and when the majority of holders realize that the emperor hasn't any clothes, there will be a run on the confidence in this dollar fiat system. As to when, I keep thinking it will happen in my lifetime, but really I am amazed at the asset deflation that occurred in 2009.

How Effective Is the Reserve Requirement at Controlling Money?

The theoretical restraint on the credit growth of bank lending is supposed to be the reserve requirement. Our fractional reserve banking system allows banks to lend out all but the fraction called a "reserve," which is nominally at 10 percent of deposits. It is assumed that banks want to earn money by collecting the interest on loans, so they would always make as many loans as they have money to do so.

It is a great business. They start with a million dollars and can immediately make loans of $10 million and collect interest on all those loans. As long as they pick borrowers who pay back the loans, they quickly get rich. The Fed is supposed to watch over this reserve requirement to keep credit in line. But the Federal Reserve changes that decreased the requirement to have reserves on deposit have become so small that there really is no control on the banks. Reserve requirements used to be 40 percent, but now through various regulations the official requirement

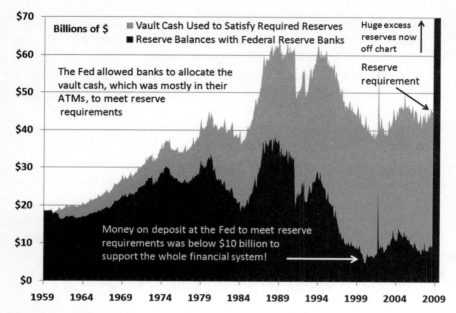

Figure 4.8 Banks Meet Reserve Requirement with ATM Cash
SOURCE: Federal Reserve.

of 10 percent overstates the actual requirement. Banks are free to expand credit greatly and have done so. Figure 4.8 shows how small reserves really were up until the big bailout, at a trivial $10 billion.

Since 1990, required reserves have fallen even while banking and deposits have grown. The Fed eliminated the reserve requirement on large time deposits in 1990 and lowered the requirement on transaction accounts in 1992. A more important source of the decline in required reserves came from the invention of sweep accounts. Funds in bank customers' retail checking accounts are swept overnight into savings accounts that are exempt from reserve requirements and then put back into customers' checking accounts the next day. This explains the relatively small size of total demand deposits and the related decline in reserve requirements.

The current credit crisis is not driven by banks' inability to meet reserve requirements. The Federal Reserve has done its job to make sure that the requirements are not limiting their ability to make new loans. Because banks are not up against the reserve requirement limit, adding more liquidity does not multiply through the banking system in additional loans. The banks have other problems that are limiting their expansion of credit.

The problem for the banks is that their losses have wiped out their equity so that the banks are close to insolvency. They made bad loans, profits were lost, and many banks will be forced to close. It was claimed by Paulson that the big banks were so important to the country that we must use trillions of dollars to bail them out or the rest of the economy would grind to a halt. I personally don't believe that. I think Paulson scared Congress and took the money from the taxpayers to bail out the corrupt bankers.

Bank lending is constrained by the capital adequacy requirement more than the reserve requirement. The Bank for International Settlements (BIS) sets this requirement for all the banks of the world, and countries apply the requirement as they can. The capital requirement is more complicated than the reserve requirement, but it explains why banks, which can create money, are going bankrupt. A bank's capital is its assets minus its liabilities. Assets are "risk-weighted," with some being considered riskier than others. The capital adequacy rule requires that the ratio of a bank's capital to its assets with a risk-weighting of 1 be at least 8 percent. In other words, the bank must have $8 in capital for every $100 in ordinary loans. Federal bonds have a risk-weighting of zero; mortgage loans have a risk weighting of .5.

If loans have to be written down, a bank may suddenly find that its assets are insufficient to support its liabilities. That makes it insolvent and unable to make new loans.

Credit default swaps (CDSs) are sold as insurance against default. When the housing bubble burst and the insurance companies couldn't meet their payments for default, the value of the derivatives protecting securitized mortgages became so questionable that they were unmarketable at any price. Banks counting them as assets on their books then had to mark them to effectively zero, reducing the banks' capital below the levels called for in the Basel Accords and rendering the banks officially insolvent.

Some numbers from the Z1 report will help explain how big the financial institution's supply of credit is. The financial sector in 2000 was borrowing $8,158 billion, and in 2008 it was $17,080 billion, which is an increase of 209 percent. GDP grew only 145 percent (from $9,952 billion to $14,441 billion).

So the reason interest rates are low is that there is a huge supply of credit from our financial institutions. That should be no surprise, considering the policy that brought us to the .25 percent overnight rate.

The problem is that this credit creation provides the money to bid up prices not just of Treasuries, but of all kinds of assets. Soaring asset prices, first in stocks in the 1990s and in houses to 2006, are the result of not only the relaxed policies of the Fed, but the expansive policies of the banks in creating lots of money (i.e., credit), which caused prices to rise and the purchasing power of our currency to decrease commensurately.

So Why Are We Seeing Deflation in Stocks and Houses Now?

In a fiat money system, with no required gold backing, there is little limit to how much money can be created. But what is not recognized by the simple paradigm is that for large amounts of money to be created, the banks have to be creating the money along with the Fed.

Deflation could occur if the Federal Reserve were to adopt a policy of raising reserve requirements and selling off assets like Treasuries to absorb money that it previously created. That is the exact opposite of what the Fed is doing now. For deflation to occur, there would have to be a contraction of credit, and that can also occur from the banking sector itself in spite of the action of the Fed. That is what we experienced in 2009: The banks were not lending.

The key problem for the Fed in 2009 was the unusual situation that the restrictions and reasons for not making loans held the banks back from the traditional process of making loans that would create a multiple of new money for the system. Quite simply, the Fed gave banks hundreds of billions of new reserve deposits, but the banks sat on their hands not making loans.

That is the situation in the lower third part of Figure 4.6 of my models of the banking system. It is like the old story of leading a horse to water but not being able to make him drink. Banks normally want to expand loans, because they make money from the interest on the loans.

But in 2009, there were fewer qualified buyers at the higher standards required of borrowers, and the banks were having the problem of not enough ready cash to cover problem loans. Also the Fed now pays .25% on deposits.

They perhaps justifiably are not making loans. The result is that the massive stimulus of the Fed has gone only to bail out the bad loans and hasn't stimulated the economy with new loans for new spending. So we experienced deflation of asset prices in the first half of 2009 in the housing market and the stock market—even in the face of the most expansive set of stimuluses ever taken by the Fed. In essence, the Fed printing-press theory isn't working, yet.

Foreigners Are Partners in Our Credit Supply

This requirement for banks to lend to grow the economy is generally understood by bankers and economists. But there is another important complexity to this model that must be covered to think about what may be the next steps in this unwinding world economic crisis. It is the relationship of foreigners to the U.S. trade deficit and their flow of money. Chapter 2, on the trade deficit, explains in more detail how foreigners reinvest their trade dollars back into the United States. In fact, they have been so generous that they bought all the new debt of the U.S. government for the decade up to 2006.

When the federal government spends more than it taxes, it is adding dollars to the private sector for business and households to spend. It is stimulative. If foreigners provide the money to buy the Treasuries, the U.S. private sector does not have to spend money buying Treasuries and the federal government could fund its deficit.

But there is a very big problem looming. The budget deficit in 2009 exploded to four times what it was in the last record year of 2008. It went from $455 billion to $1.4 trillion. The trade deficit declined to a little over $400 billion.

Foreigners may find better things to do with their dollars than buy U.S. Treasuries. They could buy U.S. mining interests. That would cause two problems: The prices of mining interests might rise as the demand rose, and the Treasury would now have to find other sources from whom to borrow the money to fund the huge deficits. Consumers have plenty of credit-card obligations to pay down, so they are not likely to expand big loans to the government. Banks now have some funds for buying Treasuries from their excess reserves, but not at the level required to cover the massive budget deficit.

Thus, the likely response is for the Federal Reserve to make new dollars available with which to buy the new Treasuries. Even though the Fed will still buy them in the open market, the net effect is the same as if they bought them directly from the Treasury.

The reason this last model is important to watch is that the significance of the foreign investment in keeping the dollar strong and rates low is not emphasized enough and not understood well enough. The process kept inflation low in the United States for the last two decades, even as the U.S. banking system went on a leverage loan spree that would otherwise have been very inflationary.

Cheap foreign manufactured goods kept prices low, and the recycling of the trade surplus by foreigners into our credit market kept the dollar strong and interest rates low. Normally, the large amount of debt creation in the United States would have forced the dollar down and rates higher and would have led to higher inflation.

The important point is that protection by foreigners is about to be unmasked. If foreigners were to sell off their holdings, it would be even worse. If they just stopped buying government debt, it would leave the Treasury with no other source of funding than the Fed printing. We can see that the long-term implications lead toward dollar weakness and inflation. The big issue is that the budget deficits can be met only by Federal Reserve printing of money. The Fed will be creating deposits out of thin air to buy Treasuries, and the government will be using those deposits to fund its programs. Foreigners have already stated their desire to diversify out of the dollar, which means that they cannot be expected to be buying as much of our financial paper.

The Government Is Supporting the Economy Rather Than the Dollar

It is generally understood that as a government expands its deficit, it does so eventually through the process of creating more of its own money to fill the gap between taxes and spending. (Here, I am including the Fed as part of the government.) That additional money chasing goods drives the price of goods up and the value of the currency down. The United States has avoided much of that inflationary pressure by the kindness of foreigners as we have bought their cheaply manufactured goods and they have dutifully reinvested their trade surpluses in our government debt. As the world's reserve currency, the U.S. dollar has avoided the typical inflationary pressures that these twin deficits would bring to the currency of other nations.

Because virtually no currency in the world has any connection to a specific anchor of value, all currencies derive their value from the confidence of the people using them. The game is that holders will be able to pass the currency (or bank check) on to the next party at somewhere near its present value.

Confidence is absolutely crucial to maintaining this house of cards of our world currency system. A fiat currency is more fragile than the banking system. One reason this fragile system works is that all the governments and central banks have a vested interest in main-taining the status quo. After all, they benefit greatly by printing their own money.

By understanding that our governments want to kick the can down the road, we see how deeply out of balance the system has become. The most obvious conclusion one can make about the many public pronouncements by Bernanke, Geithner, Summers, and Obama is that they want to maintain and grow our economy even at the cost of eventual dollar debasement.

I have been talking for years about the dilemma of a rock and a hard place, where if the Federal Reserve defends the dollar by raising interest rates, it faces a declining economy, or if it does the reverse of flooding the market and world with liquidity in which it hopes to expand the economy, it will cause the dollar to decline. We now know the direction our leaders have taken: They are fanning the flames of dollar demise with the hopes that the short-term economic situation can be patched up by adding more liquidity to specific problem areas. Although international markets have not reacted yet, I think we are close to the point of no return because of the size of these huge deficits, bailouts, and interventions.

Federal Reserve's New Inflation Policy

The Federal Reserve embarked on a new policy in the spring of 2009 of bailing out mortgage-backed securities by committing to buy $1.25 trillion worth. It is also buying $200 billion of agency debt and $300 billion of Treasuries. The shift is dramatic, as presented in Figure 4.9. The goal is to keep interest rates low and to stimulate and support mortgage lending. This quantitative easing has added a tremendous amount of liquidity. Because the other direct lending to troubled banks and other market support has been declining, the Fed's balance sheet has been steady.

The process is entirely different from how the Fed approached its early bailouts at the end of 2007, where it directly provided funds by selling off $200 billion of its short-term T-bills. So, in essence, it gave the market funds with one hand, as it drained it with the other. The net created only moderate new money for the system.

Looking to the future, there seems to be no way for the federal government to borrow $1.5 trillion in 2010 without great assistance from

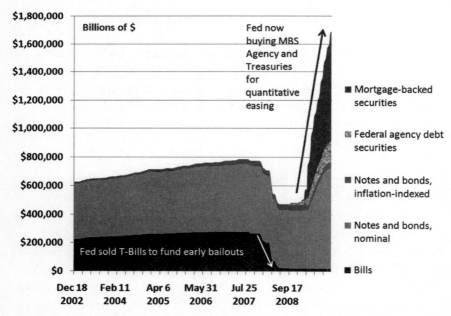

Figure 4.9   The Fed Switched from Noninflationary Actions to an Inflationary Policy in Mid-2008

the Federal Reserve. Although the Federal Reserve has announced that it would purchase $300 billion of longer-term Treasuries, the government borrowing suggests that the Fed may purchase up to $1 trillion of Treasuries to fund the federal deficit at the ongoing rate. This amount of expansion of the Federal Reserve balance sheet could damage the dollar. Tim Geithner was laughed at in China when he said that Chinese investment in U.S. securities was safe. This kind of Fed expansion will not be ignored, and the direction is toward inflation.

Who Will Buy All the Treasuries?

The huge jump in the federal government's projected budget deficit raises the question of who will buy all the debt that will have to be issued to fund spending.

Trying to identify who will ultimately step up to buy up the next wave of government debt, I look past the current holdings and focus on the recent buying patterns of the four sectors. It will, after all, have to be buying by some combination of these sectors that, in total, cover the government's deficit. So, which of the sectors have been buying more recently?

As you can see in Figure 4.10, I expect a big jump in Treasury purchases by both the *private domestic holders* and by *foreigners*. This increased buying reflects the move by investors, concerned about defaults in mortgage-backed and other securities, into the "safe harbor" of government-issued paper.

In an attempt to look forward, I've spent a considerable amount of time developing defensible projections, which are also reflected in Figure 4.10. These projections indicate that while both foreigners and domestic investors will continue to buy Treasuries, they'll do so at a lower level. Let's look at each group:

- *Foreigners:* In the case of foreigners, the trade surplus is their source of ready cash. That is in steep decline, from about $750 billion annually down to about $500 billion now. They have fewer funds available to invest, and usually follow that source.
- *Private Domestic Holders* are made up of two groups: households and businesses. Households' net worth is decimated by the economic

$ Billions

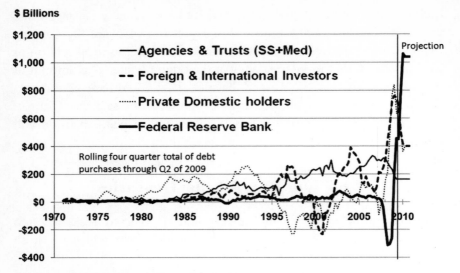

Figure 4.10   The Federal Reserve Will Have to Buy Treasuries to Fund the Deficit

downturn, and their incomes are hit by the recession, so they simply don't have the economic firepower to make new investments. There could be purchases of Treasuries by the financial sector, as they are far less willing to take on risk of new loans.

- The *Trust Funds* will continue purchases, although at slightly lower levels now that baby boomers born after 1945 are turning 65 years old. Thus, the surplus generated by these trust funds will not be as big a piggy bank for the Treasury to pillage.

In short, these sectors will not be able to absorb the $2 trillion deficit. And that leaves only the Federal Reserve to step up and buy the excess new issues of Treasuries.

Figure 4.10 also shows that in order to cover the government deficits of close to $2 trillion, the Federal Reserve will have to buy up to $1 trillion of Treasuries a year, according to my estimates. The mechanics of how this will be achieved may be more complex than directly buying Treasuries at Treasury auctions because that raises flags to the financial community about the demise of the independence of the Fed and the destruction of the dollar. It will involve the Fed buying Treasuries from the open market in what are called Permanent Open Market Operations (POMO).

The federal government is likely to put those newly created dollars into circulation more rapidly than when the Fed gives money to the banks. The Treasury spends the money immediately on Social Security or bombers. So this government spending will be an increasingly more effective stimulant than the bank bailouts. That is because the banks have been reluctant to make new loans with their bailouts, preferring to leave money on deposit at the Fed as I discussed earlier. The point is that deficits that are monetized are more inflationary than Fed loans to banks that hoard the money.

Many economists and bond dealers are operating under the "Pushing on a String" model, predicting deflationary results like those that occurred in the Depression. In those days the tie to gold kept the Fed from pursuing the kind of money creation that they have already done. For comparison, Roosevelt's New Deal spending was not nearly as big as the current bailouts, not by a big margin even after correcting for the difference in purchasing power of the dollar.

Who will buy all the debt being issued to fund the government's massive spending? The government itself (the Fed), through an equally massive amount of money creation. That will be inflationary.

When Might Deflation Turn to Inflation?

The race between asset price depreciation and the effects of the government aggressive bailout is the most important driver of whether we will have inflation or deflation. The erosion in housing and stock prices has affected the apparent wealth of everyone. Against the erosion is a wall of money emanating from the federal government and the Fed in their attempt to reinflate the collapsing bubble.

So far, the asset-deflation side of the ledger has been bigger than the bailouts.

Although I can't know much for certain, I do know that in a fiat monetary system, such as we now operate, the Federal Reserve has the

Table 4.1   Government Bailout Programs

Stimulus	Total Program Promise	To Q3 2009 Commitment/Loss
Federal Reserve Total	$ 7,766	$1,679
FDIC Total	$ 2,039	$ 358
Treasury Total	$ 2,694	$1,834
HUD Total	$ 300	$ 300
Total (Billions)	$12,798	$4,170

ability to crank out virtually any amount of money it deems necessary. Although there are obvious limitations in terms of how far creditors will allow the Fed to go before severely punishing the dollar, as long as price inflation continues to appear under control, the government can be expected to continue to spend, and prodigiously so.

To establish the magnitude of the countervailing forces, I created Tables 4.1 and 4.2. The caveat is that the numbers are fairly loose. Even so, they are sufficient for the purposes of getting a general indication of how much more money the government needs to come up with to douse the flames of collapse.

Table 4.1 summarizes the stimulus items that have been announced so far, with the amount promised by various agencies (in the middle column) and the amount actually committed by those agencies (in the right column).

Table 4.2 summarizes, using reasonable but ultimately inaccurate estimates, just how bad the losses could get at the worst (in the middle column) and what those losses are to date (in the right column).

Table 4.2   Asset and Loan Losses from Peak

Losses	Potential Losses	Losses Q3 2009
Stocks	−$ 6,000	−$ 4,000
Houses	−$ 8,000	−$ 6,000
Commercial RE	−$ 3,000	−$ 1,500
Loan loss	−$ 1,800	−$ 1,000
Total Losses	−$18,800	−$12,500

Although the losses in assets could be as bad as \$18.8 trillion, the government's total promises to date add up to only about two-thirds that level, or \$12.7 trillion. Based strictly on those two numbers, the government would have to make a similar level of commitment for the first two thirds of 2010 if it were to reinflate the bubble. That may be their track, and it may be in 2010 that we see deflationary forces overcome by inflationary.

When you look at the numbers of actual current losses, \$12.5 trillion versus the government's actual commitments today, \$4.2 trillion, you could come to the conclusion that the government has almost three years to go at current levels to catch up with the losses.

My methodology in Tables 4.1 and 4.2 is completely off the wall, but it gives me a range to consider when deflation might turn to inflation, which is to say at what point might the government succeed in outspending the deflationary pressures. Of course, there are many factors involved in this equation, and so this is little more than a mental exercise. I want to share with you some sense of the data that I look at when trying to come to grips with the current state of the economy and where it's headed next. I don't guarantee these numbers follow rigorous definitions that formal economists expect!

In July 2009, the watchdog overseeing the government bailout said the government's maximum exposure to financial institutions since 2007 could total nearly \$23.7 trillion. The headline-grabbing amount was compiled by Neil Barofsky, the inspector general for the \$700 billion Troubled Asset Relief Program. This overstates the expected actual costs because many of the programs are backed by collateral and the \$23.7 trillion represents the gross, not net, exposure that the government could face. He doesn't suggest that the full amounts would be used, but the amounts do get close to the kind of unlimited spending that the government sometimes seems to be moving toward. One of his valid criticisms is that the government is not telling us precisely what organizations are getting what money, which is a red flag to me because where there is secrecy there could be fraud.

As I look more closely at the rising stock market, up 65 percent since March 2009, housing prices rising a little and crude oil doubling from depressed levels at the end of 2008, I conclude that the deflationary pressures are ready to give way to inflationary pressure in 2010 and grow thereafter.

Political Implications of Egregious Fed Spending

The Federal Reserve has moved way beyond the authority of its original charter, which was to act as a banker's bank and to distribute our currency. It now believes it is an instrument of economic policy and is unilaterally creating credit, buying up so-called toxic waste assets, and venturing into large purchases of mortgage-backed securities and longer-term Treasuries. This is a tremendous addition to the credit markets, which will eventually lead to debasement of the dollar.

The Federal Reserve doubled its balance sheet in 2008 and could add another trillion again by the end of 2010 to meet the commitments of supporting the mortgage market and to fund the government deficit.

The complete freezing of many markets and the recognition of big financial institutions that they did not have enough capital to keep operating brought a massive response from the government. The Treasury took over Fannie and Freddie and entered the credit markets to lower rates by guarantees and new investments. To fund these bailouts, the Treasury issued massive amounts of new Treasuries. The Treasury borrowed a trillion dollars in three months. I use the word panic to describe how fast the new borrowing was accomplished. There has never been this big a jump in history except during the World Wars.

The hidden political shift in power is to concentrate wealth in the big lenders, including the banks and wealthiest people. This becomes more obvious when contrasted with the way our system is supposed to work. The big financial institutions that were overpaying their managers and traders to take unreasonable risk for short-term profits that bring personal bonuses and stock option payouts should be wiped out, including those invested in these sham institutions. Bankruptcies and investment losses would make any future institutions far more balanced with a long-term view of risk about their investment choices. We are seeing the end of capitalism and the rise of a concentrated government authority over our financial system.

After all of this it is impossible to say why money has any value at all. Before 1971, when dollars could be converted into gold at $35 an ounce by foreign central banks, there was an anchor for the dollar. Since then, dollars are merely traded on the convention of what they were worth yesterday. It is my view that the only value of dollars is from the combined opinion of all the users to agree on their value. This illusion is the greatest CONfidence game ever developed in the financial community!

It is my belief that we are on the cusp of recognizing the failures of this highly leveraged debt-based monetary system. The whole world has been caught in the economic slowing and loss of confidence in credit as this system begins to unwind.

Banks expect to take back more money in interest along with the principal that they put into the system. That is not possible on a long-term basis if money maintains it value. It would mean that bankers eventually own the world. The whole world has been captured in the debt trap of an overleveraged, too-big-to-fail banking mania and collapse.

In a fiat money system, the Quantity Theory of Money is unable to explain all that is going on. When dollars had intrinsic ties to gold, ratios of money supply to quantities of goods were sensible interpretations. But when money is whatever people think it should be worth, the mechanism of supply of money for predicting prices is no longer adequate. Prices don't calmly decline because of a contraction in the money supply. Workers are fired, businesses cut back, and the economy goes into recession. It's too optimistic to assume that the Fed can fine-tune prices by controlling the money supply. It is very difficult to control the money supply as there are independent players acting to create money. For example, the Fed now is increasing the part of the money supply it controls (monetary base), but we are not seeing inflation because banks are not lending. Banks make loans, and foreigners can purchase assets, both of which affect the domestic money measures. Adding Federal Reserve deposits to the system might not raise prices if foreign goods can be purchased cheaply.

It was the commercial banks, by their own money multiplying under the lax review of the regulators, that created this mess as much as it was the central bank. Commercial banks just create money as accounting entries on their books, as does the Fed. The crisis came when overextended housing loans collapsed, not because of a Fed policy change.

The bank bailout has proven to be no more than a handout to well-connected big Wall Street banks, and it didn't get credit flowing again.

In early 2008, outstanding derivatives on the books of U.S. banks exceeded $180 trillion. However, $90 trillion of this was carried on the books of JP Morgan Chase alone, while Citibank and Bank of America each had $38 trillion on their books. Not so surprisingly, these big banks that hold incalculable amounts of derivatives on their books, are the ones that got the majority of the Treasury's bailout money under the Troubled Asset Relief Program. Rather than getting rid of the derivatives, the trillions in taxpayer money is being used, not to unfreeze credit by making loans, but to buy up smaller banks. That means the derivative time bomb continues to tick away.

The Fed May Be Acting Beyond Its Intended Authority

It seems to me that the Fed is acting outside of the constitutional authority that gives Congress the right to allocate funds. The Federal Reserve hides behind Section 13.3 of the Federal Reserve Act talking about unusual circumstances to justify their actions. Even more egregious is that they refuse to tell us to whom they have given these special deals and buyouts, or to reveal the actual holdings of the garbage they have purchased.

Congressman Ron Paul from Texas introduced a bill into the House asking only that the Federal Reserve be subject to normal auditing scrutiny. While he has support in the Congress, and has obtained kudos from the public for his tenacity in taking on the crusade for what should be normal practice in any government operation, I am sure that the powerful banking interests will squash this bill in the Senate. We the people will be left with what we have been left since this crisis started: the responsibility for paying the bill without understanding who is getting the payoff.

The Federal Reserve Act provides for the Federal Reserve to purchase only government guaranteed securities. So it seems outside the Fed charter to be purchasing $1.25 trillion of Mortgage-Backed Securities.

The Federal Reserve is trying to drive down the cost of mortgage rates to support the housing market with this huge sum. The risk to the Federal Reserve is that many of these loans might not be paid off and many homes are in foreclosure. These securities were mostly guaranteed by Fannie Mae and Freddie Mac. Fannie and Freddie have now been taken over by the Treasury in what is called a conservatorship. The legislation allowing the Treasury takeover was rammed through Congress by Henry Paulson who said he needed the authority but claimed he doubted he would use it. Almost immediately he took over Fannie and Freddie. The legislation includes a limit of $300 billion in total, and $200 billion for each institution. But on Christmas Eve 2009, Timothy Geithner slipped out the announcement that the Treasury had unilaterally eliminated the $200 billion per institution. The result of this open-ended support for Fannie and Freddie will be that the treasury (that's you and me) will be printing up new Treasuries to cover the losses at Fannie and Freddie, which will be induced from the $ trillion + Mortgage-Backed Securities being held by the Fed. This means that the toxic waste assets purchased by the Federal Reserve will be bailed out by the taxpayer. All this is happening without taxpayer approval.

While the actual hundreds of billions of dollars involved are enough to make us cringe, I think the roughshod trampling of the Constitution is worse. Look beyond the huge dollars involved to the precedent where now bureaucrats at the Federal Reserve, and at the Treasury, are making policy decisions and allocating money without specific congressional legal authority. It's not that I believe Congress is a paragon of virtue in deciding financial matters, but at least they are a large deliberative body, whose decisions are made in public. The Federal Reserve, in deciding to purchase over $1 trillion of securities, did so with no specific authority except the assertion of the Chairman that there was an emergency and he thought it was the right thing to do. Personally, I consider this a usurpation of power, a dangerous precedent that was not delegated under the Constitution.

So the related problem of confidence in the dollar becomes more problematic as we see capricious actions taken to bailout specific industries with only the smallest oversight by Congress. I think this is a formula for weakening the dollar even as the domestic economy repairs itself.

Regardless of the legality, the court of international opinion will decide whether the world wants to own so many dollars, with the "vote" expressed in the strength of the U.S. dollar on foreign exchange markets and for tangibles such as gold and oil. It seems pretty clear to me that foreigners are already nervous, as seen in world leaders' pronouncements and actions in the news.

Conclusion

The steps being taken by the Federal Reserve are both predictable and catastrophic. Bernanke told us in speeches and papers that he was positioned to make sure that the United States had all the money it needed to avoid a deflationary collapse similar to that of 1929. On the one hand, Dr. Bernanke was given a difficult set of circumstances to manage. But on the other hand, the actions he has taken to double the balance sheet, to provide liquidity to specific markets like mortgage-backed securities and commercial paper, and to provide the resources for bailouts of specific institutions are all way beyond anything that has been done before. They will eventually be paid for by taxpayers and by people losing purchasing power through inflation. Many people are incensed that rich bankers have been the first to slop at the trough of government and the Federal Reserve for special privileges and bailouts. What is smarter is to think about how these actions will affect our future and to get out of the way of the train wreck of dollar debasement.

The basic problem of the Federal Reserve is that there is virtually no restraint against it using its very powerful ability to create money. People used to say that money doesn't grow on trees. But if you think about it for a moment, money is just a few bits in the computer. Bernanke has already abused his situation, and the only countervailing force defined by the Constitution would be actions taken by the House of Representatives to take back the management of our currency and banking system.

In fact, the opposite is being played out in the halls of Congress, by providing more powers to the Fed to mess things up even more than they already have. The Federal Reserve is the banker's bank. It allowed the egregious expansion of credit to get out of hand, and it is now being entrusted with even more responsibility to manage in the future. The

Fed does whatever it takes to manage and support the large banks that it is supposed to be regulating. We no longer have an experiment, we have results: Our banks would have failed without the support of egregious government and federal largess.

Going forward, we already understand the policy decisions that have been made to bail out our big banks and to try to stimulate economic activity, while letting the dollar be damned. Watching this system unravel will be painful. Keeping track of the various factors of our credit markets that both add liquidity and demand money for normal economic activity is at the guts of unraveling the conundrum of who the winners and losers will be. The next chapter in this section on the theoretical underpinning of how the financial markets are structured digs into the relationship between debt, money, and the economy to see how serious the current upheaval is.

Chapter 5

The Importance of Debt for Predicting Our Economy

D ebt and credit are critical to the expansion and contraction of the economy. A clear examination of the interplay between these factors will provide some important clues to what's going on, and give us guidance as to how the current crisis will evolve from here.

This chapter is perhaps the wonkiest chapter of the book, so if you're more interested in getting on with the show, you can probably just peruse the graphs to see if any catch your fancy, and move on. I consider myself a pretty wonky economist, and what I'm providing here is the data to show that debt expansion and contraction of the kind we are now experiencing provides a fundamental explanation about how this particular crisis is importantly different from the typical recession. The basic point is that we created debt at such extreme levels that it is now being unwound with serious consequences that will stay with us for a long time.

The earlier chapters set the stage by analyzing how big the government debt and international debt has become, and how the Federal Reserve has been accommodating the demands for more debt. In this chapter, I combine the debt of households and businesses into a category of public debt and point out that its growth and contraction explain how deep the current crisis is. From this point of view, the government bailouts that are funded by going more and more into debt are working against the return to reasonable balance for the level for all debt.

Traditional simplistic monetarist views give us a starting point but they gloss over the important contribution that debt expansion and contraction makes to the cycles of our system. Keynesians acknowledge the value of debt to expand government programs, but they don't offer a plan for how to manage the effects of that debt expansion. Those economists, like Nuriel Roubini and Steve Keene, who watch debt closely were able to see the credit crisis coming, while Bernanke and Paulson were not. So, if you can slog through the theory, there is the reward that you will have a better understanding of why things are happening, which will give you a better basis for extrapolating the future. This chapter shows that debt is crucial to our overall economic system functioning and explains why the system goes through extreme cycles. So, as I often say, let's see what the data show.

Debt is behind our money. Debt makes the economy grow but is also a potential destroyer. People need credit to acquire items too expensive for cash purchase, businesses need seed capital for startup and expansion, and so on. On the other hand, too much debt siphons off interest payments and is a drag on the economy, and when it overwhelms borrowers, it leads to collapse. Debt grew so large that it is collapsing during this credit crisis and in so doing threatens the whole financial system.

Most economists don't factor in debt when analyzing the economy. This is a mistake, because today money isn't based on gold or silver. As discussed in Chapter 4, we create more money simply by creating more debt.

The government's response to the present crisis has been to create great new waves of programs to bail out whatever problem pops up—from subprime mortgages to option ARMs, auction rate securities, structured investment vehicles, collateralized debt obligations, credit default swaps, commercial paper, money market funds, hedge funds, and on and on. Floundering U.S. automakers have hopped on the gravy train, while strapped states and municipalities seek their own baggage cars filled with cash.

The problems were built up over *decades* of too much debt. Now that the merry-go-round is stopping, there aren't enough real, productive sectors left in our economy to keep this many bloated institutions afloat, as well as fund a tragically expensive pair of wars, and also support the retiring baby boomer generation. There isn't enough to go around.

The supercycle of debt was enormous and globally pervasive, akin to a steroid that falsely pumped up the world economy over the past half century. Now the bursting of that bubble is affecting all aspects of the world economy.

The free market advocates think it would have been best to let the debt be unwound quickly, albeit painfully. But the cautious political establishment dreads the massive dislocations and unemployment that would result. So government reacted as it always has, by trying to paper over the situation with more government debt. Yet without new employment through business growth, it will have trouble servicing the new debt it's taking on. After all, this is the same debt that the financial community was unable to deal with. It still exists but has been shifted to the government's book.

Our Debt Has Grown Way Beyond What Our Economy Can Support

The present U.S. credit bubble collapse is the response to several decades of credit expansion reaching a point of unsustainability. The great expansion of credit for the last 60 years—which fueled ongoing prosperity, rising stock markets, and inflated home prices—has come to a halt, leaving us with a mandatory deleveraging that has few parallels. Only the Great Depression and Japan's lost decade after 1990, both of which started with imploding debt, exhibit the same debt unwinding.

The first signs of debt instability began in the housing sector, where too much credit was extended to those who found they couldn't pay.

From there, the credit crisis exploded across the financial spectrum, bringing the worst downturn since the Great Depression. Financial companies were crushed, overcapacity in manufacturing and uncompetitive compensation crushed the great auto companies of the last century, and credit markets froze for all but the most high-quality borrowers. Lenders came to distrust mortgage-backed and other paper, and defaults like never before rolled across the desks of financial managers. The traditional economic measures of rising unemployment, slowing GDP, and sinking consumer confidence confirm that we're revisiting something more like the 1930s. This is not the usual recession that we often experienced every four years or so. This is a Great Deleveraging of overbloated debt.

To confirm the historical perspective and provide a big-picture overview, I gathered long-term data on the total debt in our country (extracted from old census reports), and I plotted the size as a ratio to our economy as measured by the GDP. Figure 5.1 clearly shows us that debt is at a record in relationship to the size of everything else we do in a year. This is what caused the bubble to burst.

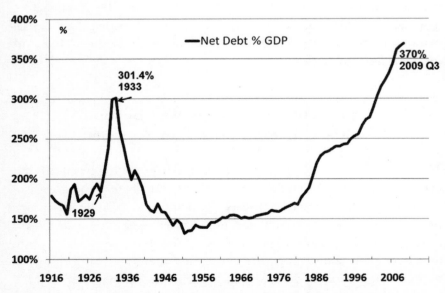

Figure 5.1   Debt as a Percentage of GDP Is at Record-High Levels
SOURCE: Federal Reserve, Census Bureau.

Debt growth supports growth of the economy as measured by GDP. Figure 5.2 shows their relationship. Credit and GDP expansion are locked together, and they grew in tandem for 40 years. But starting about 1980, they diverged, with credit growth outstripping the overall economy by an ever-widening margin. The growth of private credit reached its climax in 2009 and must be unwound, so we face a tough decade ahead. (Note: The scales in Figure 5.2 have been adjusted by using logarithms so that we can see the changes in the long-term history, as well as the nearby data, more clearly.)

Figure 5.2 shows how, during the Depression, GDP decreased even more than the debt. That is the cause of the spike in the 1930s in Figure 5.1. It also explains why the Depression was so difficult: People lost their jobs and their income, but their debts did not decrease in size. Mortgages still had to be paid. When people couldn't pay, they had to sell their houses, and prices collapsed.

One of the most serious consequences of a deflationary depression is that the debts remain fixed even as wages decline, and dollars become more valuable as prices fall. In effect, deflation makes debt that much harder to pay as the value of the dollar increases.

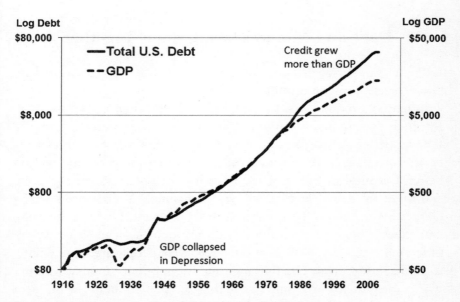

Figure 5.2   Economic Growth Moves with Credit Growth

Our Money Is Debt Today

Debt is an economic indicator that is regularly, and foolishly, ignored. It is important because it is the basis of our money supply. Money is now completely based on debt.

Any analysis of the Federal Reserve balance sheet comes down to its debt. Our dollar bills are debt of the Federal Reserve. The assets held by the Fed against this have been debt of the federal government in the form of Treasuries for decades.

The Federal Reserve identifies a vestigial asset of gold certificates that are accounted for as a value of $11 billion. Even Alan Greenspan said that the Federal Reserve doesn't own gold. If it were marked to market at today's prices, its worth would be $250 billion, but that's still small potatoes compared to the $2 trillion balance sheet of the Fed. But in the main, our dollars are debt, and that debt is backed by debt of the federal government. Chapter 4 on the Federal Reserve explained this in detail, but the point of looking at debt here is this: Since debt is the basis of our money, when we are looking at debt collapse, we are looking at monetary collapse as well.

Debt and Money Have Grown Together

In Figure 5.3, we see that long-term money growth shows a surprisingly close correlation with economic growth.

Debt and money growth have stayed closely aligned, because borrowing is done to buy something. This historical relationship is evidence for supporting the Keynesian point of view that if the government increases spending, and thus increases money, that the economy will do better. For most of this long-term history, the dollar was tied to gold, and therefore dollar fluctuations were contained. A closer look at the data after 1989 shows a less-coordinated movement. I believe the cause and effect is opposite from the Keynesian point of view: What we are observing is that when the economy does well, people are more willing to lend and to borrow and thus increase the amount of money. In other words, the growing economy caused the growth in money. The problem we will be facing going forward is that Bernanke and many politicians

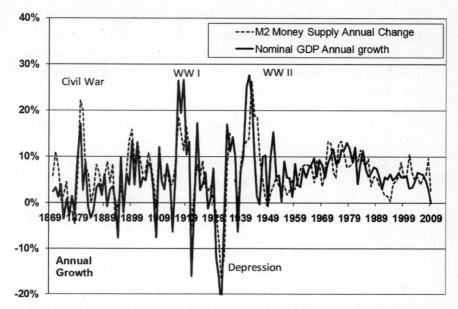

Figure 5.3   Economic Growth and Money Growth Have Moved Together for a Century
SOURCE: Federal Reserve, Census Bureau.

believe that if our government prints enough money the economy will follow. I think that is flawed because we do not create meaningful wealth by managing accounting entries. It is my thesis that the money will grow much faster than the economy in the decade ahead. That can only happen through the mechanism whereby the purchasing power of the dollar falls so that the quantity of real money moves in tandem with the real economy.

Credit Flows Predict Economic Crisis

The credit markets are unbelievably huge and complex. In fact, the bond markets are bigger than the stock markets. But because risks are considered to be less, and the credit market is less volatile, the action there is nowhere near as widely covered as its economic consequences suggest it should be. This section of this chapter presents a high-level view of the major components of the debt market in such a way that we can identify how our overall economy is being affected.

At the end of 2009, the total debt in the United States—personal, business, and government—amounted to a staggering $53 trillion, (as shown in Figure 17.5 at the end of this book). Figure 5.4 shows the annual growth in debt and the most used measure of our Money supply called M2. The chart shows the annual increase in each and the collapse to the third quarter of 2009.

We've seen the close relationship between the growth of debt and of GDP in Figure 5.2. It can be argued whether expansion of debt caused an expansion of the economy or whether the growing economy allowed for and encouraged the expansion of debt, but regardless of which is chicken and which egg, the correlation is quite high.

It is important to look at the government and private debt separately because the effects on the economy are different. Debt increases by the private sector are usually immediately reflected in growth of the economy because the debt is used to purchase output. To the extent that

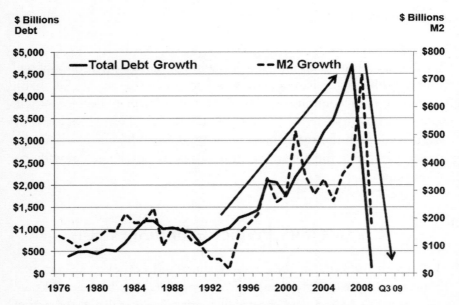

Figure 5.4 Debt and Money Grew and Collapsed Together in the Current Crisis
SOURCE: Federal Reserve Z1.

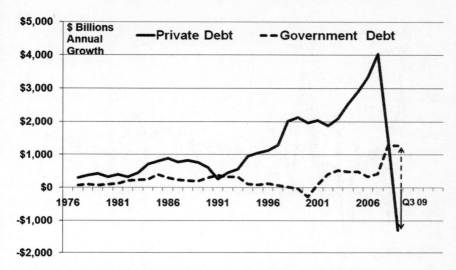

Figure 5.5   Private Debt Growth Collapsed in This Crisis as Government Debt Jumped to Bailout Problems

government spending is used to purchase goods, the economy can also expand. When the government redistributes money from one group to another, the effects on the economy can be much smaller depending on how each group ultimately would have spent the money themselves. But the more important distinction is that government debt expansion is much more likely to be directly connected to money creation and is thus much more likely to be inflationary. Figure 5.5 shows the annual growth in debt split between the private sector and the government sector. It's no surprise that government debt is expanding but the public debt is collapsing. The sizes of the movements confirm how extreme the current situation is compared to history. I've added two arrows on the right side of the graph to point out that the decrease in private debt is approximately the size of the increase in government debt. While it is not a one-for-one transference, there has been a very large takeover of debt by the government from the private sector.

It is the size of the collapse of private debt that causes some economists to predict deflation. But private debt expansion and contraction affects the growth of the GDP much more than it affects the basic quantity of money. The government spending, if accomplished by deficits that are monetized, can be much more inflationary.

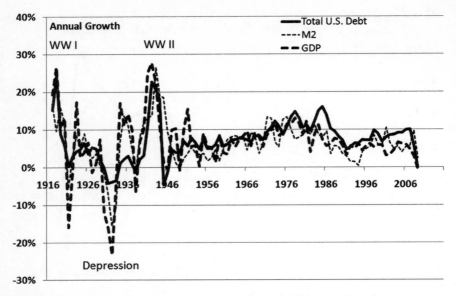

Figure 5.6 Debt, Money, and Economic Growth All Move Together
Source: Federal Reserve.

Because money is based on debt, it is no surprise that money grows along with debt, and GDP as well. Therefore, I have put all three on the same long-term history in Figure 5.6 to show the close relationship.

You can see that both World Wars and the Great Depression had a much bigger effect on our debt, money, and GDP than the current crisis—at least, so far. But a grave concern is that the present crisis might end up mirroring the Great Depression, where private sector borrowing and economic activity collapsed, and unemployment exploded to 25 percent. The debt per person in 1959 was $804 and grew to $170,000 by 2009. And M2 grew from just under $300 to $27,000. Those are pretty dramatic increases. One might point out that the purchasing power of these dollars has declined, so the dollar values are not the same. So, to confirm what our per-person debt growth has been in real purchasing power terms, I calculated the number of today's dollars that represent the debt per person, by using the Consumer Price Index (CPI). The debt per person in the United States from 1959 to 2009 grew from $20,000 to $170,000, when measured using today's dollars. That's still a pretty impressive growth.

Granted, not all of this debt is owed by households or individuals; it is the sum of *all* debt of the country, including corporate and federal. My point is that we have expanded debt more rapidly than our economy, and it will be impossible to unwind this debt to a manageable level without major distortions. This overleveraged debt that hangs on our current economy is a far more seriously negative situation than can be accommodated simply by transferring debt to our government.

Consider also that, although the $170,000 per person (which is based on the $53 trillion of all debt now existing) is large, there is another, equally scary elephant in the room: the $60 trillion unfunded requirement for future Social Security and Medicare liabilities, which are not included. Now, just because debt has grown in real terms per person, and in relation to the size of the economy (GDP), it is not absolutely clear what level is too much to handle. Household incomes have increased, so perhaps we're able to manage our debt? You might not think so, given people's problems paying mortgages and credit card bills. But what does the data say? I look at the debt of households in comparison to their income and present the results in Figure 5.7.

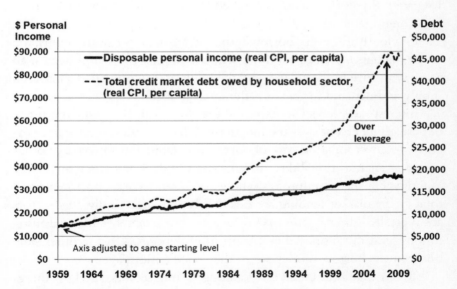

Figure 5.7   Household Debt Has Grown More Than Income, Especially After 1980

Interest rates have been falling since 1980, leading people to feel they could afford more debt. You can see from Figure 5.7 that the amount of personal debt rose much faster than income after about 1984, as the economy recovered from a difficult recession in the early 1980s. Outstanding household debt now vastly exceeds annual income.

The bottom line is that the debt explosion allowed households to consume goods and services much faster than they were earning money to pay for their expenditures. It worked for a while, but eventually spurred overproduction. More houses got built and more cars manufactured than people could afford. Which is where we are today.

Credit Expanding and Contracting Defines Our Financial Future

The current crisis has seen the greatest collapse of credit since the Great Depression, but this time around the government expansion is many times that taken during the Depression, exceeded only during the all-out World Wars. To get a better understanding of debt in our markets, I separate the borrowers from the lenders and identify how the players are changing.

Obviously, for every borrower there is a lender. So, quite simply, the credit markets match up all those who are hoping to borrow against all those who have funds to lend, and the result of the competition between supply and demand for credit is the interest rate.

Interest rates reflect an expected risk-free, real, after-inflation profit of perhaps 3 percent over the long term. That rate must significantly increase to cover inflation, risk of borrower default, and a myriad of other measures such as the ability to remarket the debt and therefore create liquidity. For the economy as a whole, total credit market borrowing and total credit market lending are necessarily the same. Individual sectors are typically either borrowers or lenders. For example, financial institutions lend the money they obtain from deposits. On the other side, homebuyers borrow money when they need a mortgage.

To illustrate how credit flows among various sectors, and how things are changing, I identified three categories of borrowers in the overall market—government, business, and households—and two categories of lenders: the financial sector and foreigners. The financial sector is broad. It includes banks and insurance companies and, indirectly, several other sources of credit. Foreigners are identified because they have become a big contributor to our credit markets, and their actions will have a profound effect on our future.

Figure 5.8 depicts borrowers and lenders, with opposing bars that extend upward away from zero for borrowers and downward for lenders. The totals of borrowing and lending must match, so the bar up is the same length as the bar down, with the sum of all the flows equaling zero. With just a little thought, you can see that the huge pool of credit is available to the borrowers in competition with each other, at the same time that the rates are in competition to bring returns to those lending. It's one big pool and you can either be a borrower or lender. All I've done is grouped all the people who typically borrow into the three categories of government, businesses, and households, and all the people that lend as being either financial institutions or foreigners. For example, foreigners could start to sell off their holdings of U.S.

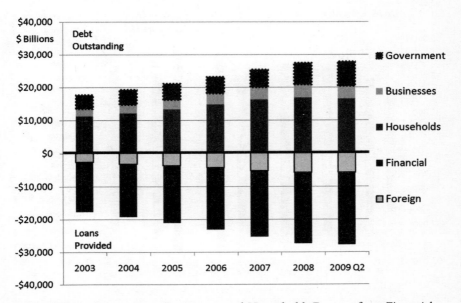

Figure 5.8 Government, Businesses, and Households Borrow from Financial Institutions and Foreigners in a Balanced Credit Market
SOURCE: Federal Reserve Z1.

debt and be a smaller contributor to the credit pool. Figure 5.8 shows the situation at the end of each year for the outstanding lending and borrowing.

Looked at in this fashion as the total aggregate lending and borrowing, the system does not appear to be in need of a major change. To see the more complex flows of the credit market, I have created Figure 5.9 with the same categories, but instead of showing the amount of *outstanding* debt, I show the *flow* of new debt into and out of each sector. The bars on the left, for the years 2004 up until the beginning of the crisis in the second quarter of 2007, have a pattern that is similar in new debt flows to the pattern of the amount of debt outstanding shown in Figure 5.8. But as we look at these flows starting in the third quarter of 2007, the action becomes quite jumbled.

First, the household sector, which had been borrowing huge amounts for housing, stopped in Q3 2007. Because Figure 5.9 shows whether the particular category of debt is increasing or decreasing, it's

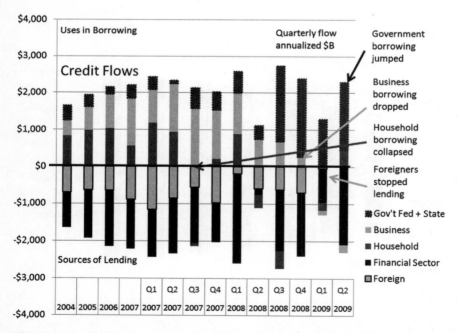

Figure 5.9   Borrowing and Lending Flows Were Disrupted in the Credit Crisis
SOURCE: Federal Reserve Z1.

possible that households paid down some of their debt, so that they became contributors to the pool of borrowing. That actually happened in both Q2 and Q3 of 2008. Figure 5.9 also shows that lending by foreigners—who have been contributing credit by lending to our credit markets on a steady basis—came to an abrupt halt in 2009 and were no longer providing new credit money by Q2. Note that foreigners have continued to lend money to the U.S. Treasury markets by buying U.S. Treasuries, but they have been selling off other holdings like agency securities (the details were described in Chapter 2). You can study Figure 5.9 to see other important shifts in credit flows, most notably that the government sector borrowing jumped in Q3 2008 and has been the biggest borrower by a large margin since.

Traditionally, the biggest sector for borrowing has been households, and their biggest borrowing has been for home mortgages. Business borrowing moves with the economic cycle most closely. But note the significant changes in Figure 5.9: In the most recent quarters, the economic slowing can be seen in the collapse of new borrowing by both households and businesses. This led to the government trying to bail out the economy, and it is borrowing huge amounts to do so. The story is all in these bars.

What does Figure 5.9 tell us about the economy? Well, business borrowing reflects the confidence and growth in the economy more directly than the others. It could be debated whether the business debt decline is a cause or a result, but the net is the same: Businesses are not borrowing, and therefore not hiring, so the economy will be weak.

Additionally, the dramatic jump in government borrowing sticks out like a sore thumb. And the key question there is where the expanded lending to the government will come from. One of the historically important sources of funds for buying Treasuries has been foreigners, which looks to be a big problem going forward.

The financial sector is identified as a source of lending in both Figures 5.8 and 5.9 Looking inside the components from the financial sector, we can see which institutions provided those loans. The biggest source of credit is commercial banks, followed by life insurance, mutual funds, and money market funds. Importantly, the direct contribution of the Federal Reserve is relatively small. It serves as an underlying enabler, whose stimulative effect is multiplied through the banks.

Foreigners are a major provider of funding, as they contribute a large portion of their trade surplus to our credit market. They are not controlled by our policies, so they could become dangerous if they should want to sell off U.S. credit instruments. The lender of last resort, the Federal Reserve, is a wild card, in that it can create new money to provide liquidity to the market. This makes money available and allows interest rates to clear at relatively low levels as described in Chapter 4.

By looking at these big-picture views as presented in Figures 5.8 and 5.9, we can see the inherent instability in this huge credit market. We are seeing an unprecedented expansion of government debt that has only occurred during all-out mobilization for war in the past. Some argue that the recession is severe enough to cause deflation like in the 1930s. I believe, on the contrary, that the government borrowing for bailouts, war, health care, and retirement is so massive that it has planted the seeds for a very serious inflation.

Economic Effects of Debt

In discussing debt, it is important to consider its effects on our economy. The following sections explain how the current crisis is unfolding badly for employment and new credit growth. The picture is grim.

Debt Drives Employment

One of the most important measures of the success of our economy is the ability to employ people profitably. Only when people have incomes can they spend to keep the economy going; thus, employment is a crucial measure of how strong the economy is.

In Figure 5.10, I take the subset of debt incurred in the private sector and compare it against annual job growth. The correlation is surprisingly close for items that are fundamentally quite different from each other. So if we can estimate the future direction of private debt, we should have a pretty good handle on the future strength of the economy as well (and vice versa).

There are two important conclusions to be drawn from the data in Figure 5.10: First, the continuing credit collapse will also mean a

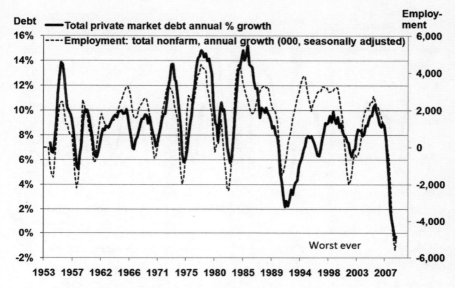

Figure 5.10 How Debt Drives Employment

continuing weakness on the jobs front. Second, both are at the lowest levels recorded since the 1950s, further confirming that this is the most serious downturn since World War II.

Credit Growth Has Collapsed

The outlook for private debt growth is pretty bleak. Banks have had to raise lending standards substantially, now that borrowers have become far less reliable about paying off their loans. Because banks have written down loans, they also face the problem of maintaining enough capital to stay in business, and that limits their own ability to make loans. And with the slow economy, businesses are not borrowing to expand.

Consumers are also sensitive to the economic cycle. They slow down their borrowing when recessions occur, making that a useful marker for the strength of the economy. Consumer credit includes credit cards and personal loans.

As Figure 5.11 reveals, despite talk of "green shoots" in the economy, consumers are decreasing their amount of outstanding credit at the fastest rate in 50 years.

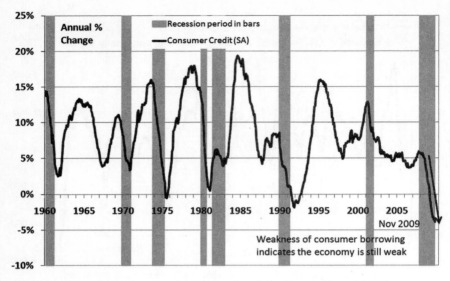

Figure 5.11   Consumer Credit Has Declined the Fastest Since WWII
SOURCE: Federal Reserve.

Where Is the Inflation?

With the bubble growth in debt and money, one would have expected to see across-the-board price rises. But that didn't happen. For example, the most important price for most people is their wage, and wages after inflation have actually been negative.

The actual inflation was in asset prices, primarily stocks and houses. That, coupled with low wage growth, makes this particular recession so much more devastating for the working and middle classes. They don't have any cushion against declining asset values, particularly their homes.

The asset inflation that we should have been worrying about was built on the availability of cheap credit in mortgages, private equity, corporate buyouts, and financial institution overleveraging. The unwinding of this leverage is a major contributor to our current crisis.

The United States is particularly hard hit by this crisis because of the magnitude of its borrowing. We are not facing the normal kind of recession that is induced when the Federal Reserve raises its interest rates to combat general inflation. That's why the further lowering of interest rates by the Fed has been ineffective as a tool to end the recession. This time, the Fed faces a burst of asset bubbles, rather than an unwinding of inventories and a cutting of overpriced wages.

Managing the Overextended Debt Leads to Inflation

Debt brings future spending to the present by allowing consumers to have now what they won't be able to pay for, for some number of years. When debt becomes too extended, and borrowers can't pay back the loans or even the ongoing interest, then the debt bubble bursts, and we get today's problems.

I pointed out that money is a form of debt, but it is important to understand a significant difference between expanding our economy by spending money we earn compared to borrowing to spend: Purchases made with debt are not really over until the debt is paid off. Thus, our GDP during the bubble years looked bigger than it would have without the debt explosion. The whole country seemed much richer than it really was. Think of your spendthrift neighbor who borrowed against his house, bought a boat, and went on a luxury vacation. That was fine until the bills came due.

Unfortunately, the bill is now coming due for the entire U.S. over-expansion of debt.

The contribution of debt to the growth of our economy tends to be ignored in most economic models because it doesn't fit with the static concept of how much money exists at a specific point in time. Here's the basic idea: If people are borrowing, they are speeding up their purchases by using debt to make their purchases. For example, a person buying a new house accomplishes that mostly through borrowing, using a mortgage. Our GDP measure will include the house as a completed transaction and include the total price in the GDP even though most of the money was borrowed. Figure 5.12 shows the outline of what is normally reported as the GDP in the standard government numbers as the highest level of the graph. To get an idea of how big the GDP would be if people were not borrowing, I subtracted the increase in outstanding debt from the reported GDP. The lower line in the graph then is how large the GDP would have been if new debt weren't included in the

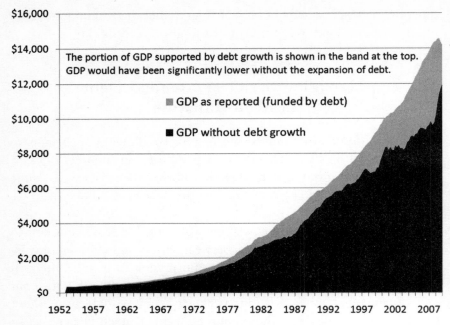

Figure 5.12   How Debt Contributed to Growth of GDP

purchasing power. Since we know that there are limits to debt, and that it is supposed to be paid back, the lower line gives a more conservative picture of how big the economy is. The point of the calculation is to emphasize how important debt is to our economic growth. Going forward one could even worry that if debt were paid down, that the economy would grow even less. The overhang of debt will be a drag as the Great Deleveraging continues.

Let's put some numbers around this borrowing binge by comparing total debt growth in the United States with GDP growth. The GDP in 2000 was $10 trillion, and the debt was $27 trillion. By 2008, the numbers jumped to $14 trillion and $50 trillion, an increase of $4 trillion in annual GDP (+40 percent), but a debt level $23 trillion higher (+85 percent).

Much of the GDP was bought with new debt. In this case, the debt grew by $23 trillion, while GDP expanded by $14 trillion. The basic idea is that the GDP is accelerated by the debt, because most debt is used to buy things. If the debt is to be paid down, the GDP will also see a slowing.

Another way of looking at it is to say that each dollar of GDP growth required the assumption of $5.75 in debt, which is not healthy.

Let's postulate two different scenarios for dealing with the problem.

First, we could merely return to the debt-to-GDP ratio we had in 2000 by paying it off. To do that, debt would have to be paid down to $27 trillion or by some $23 trillion. Over a decade, that would take $2-plus trillion per year. That would be a drop of GDP of 14 percent in the first year and an ongoing weak GDP. It was only in the Great Depression that we had anything like that. There is no one who advocates such an extreme way to rebalance our economy. It just isn't going to happen like that. But pushing these numbers suggests how severe the overleverage is, and why the government is not just letting the collapse occur without intervention. The second choice is to press on with what the government is already doing: aggressively bailing out the lenders, hoping they can add enough government stimulus with new debt that the banks will be sending new debt throughout the system. But the actions being taken by the government are making its own debt worse. That means more inflation, as government spending continues to grow. Counterintuitively, that's the whole point. Higher inflation to dilute the debt (theirs included) is what the government needs and is working to achieve.

Inflation benefits the debtor because he can pay his debt with dollars that are worth less. The effect is to reduce the implied debt downward to a manageable level. In a scenario of inflation of say 10 percent a year, GDP might drop by 15 percent in real terms, but only 5 percent in nominal terms, so things wouldn't appear as bad. The $50 trillion of debt could be decreasing in real debt load terms by 10 percent per year, or $5 trillion at the start. After five years, the real debt level would be inflated down to approaching the $27 trillion level of 2000. (The 10 percent per year for five years implies a decrease in outstanding debt in real terms to around $.9X.9X.9X.9 = 59$ percent, which times $50 trillion = $30 trillion.) GDP could be in decline in real terms even as it appears to be much better in the number of dollars passing hands. This inflationary scenario is far more likely than the hard medicine proposal of paying down the debt of my first set of calculations. Therefore, inflation is the likely result, as it makes sense from the way the leaders in Washington see the situation. The preceding calculations of future scenarios use too many assumptions to be used as predictions, but the idea that the dollar stays strong and that we continue to expand credit is not a workable policy, even if it is the story that the government stubbornly clings to.

The problem was the overextension of debt, not the collapse that followed it. The current period is extremely painful, much like the rough time a drug addict faces in detox. However, detox is not the problem, it is the drugs. Detox by eliminating the burden of debt is the solution, even though the government has chosen to put it off by expanding its own debt.

All the bailouts are giving the markets the equivalent of another fix: more debt. It won't work. These fixes just pile further future obligations on the taxpayers' backs. They don't manage the debt burden down.

In conclusion, deflation is such a damaging scenario that the government will make sure we avoid it, and that is the easy policy for the short term anyway. It just prints and spends, thereby creating the illusion that there's no need to raise taxes and cut spending. And that is just what the incentives are for the politicians to keep the populace from throwing the bums out at the next election.

The Implications of the Bursting Debt Bubble

It is said, "The pessimist complains about the wind; the optimist expects it to change; the realist adjusts the sails." I'm adjusting my sails, using the prediction of long-term inflation to support my investment decisions.

When heading into a credit bubble, the economy appears strong on the surface, where final sales are measured, but the purchases are made ahead of the necessary consumer incomes through borrowing. With easy credit, all seems well. But when credit starts to slow, and the expansion sputters, the musical chairs game stops, leaving consumers without enough income to make payments.

At that point, credit risks go up for all lenders. Lenders then tighten their credit standards, which slows the economy more. As the economy slows, businesses are forced to sell their products at discounts, and profits fall. Workers are laid off, mortgage payments go into default, and banks holding defaulted mortgages wind up with big losses.

The downward spiral is hard to stop, because it is derived from *decades* of too much debt. Borrowing expanded when the risks seemed low and the promises of returns were high, creating even more debt and inducing overleverage. The complexity of debt-based derivatives on debt-promoted phantom profits made the swing more damaging in both directions.

The problem with attempting to deleverage at this late date is that the debt overhang is so big that traditional government interventions, such as credit easing by lowering interest rates, are not able to counteract it. In fact, it was the credit easing that *caused* the original overextension of credit. The new bailouts just amount to government taking on the debt that was being held by the banking system. Banks are kept from bankruptcy, but they are not interested in taking on more debt and have become extremely cautious about extending more loans. They are making more money with leverage trading profits using the backstop of knowing that the government will be there to bail them out if they make bad investments again. Households who can't make their payments are left standing out in the cold (literally).

The current actions taken by the government are extending the day of reckoning for financial institutions that deserve to die. The banks that extended loans to people who can't pay are absolved of their crime, but homebuyers who bought more than they could afford are now facing eviction. The government is artificially extending the life of these institutions.

If insolvent institutions were allowed to die, that would wipe out their shareholders and bondholders. And yes, that would be tragic. But then *new* banks with *clean* starting balance sheets could make more careful decisions about new lending. By keeping zombies around, we ensure that these burdened institutions, which are not in a position to offer new credit even to trustworthy applicants, will only absorb huge blobs of government funds. They are saddled with the past sins of bad debts and overleveraged lending. Putting off the recognition and removal of these bad debts will result in an excessively long recovery period.

Conclusion

We have too much debt. It has accumulated over the decades and become much worse since we left the gold standard in 1971. While debt collapse is often thought of as deflationary, like in the Great Depression, the government is no longer limited in how big its bailout response to the debt collapse can be. The government is going into debt as never before and affecting the credit markets. When I add in the incentive for the holders of the printing press to make themselves and their supporters rich, the obvious path out is to keep that printing press rolling and to bring inflation on. There is now a grace period, because of the collapse of economic activity and defaults bring deflationary pressures. In this environment, government's inflationary actions do not seem so damaging. That environment allows the market to be comfortable with the government creating more debt as small amounts of inflation will soften the blow of unwinding debts. The long-term direction is not in doubt. We are sitting with interest rates at zero, with the largest jobless rate since the Great Depression keeping the government in high gear spending on new programs. These deficits will certainly cause problems for the next generation because government debt has a long-term debilitating effect on the confidence in the currency itself.

I hope I have convinced you that this economic cycle downturn is big and different from the usual recession. We will not be returning to business as usual and prosperity in the decade ahead. Rather, we will do well to avoid serious financial collapse. I offer a comment that financial collapse is much less disastrous than war. Very few people die in a financial collapse. Unfortunately, financial collapse often precedes government regime change, and sometimes wars have their roots in the scarcity that comes out of a financial crisis.

This analysis provides a useful baseline for thinking about the economy as moving through cycles over time and how important those cycles are in predicting our future. Those cycles are the subject of the next chapter. This chapter and the next focus more on the theoretical than the practical, providing evidence for where the economy is likely to go in the long term. To extend this theoretical analysis a bit more deeply, I have developed my own view of how the various pieces tie together in self-reinforcing feedback loops to create big cycle swings. That is the subject of the next chapter, where I explain how a large groups of variables all move together in predictable ways.

Chapter 6

The Big-Picture Model of Our Economy

Having a big-picture model of the economy gives us a context for interpreting the current situation to help direct which areas to pursue for investment. For example, I could see that the breakdown of the housing bubble would bring very serious downward pressure on financial stocks years before it unfolded, because of my understanding of the linkages between housing, debt, and consumer spending. This chapter expands beyond the simple supply-and-demand model to incorporate feedback to explain why markets can move to extremes. Then a few data points show the extreme position we have moved through, to set the stage for the later investment opportunities discussed in Chapters 10 through 15.

Equilibrium Is an Illusion: The Underlying Structure of Financial Systems

A basic tenet of formal economic analysis is that there is a steady state of equilibrium between the competing forces of supply and demand. These concepts are helpful in discussing markets at a point in time, but traders look beyond the limitations of simple static analysis because they know that markets are inherently dynamic. They use tools like momentum, trend following, and sentiment to evaluate positions. Economists are not considered very good market timers or investment advisors. Indeed, many economists tend to shy away from specific investment recommendations. Some laugh a bit nervously when they admit that they may have a long-term opinion about what will happen several years out, but they are unable to predict both the time and the price for a specific investment.

Part of the failure of economists is that their basic models become unmanageably complex when all the connected variables are included. Attempts at precision by adding complexity make the result so sensitive to minor shifts in parameters that it is difficult to have confidence in the results. So economists focus on overly simplistic relationships starting with assumptions like "All other things being equal..." However, I think it is essential to recognize that these main underlying concepts are inadequate to explain the real world.

There are deeper problems in relying on a model based on supply and demand. The theory of a supply curve intersecting with a demand curve seems sensible until you realize that the basic input is not available: *There is no empirically measurable supply curve or demand curve.* The only data we can measure is a single point of actual supply and price. It is difficult to explain in the basic model how there can be two different curves for the relationship of price and quantity for the same market.

I don't want to get into a theoretical discussion of the limitations of current economic theory because my goal is to discover what works in the real world. I only want to warn that basic economic analysis methods are found lacking. Economists have a weak record predicting turning points in key patterns—like the beginning of a recession or a change in interest rate. I would suggest that the underlying tools economists are taught are inadequate, and that is what explains why their predictive skills are so poor.

Here is my basic thrust: *Economic markets are NEVER in equilibrium!* They are dynamic, always in motion. The traders who look for market movement and use momentum measures have figured this out from experience. The reality is that markets go to extremes way beyond what anybody thought would be a reasonable level from looking at basic static measures like supply and demand.

There is a reason for the extreme moves: Financial systems have feedback loops that reinforce a trend once it gets going.

Intuitively, trends make sense. That there are forces that drive markets beyond equilibrium is easy to see in bubbles. For example, when the Internet was introduced as a breakthrough technology, thousands of millionaires appeared overnight. As people heard of amazing successes, others wanted to participate, and as a result more investment money became available than the fledgling industry was ready to absorb. Those who got in early and rode the trend were rewarded. Those who came in later added to the bubble in what I call a *feedback mechanism*. Investors eventually drove the bubble beyond the sustainable profits that could be generated. Eventually, it burst in what we all know as the technology bubble. This herd behavior has roots in sensibilities that are deeper than most realize. Bubbles happen because of the feedback of success, human emotions, and mob psychology. The static model using rational thinking would suggest that the price would never go to the kind of extremes that regularly happen. Extreme results do not require some surprising shock, something that economists would call "exogenous," as if it were an unexpected outside force. It is a normal part of the operation of markets. They normally go to extremes and normally swing back.

As mentioned in the introduction to this book, my engineering background gives me the perspective of oscillating systems. These oscillations are what make radio and TV possible. The circuits oscillate (albeit at very high rates) because of feedback. The electrical circuits include components that take the output and feed it back to the input in a positive or negative way, or with a delay, so that once the output becomes very big, the circuit turns back to decrease the output and the whole process turns around and starts over.

My engineer friends may cringe at this oversimplification, while my economist friends will say that such precise calculations can't be applied to a world where people's emotions are part of the equation. But my trader friends know what the purist theoretician misses: They say they don't know why it happens, but they see bubbles and extremes all the time, and that the market cycles can not only be observed, their patterns are repetitious enough to be traded. They don't need complex explanations of cause. They observe the trends and cycles and trade, often making huge amounts of money when they are right.

So my conclusion is that traders know a lot more about markets than economists realize, and that the engineers have the key as to why economic models do so poorly.

The important point may seem too simple: that *the economic system is always making cycles that go beyond equilibrium before they swing back*. It is crucial because the underlying system structure is always oscillating and never achieving a state of equilibrium. It is the internal nature of markets to be in oscillation. When we look at the economy systematically, we realize that the world is continually flowing and changing, and that these big swings are normal.

Think of a pendulum: It makes a cyclic path back and forth. A trader betting on the path would look for previous cycles, look to bet against the previous trend when it has clearly turned, and perhaps make more money as the investment goes both up and down; that trader will make more money than an analyst who thinks there is an equilibrium price that the investment should sit at. The economist who focuses on what equilibrium should be is focusing on the pendulum when it is changing the fastest and swinging through straight up and down. In doing so, the economist is ignoring how far the pendulum can swing. To properly understand the system, it is important to see the relationships and how they are interconnected, and how they provide far bigger swings than are usually expected. We are now in such a critical time where the elements of the economy are pressing the boundaries that were never predicted by the more limited and less-comprehensive view. This chapter describes these interconnections as a comprehensive overview. Chapters 1 through 5 spelled out how many of these relationships move together in pairs and in smaller models, so if you have a pretty good idea of how those work together, this section will be really just assembling those ideas into a single picture.

The Overview Model

In this section, I outline the bull and bear economic model, which results in *Virtuous Cycle of growth* or *Vicious Cycle of destruction*. I don't put all the parameters of our economic system into a comprehensive model that precisely predicts all aspects. Figure 6.1 presents the relationship between the economy to the stock market with some important inputs from housing, interest rates, trade, capital investment, and taxes to reinforce the cyclic nature.

The Virtuous Cycle of Growth

In examining key drivers of our economy, let's start by looking at the positive feedback loop between stocks and the economy. In Figure 6.1, the core feedback loop is depicted by the heavy arrows in the center,

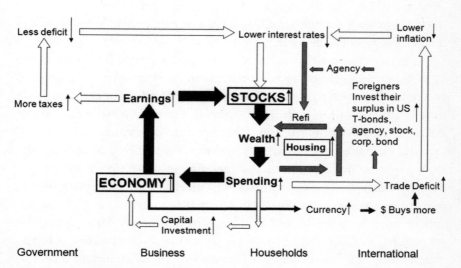

Figure 6.1   The Virtuous Cycle of Growth

where the rise in stocks makes the consumer wealthier. He increases his spending, thereby making the economy stronger, so earnings rise, which makes the stock market rise, which brings us back to the beginning. You can see the self-supportive aspects feeding on themselves.

Most simply, one drives the other, both up and down. When stocks are up, the economy does well. Stocks and the economy create the basic self-supportive positive feedback loop.

To confirm the other side of the cycle, consider what happened to the economy after the greatest rise in stocks to the peak in 1929. Many explanations for the cause of the Great Depression have been written, including how the Fed and government didn't react fast enough. But the simplest explanation is that the bubble got so big that it had to burst. Think of the pendulum that has swung way out to an extreme on one side. It will come back, regardless of the minor forces at work to help or hurt. A little push at the extreme can make the swing even wider. It's like pushing your child on a swing where you give an extra thrust at the peak as it's coming back toward you.

It is this nature of reinforcing systems that they tend to oscillate. A "bubble," as we generally use the term, is just a market that has reached an extreme—swinging way to one side. It is observable that bubbles burst, even if it is hard to say how far along the path they will travel once started. Looking for the equilibrium is not particularly valuable when the prices are so far above it.

A good example that most of us are familiar with is that there are short-term cycles connected to the presidential elections every four years as well as those tied to business inventories. But what we are witnessing now in this Great Deleveraging is quite different. We are at the end of a Supercycle of debt expansion, where private debt reached a limit and can't be expanded yet more. The government is trying to pick up the slack by going into debt itself and spending to make up for the private debt contraction. The government will meet its own borrowing limits, perhaps in the next year or two. When the government is no longer able to borrow to spend, but turns to printing money for its spending, we will have reached the end of the debt Supercycle that began in the peace times after World War II. There is one more important aspect to the Supercycle: it is a global phenomenon, and stock markets, GDP and debt expansion have been global and may be reaching limits worldwide.

This large systematic comparison of the structural variables is more important in interpreting the longer-term convulsive cycles around Vicious Cycles like the Great Depression. We can observe that it is the big swings one way (such as the boom for stocks into the 1929 peak and the run-up into the 2000 tech boom) that sow the seeds of the next big contraction. One way to predict a bust is to look for a boom and then just wait.

The next sections explain the major connections and how they are interrelated in ways that are usually mutually supportive. At other times they work together in destructive ways, as we are now experiencing. Understanding these key differences will provide the background for deciding which investments to address.

Housing

There are more interconnected feedback loops that extend beyond the stocks and the economy. The most important in the last cycle was the jump in housing prices. The housing bubble affected the markets very positively until it burst. Figure 6.1 shows that housing was supported by lower interest rates. As housing rose, households felt wealthier and spent more, just as they did when stocks rose. Part of consumer spending was financed by taking loans against the houses, and that allowed for some spending on foreign products. Foreigners reinvested their trade surplus, buying Treasuries and mortgage-backed securities, which kept interest rates low. These low rates supported housing. The success of the housing bubble brought speculators in, driving houses higher and causing the pendulum of prices to rise more than people imagined and more than most could afford. Housing kept rising with the anticipation of higher prices along with low borrowing costs and easy lending standards.

Of course, we know what happened. Just as we can see the mechanism that drove housing higher than would be considered equilibrium from a measure of, say, affordability, we can expect that in the ongoing collapse, the swing down may be larger than expected. (One of the problems of a housing bubble is that although houses are a symbol of consumer comfort, they do not produce new output like a factory, where the products can justify and produce enough profit to pay for their investment.)

Capital Investment

Another important feedback loop is the capital investment cycle of businesses. When the virtuous cycle is in full bore, a business can expand its operations in such areas as building a cement plant to create materials for houses. The normal demand for cement takes on an additional demand for the material to build the cement plant as well as to be available for new houses. This double demand for expansion makes capital investment one of the better measures of the economic cycle. It swings further than others and is at the end of the whip of cascading inputs to the economy. The feedback is that when the economy is doing well, the expansion of the productive sector gives an additional boost for the increase in capital spending, which adds momentum to drive the economy even higher.

Interest Rates

There are other positive feedback inputs during a boom. As earnings increase for both business and individuals, tax revenues rise. That means government deficits decrease, lowering the borrowing by government. Also, as the economy does well, the need for welfare payments, in the form of unemployment insurance, goes down. The result is that the government deficit is less, and there is less need for the government to borrow. That means credit markets are easier to clear, and interest rates stay down. The lower interest rates are beneficial to stocks. Companies pay less to borrow, which improves their bottom line. Also, the relative return on stocks competes better with traditional bonds, bidding stock prices higher. Price-to-earnings ratios rise in lower-interest-rate environments. All these link together as mutually supportive fuel for a boom.

Foreign Investment and the Currency

Another supportive aspect for the growth of the economy and stocks comes from foreign investments. If foreigners perceive that the economy is doing well, the investment opportunities appear more attractive to them. As a result, their investments do well as the dollar is bid up, which makes the investment returns more attractive. A strong dollar reinforces the low interest rates. Currencies include a lot of speculators and government intervention, and so are driven by other forces as well, but the collection of all the forces can make a growing bubble go to extremes.

George Soros Recognized Feedback in Trading Currencies. George Soros is one of the most successful hedge fund managers ever. He started the Quantum Fund with my Yale classmate Jimmy Rogers, and was extremely successful trading currencies. He noticed that currencies tend to continue to move in the same direction once the major shift was underway. I think the reason that currencies tend to move beyond what could be thought of as equilibrium is that they are also driven by self-supportive feedback loops. Once a currency looks attractive, returns to the investor look positive and then more investment is made. It is interesting that a man as rich as Soros is more interested in leaving behind his economic theories than his wealth. His first book, *The Alchemy of Finance,* focuses on a term he calls *reflexivity.* His term is a bit more complex than my own use of the engineering term *feedback loop*, but they both have some of the same aspect in recognizing that once a system begins to move it can move much farther than some stable equilibrium point.

I consider Soros' views important because he is the only fund manager who has tried to express the importance of how the system is affected by the traders (and the reverse) in a form of feedback loop. Economists have not adopted this approach, and that, in part, is why I believe that the underpinnings of traditional economic theories fail at describing what is going on in markets like these.

I had a chance to briefly talk with Mr. Soros after he spoke at Stanford a few years ago, and he seemed delighted that I agreed with his idea that the economic systems do operate in a fashion of reflecting back on themselves. Armed with that understanding, we as traders are able to see the economic forces that give us an edge. Soros' success supports my belief that we can profit using methods that move beyond traditional static analysis.

The Vicious Cycle of Destruction

The Vicious Cycle happens when the relationship between the economy and the stock market operate in destructive reinforcing patterns. The

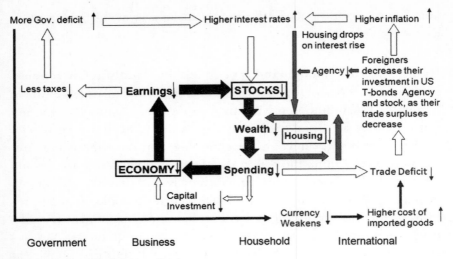

Figure 6.2   The Vicious Cycle

chart of the vicious cycle is mostly the reverse of the Virtuous Cycle (see Figure 6.2). The extreme of overvaluation leads to what will happen on the other side of the swing: when stocks show a significant drop (as they did in early 2009), losing 50 percent of their value, consumers slow down their purchases, especially of big-ticket items like houses and cars. When businesses see lower revenues, they cut back first in expansion (capital expenditures) and then on employees. Consumers seeing the slowing, and worrying about their jobs, also cut back on spending, and that slows the economy even more. So the cycle becomes vicious, as it has now become.

Politicians know that things can spiral out of control, and that is why they have taken such extreme measures to counteract the spiral, stepping in with public spending where the private sector slowed.

How does this Vicious Cycle apply to the situation we find ourselves in today? It's pretty obvious that the housing bubble breaking is the biggest driver of the current downturn. Mortgage losses on toxic waste structured investment vehicles brought huge losses to the banks and investors. Housing prices have weakened on the tightening of credit and squeezing out of investment bubble speculators. But housing is driven not only by confidence of consumers and job growth, but also by interest rates. Interest rates are now at a level that is supportive. If we had not had a bubble where people who should not have been getting loans were buying houses they could not afford, the spiral would not be continuing the way it is. The lower interest rate has, however, fueled a resurgence in the stock market as holders of investable funds cannot find better alternatives and do not need a high return to justify holding stocks. Also, there has been a resurgence of commodity prices fostered by the great increase of liquidity for the banking system, and continuing demand in developing countries like China.

The weak link that still sits out there in this vicious cycle is what foreign investors will do with their trade surpluses. Serious cracks in our economic system occurred simultaneously with monthly shortfalls in foreign investments, but a wholesale running for the exits has not occurred. That is the Achilles' heel of this cycle that worries me structurally. The United States as a country owes ten trillion dollars to foreigners, so that if the foreigners wished to cash in their positions, there could be a major dislocation of a weakening dollar and higher interest rates. I watch foreign investment very closely for this reason.

Iceland and Dubai: Two Examples of the Virtuous and Vicious Cycles

Let's look at two countries that went from boom to bust to see how the virtuous and vicious cycles apply. I had the opportunity to visit Iceland in 2007 and was amazed at the economic boom. There were construction cranes everywhere. There weren't enough workers to keep the stores open. The currency was so strong that everything seemed outlandishly expensive, with hamburgers at $15 and a tank of gas at $85. The story behind the success was that Iceland was using its geothermal energy to transform imported bauxite into aluminum. The geothermal energy was used to generate electricity that smelted the ore. In essence, the country was wealthy from exporting energy. What was not at all so obvious was that the credit expansion that built the bubble exceeded the sustainable underlying economy. People felt the boom, but then the bust was worse than anywhere else. Iceland's three banks have collapsed, destroying savings, there are riots in the streets, and the leadership has admitted defeat with resignations and new elections. The extreme boom turned to collapse in less than two years. The most important evidence of impending collapse had been the extreme nature of the boom.

At the beginning of 2010, Iceland is still in difficulty as President Grimsson vetoed the Icesave accord because 60,000 of the 320,000 inhabitants signed a petition to reject the legislation. It would have followed the United States' model of bailing out the mess created by a handful of banksters who overleveraged and caused the destruction of the county's banks and losses of savings. This is still evolving, but my sentiments are with the population.

In the spring of 2007, I saw an even more amazing boom in Dubai. I gave the keynote speech to high-paying investors from Europe and around the planet at a fabulously luxurious hotel by the Persian Gulf. There was more construction than I had ever seen in one place, including the world's tallest building. Low gas prices, huge traffic jams, and the bustle of multicultural workers who came to improve their lives were mixed with pushing sand into the sea to construct the most amazing resort-like homes and high-rises.

My notes at the time indicated that the uncontrolled expansion had the elements of a bubble. Dubai seemed like a combination of Las Vegas and Miami, indicating the potential for collapse. As oil continued rising, Middle East expansion did not appear like it would ever stop.

But by the winter of 2009, with oil down to $35 from a high of $147 in the summer of 2008, the boom ended. Dubai opened 2010 with the biggest fanfare of laser lights, fountains, and fireworks that I have seen, rivaling the Beijing Olympics, as it announced that it had built the world's tallest building that is half a mile high. Dubai has one of the least-intrusive governments, low taxes, and proximity to oil wealth, and therefore it will not collapse, but the pendulum of euphoria has swung to the other side in a severe slowdown.

Seeing the Relationships in the Data

The reliability of a model is confirmed if data of the economic measures confirms the relationship. The value of the model for explaining probable future steps is that if the direction of one aspect can be seen, other results will move in similar relationship. Although this may seem so obvious as to not need stating, it is amazing that whole books on investing and economics are written without confirming the validity of the analysis by looking at data. The following sections review what is happening.

Stocks and GDP

Here I confirm that the two central items of stocks and GDP do tend to move together. Figure 6.3 shows the annual change in both measures. There are two different scales because the stock market is far more volatile. The stock market is reported every minute of every day, but the GDP is reported once a quarter and revised several times, so we can't use GDP to predict stocks very reliably.

The hopeful stock investor might assume that all that was needed to be successful would be to see how the economy is going, and be in stocks when the GDP is rising and get out when GDP is falling. There are several problems with this seemingly logical approach: First is that the individual investor is competing with others who see the same indications and are making the same decisions. The many market

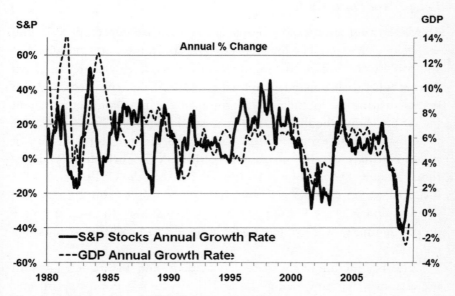

Figure 6.3 Stocks and GDP Tend to Move Together

players mean that if optimism abounds, investors will drive the market in anticipation. Hopeful future expectations for the economy get priced into the markets. So the stock market becomes one of the most leading indicators of how the economy is likely to perform.

The second problem is that we know about the stock market every minute of the day, but we only get big economic reports like the GDP on a quarterly basis. The GDP report is a compilation of the whole economy. Because it encompasses so many inputs, it is reported months after the fact, and it is often heavily revised. It is subject to government manipulation, from politicians who want to report positive news. The result is that GDP is a relatively poor predictor of anything. GDP is better predicted by the stock market rather than the reverse. But knowing that there is a feedback loop between consumers' optimism and the way the economy reacts gives us basic tools to identify the forces operating within the overall market.

Since 2006, we have witnessed the unraveling of decades of supportive feedback. Understanding that the linked pressures are big and long term keeps me confident that there are troubles ahead.

Long-Term Stock Cycles

To put the long-term history on a single chart, a log scale further clarifies the relative changes. The log scale equalizes movements up and down at any part of the picture to show the same percentage change. Investors can see what their percentage return might have been between any two points in time by looking at the slope of the line connecting them. Figure 6.4 shows the long-term rise in stocks with two large peaks.

The best way for an investor to evaluate the long-term history of stocks is to improve the microscope of history by correcting for inflationary losses. That is done in Figure 6.5, by using the CPI to show what investors would see after inflation. The biggest shift from the reported price in dollars is the big sag in the mid-1970s. Very high inflation ate up purchasing power even as stocks appeared to be flat in their nominal price.

The big picture cyclic nature is evident, and Figure 6.5 gives an indication of whether being invested in stocks is a good opportunity

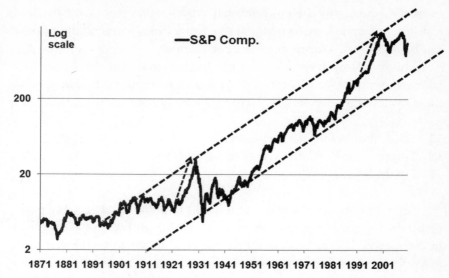

Figure 6.4   Stocks Had Two Big Bull Markets: 1929 and 2000
SOURCE: Dr. Robert Schiller and Cowels Foundation.

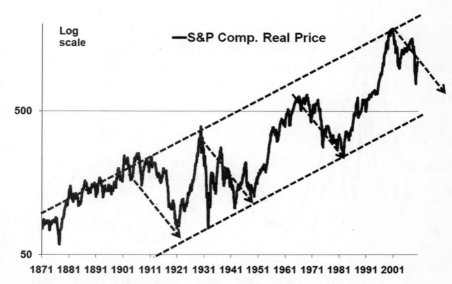

Figure 6.5   Real Stock Prices Reveal Big-Picture Cycles
SOURCE: Dr. Robert Schiller, Yale University; Cowels Foundation.

Shiller

or not. Contrary to the conventional wisdom that stocks are the best investment for the long term, there are clearly times when holding stocks can be disastrous. We are in such a period now.

The very long-term cycles of the stock market can also be seen by taking the ratio of stocks to GDP, as shown in Figure 6.6. There were three cycles when stocks got ahead of the economy:

1. The boom before the Depression
2. The rise out of World War II to the 1960s
3. The tech peak in 2000

Figure 6.6 shows that the rise in stocks to 2000 was a very big peak, being the second highest in this measure. Although the raw stock prices in 2007 exceeded the peak of 2000, this view shows a much lower peak in 2007. The level of stocks didn't show a return to new highs when compared to the size of the economy, so the fall since then is still part of a falling cycle in this longer-term view. A similar comment about the real stock price can be seen in Figure 6.5.

Figure 6.6 Stocks Were the Biggest Percentage of GDP in 1929 and 2000
SOURCE: Dr. Robert Schiller, Yale University; Cowels Foundation.

Conclusion

There are two important concepts that I want to leave you with: First is that the economic structure operates in a cyclic fashion because it is structured with feedback loops that can be mutually supportive, as in the Virtuous Cycle, or the reverse. The idea is sensible from our daily experiences, so it would not seem to require arguments in its defense. But the economic profession, by and large, ignores the concept and starts with models that are presumed to move toward equilibrium and only once in a while incur shocks. In my view, such systems will not predict important shifts in economic direction.

The second recognition is that because so many economic factors are interrelated, it is not necessary to individually attempt to identify the forces that drive each one of them. We can come to a collection of related items and see that they will move together. For example, we can construct a scenario that affects a collection of items simultaneously: If inflation is high, that means that interest rates will be high, the dollar weak, commodity prices rise, and debts inflate to lower levels. As another example, if the economy is weak, the stock market will be lower, unemployment will be higher, public credit growth will be slower, trade will decrease, housing will be weak, and we will experience a recession. The point is that so many things are related. When we make predictions, it is important to observe that many parts move together and are not individual items.

I will have more to say about how our current scenario leads to specific investment opportunities in Chapters 10 through 15. But before we get there, I offer some perspective on three of the biggest economic Vicious Cycle events historically, to see what lessons we can learn that could be appropriate for our current crisis. The next chapters describe what happened in the 1929 Depression era, Japan after 1990, and finally in a very different scenario, what happened in Germany during the high inflation of the Weimar Republic.

Part Three

RECESSION OR DEPRESSION?

art Three is a comparative history lesson. The historical perspectives of other countries' financial crises provide a filter for confirming the analysis of Parts One and Two. In fact, each of the chapters in Part Three could be read independently as their own essay on the topic of the particular event. The results are different so the more interesting comparison is to the parameters of our own situation.

Chapter 7 compares historical data from the 1929 Great Depression to our current crisis so far. The first question is whether we will devolve into such a serious state or recover to normalcy. We are already in the worst crisis since the Depression, and this story is still unfolding. The next question is whether we will see inflation or deflation from the aftermath. One important difference is how much bigger our current government and its actions now are for our economy.

Chapter 8, on Japan's lost decades, is also relevant to our current situation because Japan also experienced a simultaneous stock market and real estate bubble much like ours. Although Japan is no longer described as a miracle, it has survived, and many of its responses to crisis seem like the ones we are taking. The important difference is Japan's trade surplus.

Chapter 9, on the big German inflation (with comment on other countries), should not be the shocker that it is for most Americans. We have never experienced the destruction that hyperinflation brings. History lessons are rarely exactly conclusive, but they do give us a tapestry for thinking about our situation.

Even if you disagree with my conclusions, the extensive amount of data I have dredged up on how those historical experiences unfolded will give you a sound basis from which to make judgments about the similarities and differences for our existing crisis. I think you'll be surprised at some of the similarities.

Chapter 7

What Can the 1929 Great Depression Teach Us about Today's Crisis?

M any people have noted some of the similar characteristics of our credit crisis and the terrible times of the 1929 Depression. Some think we will have serious deflation like then. Others ask about how deep and long our current jobless crisis could drag on.

When difficult questions like these arise, my personal mantra is "Let's look at the data." In this chapter, I try to look under the hood and back in time to see if I can confirm—or refute—the positions of deflation and how deep the economic cycle might become. And then, based on my findings, I'll share some further thoughts and conclusions.

This is a particularly difficult time to interpret because the size of the continuing collapse is like nothing we have seen since the Great Depression. It is a credit bubble that is becoming The Great Deleveraging.

It is not a typical recession like has occurred about every four years in the usual business cycle (as I explained in Chapter 6, "The Big-Picture Model of Our Economy"). Those traditional recessions do not provide reliable yardsticks for severity and duration. We need to see the similarities of the two biggest stock bull markets and collapse to interpret what might happen today. So my method is to compare important economic measures then to now to see the differences and similarities. We are still living today's crisis, so some of what is happening is in real time with history. I start with an example of my view of what I expected would be our path from 2006. The example shows there is a lot to learn from history.

Comparing the Stock Market during the Depression with the Current Economy

The stock market then and now as seen in the overlay shows a similar pattern if not as damaging a drop today as in the Great Depression.

Figure 7.1 shows a stock market comparison that was published in 2006 that has already produced a valid prediction. It provided some

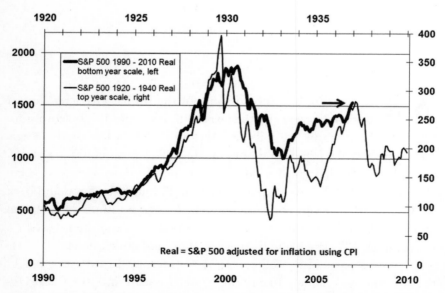

Figure 7.1   Although the Patterns of 1920 and 1990 Overlap, We Are Not in a Depression Now
SOURCE: Robert J. Shiller, Yale University.

reasons to be concerned about the direction of the stock market: It shows the stock market as it rose in 1929 and fell into the 1930s, overlaid by our current stock market to show a similar pattern. Both are in real terms corrected for inflation. The chart only shows the stock market up through 2006, but the ongoing pattern from 1937 was suggesting that the stock market would fall.

My prediction from that time was mostly right, as noted below:

Potential Concerns Going Forward

The question is whether the potential slowing we are already seeing from the housing bust will spread to other businesses, creating a longer-term slowing. The housing slowing will slow the consumer borrowing against that housing, which will cut consumer spending enough to cause corporate profits to fall. Falling profits will lead to cutting employment and that could slice spending again, in a self-defeating spiral.

A key tipping point will be how the current recession is handled. If the last recession is an example (and Bernanke gives every indication of following suit), the "Fix" will be for the Fed to lower rates and the government to add more deficits to keep the recession from becoming deep. The seeds planted by this reaction will lead to an inflationary recession, what I call stagflation. Other important drivers, like the demographics of old people putting demands on the Medicare and retirement systems, and potential skirmishes over scarce resources (energy) leading to perhaps serious war, bring us to higher deficits that cannot be absorbed, because we are on a weak platform now of overleveraged debt.

The next decade-long cyclic slowing will not spiral into a deflationary quagmire of the 1930s, but into a frothy situation of unexpected high prices but little new wealth.

What This Means for Investors

This is not a time for stock market investors to be complacent about the prospects going forward, because of the long-term cycles and the prospects for earnings and inflation. My view for the decade-long direction for stocks is that prices may appear steady, but that inflation will erode the real returns. The huge rise in stocks in the 1990s parallels the rise in the 1920s, suggesting a slowing of values of equities in the decade ahead. But the stimulus from our governing bodies is likely to hide that slowing under an inflationary cloak, more like the 1970s, thus providing nominal returns that don't keep up with inflation.

The conclusion of all of this is to be careful of traditional dollar-denominated investments like stocks and bonds, and to be looking for safety against dollar weakness and inflation in physical assets, like precious metals and energy.

While ordinary news reports only modest increases in normal Fed measures of money supply, the credit markets derivatives ballooned 30 percent last year to $370 trillion notional value. The Credit Default Swaps alone are at $15.7 trillion—a number bigger than the U.S. GDP. These markets are now in tumult, as seen in the strange reading where the guarantee plus underlying are trading less than the Treasury.

Our situation is much as I predicted in 2006, except that inflation stopped with the oil peak in July 2008. The commentary on Credit Default Swaps was more important than my emphasis at the time, but no one else was even mentioning them. It is instructive to notice that the amount of CDS tripled since then. CDS brought Lehman and AIG down. It was only $15 trillion then, which seemed huge, but it grew to $60 trillion before that stuff hit the proverbial fan.

Figure 7.2 shows how the stock market played out: The peak of 1929 is aligned with that of 2000. The drop into 1933 was far more

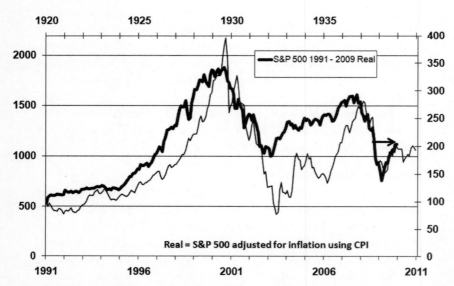

Figure 7.2 Stocks of 1921 and 1990 Overlap, with a Similar Pattern
SOURCE: Robert J. Shiller, Yale University.

damaging than we experienced into 2003. In 1933, the deleveraging of debt became severe. To fight the recession that started in 2001, Greenspan cut interest rates to 1 percent, and the administration cut taxes, provided a stimulus, and started an expensive war. The low rates spurred a housing bubble. That gave consumers a source of borrowing, so they were not hit with the slowing that started after the stock market bubbles of 2000. The crash of 1929 led directly to the implosion of the overextended debt of that time, but I think we are now just starting to look over the horizon of not being able to cope with the current debt deleveraging. That is still to come.

Comparing Prices and the Money Supply during the Depression with the Current Economy

Here are more comparisons of the 1929 Great Depression and the current Great Deleveraging. The Depression was the only time we experienced consistent deflation since the Civil War. It was worst in housing and in asset prices, particularly in stocks that dropped 80 percent. The Consumer Price Index (CPI) may not reflect all the pain of the period, as it dropped only about 30 percent. Applied to the 80 percent drop in stocks, that means the drop was less in real terms (about 75 percent). Figure 7.3 shows the different pattern of the deflation then and modest inflation at the start of the current weakness. The conclusion is that deflation today is only a modest wiggle compared to the Depression.

Because the dollar is no longer tied to gold, the government bailout can be much bigger and the inflationary pressures from government deficits and Fed money creation can be effective at decreasing the amount of deflation. The Depression case shown in Figure 7.3, at 27 percent deflation over two years, is not likely for us going forward now. The other aspect of the comparison shown in Figure 7.3 is that by 1938, the Depression was no longer hanging over the economy in the way that the current collapse is still seemingly with us. So one might suggest that the worst for deflation has not hit us yet. Also, the peak-to-trough in 2000 for stocks had a significant recovery to 2006 with the 1 percent Fed funds rate in 2003, Iraq war stimulus, and tax cut all helping move stocks higher. Having delayed the more serious collapse until 2008, some will

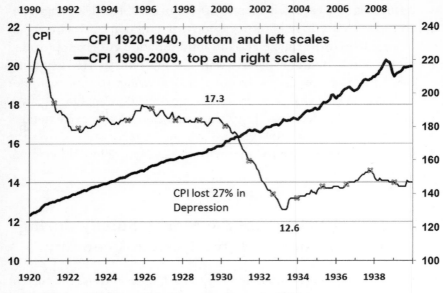

Figure 7.3 CPI Moved Up Now, But Down in 1930

argue that we may now be facing some deflation ahead, but it will be much less than the 27 percent as the Fed and Federal stimulus kicks in, even if the economy continues to collapse.

Money supply dropped in the Great Depression. Our money supply today has not dropped, and appears ready to jump on the Fed actions. You can see the difference in Figure 7.4.

The bailouts assure that money will be growing soon, and thus expecting inflation in the longer term is the proper course.

Figure 7.5 shows that M1 and CPI in the Depression dropped together.

The money supply has continued to expand through the recent recession. M1 has some measurement difficulties because the invention of Money Market Funds (MMFs) has allowed other sources to act as transactions money that didn't exist during the Depression. Money of Zero Maturity (MZM), which includes the MMF, has been growing even more. A long-term view of money supply data in Figure 7.6 gives a more precise peak to trough of money supply. Observing the MZM as

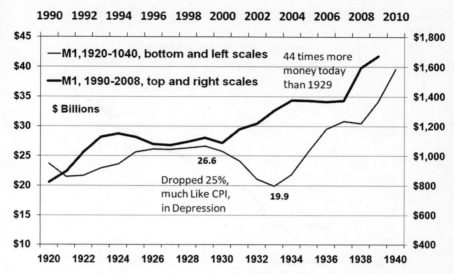

Figure 7.4   Comparison of the M1 Money Supply from 1920–1939 and 1990–2009

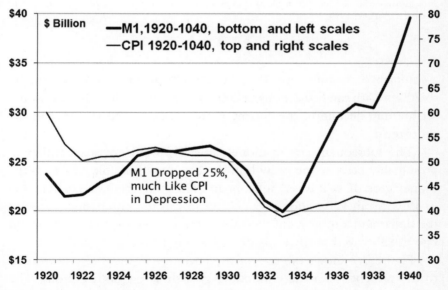

Figure 7.5   M1 CPI from 1920–1940 Moved Down Together

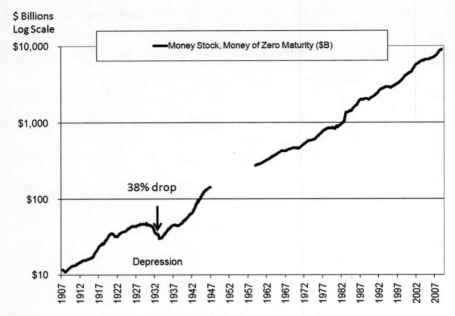

Figure 7.6   Money Stock Dropped during the Depression Like No Other Time
SOURCE: Money Stock from NEBR, Demand Deposits + Currency, Seasonally Adjusted, and Federal
Reserve MZM after 1959.

a comparable measure after 1959 indicates no slowing in money supply
to 2009. With the Fed actions in 2008, it is inconceivable that we would
see any big decline in the narrow money supply measure (M1) in the
short term.

The subsequent rise in money after 1933 did not spark inflation,
presumably because the growth in the economy was able to absorb the
money growth, so it wasn't inflationary. The gold price was raised to $35
in 1934 (from $20.67 for a 39 percent loss in the purchasing power of
the dollar and a 69 percent increase in the gold price). The conversion
rate of $35 stayed steady until 1970, keeping prices contained.

Figure 7.7 shows the size of the currency in the 1930s compared
to the present, with the continuing growth across both periods. The
growth was much better controlled before devaluing the dollar against
gold by 40 percent in 1933, from $20.67 to $35 per ounce. The

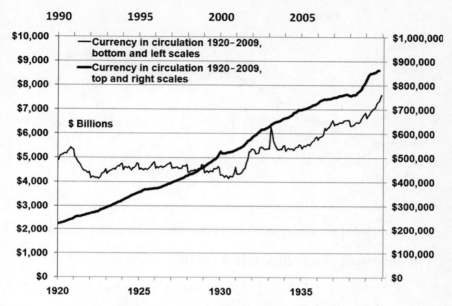

Figure 7.7   Currency Rises Now and in the 1930s Are Similar

more important difference might be the big relative size of the currency now versus then. We now have 100 times more. GDP grew less—from a 1929 peak of $865 billion to $9,817 billion by 2000, or only 11 times as much. The insight here is that inflation is not a new phenomenon.

Comparing Industrial Output during the Depression with the Current Economy

Figure 7.8 shows how industrial output dropped to half during the Great Depression, but it was barely slower in the last downturn in 2003. The fear is that the worst in the downturn is yet to come after 2008. The other comparison is that while currency is 100 times as big as that period, industrial output is only up about 10 times. That suggests that the dollar should be valued at only one tenth as much as then, and that seems to be roughly the case.

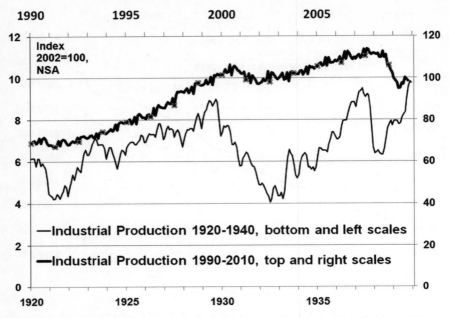

Figure 7.8   Industrial Output Dropped More in the 1930s Than in the 2000s

Comparing the Value of Gold during the Depression with the Current Economy

Figure 7.9 shows how gold has been completely stable at 262 million ounces in the current period, because there are no sales and no purchases now that gold is not redeemable for currency. Although there was volatility in the 1920s, there wasn't a panic in the value of the dollar. The supply of gold held by the central bank grew steadily after the Depression. It seems the stocks of gold were not a serious issue.

It is interesting that the amount of gold that is claimed by the U.S. government today is similar to the amount in the 1930s, but that the amount of currency is now 100 times as large. If there were a need to go back to gold at the similar ratio of the 1930s, this historical precedent might indicate a price of 100 times as high as then, or $3,500 per ounce. Although that is surprising, compared to today's price, it seems quite possible that the price could rise that much.

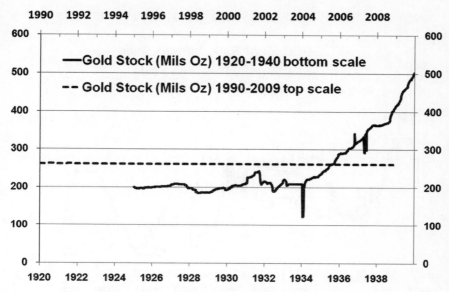

Figure 7.9   Gold Inventories Grew after the Depression

Comparing Interest Rates during the Depression with the Current Economy

Figure 7.10 is a comparison of the Fed funds interest rate in the 1920s–1930s and 1990s–2000s. The comparison shows a similar pattern, except that in the 2005 and 2006 time frame, confidence returned, and the Fed raised rates. This is further evidence that the problems of deleveraging the debt were not addressed in the first stock market slowing into 2003, as they were in the 1929 collapse into 1933. One of the reasons that we did not need to unwind in the 2003 time frame is that foreigners continued to loan us the money to keep our economy bubbling along, especially housing. Those foreign investments provided funds for all kinds of debt, including federal government debt. Foreigners loaned us the money, so we not only didn't need to unwind the extreme debt position, we were able to expand our debt to levels never seen. Foreigners are still loaning us money except for two brief periods: first, in August 2007, at the start of the credit crisis, and again in August 2008, at the escalation of

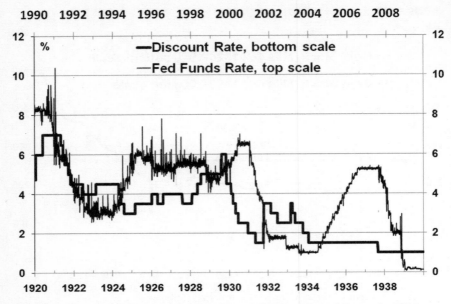

Figure 7.10   The Fed Rate Moved Up in 2006, But Stayed Down in 1936

the crisis where big bailouts and loans are now being applied to patch the system together. The overleverage debt problems are just now being forced to be addressed.

Comparing Public Debt during the Depression with the Current Economy

The sheer accumulated size of the public debt is far harder to manage now than three quarters of a century ago. The comparison of debt size movement is much smoother now because the size is so much bigger. To get one comparison of the amount of debt to the productive capacity, Figure 7.11 shows the ratio of debt to industrial output; it is 20 times larger. Much of that is reflected in the 10-times loss in value of the dollar. There is some real concern that the debt is much larger to handle now, being twice as big in real terms. The material here begs more analysis, but suffice it to indicate that we have extreme amounts of debt yet to unwind.

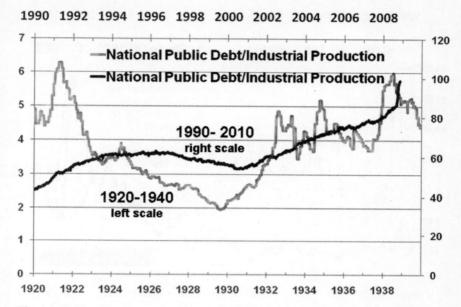

Figure 7.11 Comparison of the Ratio of Debt to Industrial Production in 1920–1940 and in 1990–2010

Comparing the Price of Oil during the Depression with the Current Economy

Figure 7.12 shows how the price of oil dropped in the deep economic slowing in the Depression of 1932, but it did not drop until 2008 in the current start of serious recession. That suggests that we are just now starting the parallel downturn because the Greenspan bubble reflation into housing of 2003 did delay the Great Deleveraging for the intervening time period to now. Figure 7.12 confirms shows how 1933 may be a closer analogy to today's 2008.

Comparing Corporate Bond Rates during the Depression with the Current Economy

Figure 7.13 takes a closer look at the aftermath of the 1929 stock market crash into the 1932 credit collapse, and it shows a similar pattern for

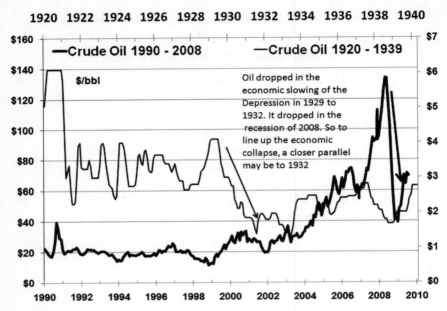

Figure 7.12   Comparison of the Price of Oil in 1920–1939 and 1990–2008

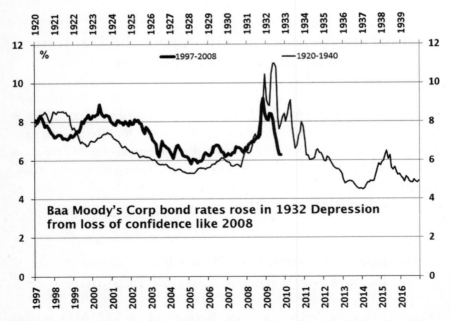

Figure 7.13   Moody's Corporate Bond Rates Rose During the Depth of the Depression in 1932—as They Did in 2008

the when matched to the 2008 credit crisis. The interest rate on riskier corporate debt rated a moderately weak Baa by Moody's jumped up as the world recognized the risk of companies going bankrupt and defaulting on their bonds in 2008. That did not happen in 2002, but in 2008. The conclusion is that the serious phase of the credit crisis just got started in 2008. The more precise comparison is to look at what happened in 1933 to see what may be the path for 2009, particularly for evaluating the path for the riskier interest rates. History showed them rising from the current 9 percent to 11 percent in the next year, and then falling back. That is pretty much how 2009 evolved with an early peak in corporate bonds unwinding in the pattern suggested in Figure 7.13.

Comparing Unemployment during the Depression with the Current Economy

Unemployment is one of the most important statistics to measure the health of an economy. During the Depression, the 25 percent unemployment seared the country and left its mark on a generation. As Figure 7.14

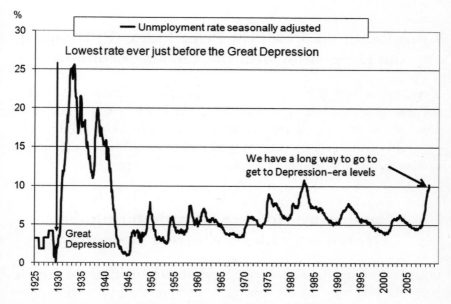

Figure 7.14   Comparing Unemployment from 1925 to 2009

illustrates, however, we are nowhere near that level today, leaving me to conclude that we are not yet experiencing the kind of deleveraging of that era.

By 1937, which was eight years after the stock market bubble peaked, unemployment was down to 11 percent. Statistical measures today tend to undercount classes of unemployed as "discouraged" and overcount multiple employers, suggesting that today's numbers should be higher for comparison. Even so, anecdotal stories indicate that we are not even close to the disaster of that era.

My interpretation is that we have not really taken the economy through the great deleveraging that occurred so terribly in that era. We could face that going forward, however, because the United States is not generating new fundamental jobs—for example, in manufacturing—that can sustain the supporting jobs in the service economy. The interpretation is that we are still to face the deleveraging of that era and that 2008 may look more like 1932.

The unemployment problems lingered up until World War II are one of the lagging indicators of recovery. Another lesson in this data is not to expect a rapid recovery in employment today.

Comparing the Producer Price Index (PPI) during the Depression with the Current Economy

A major structural difference between the Depression and now is that the dollar was on a gold standard until 1971. The PPI wholesale price index shows the shift in underlying direction after 1971 (see Figure 7.15). The structure of the Federal Reserve and government limited the size of stimulus responses that could be provided in the Depression.

Comparing Housing Growth during the Depression with the Current Economy

Figure 7.16 illustrates how housing growth slowed before the crash of 1929, and housing is already slowing. The Depression had a very negative effect on housing, and the current situation looks to continue down.

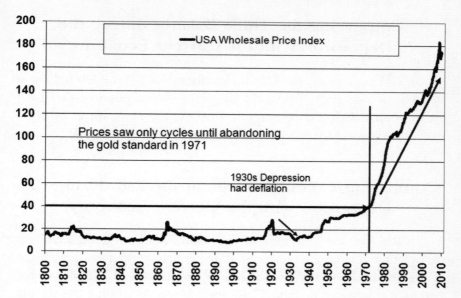

Figure 7.15 How Commodities Prices Rose Dramatically after Going Off the Gold Standard in 1971

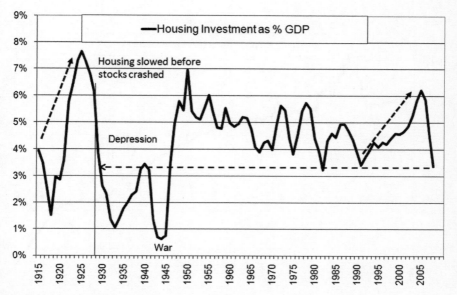

Figure 7.16 Housing Investment as a Percentage of GDP: The Housing Bubble in the Years before 1929 Was Even Bigger than in the 2000s

Comparing the Trade Balance during the Depression with the Current Economy

Figure 7.17 shows how the U.S. trade balance has left the United States as the biggest debtor to the world. In the 1930s, the position was strong for the dollar with a trade surplus. To show the comparison over the years, the data in Figure 7.17 is shown as a percentage of GDP.

Comparing Excess Reserves at the Fed during the Depression with the Current Economy

Excess Reserves are a measure of the banks having more on deposit at the Fed than the required reserves. Showing that number as a percentage of the required reserves gives a relative comparison of liquidity in the system. As illustrated in Figure 7.18, the Fed was accommodative during the Depression, during World War II, and for a brief time during the fear of problems called Y2K during the change to 2000.

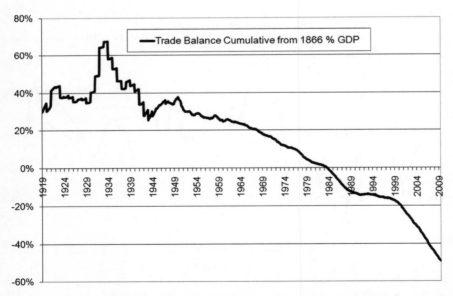

Figure 7.17   The U.S. Trade Balance, from 1919–2009: In the 1930s, the U.S. Enjoyed a Positive Trade Balance, But It Is Negative Now

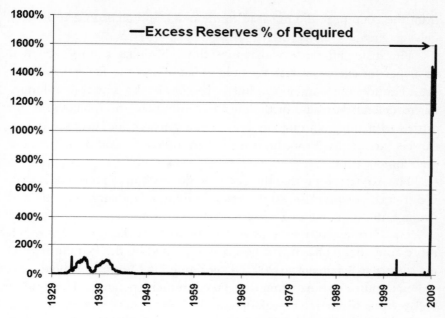

Figure 7.18   How Excess Reserves at the Fed Grew to 100% during the Depression but Reached 700% by 2009

This is one of many measures that show the Fed is acting in a new experiment that has never been done before to pump up money, avoid deflation, help the financial system, and hopefully revive the economy. It would be very inflationary if it weren't for the collapse of other debt and prices. The obvious conclusion is that the Fed is doing more to expand the money and fight deflation than was ever done before. I expect we will see that work its way through to observed price inflation in the not too distant future.

Conclusion

The current slowdown is coming under the same kind of credit collapse that forced the Great Depression to be so severe. There was too much debt, a housing bubble, and an unsustainable stock market bubble. The implication is that today, we still face a Great Deleveraging, which will also be serious and last for several years. Our stock market crash from the 2000 peak did not lead to the quick and damaging 1933 debt deleveraging.

The main difference is that now the U.S. dollar is no longer tied to a specific exchange rate for gold. That allows the Federal Reserve great latitude to expand its funding to bail out banks. The Fed no longer has to defend the value of the currency. Similarly, the Congress is not as tied to making sure taxing and spending match, because the deficit can be extended without limit if the Fed intervenes and monetizes the government debt.

The expectation is that the Fed will monetize much more debt than it did in the Depression, so the result will be inflationary, once filtered through the system after a delay.

The current collapse after the 2000 stock market peak was much more contained. That was largely accomplished by the Fed cutting interest rates to 1 percent in 2003. That ignited the housing bubble, providing a source of borrowing to keep consumers spending. The kind of collapse that washed out weak debt in the bottom of the Depression was avoided. The great deleveraging that occurred by 1934 didn't happen by 2009. *It is still ahead of us.* So the situation that is parallel to today is more like 1931, looking ahead to the unwinding of debt.

The budget deficit for 2009 quadrupled its previous highest-ever level. Funding that deficit will require money creation, and that will be inflationary. The government borrowing to fund the deficit has already started, with the damaging effect of less private credit available for those with less than the most reliable of credit records.

Another difference is that the country has accumulated a trade deficit overhang that is a negative position for the dollar. The size of the accumulated trade deficit of the United States could not have gotten so extreme under a gold standard. But in the current environment, the United States has created international debt on a scale never done before, so that the United States is the world's largest debtor.

There is a loss of confidence about the country's creditworthiness that will also make capital harder to find. The world economy is in a fast decline, as U.S. imports slow and foreign profits will be hurt. Non-government interest rates have already risen, as credit risks jumped.

The cause of the current situation is not obvious to most observers—too much debt accumulated over decades. If that were recognized, the solutions of applying more debt wouldn't be so easily embraced by the complicit Congress and the uninformed public. The cure is the reduction of the level of debt (the Great Deleveraging). But the policy the government is taking makes the disease worse by borrowing more to bail out Wall Street. The government is not even considering decreasing the debt of the country. So the disease will last a long time. The bailouts mean that many zombie financial institutions, whose poor choices should have led to their demise, will be with us for a decade. They will not be relieved of their problems by letting Shumpeterian[1] destruction take its course. The United States will move to inflation because of all the deficits.

Some argue that the Great Deleveraging could be drawn out over a decade like it has been in Japan. The U.S. dollar enjoys many strengths including the fact that dollars are used in many world transactions. But the attitude toward the dollar compared to that of the yen in the 1990 in terms of its prognosis in purchasing power is quite different. The structural weakness of the United States being the largest debtor in the world (as opposed to the largest creditor, as Japan was), leads me to predict a loss of confidence in the dollar that will not allow the elongated muddling that Japan experienced. When foreigners lose confidence in holding Treasuries (they have already lost confidence in holding agencies), the United States could face the kind of crisis that besets overindebted countries, like the Asian Tigers (Thailand, Korea, Philippines, Malaysia, etc.) in 1998 or Latin American countries that experienced currency devaluation when petro dollar debts were too big to handle in the 1980s.

Many are saying that the problem is that housing just needs to be stabilized. I think the problems need to be viewed more comprehensively, and until I hear solutions addressing the debt, I think we will not be close to moving on.

It was the extreme leverage of too much debt that was the precursor to the housing bubble bursting. The current collapse did not start in 2006 and 2007, but in the decade before when too much debt was extended. The source was in the financial engineering of inventing Structured Investment Vehicles (SIVs), securitizing, off-balance-sheet funding, and

---

[1] After Joseph Shumpeter, an economist who advocated "creative destruction."

foreign investing. We will be in recovery after massive overleveraging has been wiped out, mostly through default, and some through dollar inflation to decrease the debt size compared to the ongoing earning power of the debt holders and the economy. That view makes the path ahead more difficult to get to recovery. It will take longer than typical economists think. The deflation we have now is damaging to the debtor. Many debts and debtors will be destroyed before we recover.

The active policy of the Fed, the Treasury, and the administration is to reflate the system, with government-sponsored adding of debt (their own) and new money. Much also depends on whether foreigners slow their loans to the United States, in the form of shifting their buying from Treasuries to something else, such as gold or buying resource-producing companies.

The dollar will come under severe pressure from all these forces going forward.

The conclusion is that although the same forces of debt overleverage drove us to a bubble that burst, we are responding differently this time. With the boom now entering collapse, this particular Great Deleveraging is unfolding with a softening cushion from the massive bailouts. That has allowed some measures of the economy to appear to be recovering which are being called "green shoots." But these extreme government bailouts are way beyond what was done by Roosevelt in the New Deal. The expansion of government programs during the Depression era amounted to only about $500 billion in today's dollars. Today's $10 trillions bailouts, Fed expansions, guarantees, and now spending policies are turning the deflationary tide just as it was starting. The combined assault of all the programs will turn into an inflationary currency crisis, rather than the long deflationary period of the Great Depression. This period of difficulty is likely to extend several years.

It is not so much that the circumstances leading up to the great boom of the economy in both periods are so different. It is that the responses of the government are so much greater this time around. Make no mistake about it: the United States will be facing terrible difficulties in the years ahead. Printing up money does not create more wealth. We will be suffering as a nation from the extreme imbalances that are being unwound. It is the policy of the government to achieve the decrease of so much debt; not through default, saving and paying down debt, and productivity; but through fostering an active debasement of debt through the debasement of the dollar that decreases the debt burden. The decrease will be in real terms even as debt is paid off in inflated dollars. This process will take an extended period as it did after the Great Depression and will be painful for years.

Today's financial world is far more interconnected and aware of shifting trouble spots than in the aftermath of the Great Depression. Today we face the overhang of foreigners' confidence in our system that could collapse quickly once the active policy of dollar destruction is understood. Unfortunately, in these circumstances the confidence in the dollar is in the minds of foreigners, not in the short-term policy actions by our government. And should they wake up to how seriously damaged the dollar has become, a collapse could come rapidly.

I worry that our policymakers, particularly Ben Bernanke, do not understand the tiger they are unleashing. By leaning against the historical precedent of deflation they will get what they want: very big inflation. And once that tiger is unleashed it will have its own ravaging effects. So the conclusion I come to is that even though the initial circumstances of the stock market crash of 1929 and our current-day economic slowing are similar, the responses are different enough that the 1929 deflationary historical event is not likely to be repeated.

The other country experiencing deleveraging and deflation that seems comparable is Japan and their "lost decade." Japan's situation is slightly different because its central bank took a much more active role than did our Federal Reserve during the 1930s. The next chapter takes a more detailed look at what lessons we could learn from Japan's bubble bursting.

Chapter 8

What the United States Can Learn from Japan's Lost Decade(s): 1989–2009

I select Japan's lost decade as relevant to our situation today because Japan experienced both a stock market bubble and real estate bubble that burst not unlike our own. How well I remember a different era when I was working for the large computer manufacturer Amdahl in Silicon Valley that was 40 percent owned by Fujitsu. I studied the Japanese miracle and negotiated business in their stylized format, gaining both respect and seeing some weaknesses in their system. Economists today are asking if the deflation and long-term slow economic growth are paths that the United States might follow. In this chapter, I'll dig deeper, looking at the economic data in comparison to the United

States, and then I'll wrap up with my interpretation of the similarities and differences that may predict how our particular crisis evolves.

The United States is following an aggressive policy response to our credit crisis, much as Japan did. The Fed cut the main U.S. interest rate to as low as zero in December 2008, and then extended to nonconventional measures in trying to resuscitate the economy with buying debt and making direct loans. These moves were reminiscent of those taken by the Bank of Japan in the early part of this decade, as it struggled to end the deflation gripping that country's economy. Japan's economy went from the shining example that the world wanted to emulate in 1989, to very slow growth for almost two decades. After its credit bubble broke when both real estate and the stock market fell in 1990, Japan's economy never returned to its vibrant success. The period has been called the Lost Decade. The United States is entering a similar situation of a credit bubble bursting.

To revive the economy, Japan went on an intense fiscal-stimulus spending spree, creating big deficits so that its central government debt is now approaching 200 percent of GDP. (By comparison, the United States' debt is 65 percent.) The Bank of Japan cut its interest rate to zero, just as the United States has done. Then it made extra liquidity available to the market in what is called quantitative easing (QE), just as the U.S. Federal Reserve is now doing.

Japan's Lost Decades: How Japan's Economic Bubble Burst after 1989

Figure 8.1 shows how Japan's stock market soared to 38,000 at the end of 1989—and how it has been dropping since; it is now around 10,000, which is a 75 percent drop. Japan's real estate bubble did the same. Japan's bubble burst, and its economy has been slow ever since. Note: The charts in this chapter use the scale of 100 million yen because that's easy to translate to dollars; there are about 100 yen to the dollar, thus 100 million yen equals $1 million.

The Japanese real estate bubble burst as the direct result of credit expansion and contraction. Figure 8.2 shows how Japanese land prices peaked at the same time as stocks peaked.

Although there were many factors involved in creating the Japanese economic bubble, dominant were the same sort of inputs that helped

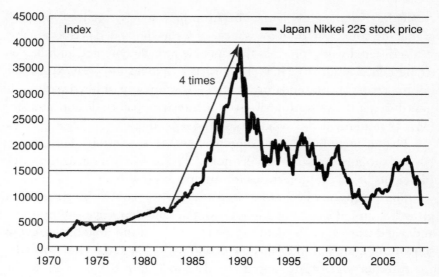

Figure 8.1   Japanese Stocks, from 1970–2009: The Bubble Peaked in 1990

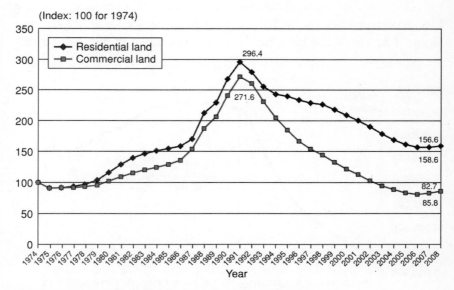

Figure 8.2   Japanese Real Estate Also Peaked in 1990
SOURCE: "Published Land Prices," Ministry of Land, Infrastructure, Transport and Tourism; http://tochi.mlit.go.jp/h20hakusho/chapter7/chapter07_eng.html.

create the extreme growth in China from 1980 to now: a cheap currency, giving the country a low-cost wage base for its motivated and reasonably well-educated work force. As the Japanese miracle emerged and the yen strengthened, wages rose in global terms. To extend and even expand the boom, Japan's accommodating central government partnered with business through the powerful Ministry of International Trade and Industry (MITI) and provided easy and inexpensive credit.

The Japanese bubble was supported by the expansion of credit way beyond proportion to the real economy. That drove real estate and stock to heights based on projections for unlimited growth.

The expansion of credit induced assets to rise, so watching the credit growth is an indicator because it drove the self-supportive rise in stocks and real estate. Once the debt in Japan hit its limit and no longer grew, as shown in Figure 8.3, the Japanese economy lost its miraculous growth.

Another way of looking at the data in Figure 8.3 is to show the annual growth rate, which rose to 18 percent just before it crashed, as shown in Figure 8.4.

The result of the collapse is best measured in comparison to the U.S. economy by showing the GDP of both on the same graph, as in Figure 8.5. This is the key chart to remember when thinking about the

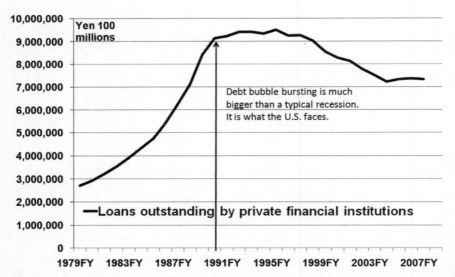

Figure 8.3   The Number of Loans Outstanding by Private Financial Institutions Shows How Japan's Debt Bubble Burst in 1990

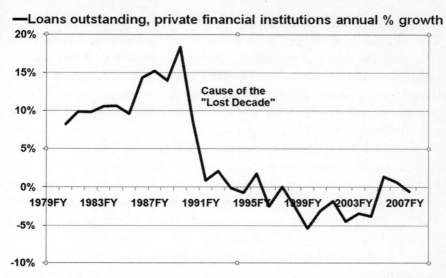

Figure 8.4 Japan's Loan Growth Collapsed from 18% Annual Growth in 1989 to No Growth

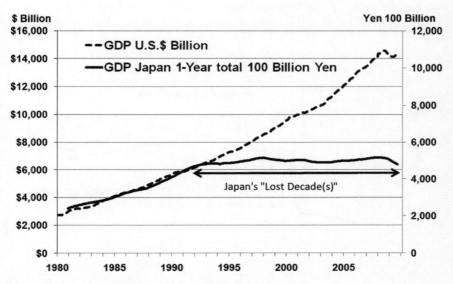

Figure 8.5 Japan's Economy Was Flat after 1990 Burst

comparison of the United States to Japan over the lost decades. (Note: The data shown in Figure 8.5 is not adjusted for inflation or exchange rate; only the nominal published numbers are provided. Adjusting for inflation would show the United States with a little less growth, but it would leave unchanged the key point of the relative sluggishness of Japan over the period. Nominal GDP is a useful base for comparison to other nominal measures within each economy.)

Japan has been unable to return to the growth achieved with expanding credit. Japan excelled in production for export. Japan's competitive edge of cheap production labor was taken over by other foreign countries. Japan bankrolled many of the Asian Tigers (Thailand, Korea, Taiwan, Philippines, Malaysia, Singapore, etc.) in setting up foreign factories to produce what was uncompetitive at their own high wage rates. China was the biggest replacement for Japan's manufacturing for the world.

The economic slowing, combined with the strength of the yen, delivered a 20 percent price drop over 23 years—from 1980 to about 2003—as shown in Figure 8.6. It is this deflation that is pointed to as a possible path for the United States, so we need to look closely at the situation in Japan. While in total it amounted to 20 percent over 20 years,

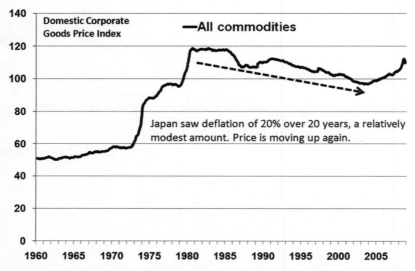

Figure 8.6   Japanese Domestic Goods Prices Dropped from 1980 to 2003

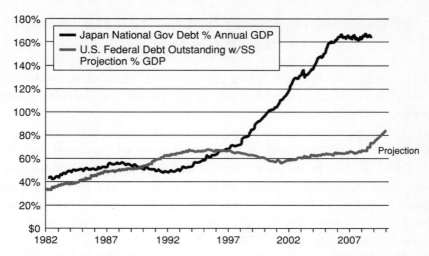

Figure 8.7 Japan's Debt Jumped while the United States' Was Flat in Terms of Percentage of GDP

that was in the 1 percent range per year—not a disruptive level. While deflation hurts debtors, the amount that Japan experienced has not been disruptive, and could be managed if the Japanese level did occur, in the United States.

Japan launched big government spending programs with stimulus packages to expand infrastructure, increasing the national government debt. The debt as a percentage of GDP is now at a very high level approaching 200 percent, as shown in Figure 8.7. While the United States worries about its federal government debt, the comparison in Figure 8.7 (which is shown as a ratio to GDP to allow comparison across the different-size economies) indicates the rapid Japanese expansion. The comparison is important because U.S. policymakers are throwing caution to the wind about expanding U.S. deficits. We are just starting on the path of quantitative easing, so the data haven't yet been compiled regarding what has happened in the United States. The stimulus probably helped Japan to avoid a destructive depression from its slowing credit bubble, but Japan's economy did not recover quickly.

The U.S. Flow of Funds data shows the total debt-to-GDP ratio at 370 percent of GDP (refer back to Figure 5.1). This is more than twice the level that the Japanese economy started with when it entered its lost decade in 1990.

Quantitative Easing Is What You Do after Cutting Rates to Zero

To stimulate its economy, Japan cut its rates to zero. Easy credit was expected to expand investment and provide loans to consumers to spend. Today, U.S. politicians tell the same story.

Quantitative easing (QE) is the step beyond the traditional lowering of interest rates. The Bank of Japan (BOJ, which is equivalent to our Federal Reserve) launched an experiment to provide extra liquidity to the banks by buying Japanese government bonds and providing even more liquidity to the weak banks that had many bad debts on their books, mostly from real estate where prices had collapsed. Figure 8.8 shows the easing on the BOJ's books as excess reserves.

Combining a closer look with the interest rate of the overnight call (i.e., a short-term interest rate) rate of the dotted line, we can see, in Figure 8.9, that the experiment got the interest rate to zero. The policy has been called the Zero Rate Policy (ZRP).

The experiment was considered bold. It lasted five years, from 2001 to 2006, providing banks with $250 billion of excess reserves to expand the economy. However, you already know the answer to what happened: It didn't work.

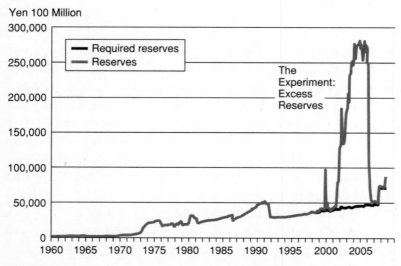

Figure 8.8   Japan's Example of Quantitative Easing

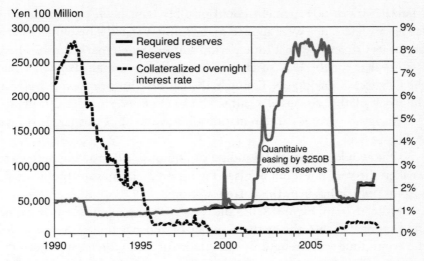

Figure 8.9   Japan's Quantitative Easing Achieved a Zero Interest Rate

So let's look further at what happened to important economic measures. The most successful comparison is to the stock market, where the rebound during the period was noticeable, as shown in Figure 8.10. This was important history and relevant for the repeat of the experiment in the United States. The astounding jump in the U.S. stock market from

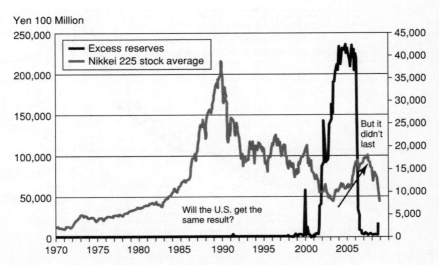

Figure 8.10   Excess Reserves Boosted Japanese Stocks

March 2009 of 60+ percent could possibly have been predicted if the Japanese experience were applied to the United States. The United States began its QE around that time period and our stock market rose. There is a message for the U.S. stock market about what might happen when the U.S. exits Quantitative Easing in the Japanese history as well. In Japan the stock market collapsed again to the level of entering the QE phase.

Also, the currency in circulation moved up—but not far, as shown in Figure 8.11.

One would expect the flooding of liquidity and growing deficits to weaken the yen, but it did not (see Figure 8.12). Japan still enjoys a trade surplus, which has kept the currency strong.

Note that in Figure 8.12, the yen is stronger with a downward movement, because this is the number of yen per dollar. A reason for the continuing yen strength was the trade surplus, which came from the attractive Japanese products that kept the yen in demand, as shown in Figure 8.13.

To confirm that the Japanese Zero Rate Policy was an unusual distortion of typical interest rate levels, Figure 8.14 compares the official central banks' overnight rates of Japan, the United States, the European Union, the United Kingdom, and Canada.

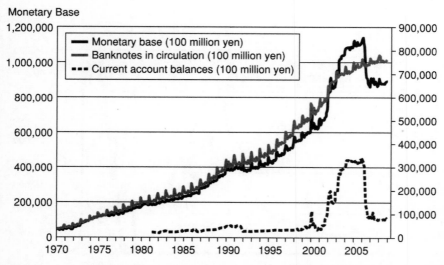

Figure 8.11   Japan's Monetary Base Increase Did Not Move Currency

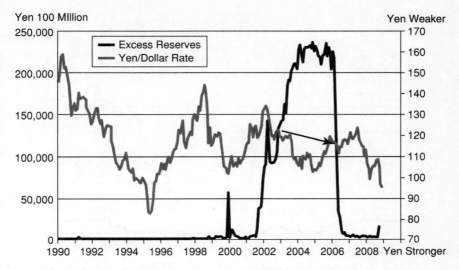

Figure 8.12   Japan's Quantitative Easing Didn't Hurt the Yen

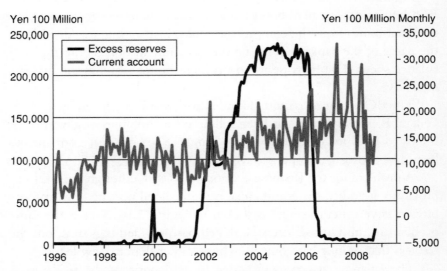

Figure 8.13   Positive Current Account Kept Yen Strong

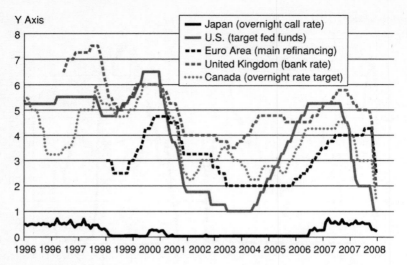

Figure 8.14   Japan's Interest Rate Has Been the Lowest of the Major World Economies

Figure 8.15 shows how the quantitative easing was funded by the BOJ buying government bonds. This was accomplished by buying government bonds from the commercial banks, by creating new deposits in the name of the banks, and taking the government bonds onto the BOJ balance sheet. The increase in government bonds matches the increase of reserves.

The BOJ's process is quite different from that being taken by the U.S. Federal Reserve, which has been selling off its holdings of government bonds to fund its loans to banks to purchase toxic assets, poor-quality loans like mortgages to people who aren't paying.

A problem for the Japanese economy was that although the BOJ was providing liquidity, the commercial banks avoided making new loans by buying government bonds, as shown in Figure 8.16. This is the same problem in the United States. The Fed has provided big sums, but the result is that money has gone elsewhere, rather than to new loans.

The Japanese government added to its deposits at the BOJ just at the start of the easing, but then removed them over the time of the experiment, as shown in Figure 8.17.

As the excess reserves were eliminated, the BOJ provided new direct loans after 2006 to maintain a stimulating effect, as shown in Figure 8.18.

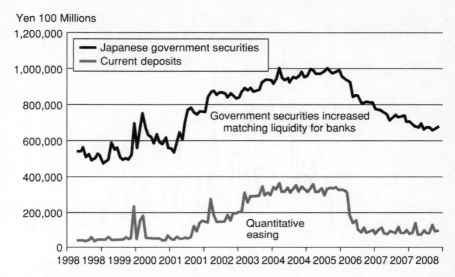

Figure 8.15   Japan's Quantitative Easing Was Funded by Buying Government Securities

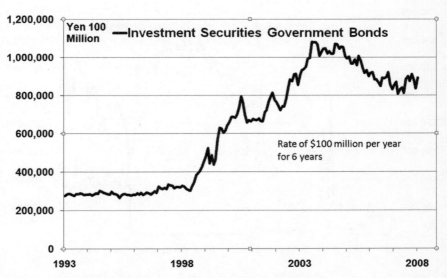

Figure 8.16   Japanese Banks Bought Government Bonds

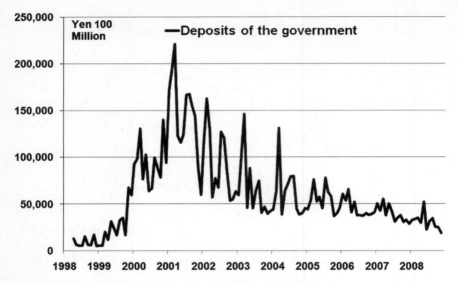

Figure 8.17   Government Deposits at Bank of Japan Declined

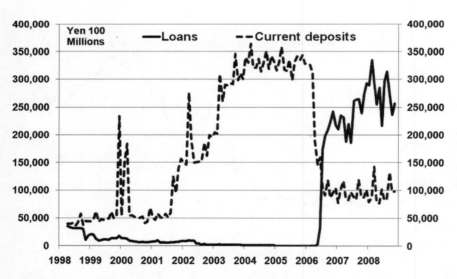

Figure 8.18   As Deposits Dropped after 2006, the Bank of Japan
Extended Loans

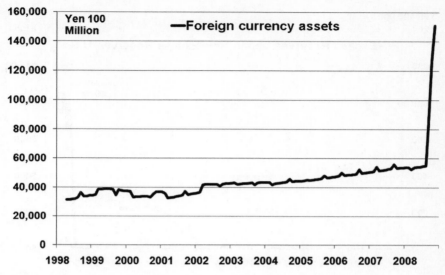

Figure 8.19   The Bank of Japan Increased Foreign Currency Assets

This is almost a mirror image of the approach of the Federal Reserve who had extend hundreds of billion of loans to financial institutions in emergency funds in 2008, and then began quantitative easing in 2009 (buying MBS, etc.) and eliminated the big direct loans.

In late 2008, the BOJ shifted its policy from not holding much foreign currency to now holding $100 billion more, as shown in Figure 8.19. One guess is that BOJ policy is to not automatically buy U.S. Treasuries, with the trade surpluses, because the BOJ has not figured out how to invest the money.

Comparing Quantitative Easing in Japan and the United States to 2009

The easing in Japan to provide excess reserves was only one-third as big as the United States so far. In this low-rate environment, there is less incentive to remove the deposits from the Fed, so excess reserves have stayed at the Fed and have grown. The latest Fed data shows a big jump in the U.S. excess reserves, much like the quantitative easing in Japan—see Figure 8.20—but it is not clear what toxic assets may have

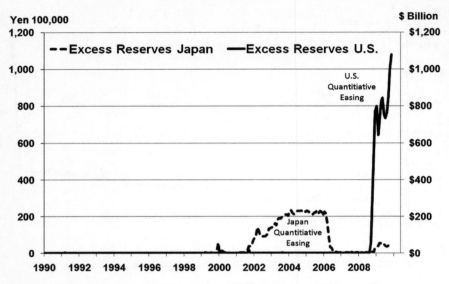

Figure 8.20   U.S. Excess Reserves Are Triple Japan's to 2009

been bought from the banks, because the Fed is being secretive. Japan's banks should be able to extend loans, but they are not doing that very rapidly. It is important to note the differences. The United States is acting more quickly in the cycle and with even bigger amounts.

Relative sizes compared to GDP suggest that Japan's increase in money was big. Because the relative size of the Japanese GDP is only about a third of the United States', the relative size of the credit expansions were about the same at the start, as shown in Figure 8.21. The United States has continued to expand more in late 2009, rising to 7.5 percent where Japan's peak was under 5 percent of GDP. The surprise is how fast the Fed expanded its programs, and since it has promised more, the end is not in sight.

Figure 8.22 shows how the Fed moved much faster and with a bigger affect on its balance sheet than did the Bank of Japan.

The bigger movement and the speed that the Fed expanded its balance sheet indicate that the affect on the United States should be bigger, too. The fear is that the U.S. trade deficit, combined with the rapid expansion of the Fed's operations, will be disastrous in terms of confidence in the dollar.

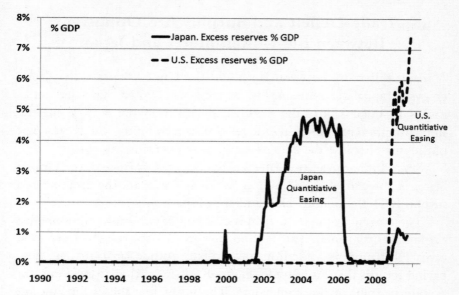

Figure 8.21   Japan's and the United States' Expansions Are Similar in Terms of Percent of GDP

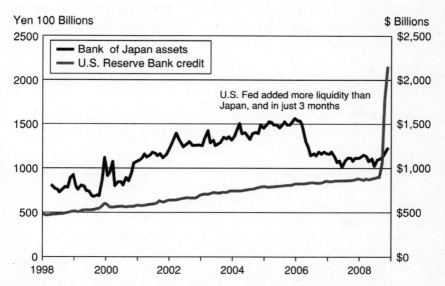

Figure 8.22   The Bank of Japan's Asset Expansion Was Less than the U.S. Federal Reserve's

Trade Deficit and Surplus Are Opposite Between the United States and Japan

A major difference between Japan and the United States is that Japan enjoys a capital account surplus, whereas the United States has accumulated a huge debt to the world, as shown in Figure 8.23. Using the similar method of comparing the relative sizes by ratio–GDP is only part of the story because the deficits accumulate over time.

Since 1985, the accumulated current account balance of the United States is a negative $6,893 billion, whereas for Japan, the accumulated surplus is $3,234 billion. The difference is pronounced.

The current account of Japan is made up of two broad components: the trade surplus and returns from investments abroad. A closer look reveals that more is made from investments outside Japan that are now paying returns than from trade. Figure 8.24 shows the Japanese current account surplus in the higher line. The lower line shows the amount of the current account surplus that comes from trade. The difference between the two lines is the amount of foreign investment income. So although Japan is enjoying a very positive current account calculation, trade surplus is less than it used to be. Japanese bankers funded much

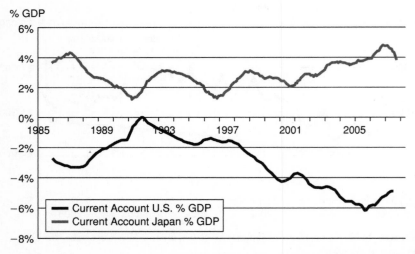

Figure 8.23   Japan's Current Account Is a Surplus whereas the United States' Is a Deficit

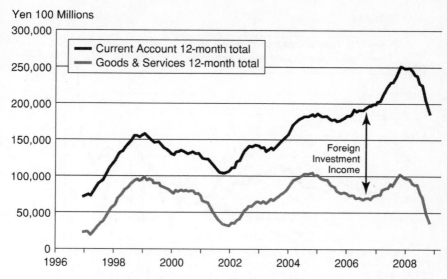

Figure 8.24   Japan's Current Account Is Much Higher than Its Trade Surplus

of the investment in the Asian Tigers' economies for their productivity and growth. Wage rates in Japan were not competitive with Indonesia, China, and the Philippines. That meant that relatively less was invested in Japan, leaving the economy at home stagnating. But the returns from foreign investment have grown to make the current account balance positive.

Figure 8.24 also indicates a drop in Japanese trade surplus.

Comparing the National Government Deficits of Japan and the United States

As mentioned earlier in this chapter, Japan's many stimulus programs ramped up Japan's outstanding national government debt toward 200 percent of GDP, but that took almost two decades. The growth in that debt compared to the United States shows how much faster the United States has expanded (see Figure 8.25).

As mentioned, the GDP of Japan is smaller than the United States, so dividing the deficit by the GDP gives a comparison based on the size of the two economies. Then the size of the U.S. deficit is not so

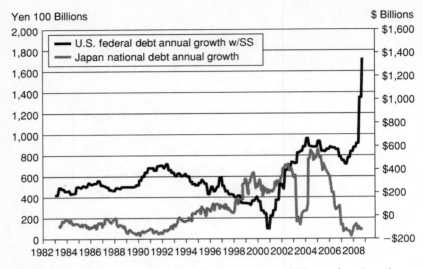

Figure 8.25   U.S. Annual Deficit Is Growing Much Faster than Japan's

much bigger than Japan's, even as the speed with which it jumps is more dramatic (see Figure 8.26). A projection for the U.S. deficit to continue at the $1.5 trillion level in the 2010 decade is assumed in this view. On the relative basis of ratio to GDP, the $1.5 trillion U.S. deficit is about what Japan grew to over 10 years. The United States jumped to this very big level of bailouts and stimulus within less than two years of recognition of a crisis. Of course, we had a head start from waging a couple of wars.

Lessons from the Japanese Experiment

The position of the United States is similar to Japan because the big debt growth of the United States is now just starting to unwind like it did in Japan in 1990. The reactions of the Bank of Japan and the U.S. Federal Reserve are similar in cutting interest rates to zero and using unconventional methods to buy assets to expand their respective balance sheets. Further, both central governments went into deficits to support their economies. From 2001 to 2006, Japan went to quantitative easing, adding $250 billion to their excess reserves, to drive the rate to zero and

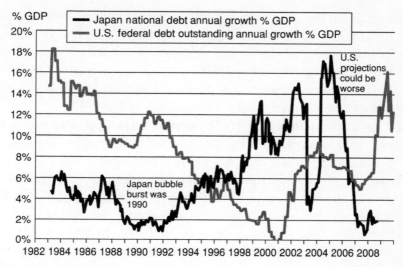

Figure 8.26   Japan Took a Decade to Ramp its Deficit to U.S. Level When Compared as % of GDP

to stimulate the economy through the banks. Japan's debt, at 160 percent of GDP, would be expected to be inflationary, but it wasn't.

The United States has acted even more precipitously, with even larger promises of intervention than Japan in its quantitative easing. Japan has taken almost two decades to do what the United States is planning to do in two years. What can we learn from these results?

1. **The Japanese economy did not react very much.** The Japanese spent trillions, but the economy did not return to robust growth. Basically, the results were less than hoped for, but perhaps they avoided a worse downturn. The Japanese stock market dropped from 38,000 in 1990 to 8,000, went back up double during the easing, and returned to 8,000. After 1990, Japan's GDP stayed level. The comparison here is that if we are like Japan, we could be in for a slow economy for a long time. But . . .
2. **Compared to Japan, the U.S. reaction is bigger.** The U.S. quantitative easing is bigger. The balance sheet of the Bank of Japan didn't rise as much as the Fed. The Fed is still adding liquidity. Deposits at the BOJ by Japan's central government didn't balloon as

they did in the United States. Obama started with a new fiscal stimulus, which is likely to be bigger than Japan's. The United States is in much weaker shape because of its accumulated trade deficits. The United States can't run big deficits and expand government programs for the financial community, for autos, and for new infrastructure without inciting inflation. So the dollar will fall.

3. **The trade deficit and trade surplus have opposite effect on the two countries.** The major difference between the United States and Japan is that Japan enjoys robust returns from its foreign investments and has consistently run a trade surplus. Together, those give Japan a strong current account and keep its currency strong. The strong yen has been instrumental in keeping the price of imports (especially oil) at reasonable levels and that, in turn, has helped keep inflation low. Consequently, despite a big increase in Japanese government debt, the yen has mostly increased against the dollar since the start of their bubble burst in 1990. Thanks to its strong currency, a modest deflation has been apparent in Japan's Wholesale Price Index. Such a modest deflation is not to be feared, because it increases the purchasing power of the citizenry without triggering the more serious consequences such as witnessed in the United States during the 1930s Depression. It is runaway inflation that is most to be feared.

4. **Foreign investment by Japan is a strength.** In the face of the accumulated trade deficits and expanding budget deficits, the United States faces the problem of attracting foreign investment to continue to buy foreign necessities like manufactured goods and oil, at the same time as the accumulated and growing government deficit for future retirement obligations leads to new federal government borrowing that cannot easily be turned off. The interest on the growing outstanding debt will make it impossible to pull back the U.S. deficit.

5. **The lesson of Japan is that even very big government interventions are not as effective in reversing economic slowdown after a big bubble created by too much debt bursts.** The U.S. disaster is extremely serious for the world economies because so many depend on U.S. consumers to purchase products of the world. The continued economic slowing is not likely to be mitigated by

the record size of the U.S. bailouts and economic reactions if Japan's rather lackluster economic growth holds for the United States.

6. **As was the case with Japan, could the U.S. deleveraging be drawn out?** The structural weakness of the United States as the largest debtor in the world (as opposed to the largest creditor, as Japan was going into its crisis) leads me to expect a loss of confidence in the dollar that will not allow the decade-long slow economy that Japan experienced.

When foreigners lose confidence in holding Treasuries—and they have already lost confidence in holding Agencies—the U.S could enter a crisis the likes of which occurs in overindebted countries, such as was the case with the Asian Tigers in 1998. The consequences of an overreaction of extreme bailouts, one after another until sanity returns, could be more damaging for the U.S. dollar.

This gives rise to the potential that the crisis will be sharp, as was Japan's in the beginning, but then—because of a weak dollar, versus a strong yen—morph into something even more dangerous: a full-blown currency crisis that shatters the dollar's global hegemony.

The longer result will be money flooding the planet, creating a currency crisis and inflation. If I am right that the situation in the United States today, of debt deleveraging being counterbalanced by government programs even bigger than Japan's and Roosevelt's New Deal, then I think the deflationary forces in the United States will be minor and short. The problems of accumulated government deficit and trade deficit leave little room for piling new debt and expansionary policies on our system without long-term deleterious effects for the dollar.

Investment Implications in Japan

The Democratic Party of Japan gained power in September 2009 by unseating the Liberal Democratic Party, which dominated Japan for half a century. Japanese Prime Minister Yukio Hatoyama named Naoto Kan as the new Finance Minister in January 2010. Japan's new central banker surprised the financial community by speaking candidly that he did not want the yen to rise. News stories have said he is on a mission to blow up the yen. The strategy is to debase the yen, which would inflate assets and, more importantly, get exports going via more competitive pricing. Kan is the sixth Japanese finance minister since August 2008. He will have to manage the world's largest public debt, as a percent of GDP.

The fiscal and economic policy shift to focus more on the economy is thought by many as a support for the stock market because as the yen weakens, exports improve. Intervention in the currency market could be possible if he sticks to his comment that the yen should not rise above the 95 yen/dollar.

So, as I always say, let's look at the data. Figure 8.27 shows the big drop in the stock market and the general rise in the yen. Analysts are suggesting that the yen may decline, so that the stock market might become a better investment as indicated by the arrows at the very right of the chart. The Nikkei 225 may rise as the yen falls. The Nikkei in early 2010 is selling at a 74 percent discount to its 1989 high (38,916). Interestingly for U.S. investors, the rise in the yen has meant that the drop in Japanese stocks from the peak was a smaller 57 percent.

I think there is more to this story than to just look for opportunities in Japanese stocks. It was not just the stock market that crashed over the

Figure 8.27 The Yen Has Been Strong As Stocks Fell. Will this Reverse?

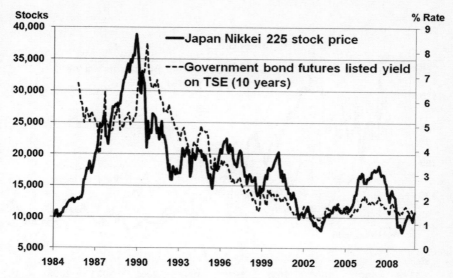

Figure 8.28 Japanese Interest Rates Collapsed Along with Stocks

last two decades; interest rates crashed as well. Figure 8.28 shows the amazing correlation in the drop of interest rates and the stock market together.

The Japanese government actively pursued easy credit policies to decrease rates with the hope of improving the economy. They were not particularly successful at reviving stocks. They would not have been successful at lowering rates had the yen not continued strong.

Figure 8.29 shows the dramatically low interest rates in Japan and the generally stronger yen. On this chart I've shown the number of yen to purchase a dollar, so that as the line drops it is an indication of a strengthening yen. The 10-year rate briefly touched a bottom of 1 percent in 2003. It would seem unlikely to return to that level considering the size of the government deficit and the announced policy by the government to keep the yen from rising. The right-hand side of the chart suggests that if the yen were to weaken, it could pressure rates to rise.

The implication of a political move of the new party to policies that will let the yen fall should be to help exporters and Japanese industry so that their stock market might recover from two decades of losses. That might be the case, but foreign investors, who might be getting

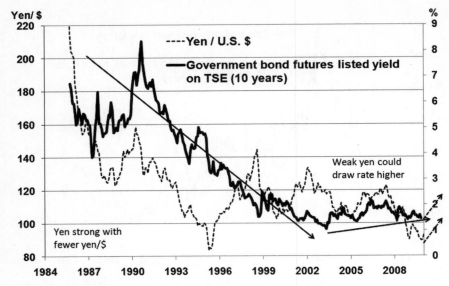

Figure 8.29   Rates Dropped with the Strong Yen. If the Yen Falls Rates Could Rise

SOURCE: www.boj.or.jp/en/type/stat/dlong/fin_stat/rate/hbmsm.csv.

significantly higher prices in Japan for stocks denominated in Japanese yen, would also be losing in the exchange rate of the yen. It's a lot less clear to me how successful a U.S. investor would be in buying Japanese stocks.

The yen has been a strong currency throughout the whole postwar period. It would seem to me that a far easier play would be to directly invest in the falling yen. It is the more direct goal rather than the two steps required for stocks to rise. Now, of course, the problem is what would the yen decline against? The whole story of this book has been that the dollar is being debased by the U.S. government. Looking back over the figures in this chapter, one can see that the Japanese government has done an amazing job of accumulating government debt of 200 percent of GDP, which would have destroyed the currency of most countries. The strength of the yen came from its value in purchasing Japanese-produced goods. Japan's trade surplus kept the yen strong. But that trade surplus has mostly disappeared. The current account of Japan has been supportive of the yen, as Japanese businesses successfully invested abroad. The returns on those investments have been very strong and those returns are part of the current account. The returns on foreign investment are probably not as effective in supporting the yen as are the trade surpluses. My conclusion lines up with analysts who suggest that the government of Japan will be successful at managing the yen downward against major world currencies like the dollar.

I look beyond the Japanese stock market and the yen for one more investment opportunity that may become a "play of the decade": I think Japanese interest rates are too low. Low rates were a policy objective of the Bank of Japan, with the goal of spurring investment and growth in the country. While Japan has avoided the kind of disaster that befell the United States after the 1929 bubble, Japan's economy has been lackluster. One of the key reasons that rates could be kept so low for so long was that there was no inflation. In fact, there was modest deflation. Bond investors look to the real yield they obtain after inflation is taken out of the nominal rate of interest that bonds pay. In Japan, with a deflationary component, the real interest-rate returns to investors amounted to the regular bond interest rate plus the deflation. That is why after the yen were returned to the investor, they were able to purchase more after deflation. And there is a small side benefit: the return from deflation flies under the government radar as if it didn't exist, and is therefore not taxed. So while the real rate on Japanese bonds was low, the real rate after tax was slightly better. There is one more twist in that the value of the yen increased against other currencies, which increased the international value of the returns to investors. That is also a benefit that is not taxed to the Japanese investor. This last point is probably the justification for Japan's ability to maintain the lowest interest rates in the world for a decade. Even though during this period the yen did not strengthen significantly, there have been expectations that the yen would do well.

So my conclusion would be that if we see specific evidence of the government actively pursuing policies that will hurt the yen, then the order of investment opportunities is: first to expect interest rates to rise to compensate for the decline of the yen. The second best investment would be a direct short of the yen expecting it to fall from around 92 the dollar toward 100. (It sounds backward but this is yen per dollar and the number moves opposite to the value.) I'm sure there are opportunities to invest in Japanese stocks in such an environment, but I think the risks are higher. The stock market success in the decade ahead starting at 75 percent below its peak in 1990 does seem like a good opportunity, and moving from 10,000 to 15,000 for the Nikkei 225 would seem a reasonable target in a few years.

The play to short Japanese 10-year interest rate futures seems like another "trade of the decade." The current rate is only 1.5 percent. It has not been below 1 percent for five decades, and good sense says it would be impossible to go below 0 percent. In 1990 the rate peaked above 8 percent just after the peak of the stock market. If, as many commentators believe, a more active government is able to produce an expanding economy, that should drive rates higher. If, as is also expected by the commentators, the yen is no longer expected to rise and may even be actively managed by the government to weaken, that would also be a reason for investors to demand higher returns. The government has already created such a huge burden of debt of its own during these last two lost decades that would seem to add pressure in funding the interest on that debt when rolling it over. And finally, Japan faces the same kind of demographic bubble of an aging population that will expect government support and that will keep deficits huge. So my conclusion from an investment point of view would be to consider expecting Japanese interest rates to rise in the decade ahead.

The Japanese experiment did not bring big inflation and that example is pointed to by politicians who say we need not worry about inflation in the United States from our expansionary influences of quantitative easing and deficits. I think the important differences between our countries explain Japan's deflationary response. So to provide the extreme counterexample, the next chapter focuses on the most famous of inflationary experiences—the destruction of the mark in Weimar Germany, along with commentary on other countries.

Chapter 9

What the United States Can Learn from German and Other European Hyperinflations, and from China Today

T he entire first two sections of this book laid the foundational economic forces and massive response to the current crisis in terms that lead toward dollar debasement. So, in contrast to the two cases of modest deflation during debt deleveraging described in the previous two chapters, I move here to show examples of inflation, and just how extreme it can become. Most of us Americans have not experienced how destructive inflation can become and so tend not to worry that it could get out of control. In fact, many of the brightest observers who predicted serious problems of our current crisis also believe that we will follow a path of deflation for quite a while. They point to low interest rates and low prices for houses as examples that deflation has the upper hand. So let's put our own situation in perspective by examining examples from the other end of the spectrum of how inflation completely destroyed several European currencies in the aftermath of World War I.

Our stock market bubble of 2000 became the housing bubble of 2006 and has now become the credit crisis. With the U.S. government trying to paper over each successive crisis, federal deficits have spun out of control. Likewise, the Federal Reserve has debased its balance sheet with all manner of toxic waste, seriously undermining the long-term strength of the currency. And now we are on the path to the next logical step in the progression: a currency crisis.

The most widely noted of the currency crises is Germany's extreme inflation in the wake of World War I. The steps that brought Germany to its currency collapse in 1923 were extreme, but they come from some of the same potential weaknesses the United States is facing. I'll make a brief comparison of the United States to Germany, Austria, Hungary, and Poland, with a comparison that may surprise you. Also, as China has become the new emerging giant, I'll examine its monetary situation.

In the early 1920s, Germany was buried under the weight of insurmountable reparations payments to the war's victors, so it took the path of huge government deficit spending, covered by the printing press. As a consequence, the German currency quickly imploded to such an extent that housewives found it more economical to burn their paper money to heat the house rather than spend it on goods at the store.

In fact, the movements were so extreme that I found it difficult to even create this chapter's figures to illustrate the situation: I had to use logarithmic scales of many cycles just to put the data on one page. The data comes from the classic book, written in 1931 by Constantino Bresciani-Turroni, called *The Economy of Inflation—A Study of Currency Depreciation in Post-War Germany*. I optically scanned pages of the book, corrected errors, and developed the charts. Although the book contains many charts, Figure 9.1 provides a summary of the major economic measures. You can see that all these measures increase astronomically over the period of a few short years.

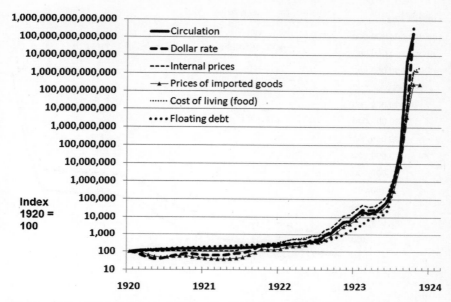

Figure 9.1   German Hyperinflation in Currency Circulation Was Matched by Its Growing Debt, Rising Prices, and Declining Exchange Rate
SOURCE: Adapted from information in *The Economics of Inflation,* Constantino Bresciani.

The item labeled "Circulation" reflects the amount of German marks being printed, and "floating debt" is the government debt, which you can think of as being similar to the excess quantities of Treasury securities currently being created by the U.S. government. Overlaid with several measures of the purchasing power of the mark, it is hard to see which line is which—and that's exactly the point: Once the deficits became too big, they were met with increases in the money, which increased the price of everything.

The message in Figure 9.1 is clear: The government can create inflation from its spending policies.

While that may seem obvious, there are many analysts today who say that Federal Reserve Chairman Ben Bernanke is pushing on a string and that no matter what he does, he won't be able to create inflation because banks aren't lending. It's certainly true that we have had a short period of asset collapse and associated deflationary pressures in the second half of 2008 and 2009. But it is wrong to believe that governments can be immune from the market forces of too much printing, once confidence in the financial system begins to erode.

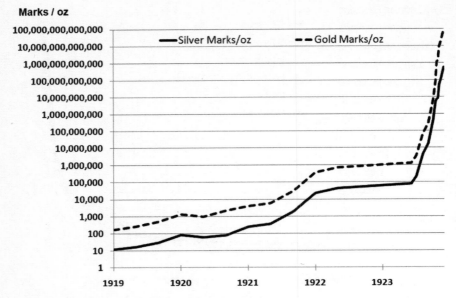

Figure 9.2   German Inflation in Gold and Silver

As you would expect to see, when the German, mark collapsed gold and silver did the equivalent of a moon shot, and that's exactly what Figure 9.2 illustrates. The prices of those metals were fixed in dollars at the time, so they soared as the value of the mark collapsed. That underscores my contention that predicting the price of gold is the wrong perspective; instead, we need to consider how gold is currently pricing the value of the dollar. (Chapter 15 expounds on why gold is the ultimate money, rather than dollars.)

Gold is understandable and relatively immutable as a globally accepted form of money. By contrast, the dollar is an instrument of the government, just as the German mark was before it. And, in the same way that the German mark was susceptible to unsound monetary policies, so is the U.S. dollar. The obvious lesson is that gold or silver can protect you against the destruction of the currency.

Of course, the key question is whether the situation of the United States today is anything like what Germany faced in the 1920s. To help in that assessment, I dug out data on the size of the German government's revenues compared to its expenditures. My goal was to understand how

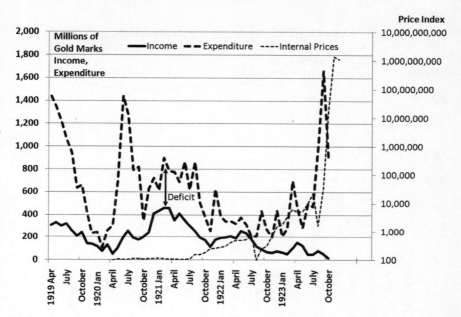

Figure 9.3   Germany's Deficit Drove Inflation, from 1919–1923
SOURCE: Adapted from information in *The Economics of Inflation,* Constantino Bresciani.

bad the gap between revenues and expenditures was in the period leading up to the hyperinflation. The data shown in Figure 9.3 has already been corrected to its equivalent in gold, rather than being quoted in rapidly changing marks. As you can see in Figure 9.3, the gap of expenditures over revenues was huge—and quite variable.

To finance its big deficits, Germany issued floating debt, which is the same process the United States is using currently in issuing Treasury securities. Calculating the size of the new German debt issues, compared to the country's expenditures, gives an idea of how bad the situation became: The deficits were running around 70 percent of expenditures, as shown in Figure 9.4.

In some sense, Germany's train had already gone off the track in 1920 because of expenditures being too high long before the actual explosive price increases took hold.

The United States is not at the danger point that got Germany into so much trouble, even though the U.S. deficit as a percentage of expenditures in fiscal 2009 (which ended September 30) was extreme,

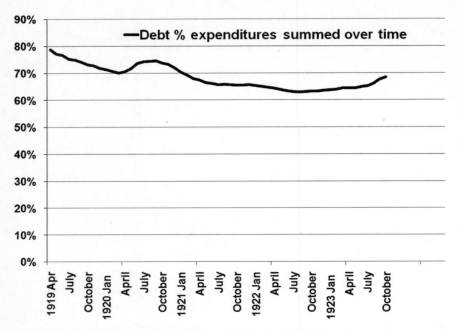

Figure 9.4 Germany Was Running Deficits of 60+%, from 1919–1923
SOURCE: Adapted from information in *The Economics of Inflation,* Constantino Bresciani.

at 40 percent. (That figure comes from dividing the $1.4 trillion deficit by $3.5 trillion expenditures.)

However, 40 percent is a dangerous level if it is to continue. The following study points out how dangerous this level is.

Peter Bernholz (professor emeritus of economics at the University of Basel, Switzerland) wrote a book called *Monetary Regimes and Inflation: History, Economic and Political Relationships,* where he analyzes the 12 largest hyperinflations. They were all caused by too much government deficit. His finding is that when government deficit exceeds 40 percent of expenditures, the government loses control of the currency, and its value declines precipitously.

It wouldn't be proper to suggest that the United States has the kind of extreme situation of Germany, but it's naïve to think it can't happen here. Because the United States has the second-oldest currency, as a country, we feel like the risk is so remote as to be impossible. The lack of widespread public concern about the potential dangers of a serious currency crisis gives the administration the latitude to pursue policies that, in time, could lead us to a much more damaging result than most people believe possible.

Before wrapping Germany together with the other countries of Europe that had difficulties, I want to briefly touch on the situation of the most populous nation on Earth: China. I had the opportunity to visit China in 2008 and was fascinated by its very long-term history with bronze-based money, paper-based money, and coins with holes in them, which are on display in the magnificent museum in Shanghai. China was happy and booming at the time.

China's Currency and Economic Expansion Actions Today

China has a special place in the world currencies because its trade affects all of us, especially the U.S. dollar. China is currently on track to become the world's second-biggest economy. With almost $1 trillion of U.S. Treasuries, China has just exceeded Japan as the largest holder.

The Chinese currency has acted differently from most other currencies of the world because it has been actively pegged to the dollar. Throughout the 1980s, the dollar was stronger against the yuan (RMB), as shown in Figure 9.5. But after 2006, the dollar decreased against the yuan, as the Chinese government relaxed some of its mechanisms to peg to the dollar. The Yuan has been strengthening as Chinese exports bring China a strong balance of reserves. Chinese officials understandably do not want to let their currency appreciate further because it might slow their exports that provide the jobs to keep their population happy.

China has hundreds of millions of workers who must be kept employed to avoid civil unrest. One tactic has been to keep the yuan low so that exports increase, providing jobs at home. In my travels to China, I was pleasantly surprised by the relative purchasing power of my dollars in Beijing and Shanghai. A subway that costs $3 in New York costs 3 yuan in Shanghai, yet the exchange rate is managed at a much weaker rate, of almost 7:1 (yuan to U.S. dollars).

We can see the results of the noticeable slowing in exports during the latest economic slowdown by looking at the level of accumulation

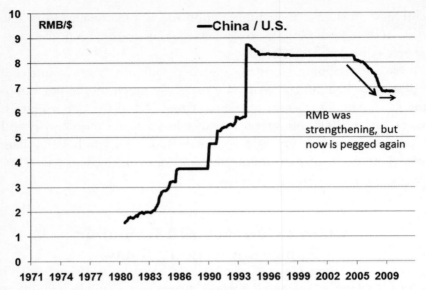

Figure 9.5   The U.S. Dollar Was Strong Against China's RMB until 1994, but Declined after 2005
SOURCE: Federal Reserve.

of foreign exchange reserves, which took a decided slowing in 2008 (see Figure 9.6). That was one of the reasons for the Chinese authorities to step up loans to keep the economy growing. That stimulus can be seen in the M2 money supply growth, which is much higher than the historical rate.

The Chinese embarked on the huge stimulus to counteract the slowing world economy, which had hurt its exports.

Even though the central banks of the world launched big stimulus programs, we have a worldwide recession—except in China. China's rebound has been boosted by 4 trillion yuan ($586 billion) of spending on stimulus programs like railways, roads, power plants, and public housing. With GDP of $4.6 trillion that is 12.7 percent of GDP, our (most recent) stimulus package of almost $800 billion was only 5.7 percent of our $14 trillion GDP. The bailout program is having a big effect: China was able to provide the big investment because of the $2 trillion of foreign currency it accumulated, so China had the money to spend. When the

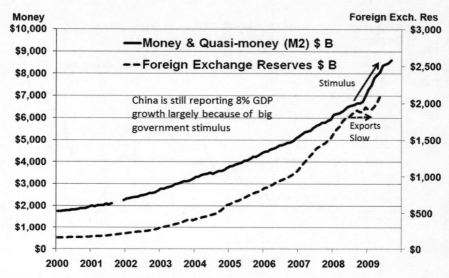

Figure 9.6   China's Money Stimulus Replaces Its Slowing Exports
SOURCE: People's Bank of China.

Chinese government dictates that banks lend, they do (which is what is *not* happening in the United States). China's stimulus-induced lending binge propelled growth in the fourth quarter of 2009, to 10.7 percent, its fastest pace in a year.

Chinese Money and Credit Spike Upward

By November 2009, the increase in money growth for both M2 and M1 had reached 30 percent year over year, as shown in Figure 9.7. That is up sharply from an already high 15 percent rate at the beginning of 2009. The resulting flood of money has supported Chinese stocks, real estate, and commodity inventories. It has also sparked an investor's real estate boom.

China is expanding its monetary base. But so is the United States, the United Kingdom, and most other countries, too. The United States has plenty of weaknesses (such as mark-to-market accounting, off-balance-sheet entities, etc.), but the Chinese are telling us even less

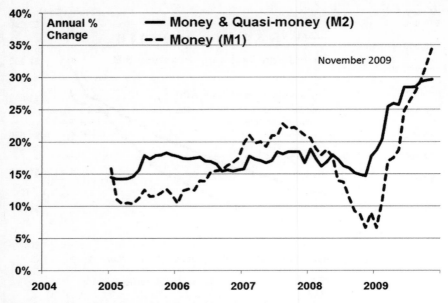

Figure 9.7   China Stimulus Caused Money to Jump in 2009
SOURCE: People's Bank of China, data to September 2010.

in their accounting about what is actually happening. Inflation could arise in a short timeframe because so much money has been added to China's system. We are seeing this in the Shanghai stock index and real estate.

Since the yuan at the official exchange rate seems underpriced in purchasing power, the Chinese can absorb some fairly high domestic inflation and not have to worry about the international effects on the exchange rate. My view is that this leaves them more vulnerable than what is generally understood. China, like the rest of the world, is facing overcapacity in a world of slowing economic consumption. So my view is that, despite announcing strong measures of its economic growth, China is vulnerable to economic slowing. China has the same penchant for government debasement of its currency that the rest of the world does. China is busy ramping up production for world consumers who are pulling back. China is printing its currency and using its dollars from trade surplus to buy commodities, and it's driving those prices higher as well.

How strong will the Chinese economy be in the long run when China winds down its stimulus? It will be facing overcapacity and slowing, just like the rest of the world.

Other Countries' Inflation after Big Government Deficits

Now, returning to Europe, I analyze summary data from the hyperinflations of Austria, Hungary, and Poland together with Germany to identify characteristics about causes of their inflation that could give us some guidelines against which to measure our own situation.

My evaluation is to look at what happened at the beginning stages of other serious inflationary periods around the world. The calculation of what fraction of the deficit is financed by borrowing in previous situations leading to inflation gives some indications of what the United States might face going forward. As mentioned, the United States had a deficit of 40 percent of spending in 2009. Comparisons help shed light on the question of how much effect these high deficits might have on the potential purchasing power of the dollar.

Using the examples of serious inflations experienced by Austria, Hungary, Poland, and Germany, I find that the first year of excessive deficit as a percent of total expenditures was 50 to 60 percent. The data is shown in Table 9.1, as is the resulting inflation that occurred in the year immediately following, shown in the last column of Table 9.1. As you can see, the outcome is not encouraging, with the best case being an inflation of 820 percent, and the worst at more than 7,000 percent.

Table 9.1 A Summary of Four Big Inflations

	Year	Government Expenditures	Deficit	Deficit % of Expenditures	% Inflation Next Year
Austria	1920	16,873	10,578	63	1042
Hungary	1920	20,210	9,690	48	1544
Poland	1921	880,852	535,541	61	820
Germany	1921	11,266	7,042	63	7475
Average				58	2720
U.S. est.	**2009**	**3,600**	**1,417**	**40**	**?**

Of course, there were different circumstances surrounding these inflations in Europe from today, but the data is revealing nonetheless. With the United States at a deficit of $1.7 trillion in 2010, that would be in the range of 45 percent of expenditures, which is important because the circumstances that led to complete destruction of the other currencies were only modestly worse, from 48 percent to 63 percent. That does not mean that inflation would get to the runaway levels shown in the comparison countries (in Table 9.1), but history certainly suggests a very significant potential for serious inflation.

That said, we are currently experiencing asset price deflation and economic slowing, but the truly extraordinary and historic level of government spending and bailouts that are being deployed to keep the economy afloat are, in my analysis, certain to lead to inflation in the not-too-distant future.

Hyperinflation occurs more regularly than most people realize, so I've collected some data on other hyperinflations in the next section.

Currencies No Longer in Circulation

DollarDaze.org analyzed 599 currencies that are no longer in circulation and found that 156 were destroyed by hyperinflation. The median age for these currencies was only 15 years. Table 9.2 groups the fates of these currencies.

Table 9.2   Currencies That Are No Longer in Circulation and Why

Currency Was...	Number of Currencies	Description
Ended through monetary unions, dissolution, or other reforms	184	Voluntary monetary unions such as the euro in 1999, or creation of the U.S. dollar in 1792.
Ended through acts of independence	94	Acts of former colonial entities renaming or reforming their currency.
Destroyed by hyperinflation	156	Currency destroyed through overissuance by the government.
Destroyed by acts of war	165	Currency deemed no longer valid through military occupation or liberation.

Looking at Other Financial Crises for Similar Characteristics to the United States

History provides a clear warning about financial crises: When things get bad, they can expand far beyond the original problem. In the current context, the subprime mortgage lending structure quickly escalated into the worst economic recession the United States has seen since the Depression.

In trying to put the situation today into the correct perspective, I looked more closely at 41 distinct financial crises over the last 30 years and found that 23 of them were also a currency crisis. To build understanding of the conditions preceding these currency meltdowns, I quantified and then took the median of several important macroeconomic conditions a year prior to the onset of the 23 currency crises identified.

With that work done, I then compared them to the United States today, which I show in Table 9.3. These macroeconomic indicators are flashing red, warning that we may not be so far from inflation.

As you can see in the column at the far right of Table 9.3, of the seven conditions that led to those 23 currency crises, six of the metrics for the United States are as bad or worse than the crisis median. The only exception is inflation. Why? Simply, the United States benefits today from its special status as the world's *de facto* reserve currency—meaning it underpins and generally sets the standard for the world's other major

Table 9.3   Summary Statistics of Other Currency Crises Compared to the U.S.

Initial Conditions	23 Currency Crises Median	U.S. in 2009	Worse (W) or Better (B)
Fiscal balance/GDP	−1%	−10%	W
Public sector debt/GDP	29%	65%	W
Inflation (CPI)	11%	2%	B
Deposits/GDP	37%	53%	W
GDP growth	2.0%	−2.0%	W
Current account/GDP	−2.9%	−3.5%	W
Private credit to GDP growth	8%	9%	—

SOURCE: IMF Working Paper, Systemic Banking Crises: A New Database, Luc Laeven and Fabian Valencia.

currencies. This prestige, which largely comes from the current lack of a viable alternative (ignoring gold, of course), has helped shield the dollar, despite the weak macroeconomic conditions. It's a major reason that the United States has been able to run such large imbalances in the other measures without currency damage—yet.

Put another way, the conditions are all there—save one—for the United States to follow the path of a currency crisis.

Review of What We Learned from the Currencies of the World

There are many lessons we can learn from looking beyond our own experience that tell us what may happen. As Americans, we don't feel the fear that Germans still remember from their experience of currency catastrophe, because we have never lived through such extremes. As it turns out, there have been many cases of currencies that were annihilated by government profligate spending. African countries, Latin American banana republics, and former communist states all faced currency crises. So the first lesson is that currency collapses are more common than most of us in the United States realize, and could happen here.

Germany went to extreme hyperinflation in 1923 due to government deficits that led to currency printing, which led to higher prices and finally to the loss of confidence that became a self-destructive spiral. The United States is not in as severe a position as Germany, but our deficit in 2009 was big enough to be raising flags of potential dollar instability.

The United States has followed the predictable path of extreme government bailouts to fight back against the Depression-like great deleveraging. By attempting to reinflate the economy, the government has planted the seeds that will grow into much more inflation in the not-too-distant future. In fact, the current situation of the United States, in terms of macroeconomic variables, is very much like the set of conditions that led to 23 other currency crises in the past. The one missing parameter is that inflation has not yet taken hold. The lesson is that we are closer than most of us realize.

In a rather unexpected twist of events, China, which has been considered a Third-World nation, is now one of the richer nations in its holdings of world currencies. It holds almost $1 trillion of U.S. Treasury issues, and with its newfound wealth, China is spending aggressively domestically and making loans so that its money supply is growing 30 percent a year. The point of the analysis is that the dollar, which will certainly be decreasing in purchasing power, may not change as dramatically against other currencies because they all are also hell-bent on bailing out their own economic systems, thereby doing their own version of currency devaluation.

The deficit spending of the United States, being financed at 40 percent by borrowing, is at the level that has destroyed other currencies. The historical strength of the United States has given us more leeway than has been afforded to other countries.

Conclusion

The obvious longer-term prediction is that the dollar will decline in purchasing power and perhaps very dramatically. At less than 10 percent per year, the changes can be easily absorbed. But at 25 percent per year, dislocation will be large enough to call out the controls of a currency crisis: limitations on international transfers and investment, wage and price controls, higher tariffs, and regulations against hoarding. Other currencies may follow the same path, if not as severely. Gold becomes the surest protection against dollar decline; also, most commodities, starting with oil and working through agricultural products, are good bets in times of inflation. If the world players lose confidence in the dollar, the logical necessary response from our Federal Reserve will be to drive interest rates higher. Because rates are so low, a move upward seems inevitable with any move of a weaker dollar. So history is warning us to protect against the demise of the dollar.

This wraps up the analysis of where we are and how the collection of forces will be driving our future. To here I have concentrated on the reasons *why* the economy and the dollar will move in the decade ahead. The rest of the book now turns toward identifying specific investing targets that should do well in the tough times ahead. It gives recommendations based on *what* is likely to happen. It concludes with predictions for the economy and how far the investments might move.

Part Four

INVESTMENT OPPORTUNITIES

The six chapters of this section can be read in any sequence, depending on your investment interest. I address stocks in Chapter 10 because that is the focus of most people's thoughts when they think of investments. My own interests lie beyond the stock market, because I think there are better opportunities in the areas that are less emphasized. Chapters 11 and 12 address the most fundamental of human needs: energy and food. Chapters 13 and 14, on the dollar and interest rates, are really the target of the previous economic analysis. In my view, interest rates will be the trade of the decade. Finally, Chapter 15 puts the capstone on my recommendations by recommending investment in gold, as the true money and the best safe haven from the dollar collapse that I see coming.

Chapter 10

The Stock Market May Be Dead for Another Decade

This chapter examines the long-run behavior of the stock market, with an eye to the strengths and weakness of various sectors. By looking at earnings and dividends and by comparing ratios to other investments, we can get a flavor of the big picture of whether stocks are overpriced or underpriced. I develop a model that can be used to assess the fundamental value of the stock market.

A Stock Market Model

The basic law of all investing is to obtain a return that is as high as possible compared to the price of the investment. It seems so obvious, but it is worth repeating, because we often respond to emotions and stories about an opportunity, rather than looking at the hard numbers to tell us what to do. The basic point is that we want a return on our investment.

For stocks, the basic idea is that a corporation will give us a fraction of its earnings for the fraction of ownership of the company that we hold. The investment is the price of the shares. The return is the earnings a company makes. Therefore, the calculation is to divide the earnings by the price and get something that looks like the return. We usually look at whether a stock is high- or low-priced by comparing the price to its earnings and calculate a price/earnings ratio (P/E). Here, I invert the ratio and divide the earnings by the price (E/P), which is called the earnings yield. To decide if the stock market is priced high or low, we need to compare that return to a measure of other investments.

For the overall stock market, the best measure of stocks comes from the Standard & Poor's 500 index. They nicely provide the actual earnings updated daily along with projections for the next few quarters on their web site: www2.standardandpoors.com/spf/xls/index/SP500EPSEST.XLS.

As with all attempts to be simple as well as comprehensive, there is one more complexity of defining the earnings of companies: Accounting requirements force companies to recognize and report their big losses and special (perhaps one-time) problems when they occur. The official earnings as required by Generally Accepted Accounting Principles (GAAP) tend to be a bit lower, especially during times of economic downturn when serious problems are recognized. The GAAP earnings are more closely regulated, and they give a narrower result for the value of the underlying stock.

Therefore, when estimating the long-term value of companies as ongoing enterprises whose underlying business produce ongoing earnings from their operations, it is better to use earnings that eliminate these one-time events. Companies report the usually more attractive operating earnings that remove the big one-time problems as well as the GAAP earnings. In looking at historical comparisons, the operating earnings track more closely with the value of the underlying shares as investors can see past one-time problems. I use the more conservative Reported Earnings in the following analysis to value stocks. Figure 10.1 shows both measures of earnings and how much more severe the drop of GAAP reported earnings was for the overall S&P 500 index of stocks.

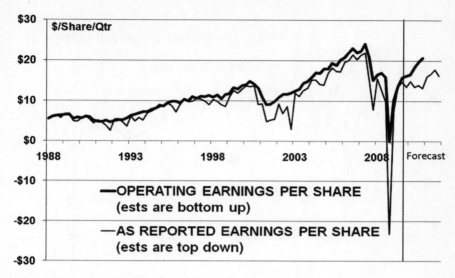

Figure 10.1   Recessions Brought S&P 500 Earnings Drop
SOURCE: Federal Reserve, S&P web site, www2.standardandpoors.com/NASApp/cs/ContentServer?
pagename=sp/page/IndicesMainPG&r=4&I=EN&B=4.

Whether the earnings yield is high or low is best judged by comparing the calculations of the stock market to the rest of the environment of
investable items. When interest rates are very high, then earnings yield
on stocks must also be high to be competitive. So to identify whether a
given earnings yield, or P/E multiple, is high or low, we need a benchmark of comparable returns. My benchmark of choice is the 10-year
Treasury bond because there is no risk of default, and it is considered
a standard in the bond market arena, against which other interest rates
(such as mortgages) are set.

So armed with this methodology, what can we see by looking at
the historical measure of the stock market earnings yield compared to
the Treasury yield? Earnings yield tends to track with the interest rate.
If stocks rose, earnings yield would be less. It is possible to provide
projected earnings yield by using earnings estimates taken from S&P,
and combine with the existing stock price to see what may be in store.
Figure 10.2 shows the interest rate dropping, along with the earnings
yield, for most of the last 2 decades. I am forecasting a rise of interest
rates in the quarters ahead.

Figure 10.2   The Earnings Yield from Stocks Tends to Move Up and Down with the 10-Year Treasury Bond Interest Rate
SOURCE: S&P.

To observe the situation in a familiar fashion, I calculated what price the stock market should be, based on the actual yield of the 10-year Treasury and the amount of earnings that have occurred. Then I overlaid that calculation on top of the actual price of stocks to see whether it is overvalued or undervalued. Figure 10.3 shows the results.

Therefore, using this model of comparing earnings returns and stock prices, the situation suggests that the stock market is reasonably valued. But then the more sophisticated analysis is to predict *what the earnings may become*, and to predict *where interest rates might go*. Here, I add my current opinions that interest rates are now rising from 50-year lows and will probably continue higher. That is a negative for stocks. On the earnings front, the Accounting Standards Board allowed the big financial institutions to avoid the restrictions of marking their toxic waste assets to the market value, thereby creating a much brighter picture of their earnings. So my belief is that the current earnings of stocks are hiding serious problems that have already occurred, and I think there are problems ahead. My conclusion is to be more cautious than the model

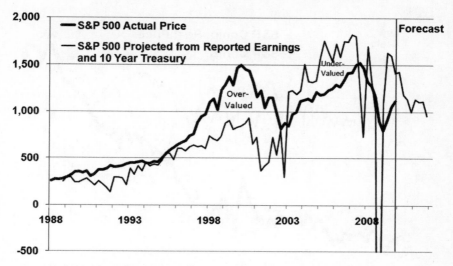

Figure 10.3   S&P 500 Earnings and Interest Rates Indicate Stocks Are Fairly Valued
Source: S&P.

indicates because of my expectation where these two items will migrate in the next few quarters.

Long-Term Cycles

A long-term view of the stock market shows a generally rising price trend, with important downturns along the way. I've assembled here the long-term history from Yale University's Dr. Robert Shiller and presented it on a log scale since 1871, in Figure 10.4. The heavy line on Figure 10.4 shows the price of stocks in the dollars of the time as usually reported.

As you can see in Figure 10.4, the two biggest rises were the big run-up to 1929 and the run-up to the year 2000. But there is something important that is missing from the chart of the raw data. An investor wants his or her wealth to grow in real terms, after inflation has been removed from the equation. When the stock market growth is corrected for inflation, we see a smaller overall growth in real terms, and we see some important differences during periods when inflation was high.

Figure 10.4   Stocks Show Cycle When Viewed in Real Terms
SOURCE: Dr. Robert Shiller and Cowels Foundation.

The thinner line in Figure 10.4 shows the value of stocks as measured in today's dollars. Overall, growth is less in today's inflated dollars.

The inflation correction also provides better insight in what was happening during two important periods of higher inflation for the dollar. In Figure 10.4, I've highlighted the two periods by solid arrows in the lower graph, where stocks appear to be moving sideways. During World War I, the stock market appeared to be relatively stable, but in inflation-corrected terms, the purchasing power of those dollars decreased quite noticeably. Similarly, during the oil shocks of the 1970s and in the wake of the Vietnam War, we had the highest inflation rates we have seen. The sideways arrow during the 1970s is replaced by a dashed downward arrow when inflation is accounted for in the value of stocks.

When looked at this way, one can see the big cycles of stock market movements up and down across multiple decades. I'm expecting our deflationary situation to move to a highly inflationary situation in which stocks may not tumble in nominal terms, but could perform poorly when inflation is removed from the returns. We have already had a decade of no returns, as our business sector has outsourced production and downsized labor contribution. My view is that we will be heading into a time more like the 1970s, where prices are relatively flat in nominal terms, but the stock market is a net loser after inflation is removed.

Dividend Yield Gives an Idea of Valuation

Dividend yield is simply the amount of dividends paid by the company, divided by the share price. The logic is that dividends are a clear cash return to shareholders, so the ratio is an indication of whether the stock price is high or low. Years ago, dividends were used as a reflection of the earning power of the corporation. But in more recent decades, many highflying technology companies did not pay out their earnings, preferring to keep the cash and reinvest it in the business. Dividends are declared by a company as a decision by the board of directors of how much they want to pay shareholders, not necessarily what the company earned in its ongoing operations.

Figure 10.5 is a long-term chart (from 1871 to the 21st century) of dividend yields. It shows typically much higher returns to investors in days gone by. When the dividend yield is low, the interpretation is that the stock price is high, and that stocks are a less attractive investment. The dividend yield in 1929 at the height of the stock market bubble dropped to 3 percent. At the height of the stock market bubble in the year 2000, the dividend yield dropped to 1.1 percent. Those were times of extreme overvaluation. The dividend yield as of this writing in 2009 of 2.8 percent is on the low side, meaning that stocks are relatively high-priced compared to the dividends being paid. But it is not just the dividend yield level that defines whether stocks are high or low; it's whether stocks offer a yield that is competitive to other investments.

It is also important to have a perspective of the environment for what can be earned via a "safe" investment, such as with government-issued Treasuries. If you are considering investing in an alternative investment, such as a 10-year Treasury note that is paying only 3.8 percent interest, then you may be justified in investing in stocks that have a much lower dividend yield—in contrast to when Treasuries are paying 14 percent interest.

The comparison of dividend to interest rate (shown in Figure 10.5) suggests that the stock market was comparatively undervalued up to

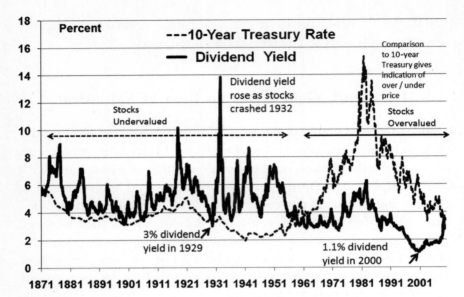

Figure 10.5   Stocks' Dividend Yields Reveal When Stocks Are Overvalued and Undervalued
SOURCE: Dr. Robert D. Shiller and Cowels Foundation.

1960, and that it has been somewhat overvalued in more recent decades. Dividend yields have fallen out of favor as an indicator, especially in valuing stocks that are experiencing high growth, but in this day of questionable accounting practices, the value of cash returned to the shareholder is becoming a more reliable measure. One concern in looking at the future is that if interest rates rise, the relative overvaluation of stocks becomes worse, as the dividend yield then must rise in competition. That then could mean that the stock prices could fall from rising rates even as dividends remain the same.

Looking at Stock Market Sectors Gives Clues about Which Sectors May Be Overvalued

The stock market can be broken into major sectors to identify the bigger trends of our system. Figure 10.6 shows the value by market capitalization of major sectors as a percentage of the whole stock market.

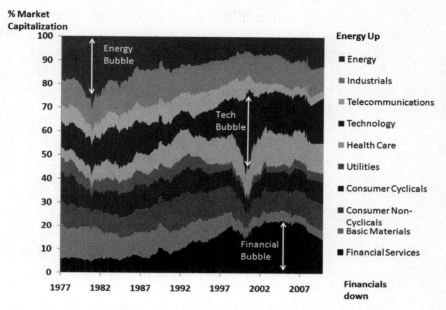

Figure 10.6   The Market Capitalization Share of the S&P 500 by Sector
SOURCE: S&P 500.

There are several interesting stories embedded in the movements of these sectors. Perhaps the most prominent is the huge technology Internet bubble that developed around the year 2000. The market value of the stocks in this sector became the largest sector. Another story is how high-priced the energy sector was during the crisis of 1980. We can also see the bubble of the financial markets as they grew from single-digit percentages to 23 percent of the total market capitalization of stocks at the height of the boom in 2006. And we can see the decline in financials that has been part of the crisis since that peak.

Looking forward, here's what else Figure 10.6 reveals:

- Technology has maintained a strong position and probably has a good future.
- Energy could still grow quite a bit more if it were to return to the levels of the 1980s, and with the importance of finding replacement for traditional fossil fuels, there will be opportunities there.
- Less obvious, because of its decline, is basic materials, although there may be opportunities in that sector to grow.

- The precious metals segment is so small that it doesn't show up on a chart of this granularity, and that in itself is a reason for big growth that this small sector could enjoy, because it is under the radar.
- Finally, health care looks like a sector that will grow, now that the government is looking to support the many people who couldn't afford coverage.

Earnings by Sector Reveal the Drivers of Performance

The whole objective of investing in stocks is that they will return earnings from their successful business ventures. We can see the story behind some of the market price movements in a more detailed look at the earnings of those same sectors in Figure 10.7.

The most dramatic event was, of course, the collapse in earnings by the financial sector. The earnings shown in Figure 10.7 have already

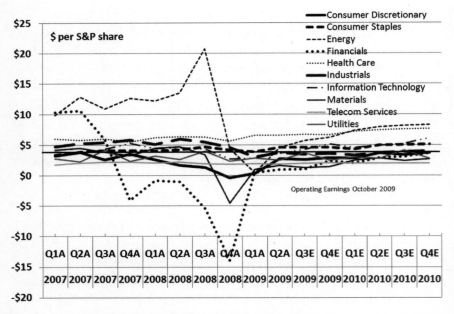

Figure 10.7   S&P 500: Financials Were a Disaster
Source: Standard and Poor's, based on Operating Earnings as of October 2009.

removed many of the one-time charges and write-offs that are normally included in what is called "reported earnings." This data is the less-volatile operating earnings. The large spike in energy earnings at the beginning of 2008 matches the price of crude oil when it hit $147 per barrel.

Analysts using guidance from companies provide some indication of expected future earnings, and they are included in Figure 10.7 as well. Energy and health care look like they have a good future in this view.

Conclusion

There are hundreds of books on investing in the stock market, so I have only been able to provide a perspective on how to evaluate the overall market and major sectors. Decisions for stock picking, however, follow some of the same formulas of looking at earnings, dividends and growth rates. I do not want to focus too closely on stocks because the ups and downs in the trades that are made by economic surprises, insiders, and even manipulators create unexpected results that can be dangerous for individual investors.

Although the stock market is the investment vehicle of choice for most people, I do not consider it the best market. As of 2010, the stock market is now at the same price it was a decade ago. In other words, the only returns were whatever dividends were collected. By contrast, gold has quadrupled and has had only one down year. Most large brokerage houses will steer investors away from things like precious metals, but their advice has been wrong for a decade. Even worse, the large swings up and down mean that many people have lost more money than just broken even, as they got in and out at the wrong times.

As I look out to the future, inventive sectors—such as biotechnology, communications, and green energy—will do well because they provide important capabilities for society. Energy is likely to push ahead, because we always need more energy. Health care is supported by the government, so it may offer some returns. The resource-extractive sector, especially gold mines, should do well with a flight from the dollar. But it is easier and eliminates one variable of possible mismanagement to invest directly in the metals themselves, rather than in stocks of companies.

Traditional old-line businesses have a lackluster future at best, especially those affected by international competition, which includes almost all manufacturers.

My only investments in the stock market in recent years have been on the short side, making money as stocks declined. I shorted many Internet bubble companies on the downside, in what was one of the opportunities of the decade where overvaluation was obvious. In the financial side, one of my best recommendations was to short the insurers of bonds like MBIA in September 2007. They were undercapitalized for insuring bond issuers against other companies' failures, and they have now all collapsed.

I also recommended shorting the big banks. As I look forward to commercial real estate falling and defaulting on loans, and to the banks having to face up to the many bad loans on their books that they have not written down because of the government not requiring them to mark their assets to their market value, I think there will be further problems for financial institutions. If I am right about a dollar collapse and rising rates sparking a new recession, they could be in renewed trouble, absent continued government support.

My conclusion is that there are much better investments than the typical group of what brokers like to call "blue-chip" common stocks. Therefore, in Chapters 11–15, I provide guidelines for specific sectors that should return far more to the astute investor.

The next chapter addresses the world's largest commodity: oil. It is a good investment and is important to understand, as its price can affect the price of everything else.

Chapter 11

Energy in the 21st Century: The End of the Petroleum Age

T he link between energy and the wealth and survival of the human species is undeniable. The growth of world population from one and a half billion people to six and a half billion people over the last century was only possible because of the availability of huge amounts of cheap, accessible energy. The utilization of fossil fuels has enabled the United States to progress from having 50 percent of its population laboring to create the food we need, to having only 3 percent of the population involved in agriculture, freeing up people for other productive capacities.

Gas and coal have both played important roles in this evolution, but oil has been responsible for the most radical changes. Everything from health care to plastics to fertilizers and most modes of transportation are dependent on our utilization of oil. Only with this abundance derived from energy are humans able to move beyond subsistence.

This abundance comes from the hydrocarbons of fossilized plants and animals, stored up over a period of 100 million years, which we are now consuming at an astounding rate. In only 100 years, with a much smaller average population base, we have used up perhaps half that stash of hydrocarbons. It only takes common sense to realize that this is not sustainable. Therefore, to be able to make any educated guess on future economic growth, it is critically important to have an understanding of the world's energy situation now and into the future.

As I've said before, all these items are intertwined, and energy is about as fundamental as food, because without one the other would not be as abundant. Certainly, human existence will be greatly changed if we do not find new sources of energy to support our bounty. The basic question is whether we can continue to expand our economy, lifestyle, and population as we approach the end of growth in production of fossil fuels laid down over 100 million years.

Peak Oil

The United States is in a precarious situation because although our 5 percent of the world's population uses 25 percent of the world's production of oil, we own only 2 percent of the world reserves, as shown in Figure 11.1.

A key question that we will analyze more closely is whether we can continue to expand our production of oil as our population and economies grow. There will be some limit to how much we can produce from the supplies that have been laid down over millions of years. Figure 11.2 provides a close-up look showing that we have not been increasing oil production since 2005. This will become more important as we look at decline in production in existing wells versus finding new oil sources.

Fundamental to whether we will be running out of oil is the question of whether we have accurately identified the crude oil reserves in the ground that we hope to pump in the future. The nations with large oil supplies are incredibly secretive about those reserves. Figure 11.3 shows that Middle East reserves all jumped in the mid-1980s, when most of

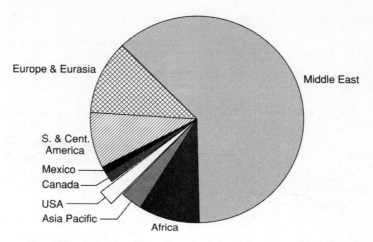

Figure 11.1   U.S. Oil Reserves Are Only 2%, Whereas the Middle East Has 62%

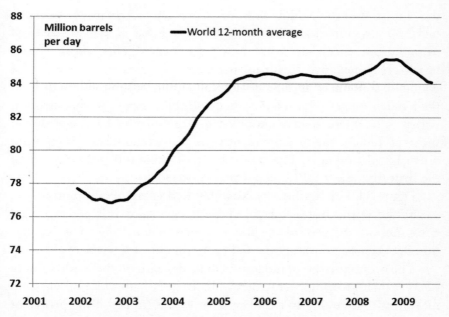

Figure 11.2   World Oil Supply Has Been Flat for Four Years

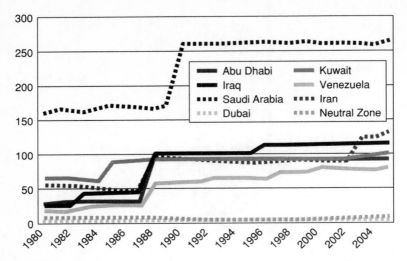

Figure 11.3   OPEC Reserves Jumped One Time and Are Now Flat
SOURCE: BP "Statistical Review."

the countries in the Middle East magically doubled their reserves. The more oil a nation claimed to have, the more that nation was allowed to pump out, according to the new OPEC rules. Thus, those nations had a great incentive to inflate their reserve numbers. None of the countries announced specific geological oil finds when they announced their much bigger reserves. Another disturbing aspect of this situation is that, after these reserves doubled overnight, they have not shown the expected decline in subsequent years that would be consistent with normal depletion rates. The reasonable conclusion is that the reserves of the majority of key OPEC states are overstated.

Figure 11.4 shows how inextricably tied energy consumption and wealth are in the world today. On the horizontal axis is per-capita oil consumption; the vertical axis denotes per-capita income. The correlation between oil consumption and economic success is obvious.

The economic rise of India and China depends on the world's ability to meet their growing energy demands. To get a better idea of what this means, it is interesting to calculate what would happen if the people of China were to use as much energy per person as the people of Mexico currently use—an upgrade of lifestyle that is not an unreasonable long-term aspiration for the Chinese.

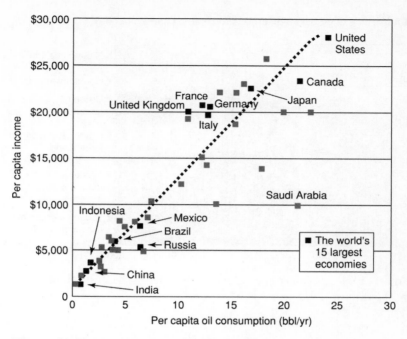

Figure 11.4 How Per-Capita Wealth Corresponds to Oil Consumption in Various Countries
SOURCE: IEA "Key World Energy Statistics."

Mexico currently uses 7 bbl (barrels of oil) per person per year, whereas China uses only 1 bbl per person. There are 1.2 billion Chinese, and if they increased their usage by 6 bbl to match Mexico, that would require 7.2 billion bbl more per year (1.2B × 6). How big is that? For comparison, the United States uses 20M bbl/day, multiplied by 365 days, equals 7.2B bbl per year. So, for a modest move by China—to use oil like Mexico—that would require as much new oil as what the United States uses today. We simply don't have that much supply.

Another key observation to consider in conjunction with Figure 11.4 is that although the United States uses more per-capita oil than any other country, the United States imports 75 percent of its supply, leaving America particularly vulnerable to shifts in world energy supply and demand.

As shown in Figure 11.5, the supply of new oil needs to not only rise with the economic growth of the world's expanding economies, it must

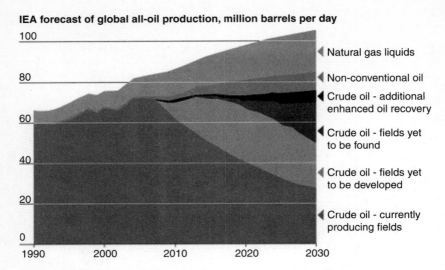

IEA forecast of global all-oil production, million barrels per day

- Natural gas liquids
- Non-conventional oil
- Crude oil - additional enhanced oil recovery
- Crude oil - fields yet to be found
- Crude oil - fields yet to be developed
- Crude oil - currently producing fields

Figure 11.5   Existing Oil Field Production Decline Must Be Replaced by Discoveries
SOURCE: IEA 2009.

keep pace with the amount of oil needed to replenish the decrease in current production from older, shrinking oil fields. Together, these two requirements create the need for a prodigious amount of new discovery and production. This chart was published by the International Energy Agency in November 2009 and immediately brought controversy from those who believe that prediction is too optimistic. The key point of contention is that future oil production has to come from fields that are yet to be found. It takes time once a discovery is made to build infrastructure and actually produce oil, and the rate of potential growth seems optimistic, to say the least.

Discovery of New Oil Is Key, but It's Not Happening

Before we can produce new oil, we have to discover it. It would seem obvious that if we believe that we will peak in production of oil in the not-too-distant future, that we would also find a peak in discovery before the peak in production. Figure 11.6 shows the two peaks schematically.

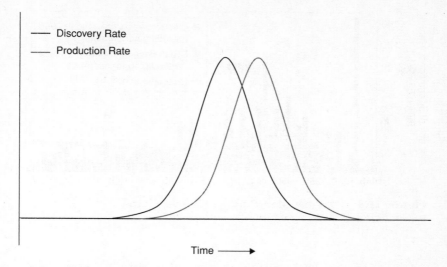

Figure 11.6   There Will Be a Peak in Discovery That Precedes the Peak in Production

A careful look at oil field discoveries over time shows a big problem: We are no longer making big finds—and we haven't been for decades. Figure 11.7 shows the total amount of oil discovered in each decade. It's evident that, in terms of our ability to discover new oil reserves, we are well beyond peak. The peak of discovery has already happened—in the 1960s!

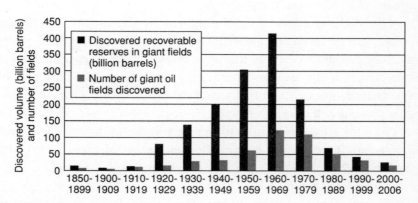

Figure 11.7   Oil Discoveries from 1850–2006: The Peak Years Were in the 1960s

Source: Uppsala Hydrocarbon Depletion Study Group, Uppsala University, 2004.

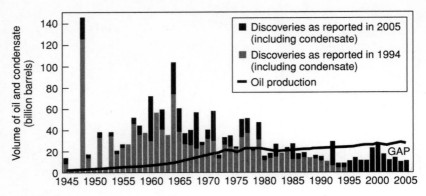

Figure 11.8 Oil Production Outstrips Discovery Rate
SOURCE: IHS Energy, ASPO and Oil & Gas Journal.

By combining the rate of discovery with the rate of consumption, we can see another problem. Namely, that we are using three times as much oil as we are finding. This can be seen to the right in Figure 11.8, where the usage is at a big gap over the oil discoveries, if you look closely. That is clearly unsustainable. We are continuing to grow production by using up oil that was discovered decades ago. Since 1986, we have been finding much less oil than we are consuming. Unless something very significant changes, and soon, the world will not have enough energy to support all of the human life on this planet. We are no longer finding enough oil to meet our consumption.

New discoveries must also be judged by the quality of reserves. It takes a huge amount of energy to extract oil from some deposits, especially tar sands, such as the ones found in Alberta, Canada. The point is that if the process of finding and extracting a barrel of oil requires more energy than that barrel of oil can produce, then that oil in the ground will never be extracted—regardless of the price.

The harder-to-extract oil is what remains toward the end of the peak oil scenario. This kind of oil provides less net-usable energy. It makes a declining contribution in the race to meet our growing needs, and it costs a lot more to extract.

Oil fields that are currently producing naturally deplete over time, producing less and less as they age. An example would be the North Sea, where the United Kingdom obtains its oil. There, the peak in discovery

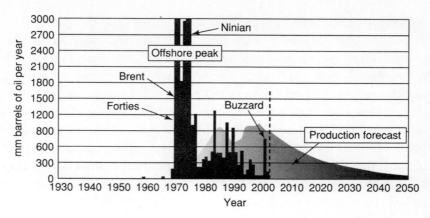

Figure 11.9 Oil Discoveries by the UK Since 1930, Projected to 2050
SOURCE: EnergyFiles, www.energyfiles.com.

was followed only a few decades later by a peak in production, as shown in Figure 11.9.

Supply Is Constrained

Excess oil production capacity has disappeared. The world currently has less than 2 million barrels per day of excess capacity, whereas a few years ago it had more than 10 million. With our current consumption rate of 80 million barrels per day, we are pumping oil flat out, all we can. Peak production may already have passed, as the production has not grown since 2005 (as shown in Figure 11.2).

A look at world oil reserves shows equally troubling problems. As pointed out in Figure 11.1, the United States has only 2 percent of the world's oil. Figures on the average depth of oil wells have continued to increase in the United States. Although there is some promise of offshore reserves, the sparse data that we have does not indicate that the United States would be able to find a significant portion of its daily requirements in its own offshore sources.

Saudi Arabia is key, because it has been identified as the swing producer that could help meet the growing world demand in the decades ahead. However, a detailed examination of previous geological data indicates that Saudi Arabia may not be able to ramp up production to the level we need. Most big producing countries keep the size of their reserves a secret because they see their oil as a strategic asset. Thus, the world is left to guess how much oil might be in Saudi Arabia's (or Iran's, or Venezuela's, or Russia's, etc.) reserves. That is dangerous, considering how dependent the population of the planet is on energy.

It is now countries, not companies, that control most of the world's oil. There are 13 countries whose national oil companies are bigger than Exxon, which is the world's biggest private oil company. What this means is that oil supply is driven more by political considerations than by basic economic principles. We know from the past that governments are less efficient than private corporations, meaning that the oil reserves under the control of these entities will underproduce and cost more than if they were under the control of the free market.

Hubbert's Curve and the Timing of Peak Oil

In the 1950s, world-renowned geophysicist M. King Hubbert predicted the peak of U.S. oil production would happen in 1970. He based his estimates on when half of the total U.S. oil supply would be used up. No one believed him at the time, but he was proven right: U.S. oil production reached its peak in 1971 (see Figure 11.10).

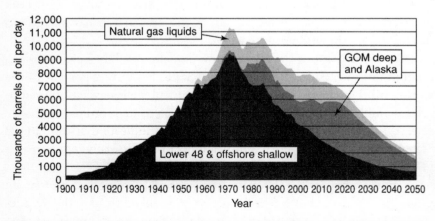

Figure 11.10 Oil Production and Forecast for the U.S. from 1900 to 2050
SOURCE: EnergyFiles, www.energyfiles.com.

Table 11.1 Geophysicist Hubbert's Projections for
When the World Will Run out of Oil

Ultimate Recoverable Oil	Production Peak In
1.3 trillion bbl	1990
2.1 trillion bbl	2000
4.1 trillion bbl	2015

Hubbert's original projections of when the world oil production would peak were calculated with alternative estimates for the total amount of oil in existence. His calculations are summarized in Table 11.1. The world has used up about a trillion barrels of oil so far. We are pretty confident we know where there is another trillion. There are arguments about whether we might find a third trillion. Using Hubbert's model, it's possible to calculate the peaking of the petroleum age, according to the total amount of oil that humanity can recover. Note that Table 11.1 shows that even if we double our oil reserves, peak oil will still happen by 2015. The reason that doubling the resource does not extend the time to peak very much is that with greater total supply, the growth in usage expands, using up the supply more rapidly.

The big question remaining is whether we can discover and produce an increasing amount of cheap oil, or if we are close to a peak in production right now. Putting together estimates of the various oil supply sources combined with the likelihood of decline in production, an image of how future production may reach its peak and decline is shown in Figure 11.11.

For oil-importing countries, the shortages of oil become more severe earlier, because the exporters will continue to expand their own usage, thereby leaving less oil to be traded on the world market. My friend Jeffrey Brown, consultant to the oil industry from Texas, has done the theoretical work, which he calls the Export Land Model to describe how declines in world-traded oil will precede the decline in production. When you add this twist to the inevitable flattening and decline of energy, you become even more concerned for the importing nations (like us).

As oil production slows to less than the population growth, the amount of oil available per person declines. This will occur before peak

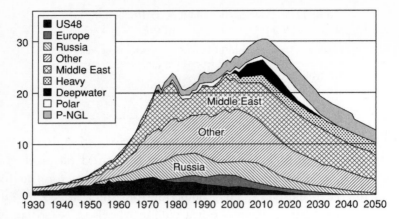

Figure 11.11 Projected Decline of Regular Oil and Natural Gas
Liquids Around the World, after 2010
SOURCE: Colin Campbell, Association for the Study of Peak Oil & Gas.

oil production. Calculations suggest the decline in per-capita usage may
occur years before production peak, so we may feel personal decline
before all of humanity sees a production decline.

Natural Gas

Natural gas faces the same kind of physical limitations as oil. It will go
through the same cycle of exploitation and be used up. Natural gas is
particularly attractive because the amount of pollution is very low. Many
new electrical plants have been scheduled with the ability to use natural
gas. An important difference for handling natural gas is that it is difficult
to move across large bodies of water. Pipelines can be used to move
natural gas across land, but to use ships, the gas has to be compressed
into a liquid form, which increases the costs and adds some danger once
it is being released.

World reserves of natural gas somewhat emulate those of oil and
demonstrate a similar problem for the United States, specifically, that
we may not have the abundance of resources that we would like.
Figure 11.12 shows the distribution by major area of reserves. The area
called Eurasia includes Russia, which supplies much of the natural gas
for Europe.

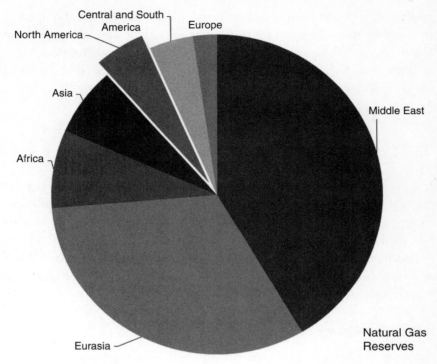

Figure 11.12   World Natural Gas Supplies by Region Show Limited North American Reserves
SOURCE: U.S. Department of Energy, IEA.

Natural gas has been easier to find than oil, but the productivity of successful gas wells declines faster than oil wells. A 30 percent decline in a single year is not unusual. Thus, new wells have to be brought on line for gas more frequently.

The latest technological development promises to be able to remove more of the gas trapped in the Earth's crust than in the past. It applies to what is called shale gas. The U.S. geological service proclaims that an area called Bakken Formation in Montana and North Dakota could produce a tremendous supply of natural gas, and there are other shale gas areas. The process requires water and lots of drilling and has not yet been developed on a large commercial scale. But the effect is noticeable in keeping the price of natural gas low. It is well below the cost of oil when compared to the amount of energy available in units of heat that can be produced. If this technique does succeed, natural gas will be abundant in the United States. It seems to me that for important uses, like producing electricity, the cheaper and cleaner natural gas wins out over petroleum or dirty coal. So my view is that natural gas is underpriced at this level of about $5.60 at the beginning of 2010.

Coal and Uranium Will Be the Major Energy Sources of the Future

It is clear that if the world's need for energy is to be met, oil and natural gas will be a greatly decreasing part of the solution over time. In order to meet this demand, other fuel sources and technologies will have to take up a large amount of the slack. It is uncertain how fuel sources such as alternative energies will manage to ramp up their production. Wind and especially solar are still costly technologies, and their application on a large scale is questionable.

Alternative Energy Sources

Alternative energy sources are still so small that they are not able to contribute much to the overall world energy demand. But if the basic analysis of oil production peaking is even close to right, finding other sources for energy is a necessity for humanity. If any of the creative ideas that are being tested in research laboratories turn out to be viable commercial sources of energy, they have the world's largest market in which to grow their business. Figure 11.13 shows the amount of kilowatt hours produced by some of the alternative technologies, and the old hydroelectric dam is still way ahead of all the others.

None of these many ideas look like they would become big enough to substitute for world growing demand. For example, if we decided that biofuels from switch grass could provide an important energy resource, we would have to grow it in areas the size of several Midwestern states to have an effect on world supplies. That just isn't likely to happen. Similarly, photovoltaic solar electric cells seem like a nice alternative to dirty coal burning, but they are very expensive, at triple the cost of conventional power. They are only installed because of special tax incentives.

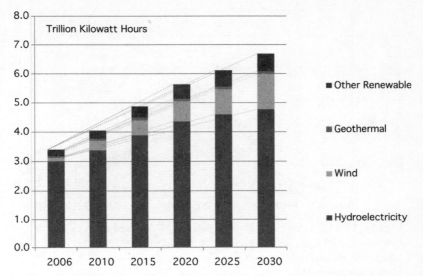

Figure 11.13   Alternative Energy Sources Are Still Relatively Small

One of the most promising for the areas where it can be used is geothermal. Most of the country of Iceland is run on the energy it gets from below the ground. Geothermal has no serious carbon wastes, and it tends to be long life. New technologies offer ways to extract the heat more efficiently, but large amounts of water are needed for cycling through the system. We already know it works in certain places, and as energy prices rise, this could be a future opportunity. Wind, solar, and biofuels all work but are intermittent and hard to scale.

The point is that there will be some big successes for the astute investor in energy plays that are now unheard of. So keep this area as a place to look for investments, and look for knowledgeable sources to help pick the right ones.

Putting the Scenario Together

No one knows the future, but Figure 11.14 is one attempt at conceptualizing a way for the world to have its growing energy demands met while oil and natural gas are in decline. As you can see, technologies and

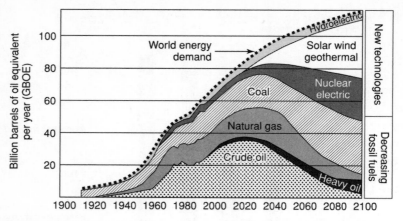

Figure 11.14   How New Energy Sources Will Need to Supplant Decreasing Oil and Gas Production, as World Energy Demand Continues to Increase
SOURCE: Edwards, AAPG.

energy sources such as nuclear, coal, geothermal, and others will have to grow significantly from their participation level of today. This shows the best-case scenario. The following calculations show that, with the known sources of oil, we are precariously short on time before we run out of supplies to meet both world and U.S. demand.

- Oil used since 1850—about *1,000 billion barrels*
- World reserves remaining—about *1,000 billion barrels*
- Amount of oil currently in production that was discovered before 1973—*70 percent*
- Time left from the world's current reserves with current world usage (which is 30B/year)—*33 years*
- Time left if the United States (which consumes 7.2M bbl/yr) used only oil from Iraq's reserves (112B bbl)—*15 years*
- Time left if the whole world used oil at the same rate as the United States currently does—*6 years*
- Time left if the United States used only oil from domestic reserves (21B bbl)—*3 years*
- Time left if the United States were to consume only oil from its strategic reserves (0.66 billion)—*1 month*

Perspective from a Nobel Laureate

The energy problems humanity faces become even more perilous when we look at how big the alternatives have to be if we need to move beyond the age of oil. As it now stands, there are a half dozen bright ideas being discussed, but no one of them would be big enough to make a difference. I think the best summary of how serious the situation comes from Richard E. Smalley, 1996 Nobel Prize recipient in chemistry. His statement says we have not found good answers for energy sources of the future.

> *It is easy to understand that energy is a big issue. We have to somehow wean ourselves off our dependence on oil—and the sooner, the better.*
>
> *What is less well known is the incredible magnitude of the worldwide energy challenge that is before us. The problem is not just oil. Somehow, within the next few decades, we must find a new energy source that can provide a minimum of 10 terawatts of clean power on a sustainable basis, and do this cheaply. To do this with nuclear fission would require no less than 10,000 breeder reactors. Assuming we don't get it all from nuclear fission, where is that 10 terawatts of new power going to come from? Who will make the necessary scientific and engineering breakthroughs? Can it be cheap enough to bring 10 billion people [world population at that time] to a reasonable standard of living? Can it be done soon enough to avoid the hard economic times, terrorism, war and human suffering that will otherwise occur as we fight over the dwindling oil and gas reserves on the planet?*
>
> *Energy may very well be the single most critical challenge facing humanity in this century.*

Forecasting Energy Prices

For First-World countries, such as those that make up the OECD, dependency on imports has grown. At the same time many of the supplying regions have less-than-reliable political situations. Many countries are downright hostile to the United States and, as observed previously, many of these countries have nationalized their oil industries. Supply disruptions, whether a result of internal strife or of geopolitical tensions, can cause shortages and quick spikes in the price of crude.

Oil and gas flows may have now peaked. Few new exploration sites of sizable new energy supply exist. What we currently have are costly and risky to produce. Costs to drill will rise. The richest nations, with a tenth of the population, use half the world's fossil fuels. The rest of the world wants to expand its lifestyle, and the demand growth from developing nations like India and China is undeniable. Their energy use will grow. Forecasts of global oil and gas demand rising from 83 M bbl/day to 105 M bbl/day over 20 to 30 years (as indicated by the International Energy Agency in November 2009) might be conservative. The physical limitation of finding the supply may not allow us to meet even that demand.

Most nonconventional oil and gas supplies will still be small compared to the needs. Black coal is rapidly depleting. Nuclear is very capital intensive and controversial.

Viewed in terms of price, oil is below its previous peak in 1980 on an inflation-adjusted basis (see Figure 11.15). It is still relatively cheap, compared to most things. Where else can you get a gallon of something for $3 that will move you and your friends and thousands of pounds of metal 25 miles?

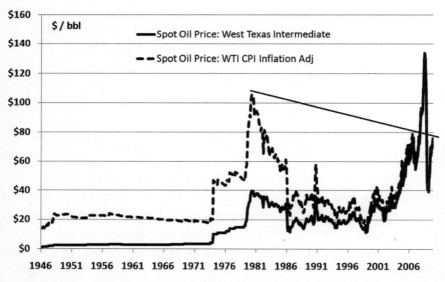

Figure 11.15   Crude Oil Price Spiked and Crashed in 2008 and Looks to Go Higher

The volatility that global politics brings to oil prices makes projections difficult. Having said that, at the beginning of 2009 when oil was $40 per bbl, I predicted that it would go to $80 at the end of the year. This is exactly what happened. A price of $100 per barrel by 2011 is likely.

The EIA provided its predictions for oil prices over the long run, as shown in Figure 11.16. It has often predicted prices below the actual. But here, the EIA offers a floor of $50 per bbl and a high case of $200. I tend to think the problems are serious enough, and the value of energy important enough, that the higher price will be exceeded in the time frame of Figure 11.16.

Natural gas prices hit a low below $3.00 in 2009, a level that has not been seen since 2002. The price is being held down by the promise of new shale sources. Natural gas reached $14 in 2005. It is even more volatile than oil because movement and storage are more difficult, so scarcity and oversupply have bigger effects on the price. If we have a cold winter or two, prices could jump, if only because they are so low.

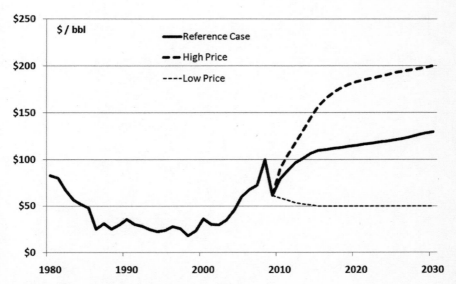

Figure 11.16   Price Projection for Crude Oil
Source: EIA Annual Energy Outlook, June 2009.

Conclusion

The pure-play investment vehicle for most of the energy commodities is in the futures market. Futures trading requires its own expertise, but the returns can be immense because the leverage is very high, approaching 20 to 1. Contracts as far out as December 2015 have large volume and trade around $90 a barrel as of the beginning of 2010.

There are several exchange-traded funds (ETFs) that invest in a broad collection of stocks. For example, iShares has four indexes in the area of energy, and there are many more. iShares (IXC) has a billion dollars invested in the big oil companies, like Exxon. If scarcity becomes obvious and new exploration becomes key, the Philadelphia Oil Services Sector Index (OSX) would rise. Of course, there is the long list of oil companies that are traded on the major exchanges as potential investments as well.

Investment in energy will be positive for at least a decade into the future. The future of humanity depends on it. As the petroleum age ends, demand for uranium, coal, natural gas, and other energy sources will rise, and oil will become increasingly expensive. In our current situation, higher prices are inevitable.

Chapter 12

Food, Grain Trading

In scanning the horizon to look for the best physical commodity investments, food presents itself as one of the underpriced opportunities for the decade ahead. There is probably nothing more basic to our well-being than food. Even back in biblical times, famine was feared. But we have achieved abundance through technology and transportation so that the fears of shortages that Malthus predicted centuries ago have not been visited upon us.

The United States is the world's biggest exporter of wheat, corn, cotton, and many other food products, which makes agriculture one of America's great economic strengths. We may depend on others for oil, but others depend on us for food. Even so, agriculture hasn't yet caught the limelight that the spicy dotcoms did in the 1990s or that the metals and energy have in the 2000s. But agriculture's rumblings are being felt.

The price of corn tripled from mid-2006 to mid-2008. For soybeans and wheat, the gains were 2.5 times and 2 times, respectively. Prices of most other agricultural commodities have also risen sharply. For investors who made the right moves, big money has already been made in the agricultural markets.

Land dedicated for agriculture has not grown, but yields per acre have steadily increased. For the past several generations, genetic manipulation of plant strains and improved fertilizers and farming techniques have yielded a growing supply of food. The Green Revolution has worked, and worldwide the share of personal income spent on food has declined. Figure 12.1 shows the very long-term history of the relative prices of corn, gold, and oil by developing a ratio where the average price of each was adjusted to 1 for the period of 1875 to 1910. By 2009, the price of corn is 8 times higher and oil is 67 times higher than then. You can see the periods of inflation around wars, and that the general price movements have similar patterns in the long term. The point for corn, and indeed most agricultural products, is that there is some catching up to do. With population growing, and eating more meat (which requires 10 times more grain input per pound consumed), demand for food will be rising. It is my view that even small shortages could create big price

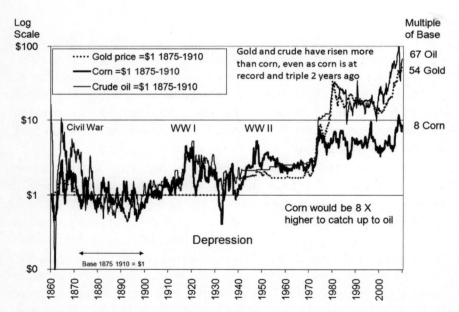

Figure 12.1   Oil and Gold Rose Much More Than Corn over the Last 100 Years

rises if there were any disruption in productivity caused by anything from climate change to political instability.

The comparison with oil isn't arbitrary. Agriculture is closely tied to energy because farming is a gas guzzler. Oil and natural gas are needed to make the fertilizer that feeds the crops, and diesel is needed to run the tractors and other machinery that plant, tend, and harvest them. Then more fuel is needed to bring the crops to market. As energy prices have skyrocketed, so has the cost of farming.

Relative to other goods, food is much cheaper than 75 years ago— even after the recent run-up in prices. For corn to catch up to oil, for example, corn's price would have to increase by a factor of 8, to $32 per bushel. And that's on top of its doubling from $2 to $4 over three years, up to 2009.

Grains: Tight Supply Drove Prices Higher Worldwide

Grains tend to trade quietly until a shock hits, most often delivered by nature. But even beyond such shocks, things have been changing. Since about 2001, the world has moved from chronic excess supply—with costly government programs supporting prices and accumulating huge stockpiles—to shortage, with consumption outrunning production and stockpiles shrinking. Figure 12.2 shows how tight the stocks of grains are across the planet. It is made from adding together the world supplies of all the major grain types and showing the stocks as a ratio to the amount of usage.

Not surprisingly, this scarcity has sharply driven up prices of all the grains.

Pricing Model for Grains

I call myself a grain trader, and in so doing, I developed a model for estimating prices, which I will demonstrate. I made big sums of money trading this methodology in 1995–96 during a big rise in grain prices. The market had a big move up in 2008 that I will show validates the

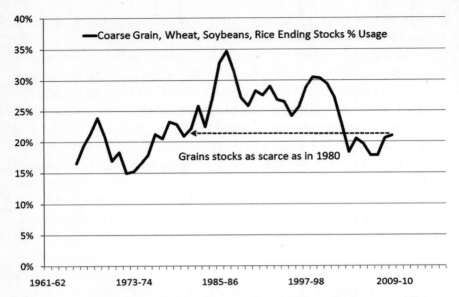

Figure 12.2 Stocks Worldwide of Coarse Grains, Wheat, Soybeans, and Rice Are in Short Supply
SOURCE: USDA.

model. The model gives a basis for price expectations. Comparing what the model expects and the actual price gives an indication of whether the price should rise or fall from where it is now.

The approach here is on the long-term fundamentals, to identify situations that should be profitable for months to come. It is based on world supply and demand. Many traders of these highly leveraged futures markets watch with detailed real-time quotes and technical analysis such as moving averages and indicators. I focus on finding the long-term relationships that drive prices, and leave short-term details to others.

The harvesting of U.S. grain crops starts in September each year, so that's when inventories from the preceding year approach their low points. The nominal harvest date for each particular grain, as cited by the U.S. Department of Agriculture, is a little different, but for each grain the inventory remaining at that date is called the carryout, or ending stock, for the season.

A grain's scarcity at the end of the crop year can be measured by its *usage-to-stocks ratio*, which is found by dividing its usage for the season by its worldwide (stocks) carryout. The industry often quotes the stocks-to-usage ratio, much like I used in Figure 12.2. But here I am looking for an indicator that moves up with price. The usage-to-stocks ratio does that. For mathematical reasons, it also correlates with the pressure on price better than the other ratio. When scarcity comes along, the effect on price of small movements in carryout can be large. Using this inverse ratio is what is key to my method.

Figures 12.3 to 12.7 show the comparison of this calculation to price for corn, wheat, rice, and soybeans. In each of them, the grain's usage-to-stocks ratio, which measures the fluctuating level of scarcity, is shown by the dashed line. Each figure also shows, in the solid line, the grain's price history. In general, prices have risen and fallen fairly reliably along with the usage-to-stocks ratio. Exceptions to that general rule indicate times when a grain may be underpriced or overpriced. When the dashed line for the usage-to-stocks ratio is above the price, it indicates possible scarcity and a likelihood that the price will move up toward the dashed

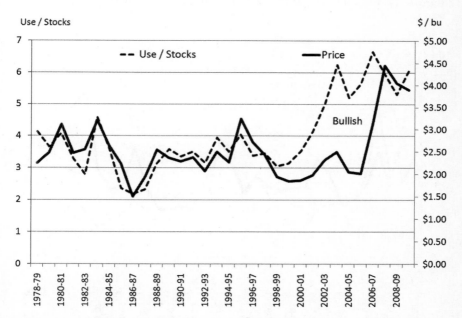

Figure 12.3   Corn World Usage to Stocks Justified Higher Price, but No Longer Bullish
SOURCE: USDA.

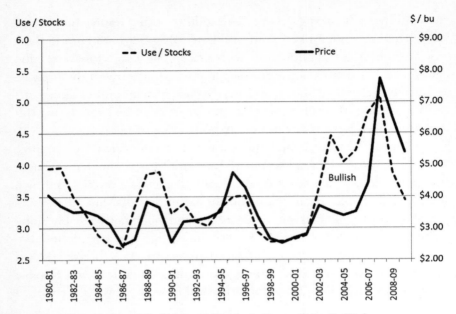

Figure 12.4   Wheat World Use to Stocks Indicates Price Is High
Source: USDA.

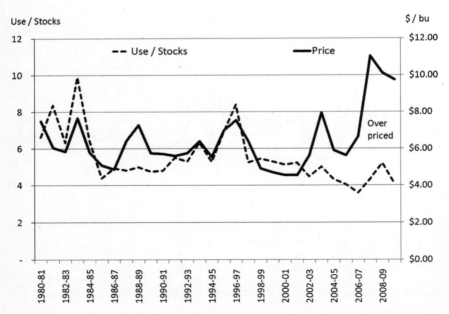

Figure 12.5   Soybean World Use to Stocks Does Not Support High Price
Source: USDA.

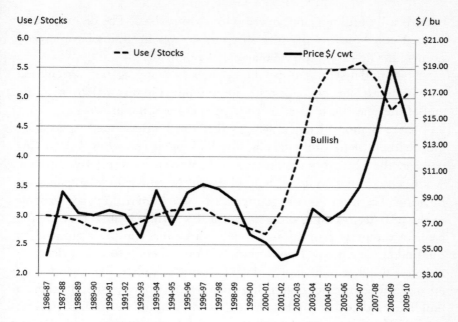

Use / Stocks

$ / bu

Figure 12.6   Rice World Use to Stocks Is Tight, But Price Seems High Enough
Source: USDA.

line. (It was because of such a situation in August 2006 that I predicted a rise in the price of corn. And in May 2007 a rise in wheat.)

Except for the ending points (at the right side of each chart, showing figures for the 2009–2010 crop year), the chart lines reflect actual historical data. The ending points reflect forecasts. The forecast for the usage-to-stocks ratio is based on the U.S. Department of Agriculture's (USDA) monthly estimate of the coming carryout. The price is the latest futures market price for the year. (The USDA's monthly forecast comes from what is known about existing inventories, rates of consumption, and the size and condition of plantings around the world. The data for these charts are updated in the World Agricultural Supply and Demand Estimate released around the 10th of every month.) The forecast is available on the web here: www.usda.gov/oce/commodity/wasde/index.htm.

The big price jumps we saw in 2008 were predicted by scarcity. Unfortunately, by late 2009, the shortage has been reflected in prices, so the investment opportunity is no longer with us. Corn and rice appear to be in line with the fundamentals; wheat has already had a pullback, but it is still a bit high; and soybeans look overpriced. The disappointing general conclusion is that the sharp up-moves in grains have already occurred. The easy money has already been made.

This model structure can be applied to many of the agricultural commodities, like cotton or other items where the seasonal stocks at the end of the year can be used as good predictors of the price.

There is more detailed analysis that can be developed by looking more closely at monthly data and by looking at countries'—most important, the United States—usage and carryout to refine the analysis. A refinement that could be helpful would be to correct the prices for inflation. The most valuable refinements come from making adjustments to the near-term USDA projections for the current year, as they are the base for the price projection. Money can be made at the margin if we can find factors that will adjust the USDA numbers before they do, such as better weather than expected or a change in policy, like abandoning ethanol subsidies that could bring corn down. I have pushed further to building models that predict what the price should be from regression on the historical numbers using the model described here.

There are many other factors that are added into the revelation of price throughout the growing season. Weekly reports update conditions. Correlations between expected yield and crop conditions can refine the expected size of the crop.

Ethanol

The interrelationship between factors is evidenced in the ethanol situation that was set up to find nonpetroleum sources for automobiles. Ethanol was supposed to meet some of the demand for gasoline. Government subsidies brought new demand to the corn market but didn't really cut gasoline usage much, because gasoline is a much bigger market. Growth in ethanol production has made carryover feed grain supplies very tight by historical standards. Figure 12.7 shows just how large the ethanol production is compared to feed usage for corn. Ethanol was behind the start of the big jump in corn prices, and one of the reasons I became so bullish on corn in 2006.

Government incentives for the domestic production of ethanol have caused a big increase in the demand for corn, as Figure 12.7 shows.

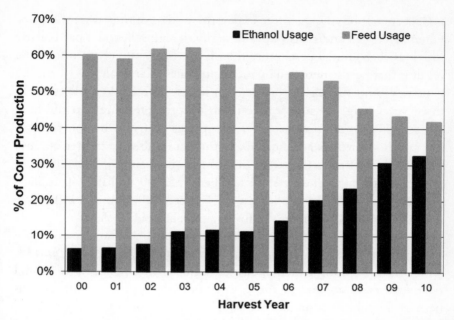

Figure 12.7   Ethanol Usage Is Approaching the Amount Used for Animal Feed

A closer look at grains markets can be found in the U.S. supply and demand. We'll usually be trading in U.S. markets, so we can get a better look by using the same method on the data for just the United States and, if you are trading, updating the latest projection with each USDA report on the U.S. supply as opposed to the worldwide supply that was used in Figures 12.2 to 12.6.

Grains are as basic an investment item as I can think of because they are the basis of the food chain and our lives. With prices at one-eighth of competitive commodities compared to 100 years ago, the long-term upside potential is likely. Most grains are fed to animals for our meat. Sometimes meat is called processed grain. So I want to take a little effort to review the situation of meat.

Cattle and Hogs

I point at the meats because their prices are low as of early 2010. In general, meat prices have not kept up with the inflation in other commodities in the last three decades. With a worldwide economic slump, people are not buying the more expensive foods. For the meat producers, when prices fall and costs of grains are high, times become particularly tough as each animal costs more than it can be eventually sold for. The result is that herds are culled by increasing sales of animals just to cut the expenses. And that drives prices even lower. The cattle cycle is about three years long, because it takes that long for breeding and finishing the animals. So after a period of low prices that cuts inventories, we can see the shortages are more likely to occur a few years later because the fewer new calves that were bred mean short supply. The USDA is predicting that the ending stocks of beef in 2009 will be 460 million pounds, which will be the lowest level since 1999. The stocks hit 691 in 2002. Figure 12.8 shows the history of beef stocks.

Cattle traders watch weekly slaughter counts and how many cattle were put on feed getting ready for market, and they look for periods when sales are low, which indicates scarcity of supplies. The model of inventory as applied in the grains does not apply to meat, as it is necessarily sold as soon as it is slaughtered. Grains can be stored for years. The inventory that is watched is the quantity of animals on feed and on ranches. More details of the weight of the animals is helpful

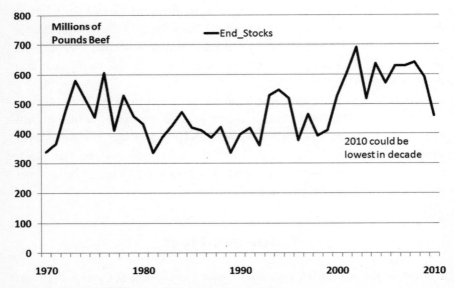

Figure 12.8   Beef Inventories Are Lowest in Years

in deciding whether they have been fed for a long time or are being shipped off to slaughter early, suggesting smaller supply.

The situation we are in is clearly one of low prices, and if economic recovery brings prosperity and more demand, one could easily see a significant move in meats.

Conclusion

In this chapter, I focused only on some agricultural products traded on the futures exchanges. They provide the easiest vehicles and biggest markets in which to invest. I suggest some caveats about futures trading because it offers extreme leverage that can wipe out an inexperienced investor.

Everything that touches farming was doing well by mid-2008. The fertilizer industry was booming; shares of potash moved up twentyfold since 2003. Stocks of farm equipment companies, such as John Deere and Caterpillar, moved up. Specialized agribusiness companies like Archer Daniels Midland (grain processor and ethanol producer) and Monsanto (seed supplier) all had their own profit harvest with their stock price up 5 and 10 times, respectively. All dropped into 2009, as crops fared well.

Great as it has been, the prosperity of each of these companies is derivative. It's fed by rising prices for agricultural commodities, so any position you might take in their stock, long or short, would depend primarily on your assessment of ag prices. So whether you are considering investing in companies tied to agriculture or in the commodities themselves, it all comes down to the question of where, commodity by commodity, the fundamentals of supply/demand are leading us.

Farmland is typically a long-term investment and requires many management decisions, such as finding a land tenant, deciding what to grow, and so on. Agribusiness stocks can be bought and sold easier and have fewer management issues than farmland.

One exchange-traded fund that is large and liquid is the power shares DB agricultural fund. It has a $2 billion market capitalization and trades in volume. It is not exciting, and frankly not the kind of thing that has the laser focus and potential big move of picking a specific agricultural commodity, but it did double during the rise of grains in 2008. It's now back where it started and would participate in a big rally should one occur.

It is in times like these, when hardly anyone is noticing what is going on in agriculture, that the opportunities for long-term gains can be better than things that are the current focus. Dr. Mark Farber, who is often in the media commenting on the economy, and who spoke at our Casey Research Conference in Denver in the fall of 2009, says that investing in agriculture today will be like investing in the oil sector in 2001–2002. The agricultural area of the globe that can grow food is limited, but the population has grown four times over in that last century. With those basics drivers, agricultural investments are likely do exceptionally well through 2020.

The most fundamental of resources for humanity of food and energy will be solid investments in an era of financial instability. As confidence is lost in the paper money systems, the prices will appear to rise even more in the depreciating dollar they are priced in. And that is the subject of the next two chapters: where investment can be made directly in the demise of the dollar and rising interest rates.

Chapter 13

The Demise
of the Dollar

Predicting the future of the dollar is the fulcrum of this book. It puts together how the economic forces of the budget deficit, the trade deficit, and the required responses to the credit crisis from the Federal Reserve and Treasury will work together to damage the dollar. These actions are part of a greater economic cycle that will affect us all, and so the historical reviews of our Great Depression, the Japanese lost decades, and Germany's hyperinflation all provide context for interpreting how markets will judge the state of our currency.

If we have those foundations interpreted properly, we should be able to invest with confidence for the long term in the specific items of energy, agriculture, and gold that are described in other chapters in Part Four. The demise of the dollar is not just a measure of the sins of the past, but an opportunity for direct investment against the currency itself. The fate of the dollar is today's most fundamental economic question, as it affects our wealth as a country and the ability of our economic systems to function. On a more personal level, erosion in the dollar's value can have a devastating impact on your personal wealth.

The mainstream media would like us to believe we are nearing an end of the economic crisis. But my research leads me to fear that the current credit crisis will evolve into a currency crisis. If the dollar is revealed as the paper weakling I think it is, the consequences will be very serious. And not just for the United States, but for the world economy.

This chapter reviews the dollar's current situation, showing its decline against other currencies and its purchasing power as measured in price indexes. Then the forces that move the dollar are described, including the most important force, the government deficit. I then identify some of the foreign connections, including how well entrenched the dollar is as a reserve currency. I go into a specific detailed analysis of why the dollar strengthened unexpectedly in 2008, which goes beyond conventional wisdom in the press. I conclude with an example of how a trader could invest directly in the exchange rate of the dollar.

U.S. Dollar Exchange Rates and Purchasing Power

While a rapid decline in a currency can be a disaster all the way around, a moderate decline in a currency over time helps debtors at the expense of creditors. No entities benefit more than heavily indebted central governments.

The real problems begin, of course, when an orderly, almost undetectable depreciation in a currency morphs into a very noticeable slide, and then the slide further accelerates to the point where holders of the currency begin to anticipate a looming cliff. At that point, a negative feedback cycle is likely to begin, with dumping of the currency leading to an even steeper decline, leading to more dumping, and so on.

The situation with the U.S. dollar is particularly precarious, due to the fact that more than $10 trillion is now in the hands of foreigners. The current U.S. administration and its Congressional cohorts are openly projecting year after year of record levels of deficit spending, so this pressure is going to continue.

While the administration talks about the need for a strong dollar, the actions it is simultaneously taking in plain sight expose those words as nothing more than insincere jawboning. Foreigners and deep-pocketed domestic institutions are, as a result, actively looking to protect themselves by moving money into alternative currencies and tangible assets. It is not surprising, therefore, that gold is trading at record highs (see Chapter 15 for details), or that oil—the world's most heavily traded commodity—has more than doubled from its December 2008 low of $37 to more than $80 at this writing (as discussed in Chapter 11).

Meanwhile, hardly a day goes by without more news of senior officials of some foreign government advocating for an end to the dollar's special role in global commerce.

One of the most unusual has been China openly advocating using Special Drawing Rights (SDRs) from the IMF. SDRs haven't really ever gone anywhere in commerce and would be declared all but a dead currency if it were not for the desperate move by China to look for something that "wasn't the dollar."

The key point is that we are entering the first stages of a currency crisis. And the currency crisis won't be limited to just the U.S. dollar, because most of the G20 countries have been engaged in largely unrestrained printing of their fiat currencies—a situation that will only worsen as they engage in a competitive devaluation in order to avoid being priced out of export markets.

Figure 13.1 shows an array of exchange rates of other currencies against the dollar. You can see major cycles, but with a general downward trend indicating a relative decline in the value of dollar. The trade-weighted index of the dollar against the major currencies is shown in a thick line in the middle of the pack. I've highlighted it because it is an easy way to discern the trend of the declining dollar against other currencies.

A closer look at the action beginning in 2000 shows a steepening of decline in the value of the dollar (see Figure 13.2). To a foreigner holding a bond earning 3 percent, or a T-bill earning nothing, the exchange losses of 35 percent since 2001 must create big concerns.

Clearly, each day this trend continues—and especially if it should begin to accelerate—gives rise to the risk that the negative feedback loop will begin spiraling out of control.

Of course, from the big-picture perspective, since going off the gold standard in August 1971, the purchasing power of the dollar has been on a slide, as shown in Figure 13.3.

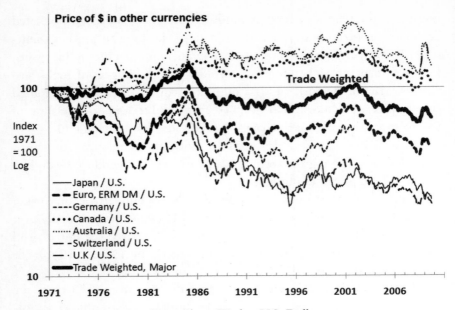

Figure 13.1 Exchange Rates Show Weaker U.S. Dollar
SOURCE: Federal Reserve.

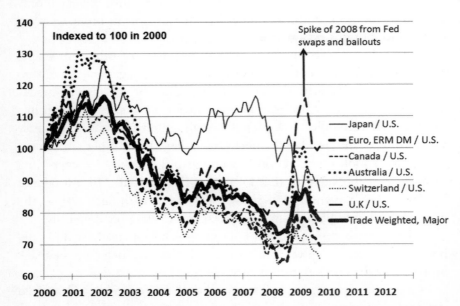

Figure 13.2 How the U.S. Dollar Declined against Most Currencies after 2001
SOURCE: Federal Reserve.

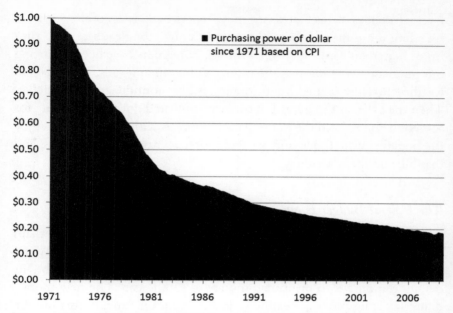

Figure 13.3   The U.S. Dollar Will Purchase Only $.20 of What It Did in 1971

Which begs these questions: What are the key drivers of the dollar today, and where might they be driving it to?

What's Driving the Dollar?

To answer this question, I've analyzed the historic relationship of important economic measures against the changes in the dollar exchange rate. Fundamental to this collection of historical data is the recognition that dollars are issued by edict of the central bank, with no clear limitations on the amount it can produce in the pursuit of its policies.

The U.S. Is the World's Largest Debtor

One of the biggest problems for the United States is that it has been spending much more on imports than it has been able to sell as exports, leading to the biggest trade deficit and the biggest outstanding debt of any of country in the world. There is no debate that, over time, this level of debt will hurt our currency. In essence, as a country, we are spending more than we earn abroad, not unlike the deadbeat who runs his or her credit cards out to their limits. Foreigners have been financing our purchases by lending us the money to buy their goods. The problem for the currency comes when foreigners lose confidence in the dollar. Then they all want to get rid of their accumulated dollars by looking for someone else to hold the hot potato. Countries with large exports enjoy the benefits of high demand for their currency to buy their goods, and that bids up their currency.

The Federal Budget Is out of Control

Whether a country's budget is in balance, a deficit, or a surplus is perhaps the most important input in defining the value of a currency. When a government operating a fiat monetary system has a huge debt, its default response is to print new money to fill the gap. The new money dilutes existing money, creating inflation and, over time, decreasing the currency's purchasing power relative to tangible goods and to other currencies.

The current budget deficit is approaching $1.5 trillion a year, which is the biggest since World War II. At this point, the government is borrowing 40 percent of the money that it is spending—a level that has created currency collapse in other countries.

The worrisome part of this important Figure 13.4, showing a clear correlation between deficits and the dollar, is that the U.S. deficit is already big enough to trigger significant further dollar weakness. The administration has announced plans to continue deficit spending at close to these levels for years to come, and that means the dire situation extends for years ahead.

The Dollar's Reserve Currency Status

One of the reasons the United States has been able to spend such large sums is that its currency is the standard of the world not only for trade, but also as backing for the issue of other countries' currencies. The United States still constitutes 63 percent of the foreign currency reserves held by other central banks. In Figure 13.5, we can see that its use as a

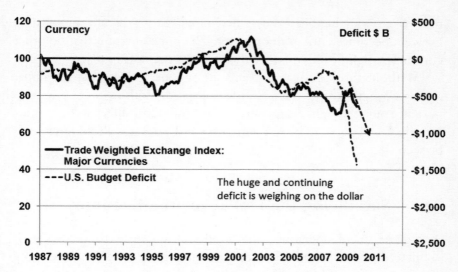

Figure 13.4 How a Budget Deficit Often Damages the Value of a Country's Currency
SOURCE: Federal Reserve.

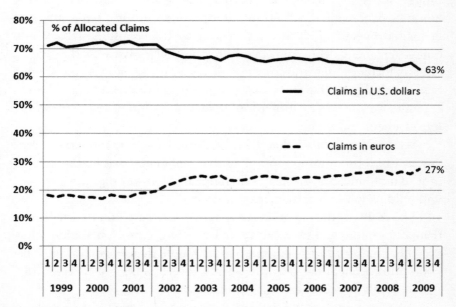

Figure 13.5 Currency Composition of Official Foreign Exchange Reserves (COFER)
SOURCE: IMF, www.ifm.org/external/np/sta/coer/eng/index.htm.

reserve currency has been slowly declining, but it will take a long time before it becomes only a minor player. The impediment is that no other currency is significantly better suited to take the dollar's place.

Without this special status, and the support it provides, the dollar almost certainly would have already collapsed. With it, there is an important counterweight against such a collapse. How effective this counterweight will prove to be in the months and years just ahead remains to be seen.

Sacrificing the Dollar for the Economy

As a government operating a fiat monetary system expands its deficit dramatically, it eventually reaches the point where it must create more of its own money to fill the gap to allow the government to continue its operations.

As I've tried to make clear in Chapter 2 on the trade deficit, the United States has avoided much of that inflationary pressure thanks to the kindness of foreigners who dutifully reinvested historic trade surpluses generated by selling all manner of stuff to U.S. consumers back into our government debt. And, thanks to the dollar's status as the world's reserve currency, demand for the dollar has largely allowed the United States to dodge the currency depreciation bullet that would have been a certainty for any other nation running such large cumulated twin deficits (government and trade).

Yet, the simple fact is that the fiat U.S. dollar, like all modern currencies, is based on nothing more than the confidence that end users have in it. The foundation of that confidence is the belief that the currency will hold its value over the period it is held.

The reality is that all modern currencies are based on nothing more than an opinion, and opinions can change in the proverbial blink of an eye. That makes any fiat currency more fragile than most assume. That assumption is encouraged by the world's governments and central banks, which have a vested interest in maintaining the status quo.

When you understand that the status quo has been for governments to essentially kick the can down the road for decades by addressing each new crisis with a fresh wave of currency creation (read: devaluation of the existing monetary stock), you can begin to get a sense of how deep is the hole they have dug for all of us. Make no mistake, the current shepherds of the U.S. dollar don't want to be running $1.5 trillion deficits; they are being forced to it out of desperation. It is a clear signal they are running out of rope.

I have been talking for years about the dilemma of a rock and a hard place; where the Federal Reserve can't defend the dollar by raising interest rates without ruining our indebted economy, and it can't do the opposite, which would be to flood the market and world with liquidity in the hope of expanding the economy, without destroying the dollar.

As I predicted, our leaders are set on the route of sacrificing the dollar. They are fanning the flames of the dollar's demise, with the hope that the economic crisis can be ameliorated—at least until after the next election—by pumping massive amounts of liquidity into targeted problem areas. Although international markets have not fully reacted yet, given the magnitude of these huge deficits, I think we're close to the point of no return.

Was the Fed Intervening for the Dollar? Federal Reserve Swaps

One of the surprises of 2008 was that the dollar reversed its long slide against most of the world currencies (as shown earlier, in Figure 13.2), and almost all individual currencies took a fall. This section provides an explanation that is not in the mainstream. To get to my explanation, I need to give some background on some unusual actions of the Fed. As the credit crisis became critical in late 2008, the Federal Reserve swapped currency with other central banks. For example, the Fed sent dollars to the European Central Bank (ECB), and the ECB sent euros to the Fed. These arrangements with other central banks around the world allowed them to extend further loans to their regular banks with the newly created dollars, as they saw fit. Although the specific reasons for these unusual arrangements were never provided, they clearly helped to calm markets.

Figure 13.6, from the Bank of International Settlements, shows how extensive these swaps and connections were.

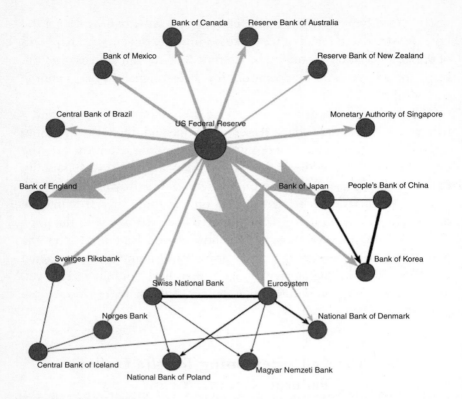

The light shaded arrows represent U.S. dollars provided to other central banks; dark arrows represent other currencies. The thickness is proportional to the size of swap lines. The ASEAN swap network is not shown.

Figure 13.6   Central Bank Network of Swap Lines
SOURCE: Bank for International Settlements Working Paper No 291.

Our central bank traded dollars for euros, yen, Swiss franks, Australian dollars, New Zealand dollars, and other currencies. In providing U.S. dollar swaps to central banks around the world, the Federal Reserve effectively became the international lender of last resort, providing those banks $538 billion at the peak, with the loans backed only by fiat local currencies.

Figure 13.7 shows the major currencies' exchange rate of the dollar compared to the swaps issued by the Fed. The dollar was in steady decline from 2001 because of the pressures of budget deficits and trade deficits.

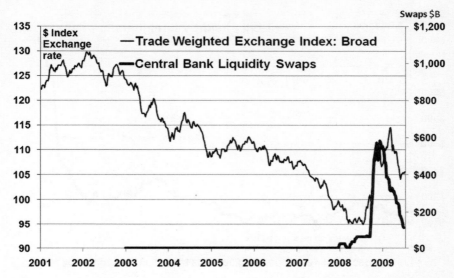

Figure 13.7   The Dollar Rose in 2008 as the Fed Swapped with Central Banks
SOURCE: Federal Reserve.

You can see the surprising jump upward in 2008. The usual explanations, such as an obvious improvement in the financial condition of the United States, were nowhere to be found. In fact, the circumstances became even more dire. So the question is this: Was it the swaps that drove the dollar higher?

It's my belief that the swaps gave the Fed a less transparent way to support the dollar, by first providing foreign central banks with the money, and they, in turn, through loans to other institutions, used the loans to invest in the United States and in some cases buy U.S. Treasuries. The circumstantial evidence is that the surprising rise of the U.S. dollar against almost all foreign currencies matches up in time, almost exactly, with the size of these large swap agreements.

When Fed Chairman Ben Bernanke was asked where the half-trillion dollars of swaps went, he acknowledged he knew which central banks were involved in the swaps, but he proffered he had no idea what those central banks did with the more than $500 billion they received. As to why the unprecedented swaps had been undertaken, there were

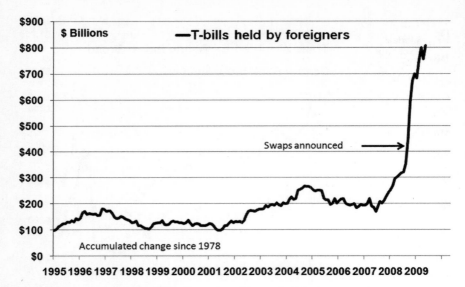

Figure 13.8   T–bills Held by Foreigners Jumped with Currency Swaps
SOURCE: Treasury TIC Data.

some very vague words about a shortage of dollars. That doesn't make sense, because dollars can be obtained any hour of the day in foreign currency markets that trade $3 trillion a day.

It may not be a coincidence that the demand for short–term T-bills by foreign investors at the U.S. government auctions spiked higher during this period, as shown in Figure 13.8. That happened despite the interest rate on T-bills dropping close to zero and on 10-year Treasuries falling to a record low of only 2 percent by December 2008. The spin was that global investors were piling into the dollar as a safe harbor, despite the fact that it had been weak for the six preceding years. That doesn't hold water. The alternative explanation that makes more sense to me is that these huge swaps eventually wound up as investments back in the good ol' U.S. of A.

Bernanke may not be talking about what happened, but the evidence strongly suggests that dollar swaps with foreign central banks provided those central banks and the banks of those countries with the funds needed to dramatically increase their purchases of U.S. government debt. They focused on short-term Treasuries, which is consistent with the fact that the swaps were only for short periods of six months or less.

Regardless, there is no disputing that the large foreign purchases of government debt kept U.S. interest rates low, in spite of huge government borrowing demands. That some large percentage of the money appears to have then been reinvested back in U.S. Treasuries helped the United States avoid the overt monetization of the new stimulus spending. Absent the swaps, the precarious slide of the dollar before 2008 that you can see in Figures 13.2 and 13.7 could have accelerated, triggering a currency crisis.

Taking a closer look at Figure 13.7 you can see that the Federal Reserve has been unwinding its swap arrangements. And, as that has happened, the U.S. dollar has resumed its slide. This is likely to continue. If the Fed were to be audited and required to explain itself, I think confidence in the dollar would weaken more. I think Bernanke knows more than he is telling and the evidence is that the dollar spike was part of a one-off deal. That deal is being unwound, and the dollar may resume its natural course—down.

All of this highlights just how little is understood about the structure of banks' international balance sheets and their interconnectedness. The globalization of banking over the past decade and the increasing complexity of banks' international positions have made it harder to construct measures of funding vulnerabilities. This obfuscation allows the central banks of the world to manipulate currencies to fight the fundamental trends. Although the use of swap lines has subsided from its peak in December 2008—as of October 2009 they stood at only $50 billion—the Fed could balloon the swaps again should it feel the need to do so.

Although one can argue against these extraordinary actions, it is important to recognize these swaps as another potential circuit breaker to be deployed against a free fall in the dollar. Whether the Fed will retain the credibility and clout needed to achieve its objectives within the international community is another question altogether. The Fed acted in panic mode, showing a willingness to go where no previous U.S. government has been willing to go.

Also, it's too early to say which (if any) of the many machinations and outright abuses by U.S. monetary authorities will send these dollar holders rushing for the exits, but there's no denying that there are more straws in the wind that this could occur than at any time since Bretton Woods cemented the dollar as the world's reserve currency.

Global Enthusiasm for the Dollar Wanes

China has now become so important to the world and to the direction of the dollar that we must look closely at its announced plans and its actual policies. China holds $800 billion of U.S. government debt as part of a total $2 trillion of foreign currency denominated investments. This is, again, unprecedented, and dangerously so for the Chinese government. It is no surprise, therefore, that it has recently announced a firm intent to reduce its reserves and diversify out of the dollar by actively seeking to purchase resource companies to provide the raw materials necessary for future growth. Last year, China invested $40 billion in outside investments as part of a policy the Chinese government calls "Going out."

China is taking several monetary actions as well, including setting up currency swap agreements with Argentina, Brazil, Malaysia, and some European countries so that China can trade directly without using dollars as any part of the transaction. China has also set up loan facilities from banks in Hong Kong to support international trade. Combined, these actions decrease the need for dollars and raise the value of the Chinese yuan.

Demonstrating its desire for a broader-based alternative to the dollar as the global reserve currency, China initiated a request that the world support a new basket of currencies to act as a reserve currency for the world, pointing to the SDRs of the IMF as a possible model. If SDRs became widely used, China could trade dollars for SDRs to lighten its dependency on the United States. The SDR is based on a basket of currencies depending on the amount of trade in that particular currency. To that end, China would like its own yuan to be included at a high portion in the SDR. It is actively pursuing expanding yuan trade, so that in 2010, when the next rebalancing occurs, China will have a better stake.

China has also dramatically expanded its holdings of gold—by about $400 billion from 2004 to 2009. This is diversification out of the dollar, although it is generally not described that way. Given its clearly stated goal to continue selling its goods for dollars (thus continuing to fuel its dollar reserves), China appears to be the logical purchaser of future IMF gold sales.

The United States faced a currency crisis in the latter half of the 1970s in the wake of two oil crises. In those days, the big holders of excess dollars were Saudi Arabia and Japan. The United States held the unusual position of providing the military support for both countries. So when push came to shove about whether these countries would continue to hold dollars, the United States held a veritable ace in the hole to ask them to keep purchasing our government debt. Today the situation with China is quite different as China is not at all dependent on U.S. military support. The Chinese have a strong centrally controlled government that will do what is in the best interests of China. China has not taken major action to hurt the dollar, but they are far more independent than our previous creditors. The situation is just more precarious for the U.S. dollar this time.

Taken together, these actions confirm that, despite public pro-nouncements by China of supporting the dollar, China is actually showing clear signs of losing confidence in the dollar's ability to hold its value and taking actions to rid itself of its greenbacks before any steep slide occurs. Highlighting the shift in confidence can be seen in the incident when Tim Geithner told Chinese students the United States would maintain a strong dollar, and they very publicly laughed him down.

Oil Countries Are Turning Inward

Another important group of friends to the dollar over the last few decades have been the oil countries who (like the Chinese) steadily recycled their profits into U.S. investments. But all the oil-rich countries have become a lot less rich with falling oil prices. This is of no small concern, as socialist domestic programs initiated during periods of abundance now require large amounts of funding to be maintained. If those domes-tic programs were to be curtailed, the social fabric in many of these countries—including Saudi Arabia—could tear. The situation has been exacerbated by the world recession.

Regardless, lower oil prices and the need to focus on inward spend-ing initiatives greatly reduces the amount of funding left over for direct investment in the United States. I don't see that there is that much the U.S. government can do to get the oil countries to step up their buying of U.S. Treasuries, meaning they will be of little help in sopping up the unprecedented quantities of paper headed for the market.

Turkey is switching to national currencies in trade with Iran and China, ending its use of the U.S. dollar. It had already switched to settling with Russia in national currencies. The amounts are small (at $56 billion a year in trade), but the structure change is important if Turkey becomes a model for other countries that want to distance themselves from the United States as it removes the dollar from the center of world transactions.

Saudi Arabia announced it will drop the widely used West Texas Intermediate oil contract as the benchmark for pricing its oil. Instead, Saudi Arabia will base the price of oil for its U.S. customers on a new index developed by Argus, a London-based oil-pricing company based on the physical market of a basket of U.S. Gulf Coast crudes. Those prices against oil on the water in boats are more closely related to the pressures away from the supply inside our country.

Elsewhere, countries as diverse as Russia and India have called for new alternatives to the U.S. dollar, and even the former stalwart Japan has not been increasing its purchases of Treasuries.

Thus, it increasingly appears that the U.S. government will need to fund a large share of its massive deficits by overtly monetizing the debt through the mechanism of the Fed stepping in as the buyer of last resort. And that will only further damage confidence, risking setting up a vicious downward spiral. Simply, although the U.S. government may want to kick the can down the road by spending its way out of trouble, it may soon find that option closed to it.

In fact, the Federal Reserve has been supplying the credit needed for other financial institutions to buy the new treasury paper associated with the large deficit. This is how it's working: the Federal Reserve is buying up $1.5 trillion of Mortgage-Backed Securities. Those institutions that sold the mortgage-backed securities now have the dollars to invest in the new Treasury offerings. So while the Federal Reserve is not directly buying as big a chunk of the Treasury debt as it seems on the surface, through these intermediaries in the credit market the same thing is being accomplished. To some extent the credit market is a big pool of lenders and borrowers. The Federal Reserve is dumping lots of dollars into that pool.

Is the Euro a Viable Alternative to the Dollar?

The euro is clearly in contention as a currency that could assume a more important role as a reserve currency. The euro represents an economic community about the size of the United States, so its size and use in considerable amounts of commerce make it the next logical alternative to the dollar. It already represents on the order of one-fifth of the world's foreign currency reserves, while the dollar is about two-thirds (as described in Figure 13.5 earlier).

I have emphasized the risk to the dollar from the United States' huge current account imbalance, which is the result of a decade of importing far more than we export. The current account reflects the flows of money across borders, as shown in Figure 13.9. On this one measure, the European Union is in much better shape than the United States. Although that's not the only measure of the value of a currency, this big difference is supportive for the euro.

Of course, a view such as this (in Figure 13.9) might lead an investor to think about diversifying into other currencies. Unfortunately, a quick look at the range of other fiat currencies finds few compelling alternatives. For instance, due to bad loans to Latin America and the Baltic states, European banks are arguably in as bad a shape as U.S. banks. China has attained more status than it deserves, in my opinion, and the situation reminds me of how enamored we were with Japan in the 1980s. China is outdoing even the United States in its expansion of its money supply by spending money like there is no tomorrow, and by encouraging banks to make loans on very loose terms. China's money supply is growing at 30 percent from its $587B stimulus. That compares to the United States, M2 money supply growing at 7 percent. Japan has a graying population, declining exports, and government debt about three times worse than the United States relative to GDP. We're all on the same path.

In addition, other central banks are going to increasingly feel pressure to undertake competitive weakening for their own currencies in an

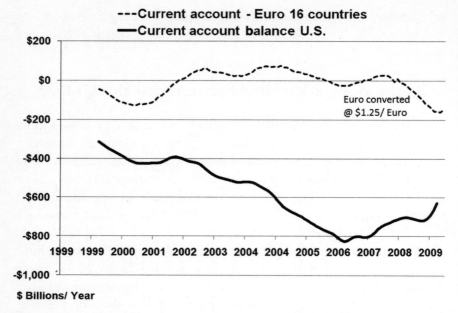

Figure 13.9   U.S. Current Account Is Much More Negative than the Euro

attempt to stabilize against the dollar and remain competitive in global markets.

How Gold Stacks Up against the Dollar

Physical assets, such as gold, are far safer to hold than the paper currencies (as I'll discuss in detail in Chapter 15). I expect demand for gold will grow and the price continue to rise, unless and until our leaders implement much greater fiscal and monetary restraint than appears likely. Gold would soar if the dollar sell-off gains momentum and it turns into a genuine crisis.

To provide a visual confirmation of gold's relationship to the dollar, in Figure 13.10 I have inverted the exchange rate by dividing it into 100, so that a weaker dollar is seen as a rising line. The relationship is obvious, but which is the cause and which the result is not obvious. In some cases, it appears the weak dollar drives gold higher, and sometimes the opposite might be the case. The axes of the chart have been aligned

Figure 13.10 Gold Rises as the Dollar Weakens
SOURCE: Federal Reserve, London PM fixing.

to show the relationship, so it should be noted that gold moves more than the dollar. Regardless, the clear, inverse correlation between the two forms of money is obvious and helpful to our analysis. Simply, when the dollar weakens, gold is the place to be.

How Stocks Compare to the Dollar

When the dollar weakens, it is thought that U.S. exporters can do better in the global competition due to a relative price advantage. Figure 13.11 looks at this assumption and finds the evidence less than conclusive, even if the logic makes sense. In recent years, there does seem to be more of a relationship that the weaker currency has supported a stronger stock market.

Where Could the Dollar Go?

The hard facts suggest that the huge federal budget deficits will remain a problem well into the future, adding strong pressure for the Fed to

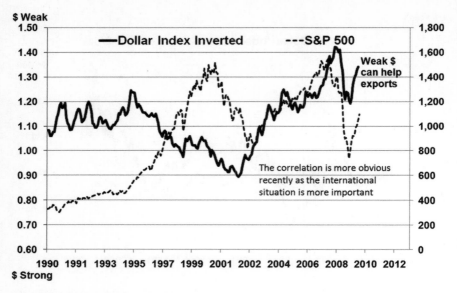

Figure 13.11 Stocks Sometimes Do Better with a Weak Dollar
SOURCE: Federal Reserve, Yahoo! Finance.

weaken the currency to fund the government's persistent deficits and to inflate away some significant amount of the debt owed.

This overhang is too big to be legislated away or covered through tax revenues, and so the simplest path is for the government to default to printing dollars. That allows it to appear to be meeting some of its many obligations while quietly behind the scenes letting a steady devaluation knock down the value of its fixed obligations.

That, at least, is the plan. But, as we have seen, history has a way of foiling such plans with rising price inflation and even the total loss of confidence in a currency.

The Fed's toxic portfolio gives rise to two problems: the first being that it will lose money on the bad assets. More important, it won't be able to use those illiquid assets when it comes time to reverse the current easing. Simply, it won't be able to sell the assets for anything like what the collateral is supposed to be worth. When the Fed owned only Treasuries, the process was a simple matter of unwinding previous purchases.

The Treasury has problems of its own, and they add to the Fed's challenges. For one, in order to keep its own financing cost low, the

Treasury has dramatically shortened the duration of its debt offerings. As a result, when higher rates return, the interest cost on Federal deficits will adjust upward much more quickly than would otherwise be the case. Consequently, if the Fed tries to support the dollar by raising rates to keep foreigners buying our debt, it will immediately translate into higher interest costs to the government. It is an interconnected web that has no easy out.

Of course, should demand from foreign buyers for U.S. debt continue to fall off, the Fed will have to increase its participation in the Treasury auctions. And that participation is already significant, with the Fed having purchased $300 billion of Treasuries from March to October of 2009. Of course, these purchases are made with newly created money, all of which dilutes the dollar and pushes the country closer to the negative feedback loop of a currency crisis.

Although we like to think such a crisis can't happen here, there's no denying that the elements of a currency crisis are now present in the United States. We have the biggest deficit since World War II and a government committed to deficit spending on a grand scale. It includes spending of targeted stimulus, which is sure to be misallocated. In addition (as discussed in Chapter 3), we have retirement programs we can't afford, which are likely soon to be compounded with a massive new health care initiative.

It is at that point where I would expect to see the concerns of world leaders move to the forefront and into the headlines. At that point, they'll either begin actively working together to create some stability, or they could start to panic, wanting to unload their large dollar holdings before the collapse begins in earnest. That latter scenario is less likely, but with the United States actually secretly wanting to have some competitive advantage from devaluing our dollar, there is a real risk things might get out of hand. Looking at Figure 13.12, the steep slide looks like the dollar index could slide to 70 in 2010.

Putting the Trends Together

All of this gives rise to the global *credit* crisis now becoming a global *currency* crisis, with the units of measure to watch being gold and other

Figure 13.12   How Far Could the Dollar Drop?
SOURCE: Federal Reserve.

tangible commodities. At the sharpest point of the crisis in 2008, Hank Paulson strong-armed Congress into approving his $700 billion bailout by warning that the nation might see martial law declared if it failed to do so. But the foreigners sitting on trillions of dollars of U.S. debt will be nowhere near as malleable. If the currency crisis begins to get out of hand, a distrusted Fed and Treasury could find themselves hard-pressed to forge a coalition to act in concert in a way that benefits the dollar.

This collection of economic factors forms a consistent pattern of aligned trends.

The fear is that the collection of forces could coalesce into a crisis, the fuse for which may very well be foreign holders losing confidence in the dollar. The economic forces are already released, and although it is unclear whether it will be lit next month, next year, or several years from now, the continued demise of the dollar seems inevitable.

Considering the extreme measures now being taken by the U.S. government, measures which will result in truly extraordinary deficits, they raise the potential for a currency crisis to emerge sooner rather than later. If we truly are in the early stages of a currency crisis (as I suspect we are), it will make itself known first in the daily exchange rates of the dollar and in the price of gold, silver, oil, and other tangibles against all the fiat currencies.

You shouldn't wait for the crisis to emerge to position your investment portfolio. The simple investment advice is to diversify out of dollars.

Investment Recommendations: Advice for Traders

As far as how to play the dollar weakness, because most investors don't have the risk tolerance to directly short the dollar, a less volatile opportunity could be investing in the Merk Hard Asset Fund. It holds foreign currency invested in foreign government debt, as an alternative currency play, in a simple mutual fund that allows you to profit as the dollar falls against competing currencies (including gold).

The speculative advice to profit from the dollar's fall is to take positions in foreign currencies, and of course, the hard alternative currencies of gold and silver (which I'll discuss in more detail in Chapter 15, focusing mostly on gold).

The Dollar Index (DX) is a way to invest using futures contracts. Figure 13.13 shows the slide from 89 at the beginning of 2009 to 75 toward the end of the year. That is 16 percent. From a technical trader's standpoint, Figure 13.13 would put the dollar at a historic low if the index dropped below 70. That is only a 7 percent further drop, and with the pessimism surrounding the dollar, that seems quite possible. The short sharp rise in the dollar over 2008 has pulled back, and any level above 70 could be a good position to take an investment position to short the dollar. Of course, that could be done by shorting the DX, or going long any of the other strong currencies.

The DX contract is $1,000 times the price, so today it has a notional value of about $75,000. Margin is a bit over $2,000, so an investment of one contract that dropped from 75 to 70 (which was the price in 2008) would return $5,000. An account should have $10,000 to $15,000 to trade, which would protect against losses of the dollar rising to the high at the beginning of the year.

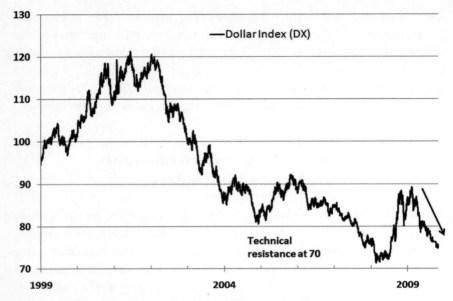

Figure 13.13   The U.S. Dollar Index (DX) Futures Contract Has Fallen Since 2001

All the major currencies can be traded on the futures markets and have similar trading ratios.

Conclusion

In summing up, the key takeaway of this chapter is that the focal point of the crisis is now moving beyond the still-problematic issues related to credit, and toward the dollar as a potential new epicenter for a major new systematic shock.

The factors driving us to this next phase are as clear as they are tenacious. Historic levels of debt, low interest rates with a politically motivated policy to keep them that way, soaring deficits as far as the eye can see, a self-serving and self-dealing political class, and unprecedented foreign holdings of the dollar are in place to keep the dollar under pressure. If confidence were lost, that could lead to serious collapse.

This chapter brings together the many diverse threads of current destructive economic forces and historical precedent to get to the central point of this whole book. After putting all the evidence together, it should be so obvious that even a child would see: The dollar is in fact worthless. The government has officially told us that the dollar is not convertible to anything. What more do we need to know? As if in a strange world of pretense, we all use dollars to buy and sell, to pay taxes, and to denominate our possessions. We extend the pretense by believing that dollars have value, as in having a lot of money makes us rich. Dollars *don't* have value. It is my contention that the whole system is the largest financial CONfidence game ever foisted on the planet. It is amazing to me that we all continue with this unfounded system that is based only on the commonly agreed-on convention that dollars were worth something yesterday and so should have some value in the future. We are all using dollars, relying on the belief that future trades with dollars will have some value, so that we can pass on a worthless computerized accounting entry to someone else.

The basic fact cannot be refuted: *The dollar is not redeemable for anything.* The Federal Reserve can create dollars out of thin air, and it is doing so on an ongoing basis. That makes the Federal Reserve all-powerful in financial matters, as long as dollars are considered to have value. But if, at some time, the child looks at the Emperor and sees that he is not wearing any clothes, then more printing of worthless paper by governments will have the same effect in the United States as in Zimbabwe. In other words, the Federal Reserve can destroy its golden goose by forcing it to lay too many eggs.

This probably looks like an extreme position to most of you who are accustomed to thinking of things as being priced in dollars, rather than thinking of dollars as merely historical convention. But once you look at the foundation of what the dollar is based on—nothing—you come to the conclusion that the dollar will be inflated out of existence just through the natural process of people waking up. Furthermore, the incentives are all in place for the government to print money for itself and its friends at the expense of the rest of us, and those incentives are too powerful to be ignored, even if it leads to destruction of our financial system. The powers of money are too enticing to avoid the Faustian self-serving bargain.

Of course, I may be well ahead of my time. Such destruction may be decades away. But in this world of electronic information and funds transfers, a collapse could happen not over a matter of years and months, but in a matter of weeks.

If the process of dollar debasement just continues as it has been going, we will muddle through. But if, as I expect, more participants wake up to the fundamental reality that the dollar is collapsing at a rapid rate, then even more players (especially the foreigners who have not been watching the interiors of our economy closely) will pile onto the negative sentiment in a self-feeding destructive loop. In other words, as the dollar falls, more people will bet on the dollar falling, making sure it falls farther than some economist's opinion about what equilibrium should be for the dollar.

It is really the destruction of the dollar that drives all of my investment plays that I recommend in this section. World commodities, such as energy and agriculture, are driven by both fundamentals and the value of the dollar. Interest rates will rise to accommodate inflation. And the final investment section chapter confirms what has been happening for years: Gold is the preeminent anti-dollar play. All are based on the same prediction: dollar weakness.

Even though dollar weakness is the central theme of this book, and investing directly against the dollar is a recommendation of this chapter, there is the serious flaw that all other currencies face many of the same weaknesses as the dollar. So betting against the dollar usually requires betting on another currency, and other currencies are also fatally flawed. So I offer two more chapters that give opportunities to invest in anti-dollar plays that do not require investment in another currency. The next chapter, on interest rates, is based on my projection for the demise of the dollar.

Chapter 14

Interest Rates: The Trade of the Decade

Almost directly because I see a dollar collapse, as described in the previous chapter, I also expect to see interest rates rise as compensation for the dollar losses. What I'm getting at here is that interest rates reflect the "price of money" and must include expected inflation of the underlying currency. What makes this time so special is that we have the lowest interest rates for a generation and the worst fundamentals of egregious government spending and deficits that have ever been combined in our history. I'll start with a review of interest rate history, add some further analysis of what causes interest rate movements, and conclude with some investment recommendations.

Out of all the data points that regularly cross my screen, it is interest rates that are the most out of step with the macroeconomic forces. As you can see in Figure 14.1, interest rates are at multigeneration lows.

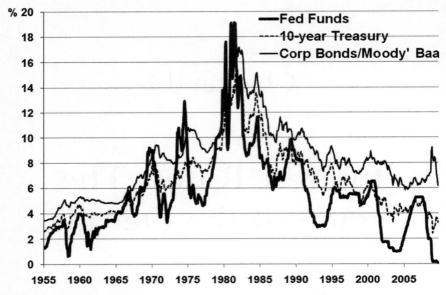

Figure 14.1   U.S. Interest Rates Are as Low as in the 1950s

If the overarching economic condition were simply normal, we would expect interest rates to be significantly higher. But conditions are anything *but* normal; despite massive existing debt, the government has told us in no uncertain terms that it will be spending a prodigious quantity of money, enough to destroy the value of the currency. That alone indicates rates should rise by a lot—enough, in fact, to push rates to the high end of the historical range.

The real interest rate is measured by subtracting inflation from the nominal interest rate that people pay in the market. Figure 14.2 reflects subtracting the annual rate of change of the consumer price index (CPI). The two deepest spikes downward were during the two biggest rises of interest rates, because inflation was pushed higher than was expected from spikes in the oil price. The inflation turned out to be even larger than the interest rate. To obtain a real return of purchasing power when inflation spiked to 15 percent, borrowers had to pay 18 percent to the lender. Even with a huge nominal interest rate of 18 percent, the lenders were not getting rich because most of their return was lost to decreasing purchasing power of the dollars they got back.

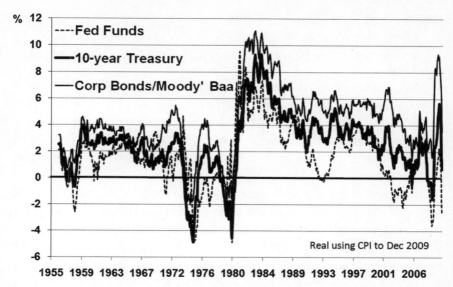

Figure 14.2   Real Interest Rates, after Removing CPI, Are Low

Over this time frame (in Figure 14.2), the average nominal rate for the 10-year Treasury note was 6.5 percent, and the CPI measure of inflation was 4 percent. For guaranteed money (such as U.S. government-issued 10-year Treasury notes), the long-term average rate of return to investors, after inflation has been deducted, is the real rate of about 2.5 percent per year. The inflation rate accounted for more of the level than did the return to the investor for making his loan.

Measuring inflation is controversial because there are many different baskets of items that can be selected to compose a price index. The government numbers for the CPI are flawed in several important ways:

1. They replace a straightforward measure of housing prices with something they call the rental-equivalent rate. That meant the CPI did not reflect the large housing bubble.
2. Improvements in quality of products are subtracted out from prices. This becomes most important in technology products like computers, where we spend approximately the same amount for a new computer but get quite a bit more computing power.

3. The basket of items measured is shifted due to what are called "hedonic" changes. For example, if the price rises for steak, the assumption is that people will switch and will buy more hamburger.

Such calculations are complex, but close observers conclude that the government has marked down the official CPI number to make it appear that inflation is lower than what most of us experience. This is a benefit to the government that indexes Social Security payments to the CPI. It also looks good to policymakers that inflation appears to be not much of a problem.

Inflation is the single-biggest driver of interest rates, and in 2009, prices of many assets are collapsing from the damaging recession. That has put downward pressure on most interest rates. Figure 14.3, which shows the overlap of the CPI and the 10-year Treasury and Fed funds rates, confirms how important that relationship is.

When the huge money creation by the Fed and federal government are recognized, the picture will turn around, and in the decade ahead rates are much more likely to rise than fall.

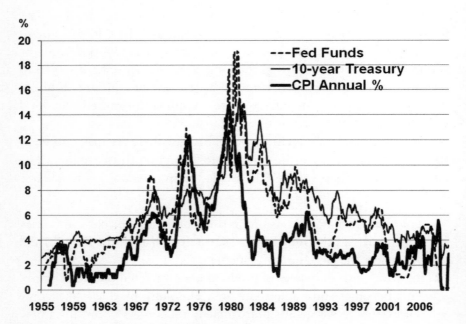

Figure 14.3   Inflation Drives Interest Rates

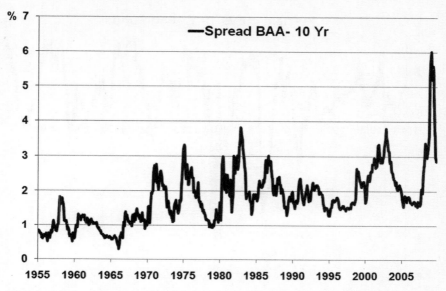

Figure 14.4   Corporate Bonds' Spread Jumped in 2008, Indicating Fear of
Default by Corporations, but Has Come Back to a More Reasonable Level
SOURCE: Federal Reserve.

More in line with circumstances, corporate bond rates have risen
during the credit crisis, reflecting (correctly) the heightened risk that
corporations will default on their debt. Corporate bond rates have fallen
back by the beginning of 2010 as fears of corporate bankruptcies have
subsided since the peak of the crisis.

As you can see from Figure 14.4, there has been some improvement
in the spread between 10-year Treasuries and corporate bonds.

The speed of the jump and fallback in corporate bonds was a surprise,
so the level at the beginning of 2010 is less dangerous. If the lender
can manage the risks, there could be returns for banks making such
loans. The T-bill has not been at zero since the 1930s, when we were
coming out of the Depression. There really is no place for rates to go
but up.

In times of crisis, the Federal Reserve cuts the federal funds rate,
which is the very shortest of overnight interest rates, to try to help banks
and thereby stimulate the economy. So it often happens that the yield
curve gives some indication of the next phase for the economy: When

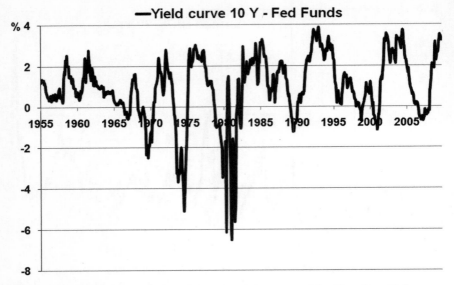

Figure 14.5 Treasury Yield Curve Is High Because of the Very Low Fed Funds Rate
SOURCE: Federal Reserve.

the long-term rate is significantly above the short-term rate, that is a steep yield curve and the economy is usually going to do well from the Fed stimulus (see Figure 14.5). But in these times, both the longer-term and short-term government Treasury rates are low due to Fed intervention and lack of demand from the private sector to borrow during a recession, so that the higher yield curve is probably not as good an indicator of healthy times ahead.

How the Growth of Public Debt Has Affected Interest Rates

Governments who spend too much and run up huge debt are the biggest source of currencies losing their purchasing power. This section confirms how important government deficit expansion is to the destruction of the dollar. Long-term histories of hyperinflations, when the purchasing power of currencies dropped rapidly, show a close correlation between government debt, money supply growth, and interest rates.

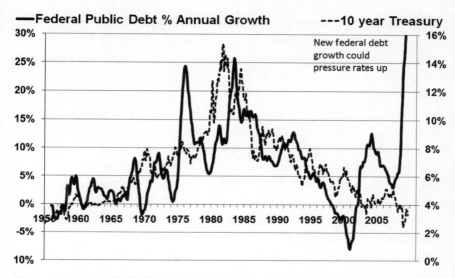

Figure 14.6   Federal Debt Growth Has Moved with Interest Rates
until Recently
SOURCE: Federal Reserve.

If inflation expectations are the important driver of interest rates, the
question is this: How can we predict what the inflation expectations
will be? Government issuance of too much debt is an important source
of inflation, so predicting government deficits is helpful to predicting
interest rates.

Figure 14.6 compares the U.S. federal government debt growth
to the interest rate. The correlation is ragged but obvious from the
1960s through the 1990s. But in the 2000s, the government deficit is
skyrocketing and with it the public debt, even as interest rates are falling.
The traditional relationship is not working today. Figure 14.6 shows one
more reason why interest rates in the long term have a big risk of moving
higher.

Figure 14.6 leaves open the question of why the huge current government deficit is not pushing interest rates higher yet. The first interpretation is that the collapse of the debt in the private sector is offsetting
expansion of government debt. The related component is that the banks
have raised standards and are not making loans to anybody, so the money
that was generated by bailouts is not supporting economic growth.

A more sophisticated nuance looks at the four-year business cycle, and notes that government spending jumps in recession, and as such becomes countercyclical, so that the wiggles on Figure 14.6 often move in short-term opposite directions if confined to the short-term of two to three years.

The big-picture assertion is that government deficits will eventually overwhelm the private sector debt destruction to create the inevitable inflation that could grow to hyperinflation in the years ahead. I have been looking for metrics to identify at what level the government deficit gets out of hand and leads to a country's currency self-destruction. One metric is the percentage of government expenditure financed by debt. At 50 to 60 percent debt financing of expenditures, inflation often takes off toward unmanageable levels. By that measure, 2009 was a dangerous year, because the borrowing was $1.8 trillion on spending of $3.6 trillion. Of course, we have many other problems like bankruptcy, asset price implosion, and no wage growth that are keeping us in Depression-era deflation. The battle between deflationary great deleveraging and the government expansionary inflationary spending may take a year to play out, but it seems likely that the inflationary forces will win because the government has almost no limitation on how much it can apply to the markets.

An important measure of whether the Fed's bailouts are working is to monitor whether banks are expanding their lending. It's important because it's the basis of the administration's goal to get capital markets working again. As you can see from Figure 14.7, they are trying to reinflate the bubble, but it's not working—the banks are still not making new loans.

Government Credit Expansion Is Huge

As I have forecasted for some time now, the 2010 federal budget deficit is on track to be huge, approaching $1.6 trillion, an amount confirmed in President Obama's official budget. To put it mildly, government spending is out of control in a huge way.

Not surprisingly, the government's projections are for the $1.6 trillion budget deficit to improve to being "only" $1 trillion almost immediately. Revenues are supposed to rise, and spending is supposed to

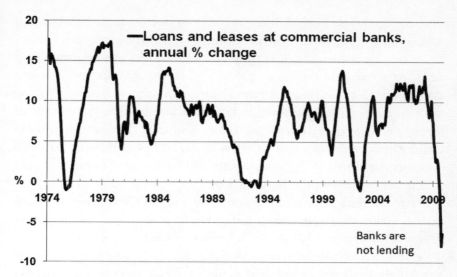

Figure 14.7   Banks Stopped Lending, Slowing Money Growth despite Fed Programs to Stimulate
SOURCE: Federal Reserve.

decline. For that to happen, the government has to dramatically cut back its big spending programs, and the economy has to recover to reignite flagging tax revenues.

Given Washington's long history of missing spending projections on the upside, and by a wide margin, coupled with an attitude toward fixing the entire world's problems that now permeates the government, my prediction is that the budget will stay way out of control.

Already, the government and the Federal Reserve have come up with a grab bag of programs to guarantee loans, buy toxic assets, and bail out the banks—to the tune of approximately $12 trillion. It has committed approximately $4 trillion of these programs of announced stimulus.

The Debt Trap

A big problem for a person running a large credit card balance is that the "miracle" of compound interest begins to work against them. As anyone who has credit-card debt knows, the interest due on those balances gets added to the debt, so that the debt grows even without new spending.

Our government is in that same situation, and on a huge outstanding debt. As a result, in the same way that a credit card company can lose confidence in an overindebted cardholder, and either cut off that person from further credit altogether, or raise that person's rates to exorbitant levels, the U.S. government (as an issuer of new Treasury debt) risks losing the confidence of the world's lenders. Should that happen (and I expect it will) the U.S. government will be required to pay a higher interest rate to attract the funding it needs.

The last time the world lost confidence in the United States (which was in 1980), short-term rates spiked to 20 percent, as you can see in Figure 14.1. Figure 14.8 shows the effect of interest rates rising by just 1 percent a year over the next decade, and that, with compounding, would result in outstanding debt doubling. With $20 trillion in debt at 10 percent interest rate, the government would be paying $2 trillion in interest, which is about the amount the government collected in taxes

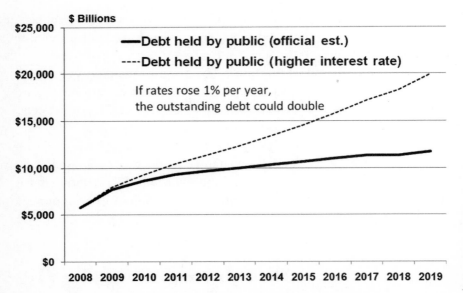

Figure 14.8   Government Interest Expense Compounds if Rates Rise
SOURCE: Congressional Budget Office March 2009 analysis, author's calculation.

in 2009. For that to be the case, the dollar would be worth a lot less, and the fears of further erosion would feed back into higher interest rates.

At that level, lenders to the U.S. government could start asking whether they will get their money back or not. After all, should government debt indeed reach the $20 trillion level, that would add up to about $200,000 per U.S. household, and it's hard to imagine the government would be able to squeeze that much out of the public—at least not in dollars worth anything close to what they are worth today.

Health Care Is Bankrupting the United States

As mentioned in Chapter 3, health care is the biggest segment of our economy. In the debate over who should pay for what (or increasingly, for whom), most people don't stop to understand just how large a portion of our society's money is dedicated to health care. As I showed in Chapter 3, the United States spends about twice that of other advanced nations as a share of GDP. This is an important reason why the United States is increasingly uncompetitive in global manufacturing. For instance, paying for health care is the most important factor (besides poor management) that caused General Motors and Chrysler to go bankrupt.

Going forward, the situation is guaranteed to get worse. The Obama administration is committed to major reform to cover the 40 million people not now covered by insurance. Using a low estimate of $4,000 a year per person, that would add $160 billion to outlays. Once everyone has insurance (with many paying nothing at all for coverage), patients won't care what it costs, and the system will spin even more out of control. The government estimate of combined Social Security and Medicare is projected to grow to $48 trillion by 2083, as shown in Figure 14.9. Clearly, something will break.

It's a safe bet, based on history, that the government will once again try to print its way out of the problem, but all that will do is further destroy the dollar and drive interest rates up more. Just to be clear, this is not just about a government program gone awry, but as much or even more so about a demographic problem, which makes it all the more intractable.

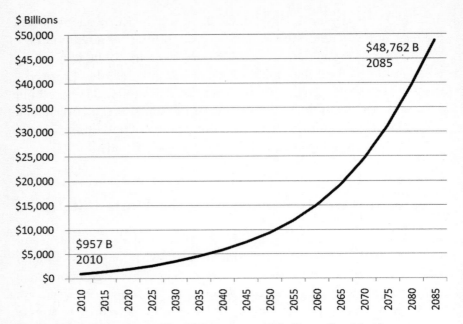

Figure 14.9   The Cost of Social Security and Medicare, Combined
SOURCE: The 2008 Annual Report of the Board of Trustees of the Federal Old-Age and Survivors Insurance and Federal Disability Insurance Trust Funds Table VI.F9 OASDI.

The U.S. Treasury Debt Is Short Term

The debt of the United States held by the public is $7 trillion, and 40 percent of that debt is due in less than one year, which means that $2.8 trillion rolls over in the next year. The Obama budget envisions $1.5 trillion of additional borrowing. Combined, that amounts to $4 trillion that needs to be raised. Of course, absent an unforeseen and very negative development, much of the debt coming due within the year will simply be rolled over by the current holders, the largest of which include foreign central banks, money market mutual funds, commercial bank holdings, and others.

But it is not inconceivable, with the extreme excesses of government spending now under way, that a third of the current holders might want to take their money and run. That would add $800 billion on top of the $1.5 trillion to be placed in new hands. I don't see a source of $2.3-plus trillion of new money.

Therefore, the Fed will have to print up money for the Treasury. If the Fed ends up printing only $1 trillion for the Treasury, it will be enough, in my opinion, to damage the dollar. But if they print $2.3 trillion, the result could be disastrous.

Specifically, the Federal Reserve balance sheet, which was below $1 trillion in September 2008, but which has grown to $2 trillion today, would have to grow to $4.3 trillion just to cover the Treasury debt. In addition to that amount, the Federal Reserve has committed to buying $1.55 trillion of mortgage-backed and agency securities, and it has other programs that could grow to $1 trillion. As things now stand, the Fed is heading toward being forced to create $2 trillion to $5 trillion of new money.

It's not a surprise that China is looking for an alternative currency. China is buying international natural resources companies and, per its recent announcement, gold bullion. I think confidence in the dollar will begin to seriously erode, marking the beginning of the end for the dollar as the world's reserve currency. After that, inflation becomes endemic.

Tax Receipts Are Falling

Another contribution to the deficit is that, in recession, earnings are lower and therefore tax receipts are lower. As you can see in Figure 14.10, there was a 25 percent drop in tax revenues from 2008 to 2009. In Obama's budget, he anticipates raising taxes on the wealthy, as well as industry, in the form of carbon taxes of one sort or another. Although only time will tell, these taxes could turn out to be counterproductive, with a neutral to even negative result as economic growth is crimped by high taxes.

Other Central Banks, Money Expansion

The credit crisis has grown to become a problem for all the central banks of the planet. It is not just the Federal Reserve that has expanded its balance sheet to provide loans and money to stimulate their economies. Figure 14.11 shows that the jumps for the European Central Bank,

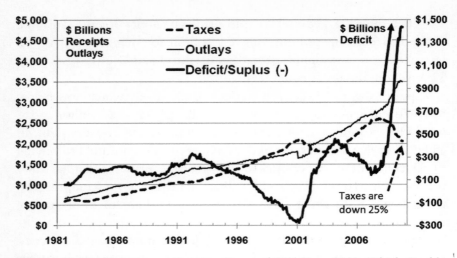

Figure 14.10 Government Receipts Dropped 25% Since 2008, Which Could Cut Revenues by $600 Billion

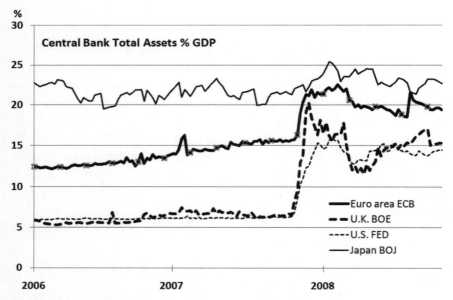

Figure 14.11 Central Banks of the World Are Inflating
SOURCE: IMF Global Financial Stability Report.

the Bank of England, and the BOJ have all increased their balance sheets.

I have been emphasizing the extreme expansion by the Federal Reserve of doubling its balance sheet since September 2008. The meetings of the G-20 bring out the need to look internationally at what the central banks are doing. The United States has about doubled its central bank balance sheet. Of course, there is more done by the government spending programs and deficits on top of all of this.

Data from the IMF in mid-2009 shows an even bigger jump in the United Kingdom. The pound has been weak and looks like it could become even weaker. Already, central banks have started a modest reversal of policy. They are no longer cutting interest rates aggressively to expand their economies (in some cases, because they are already so low they can't cut more). The Reserve Bank of Australia has already raised its rates, as have a few other countries such as Norway and Israel. The world economy is still weak, so this is not yet a landslide, but it is just a trickle of what might become a new direction.

The Fed Pushes Mortgage Rates Down by Buying Mortgage-Backed Securities

Chapter 4, which is devoted to the Federal Reserve's response to the credit crisis, describes their very big purchases of mortgage-backed securities. In this section, I show more detail of that program and the effect on mortgage rates. In my discussions, I emphasized how important foreign credit was to our own credit markets. Although foreigners have continued to buy Treasuries, they are no longer buying our agency debt. Agency debt is typically from Fannie and Freddie and used for supporting mortgages. Figure 14.12 shows how foreigners have stopped buying this mortgage-based debt. This is another reason that the Federal Reserve was required to move so aggressively to provide funding for this sector.

The Fed has promised to purchase $1.55 trillion mortgage-related paper by early 2010. Figure 14.13 shows that the Fed has purchased $900 billion toward that goal. It is making a difference in mortgage interest rates. Part of the funding came from selling off the much more

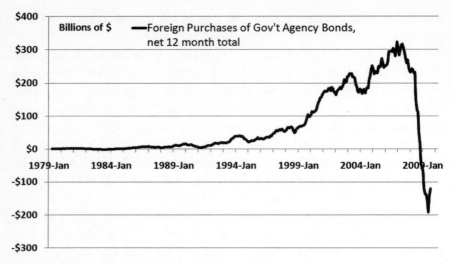

Figure 14.12 Foreigners Stopped Buying Mortgage Debt
SOURCE: U.S. Treasury.

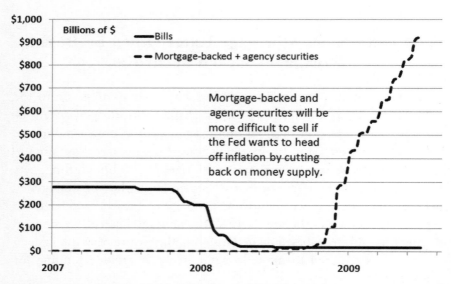

Figure 14.13 The Fed Sold Off Treasury Bills and Bought Mortgage–Backed Securities
SOURCE: Federal Reserve.

secure securities of the Treasury. When the Fed first started intervening in markets in 2007, one of their biggest sources of funding was
to sell off short-term Treasury bills. They dropped from $275 billion
to a trivial $25 billion. The combined implication is that the Federal
Reserve's balance sheet now contains the much more difficult to sell
mortgage-backed securities and agency debt. If the Fed felt that the
inflationary pressures were getting out of line, it will have a harder time
dumping these much more difficult to value securities on the market.
In essence, Fed Chairman Bernanke's assurance to the market that we
will be able to control inflation in the future, by merely draining liquidity, way understates how difficult this has now become for the Federal
Reserve.

The implication for the future is that the Fed has corrupted its
balance sheet with toxic waste to such an extent that backing out of
these huge investments would be a difficult problem, cost the Fed (and
thus the taxpayer) huge amounts of money, and will be difficult to
achieve. The point is that by 2010 or 2011, theoretically when the Fed
is no longer fighting deflation, the Fed will find it very difficult to fight
inflation. This is one more important example of why the long-term
situation is heading toward inflationary pressure.

The Federal Reserve's policy has had its desired effect: By throwing
almost $1 trillion at the mortgage market, the interest rate on a 30-year
bond has dropped from 6.5 percent to 5 percent (see Figure 14.14).
Personally, I don't think printing up new money to bail out a specific
sector actually benefits the whole economy. The problem is that the
new money comes at the expense of diluting the old money so that
everybody else loses some purchasing power.

A Close-Up Look at Commodity
Price Inflation and Rates

The worst recession since the Great Depression brought a slowing in all
kinds of demand for products, especially commodity items. That can be
seen in the 2008 dip in commodity prices of Figure 14.15. But there
has been a surprising resurgence in the price of commodities in 2009.
It's still too soon to tell if this will continue because the economy is still

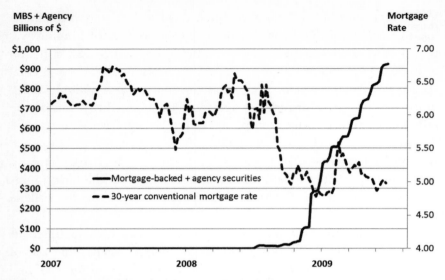

Figure 14.14   Fed Buying Mortgage–Backed Securities Drives
Mortgages Down
SOURCE: Federal Reserve.

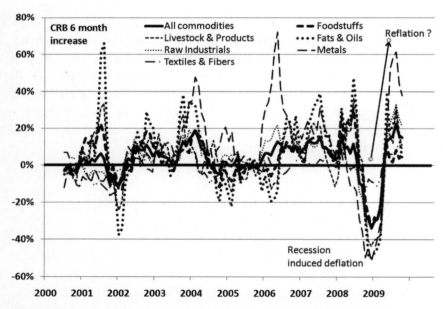

Figure 14.15   Commodity Research Bureau Prices Collapsed in Recession,
but Are Now Reflating

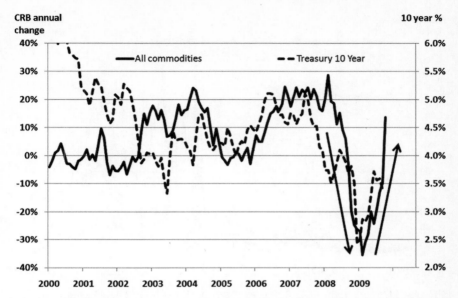

Figure 14.16 Recession Brought Commodity Prices Drop Along with Interest Rate Drop, Which Are Now Turning Back Up

weak, but it is important to watch prices if we are to estimate the effects of inflation on interest rates.

Long-term interest rates also hit record bottom at the worst of the credit crisis. Figure 14.16 compares the prices of all commodities to the interest rate for the 10-year Treasury. When prices were declining, the rate on the 10-year Treasury also declined, to 2.2 percent. If, as I expect, prices continue to climb, interest rates could also climb. As of late 2009, that seems to be the trend.

The credit crisis of 2008 has calmed down, largely from the help of direct support from the government. One good measure is the price that is paid for insurance against banks and insurance companies defaulting on their debt. The price of this insurance is publicly traded, so that we get quotes that describe how much the insurance costs. When fears are high, as they were in late 2008, the cost rose to 1,000 points, which is roughly 10 percent of the underlying bonds for a year's insurance. As you can see in Figure 14.17, that extreme rate is now closer to 300 points, or 3 percent. The main point of the graph is that fears have declined.

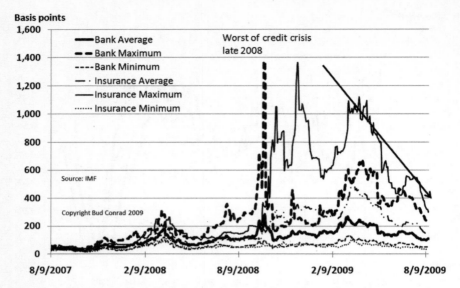

Figure 14.17   Credit Default Swaps Have Declined from Their Extreme at the Height of the Panic in Late-2008
SOURCE: IMF.

Interest Rates Rise as the Dollar Falls

A weak dollar usually turns investor attitudes against holding dollars or investing in dollar-denominated assets like Treasuries, and that turns to higher rates to compensate for the loss in exchange rate. The dollar weakness that I predict in Chapter 13 is part and parcel of putting upward pressure on rates.

Although there are many opportunities for investment, betting on rising interest rates seems especially attractive. The long slide of the dollar from 2001 to 2008 is evidence of long-term weakness, and if it continues there is the obvious expectation that, in time, rates will have to rise to offset dollar losses from anticipated future losses. If foreigners decide to divest their dollar holdings, they'll do so by selling Treasuries, and that will drive rates higher.

The problem is that rising rates are the last thing the Fed and the Treasury want to see at this point in the crisis. Thus, until they are absolutely forced to it, they'll do everything in their considerable power to keep rates at today's levels. In time, they'll lose control of rates, but gauging how much time that will take is impossible. One gauge will be when we see longer-term rates rising even when the Fed is still holding short-term rates at a low level. That means investors have lost confidence in the Federal Reserve's control of rates. That will also mean that the Fed will have to raise rates to give confidence to the bond vigilantes who are requiring higher long-term rates.

Thus, you should use caution, knowing that we may have to be patient, and could even suffer some losses, before the upward cycle in rates kicks off in earnest.

International Interest Rates and Currencies

For major currencies, one of the important drivers of the change in exchange rates is the interest rate that can be returned to investors. If rates are higher, then world hot money is more likely to move to obtain that higher return, and the currency appreciates. Traders often stop their analysis at the nominal interest rate differential. But a good added sophistication is to include the effect of inflation. In this method, the inflation is deducted from the interest rate to obtain the real interest rate, and then interest rates are compared across the different currencies. To be even more precise, the expected inflation over that period of time should be used. In practice, we don't have reliable inflation predictors, so I suggest using the most recent inflation measure.

Figure 14.18 illustrates the comparative interest rate situation and how short-term rates in the Euro area, Japan, and the United States have all declined rapidly in the credit crisis. The slowing economy has decreased the demand for credit, at the same time that world central banks have been flooding their economies with new money in the hopes of stimulating economic recovery. When rates are low everywhere, the differentials that could drive the relative exchange rates of the currencies are not as obvious.

As I said at the start of this chapter, an important driver of interest rates is the amount of inflation. Despite large stimulative measures on the part of governments, the collapse in asset prices and the generally slow economies has meant that inflation has dropped dramatically during this crisis, as shown in Figure 14.19. Probably the major harbinger of

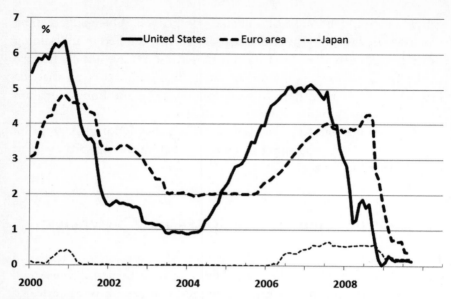

Figure 14.18   Short-Term Interest Rates Have Collapsed Across the Planet
SOURCE: BIS.

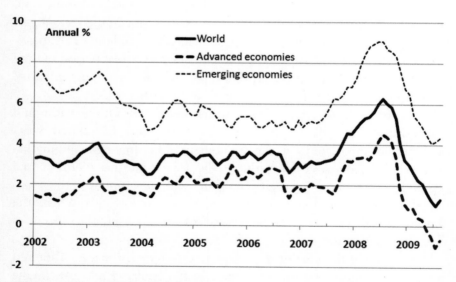

Figure 14.19   Global Inflation Is Down
SOURCE: BIS.

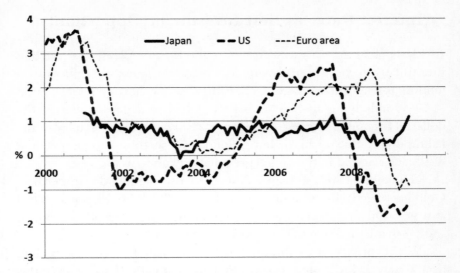

Figure 14.20   Comparison of the Real Short-Term Interest Rates of the
United States, Japan, and the EU
Source: BIS.

the drop was the world's largest commodity: Oil dropped from $147
to $37 in the second half of 2008, affecting all kinds of things from
transportation to plastics. This pressure is turning around, with crude
doubling, the U.S. stock market up 70 percent, and many commodities
rising.

The point of Figure 14.20 in this series is to notice that higher real
interest rates are supportive of a country's currency. Even though interest rates in Japan have been the lowest in nominal terms for years,
with Japan's deflation, the real interest rate is actually higher than
in other countries. The result of this is that investments in Japanese
yen have made sense because the purchasing power of the yen has
risen. Or, turning this around, the higher real rate adds support to
the Japanese currency. Also, although the differences aren't as obvious, the higher interest rates in Europe have also supported the euro
compared to the dollar. Of course other factors affect currencies,
such as trade deficits and budget deficits so there are many factors to
evaluate.

Interest Rates as Best Investment Opportunity

As I look at all the various scenarios, I also try to look at what the best investments in those scenarios might be. Which most warrants our attention: foreign currency, gold, oil, natural gas, or shorting interest rates?

My underlying analysis ultimately points to a debasement of the dollar. That might suggest a foreign exchange investment to play the falling dollar. But further investigation shows that most foreign central banks are engaged in the same egregious expansion as the Fed.

Gold and oil are also logical choices in a weakening dollar scenario. Gold has staged a pretty impressive rally since 2001. So, it's not as cheap as it was. Oil and natural gas are closer to the lower end of their range, and on that basis alone they might be a safer investment.

Which brings us to the potential investment that is now trading near a 50-year low: interest rates. Look at Figure 14.21 to see how this opportunity to bet on interest rates is a once-in-a-lifetime event.

When you recognize that the rate cannot go below zero in any meaningful way, so that rates rising is the only direction they can go,

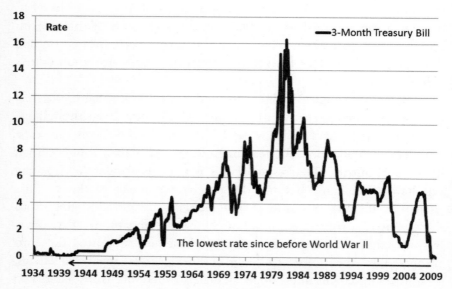

Figure 14.21 The 3-Month Treasury Bill Rate Has Not Been This Low Since the Depression

you begin to see why this is an opportunity of a lifetime, and it is not likely to last forever. Of course, it is the manipulation of the rates by our Federal Reserve that has forced these rates below what would normally be decided by free markets. We still have some time because the Federal Reserve has announced its intention to keep rates low for an extended period. But I don't think it will last.

There are several exchange-traded funds (ETF) that track interest rates in an inverse way such that as interest rates rise, the value of the fund rises. As with all ETFs, they are easily bought and sold like shares. They are relatively slow moving, so are neither big-risk nor big-return investments. Both RRPIX and the Rydex Inverse Government Long Bond Strategy (RYJUX) track the inverse of the daily price movements on long-term T-bonds. The ProFund Rising Rates Opportunity 10 (RTPIX) tracks the inverse of 10-Year Treasuries. I offer a word of caution for some of the ETF, especially those that are leveraged. If the market moves erratically up and down, the tracking mechanisms can lose money even if the direction of the underlying is moving as expected. It is not just poor management of the fund that can cause loses. The math is complicated, but it is the structure that a 10 percent loss is not recovered by a 10 percent gain.

Futures markets offer a complete array of ways to speculate in interest rates. Commission is very low and leverage is very high, so returns (and losses) can be very high. There are contracts for 30-, 10-, 5-, and 3-year Treasuries and 3-month Treasuries, as well as interest rates for most of the foreign currencies. There is a contract for the 3-month interest rates in dollars called the Eurodollar, which has contracts as far out as 10 years. It is probably the largest and most liquid of all the futures investments. There are options on the futures contracts that limit the risk, but they are typically expensive, sometimes of low liquidity, and sometimes difficult to fill at specific prices.

All these futures contracts are listed kind of backward from the actual interest rate, because they quote the price of the underlying instrument. For example, the Eurodollar contract may be listed at 99, and so to calculate what that is as an interest rate, you need to subtract the 99 from 100, in this case yielding a 1 percent rate. All this is a bit confusing and shows that you do need to study how instruments operate if you should decide to trade them. The professionals are trading these in monstrous quantities, thus providing an extremely liquid market for all of us. Futures are my preferred way of investing in interest rates. I would recommend against anyone trying such investments who cannot dedicate a significant amount of time to doing it.

One source for futures quotes that is free is futuresource.quote.com. The exchanges offer lots of information as well. This is the web site of the Chicago Mercantile exchange: www.cmegroup.com/.

Conclusion

So here we are almost at the end of my saga. I call the interest rate investment "the trade of the decade" because it is so obviously extreme in the opposite direction from what I would expect from the fundamentals. I expect it will take more than a decade of reversing the trend from interest rate peaks almost 30 years ago for this to play itself out, and I predict that rates will be above the level of 1980 because conditions are worse. Things can move fast in this new electronic world once momentum is in place. I believe the lows for the 10-year Treasury in December 2008 will not be seen again.

I have one final investment recommendation in the next chapter, where gold has already proven itself as a much safer holding than dollars. Gold is not only the metal of kings, but in my opinion, the safe haven for all of us in these times where we cannot trust our government's actions. Let me give you my best insights on this most precious metal.

Chapter 15

Gold Is the Only
Real Money

This chapter on gold is sort of saving the best for last. Despite raising images of kings with crowns and treasure chests, gold is really only a beautiful scarce metal. Less than $100 million worth of gold is mined in a year. By itself, that would not make gold magical. But with the world's biggest financial confidence game cracking around the foundations (as described in Chapters 1 to 6), gold becomes the safe haven that is not big enough for all the ships that may want to come to its safe haven. So in these tough times, all the lessons I've been trying to explain lead to gold as the alternative to paper money. I give gold the capstone position in my book because gold was the original base of our monetary systems, and it's playing a role in the evolution going forward.

I started my heavy investment gunslinging with the best investment return I ever made by buying precious metals futures contracts markets in 1978. I've always been interested in the theory of money and its value, and in those days, it was really being tested. I had the title of new business development manager at TRW, and I traveled from sunny California to blizzard-engulfed New York City to evaluate a new idea of providing futures quotes to traders on remote computer screens. New York City was being closed down on this wintry day, and it was a challenge to get to Connecticut, where a successful small business, which was the forerunner of many others, was delivering online charts. The technology was exciting, but even more interesting to me was a dinner with the entrepreneur, who seemed quite wealthy. I inquired about whether this was the success of his charting service, and he said, "Only indirectly." He described that he had been buying silver futures and had made much more money actually trading.

In the days thereafter, I learned enough about futures to be dangerous, and I opened my first account. They required $5,000 to open the account but allowed me to request $3,000 to be returned to me once the account was established. That left enough money for one futures contract. Those were heady days for precious metals, so with pyramiding, my initial investment eventually grew to more than $100,000 by 1980. I started with buying gold at $278 an ounce and finally got out around $600 an ounce. With 5,000 percent returns, I wondered why I bothered to work for a living!

In this chapter, I'll cover the connection between gold and the dollar and between gold and oil. I'll also discuss gold mining and how to invest in gold; and I'll touch briefly on other metals, including silver. I explain how central banks have combined with mine hedging in complex transactions that add supply. I provide a model for evaluating mining stocks. And I conclude with my price projections for the decade. It's a long chapter because gold is so important.

So let's look in more detail at what is going on in the precious metals markets these days, with some thought about how the loss of confidence in the dollar could affect us now, as it did in 1978.

How the Price of Gold Reflects the Macroeconomic Forces

The most basic view of gold is its price in dollars since we went off the gold standard in 1971, as shown in Figure 15.1. The arrow on the left is

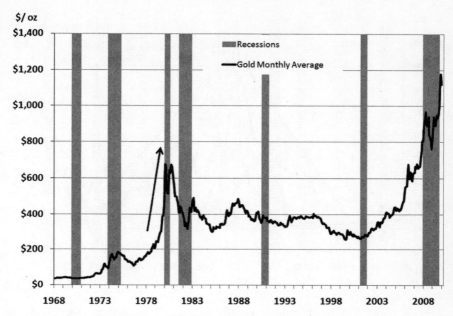

Figure 15.1   The Price of Gold Often Rises during Recessions
SOURCE: Federal Reserve.

the last big run up, during which I was so successful in trading futures. As we look through the next few charts, it's helpful to remember which end of the telescope we are looking through; usually people talk about the price of gold going up and down, but from my point of view, it's important to look at it from the other side—namely, that as gold price increases, it is really the dollar value that is decreasing in purchasing power. Try thinking of it the other way: The dollar is priced in gold, so the gold price gives value to the dollar.

The period of the late 1970s was one of large inflation and loss of confidence in the dollar. Gold reacted even more than other measures, and it was a bellwether for the psychology of the markets. Another observation is that gold was rising as often in recession as not, and that was a point that has kept me invested in gold, even as commentators were emphasizing the deflationary aspects of the credit deleveraging we are experiencing.

Figure 15.2 shows two other measures: the interest rate and inflation along with the price of gold to show that higher inflation went with higher interest rates and higher gold to the peak of 1980. Since that

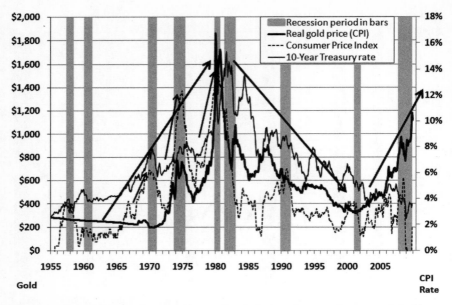

Figure 15.2   The Big Picture Shows that Inflation, Interest Rates, and Gold
Prices Move Together
Source: Federal Reserve.

time, we have had a significant downturn that brought interest rates and
inflation to record lows since the 1950s. Gold has been moving upward,
and it is my opinion that loss of confidence in the dollar will mean
higher interest rates and inflation in the period ahead.

To unravel the complexities of the shrinking yardstick of the dollar,
I've recast the price of gold based on today's dollars (i.e., at the time
of this writing). The bottom solid line of Figure 15.3 shows the price
of what gold was selling for in the dollars at that time. It is the same
line as Figure 15.1. The purchasing power of the dollar has decreased to
today, so to buy gold in 1980 with today's dollars would require *more* of
today's dollars. The middle line in Figure 15.3 shows the price of gold as
measured in today's dollars, as calculated from using the Consumer Price
Index (CPI). With that calculation, the price of gold in 1980 peaked at
about $2,000 of today's dollars.

I personally don't trust the government's calculations for this inflation
measure, and I have looked at details of hedonic pricing and rental-
equivalent housing pricing that are used in the CPI, and I conclude

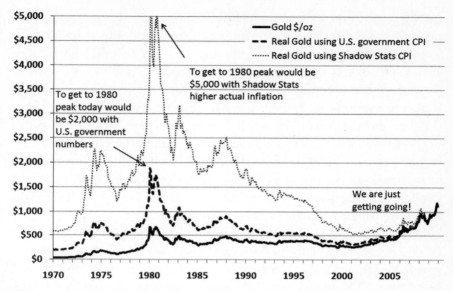

Figure 15.3   In Inflation-Adjusted Real Terms, Gold Has a Long Way to Go

that inflation is probably much higher than the government is telling us. One person who provides better estimates is John Williams, who publishes his estimate of CPI on his web site at www.shadowstats.com. With his numbers, the price of gold in today's dollars would be closer to $5,000. My conclusion is that while we had a bubble driving gold to surprisingly high prices at the beginning of 1980, we now face a situation that in economic terms is significantly more destabilized, and therefore, the price of gold could rise significantly more just to reflect historical equivalent levels. I think the price of gold can rise much, much higher.

Gold Was Used by Central Banks to Back Their Currencies

Students of gold note that the history of paper money includes the issuing of paper depositary receipts that could be redeemed for gold. We also know that the banks have found it much to their advantage to print far more paper than there is gold to back up this paper. Figure 1.1

(in Chapter 1) shows how much more money has been created than physical wealth, as measured by industrial production. In a similar fashion, Figure 15.4 tells us more of the story about the world issuing more currency than was able to be backed up by gold. Figure 15.4 compares the quantity of currency (as measured by the reserves of all the central banks) to the amount of gold stored in their vaults. I value that gold at the then-current price. The result is starkly obvious: The central banks of the world have printed far more currency than there is any promise or hope of ever being redeemed for gold. Figure 15.4 is fundamental to my thinking because it explains why we will not go back to a gold standard anytime soon. There is just not enough gold to be a standard for all the paper currencies that are now circulating.

Central banks used to issue paper currencies, claiming that they could exchange the currency for gold they own. After World War II, when the United States was the most reliable central bank and offered to exchange $35 for an ounce of gold, many other central banks took the United States at its word, so instead of holding gold, they held

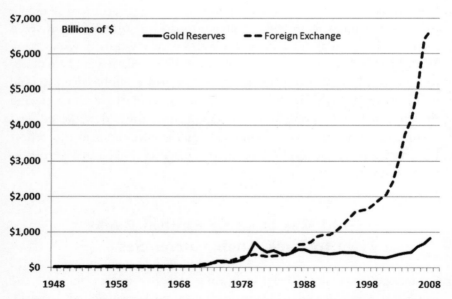

Figure 15.4 Central Banks' Foreign Exchange Reserves Could Never Be Redeemed for Gold
SOURCE: IMF.

U.S. dollars as backing for issuing their own currencies. As we all know, the world paper money systems lost their anchor of a specific convertibility to a physical asset in 1971. Yet world commerce has survived, and monetary regimes continue on. The gold holdings of central banks have been relatively flat in terms of total ounces. They grew a bit after World War II and declined a bit in more recent decades.

On the other hand, central banks have accumulated massive amounts of foreign exchange to back their issuance of their own paper currency. Figure 15.5 shows the fraction of reserves held by central banks of the world that is made up by gold. In 1948, gold was approximately 70 percent of the backing of currencies. That has dropped to only 10 percent, as the expansion of all kinds of currencies has been accomplished by issuing more paper. The backing of one brand of paper money by another brand of paper money is a central mechanism of what I call the greatest financial confidence game ever foisted on the world. Because there is no convertibility promised by any central bank, there is no requirement for any amount of physical gold to be used as backing. The central banks

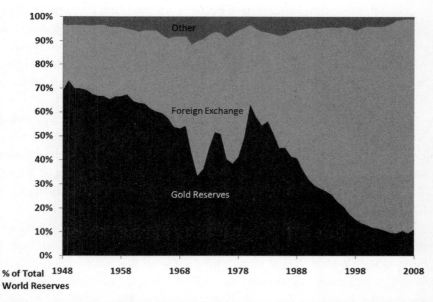

Figure 15.5   World Central Banks' Gold Reserves Dropped from 70% to 10% over 60 Years
SOURCE: IMF.

aren't lying or being deceptive; they have outright told us that paper currencies are not redeemable for anything but more paper money. It is surprising that people have barely flinched and continue to use these paper money systems as if they had some intrinsic value.

The jagged swings in the percentage of total reserves represented by gold in Figure 15.5 were entirely due to the price gyrations when gold shot up to $800 an ounce. A closer look shows the amount of foreign exchange (paper) reserves climbed exponentially throughout all this time frame.

Figure 15.5 reveals one hidden aspect of a calculation about what the price of gold would need to grow to. If the price of gold were to increase by a factor of seven times, it would return the quantity of gold as a percentage of total reserves to 70 percent, as it was back in 1948. That level would then be over $7,000 per ounce. That is not a projection but a calibration of how far paper money systems have been able to continue to operate without gold as an anchor.

Alternatively, one can look at the quantity of paper that has been created over this time frame (i.e., 1948–2008) as an example of how successful the central bankers have become with turning on their printing press. Over the 60 years from 1948, the foreign exchange component has multiplied 485 times. It has increased from $13.7 billion to $6.6 trillion. Most of this was issued out of thin air, making the central bankers richer and covering over government deficits. Central banking is big business for those who have the special authority to print currency.

Figure 15.6 shows that the total ounces of gold holdings by central banks has only declined by modest amounts. Most of that has come from European banks selling off portions of their holdings. The United States sold off more than half of its very large stash from after the end of World War II to the time of closing the gold window in 1971. Since then, it has kept its holdings relatively flat.

The United States has 262,000,000 ounces of gold in Fort Knox that the Federal Reserve supposedly has access to. Since no audit has been done at Fort Knox since the 1950s of the physical gold, one questions whether it has been maintained or siphoned off secretly for some other purposes. But even if it is there, the $850 billion of United States paper currency would then be backed one for one at a gold price of about $3,000 per ounce. If the United States tried to pay off $7 trillion

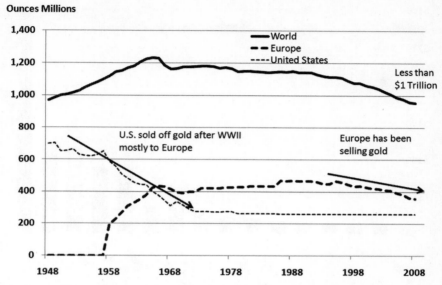

Figure 15.6   Central Banks Sold Gold despite Currency Growth
SOURCE: World Gold Council, author's calculation.

of accumulated trade deficit to foreigners, the price would be almost 10 times that, or $30,000. It is not likely that the United States would do either of these things, but these calculations give an idea of the scarcity of our gold.

Figure 15.7 shows that gold holdings, even denominated at the much higher price level today, are still only small amounts compared to the world money flows. The less than $1 trillion of gold held by all monetary authorities is small compared to the $7 trillion of monetary reserves. The United States enjoys the biggest position at $300 billion, but this seems trivial compared to our trade deficit that was running double that amount a year. In the days of a gold standard, gold would have been used to settle the international accounts. That obviously could not be done today.

Figure 15.8 points toward the flaw of modern currency systems by showing that the very large growth in world paper currencies tended to lead to increases in the price of gold. In the current instance, world banks are heading back toward printing more money, so it is reasonable to expect gold to continue to rise in price.

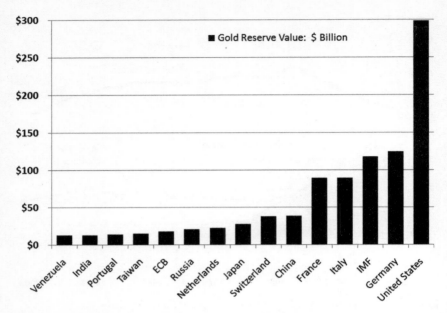

Figure 15.7 The Total Gold Reserve Value Is Only $930 Billion for the World's Top 15 Central Banks
SOURCE: CNBC from World Gold Council, using price of gold at $1,042/oz.

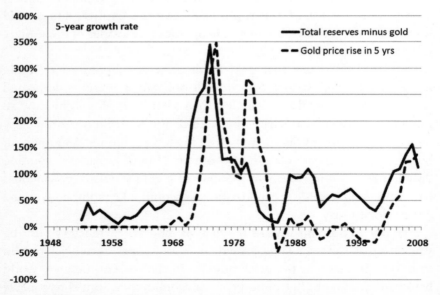

Figure 15.8 Central Bank Reserves Preceded Gold's Price Rise
SOURCE: IMF.

Most of the central banks of the world took the unusual undertaking of agreeing, at a meeting in Washington, DC, not to sell more than a combined 400 tons of gold per year, starting in 1999. This Central Bank Gold Agreement (CBGA) lasted for five years and was succeeded by another five-year agreement that also limited gold, this time to 500 tonnes per year. They announced a new agreement starting in October 2009 that has lowered the limit again to 400 tonnes per year.

In 2008, the central banks sold as little gold as they had previously done only in 1999. Nations outside the CBGA have long turned into net buyers of gold. In 2009, only about 100 tonnes were sold. This means that the large selling programs of the central banks have come to an end. This is bullish for gold, as their supply is drying up.

Due to the global economic crisis, the International Monetary Fund (IMF) has gained importance again. The IMF currently holds more than 3,200 tonnes of gold. The Fund has repeatedly pointed out that it wishes to sell 403 tonnes (i.e., 13 million ounces) to fill its empty coffers. The IMF says it wants to make loans to poor countries. It seems to me that selling off its most valuable asset is a poor financial decision, but the IMF didn't ask me. It also seems to me that the IMF has talked about this for so long that it is as interested in scaring the market as it is in picking up $13 billion in sales. The IMF sales of 403 tonnes are to be processed under the third CBGA. India surprised the market by buying 200 tonnes from the IMF at the market price of around $1,045. Gold moved up, so there will be little problem absorbing those sales.

But this all seems like a sham, because some important central banks are buying, including China, Russia, and India. It seems unlikely that the CBGA limitation will have any effect on the decisions of central bankers.

How Gold Moves with Other Parts of the Economy

While we intuitively understand that gold tends to rise in dollar terms when the dollar is weaker, it is not quite so obvious how to measure these changes. Other currencies have their own weaknesses, and there are many differences. To get a comparison, I used the dollar index of major currencies, as weighted by their trade, as shown in Figure 15.9. To make the visual comparison, I inverted the exchange rate of the dollar

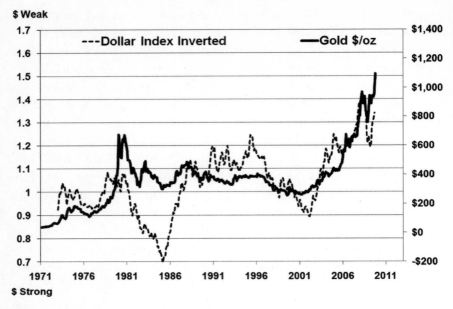

Figure 15.9   Gold Rises as the Dollar Weakens

in such a way that the dashed line rises as the dollar decreases, compared to other currencies. It's no surprise that in the bigger picture, gold rises as the dollar declines.

Oil is often called "Black Gold" because it is the world's most widely traded commodity, so in some sense it's an excellent definer of the value of the U.S. dollar. With that point of view, it's no surprise that gold and oil generally move together in price, as seen in Figure 15.10.

Gold Supply and Demand

Gold is a relatively small market, with production of 2,300 tonnes a year. Multiplying that by 32,150 ounces per ton and $1,100 per ounce, that is only $80 billion. The stock market value of all the gold mining companies is only a couple hundred million dollars. If there is a panic out of traditional paper currencies to gold by even a small fraction of people, the demand will outstrip supplies and force prices much higher. Gold is not used up as, for example, oil or lumber is. It is estimated

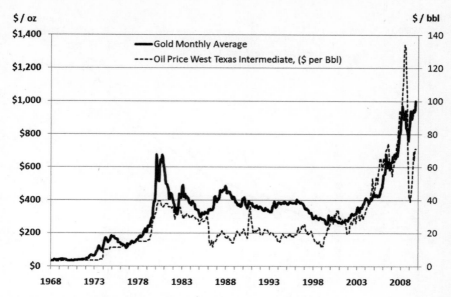

Figure 15.10   Oil and Gold Tend to Move Together
SOURCE: Federal Reserve, Moody's.

that about 5 billion ounces of gold have ever been mined, as shown in Figure 15.11. The biggest use for gold is in jewelry. In some cultures, for example, India, this jewelry doubles as an investment and can be thought of as a bank account.

Figure 15.12 points out dramatic shifts in the sources of new gold production. South Africa, which dominated the scene for decades, is having problems of very deep mines that are no longer producing as much, as well as infrastructure problems with supplying electricity to mining operations. Despite the incentive of higher bullion prices, gold production is flat and falling in most areas. Flagging production reflects the difficulty of finding and producing gold, despite the incentive of markedly higher prices since 2001. Now that the easy deposits are largely mined out, new mines of any significant size are difficult to establish. The most salient point is that world production is in noticeable decline.

Figure 15.13 shows that mining costs are increasing, especially the cost of the fuel needed to move ore. Higher costs keep marginal deposits out of production. New mine supply is not projected to grow because financing is hard to arrange.

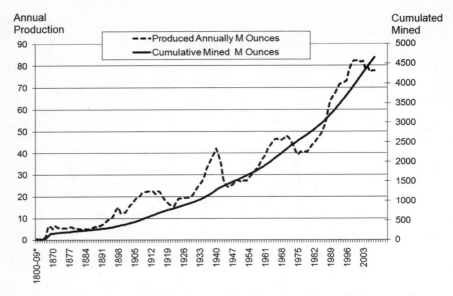

Figure 15.11 How Gold Production Has Slowed and Is Small Compared to Total Inventory
Source: CPM Group.

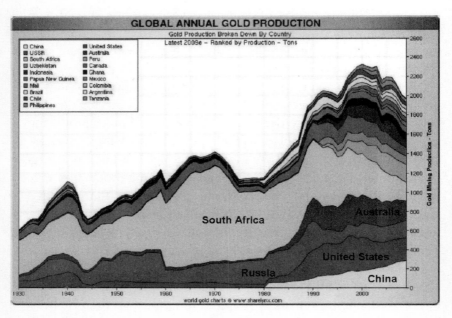

Figure 15.12 Global Annual Gold Production

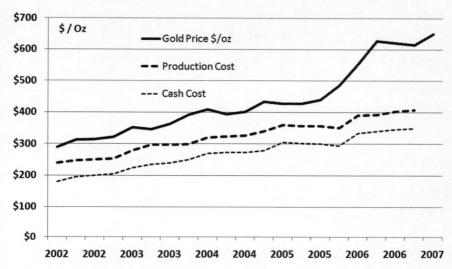

Figure 15.13 Gold Mining Costs Have Risen

One of the big reasons that costs are increasing is that the ore is of lower yield. The grams per ton in 2000 were approximately 2.2, and that has steadily declined to about 1 gram in 2008. That means processing more rock for the same amount of gold.

Investment Demand Drives Price

The major categories of gold supply are mine production, scrap, and official gold sales. Against that, we have demand for fabrication (mainly jewelry) and investment demand. Investment demand isn't measured directly. Instead, it is estimated as the difference between total supply and gold used in fabrication (supply *minus* fabrication). Figure 15.14 shows how investment demand has grown relative to fabrication: Fabrication has decreased as the price of gold has risen. People are still spending as much on gold for jewelry in dollar terms but less in ounces.

The growth in investment demand is the new demand. With monetary systems leaving people questioning if currencies are safe, they are increasing their investment in gold. Although the investment demand has grown quite a bit, it is still small in total. The Fed and Treasury

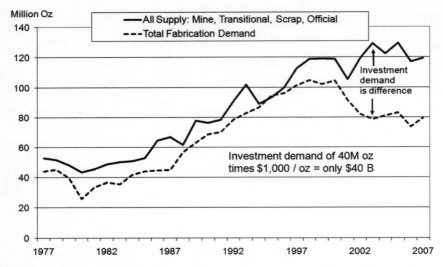

Figure 15.14 Gold: Supply — Fabrication = Investment Demand
SOURCE: CPM Group.

throw around sums in the trillions, but the 40 million ounces of gold purchased for investment amounts to only $40 billion.

Gold demand has been outpacing gold mine and scrap supply by more than 1,000 tonnes per year for the past decade. The difference has been met by official bank selling and clandestine central bank lending. Bullion banks like JP Morgan Chase have been borrowing gold from central banks at extremely low interest rates and selling it into the physical market, using the proceeds to make higher return investments. As a result, the central banks probably have less than half of the 30,000 tonnes of gold they say they have.

One important measure of investment demand is that the new Exchange-Traded Funds (ETFs) for gold have been growing and purchasing gold for their accounts. Some 1,600 tonnes (which is 51 million ounces) are now held by various ETFs, as shown in Figure 15.15. The dramatic growth is expected to continue because these vehicles are now readily accessible to the public.

If investors in our $14 trillion market capitalization stock market decided to allocate a modest 10 percent to gold, that $1.4 trillion demand would exceed the annual supply of mine production by a factor of 19 times.

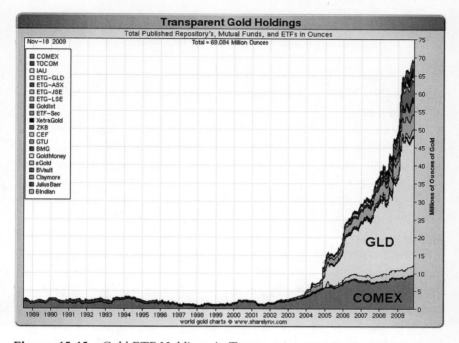

Figure 15.15   Gold ETF Holdings, in Tonnes

SOURCES: www.isheares.com; www.exchangetradedgold.com; www.etfsecurities.com; Zurich Kantonalbank; www.Deutsche-Boerse.com; www.juliusbaer.com; Global Insight; World Gold Council, www.gold.org.

Foreigners who are holding too many dollars would like to consider alternatives as a store of value, and gold would appear logical on the surface. But foreigners couldn't find enough gold just to get rid of their dollars either. Foreigners hold $3.6 trillion of U.S. government Treasuries. If they bought gold for, say, $1,000 an ounce, they would be looking to buy 3.6 billion ounces. Compare that to mine production of only 74 million ounces a year: That would be 48 times the amount produced in a year. The net is that a sensible diversification program into gold cannot be implemented, at anything like current prices.

China is a big enough buyer of gold to drive the price up. Its holding of 1,054 tonnes (multiplied by 32,150 oz/tonne × $1,000/oz) is a trivial $33 billion. Compared to the $2 trillion of foreign reserves, they have a long way to go. With world mine production at about twice that $33 billion level, there isn't enough gold to diversify the Chinese holdings.

Summarizing Some of the Gold Supply and Demand Forces

Higher bullion prices have reduced demand in terms of ounces sold, especially for jewelry fabrication, but increased the overall dollar value of the gold sold.

The key driver of future gold demand will come from investment. Even if only a small percentage of available capital shifts toward gold, demand will quickly overwhelm the supply that's available anywhere near current prices.

The demand for gold ETFs is growing, with bullish implications as small investors begin to pile in with their online and traditional brokerage accounts.

While central banks don't like to highlight the fact, their selling is decreasing, which is also bullish. Estimates of the extent of gold leasing by central banks are largely guesswork, but the true size is probably bigger than generally thought.

The aggressive unwinding of hedges by gold producers—most notably champion hedger Barrick, after its acquisition of Placer Dome—is beginning to slow down, reducing one source of upward pressure on gold.

Gold Leasing and Forward Hedging

Central banks have been leasing out their gold at extremely low interest rates. In theory, such a practice would give the central bank a return on its investment that it does not gain from keeping the gold in its vault. People who mistrust the motives of these national banks believe that they are actively trying to keep gold's price from rising. As central banks lease gold to a bullion bank, the bullion bank sells the gold in the open market immediately and then invests the proceeds in some other asset that would have a reasonable return, such as government Treasuries. Then at the end of the period, the bullion bank buys back the gold to return to the central bank.

Gold mines need capital up front to incur the big development costs to bring a mine to production. In years gone by, it was a common practice to sell a portion of the expected mine production for forward delivery, with the idea of using proceeds to invest in the mines they develop. As the price of gold has risen, this has turned out to be a poor strategy because the mines have given up the ability to sell at much higher prices. The linkage involves bullion banks who take the other side of such a transaction by setting up the purchase from the mine for a future period.

Figure 15.16 shows how a mine can put on a forward position, at the same time that a central bank leases gold to the market. The biggest bank in gold derivatives is J.P. Morgan and is shown at the center of this set of transactions. The start is a central bank leasing gold to J.P. Morgan at an extremely low interest rate that is typically only a fraction of a percentage point. J.P. Morgan then dumps the gold into the physical bullion market, obtaining dollars that it can invest; in this example, J.P. Morgan buys a 5 percent Treasury. The problem for the bank is that it needs a way of protecting itself against gold price rising; in other words, it needs a long position in gold. That position was provided by gold mines hedging, where they promise to deliver at a future date. For the mine, this was locking in its price for gold, to potentially enhance finding some

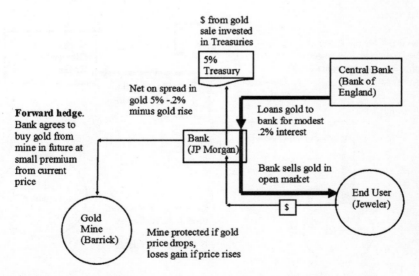

Figure 15.16   Central Bank Lending through Banks Adds Gold to Current Market

investment money by showing guaranteed buyer, and hedging against potential decreases in the price of gold.

Figure 15.17 shows the steps to unwind the transaction when gold is delivered back to the bullion bank, who then returns the gold that was leased from the central bank. In times when the gold price is relatively stagnant, this operation provided a profit to the bank and allowed the mine to produce its gold at an adequate price. But with the big jumps in price, the mine has lost out on the price rise. Having to deliver gold at under-market prices, with increasing mining costs, has been a bad consequence for mines. Investors, who are looking for returns as gold prices rise, avoid mines with hedges, keeping share prices low. So most gold mines have been trying to unwind their hedge positions. The unwinding requires gold mines to deliver gold or buy back positions by buying futures positions, and that puts upward pressure on gold. Having found how disastrous the hedging has been, the amount still hedged by mines is now much reduced so the pressure from unwinding hedges will be less going forward.

Figure 15.18 confirms that mines have been unwinding their hedges. In this presentation, a large negative number is thought of as decreasing

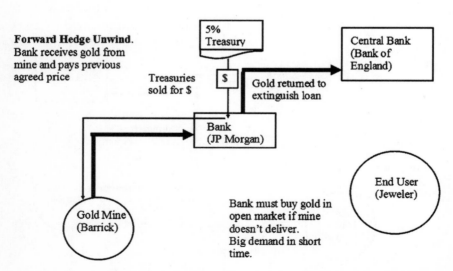

Figure 15.17   Gold Mine Unwinding Hedge Returns Gold to Central Bank

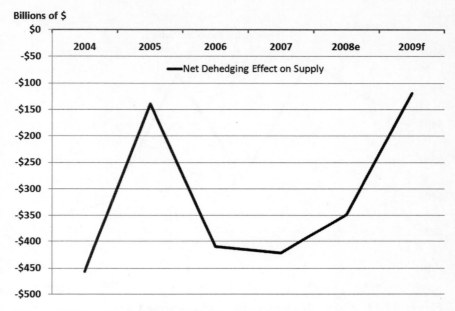

Billions of $

Figure 15.18   Net Dehedging Is Taking Less Supply
SOURCE: Fortis Bank.

the supply of gold because the mine identifies a way to remove its forward-sale hedge. In essence, this is a new demand for gold to meet the hedge and can be thought of as bullish to the extent that mines are unwinding their hedge positions.

Figure 15.19 shows that central banks are decreasing the quantity of gold they are selling, which means that there is not as much supply to the physical markets. With the newly disclosed purchases by China of 454 tonnes of gold, and the 200 tonnes by India from the IMF, we can safely say that central banks are now net buyers of gold. That is bullish for gold.

As a prime example of how bad the mess became for mining companies, look at unwinding of hedges at the world's largest gold miner; Barrick Gold removed its troublesome gold hedge book with a massive equity issue worth as much as $3.45 billion.

Barrick is selling 81.2 million shares at $36.95 each. It use the proceeds to buy back more than half of its hedge contracts, which had

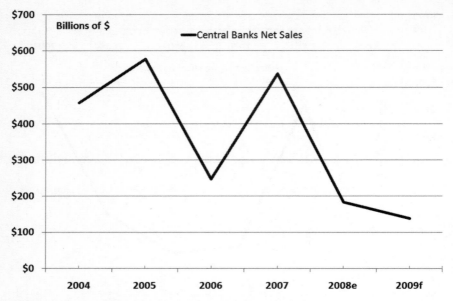

Figure 15.19   Central Banks Are Not Selling as Much Gold
SOURCE: Fortis Bank.

locked the company into receiving a fixed price for some of its gold production.

Barrick produces about 8 million ounces of gold a year. The problem is that Barrick sold off much of its future mining production years ago, at much lower prices. Its hedge book totaled 9.5 million ounces. Barrick said it will use $1.9 billion of the net proceeds to eliminate all of its fixed-price contracts in the next year and $1 billion to eliminate a part of its floating-price contracts.

The proceeds from the stock sale probably won't be enough to rid Barrick completely of its contracts, which have a market value of approximately $5.6 billion.

The Seasonality of Gold Demand Also Affects Prices

Just like its bigger brother the stock market, gold reflects a seasonal bias in the amount of increase, depending on the time of year. It seems that

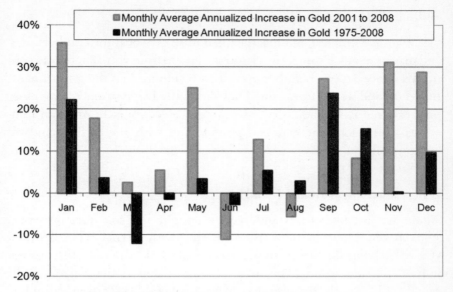

Figure 15.20   Gold Stocks Tend to Rise More in Winter

many marriages occur around the beginning of the year, and that it is custom to use gold in celebrations around the New Year. This backs into higher prices, as fabricators look to obtain gold to manufacture jewelry. Regardless of the logic, the observed increases in gold on a monthly basis are much higher starting in September through the springtime than they are during the summer months, as shown in Figure 15.20.

How to Invest in Gold

There are many different ways to invest in gold, and the right one depends very much on the personality as well as the investment structure of the person taking on the positions. Therefore, I want to emphasize that I can't tell you what you need to do; you need to figure it out yourself. Here are just a few of the many alternatives so you know what you may want to research further. Without doubt, however, I strongly believe you should be holding a significant chunk of your own assets in gold, gold shares, futures, options, ETFs, or other instruments just to protect yourself from the demise of the dollar.

Bullion Coins and Bars

Coins are the simplest, but in large quantities, they become cumbersome and may be at risk if someone tries to steal them from you. Therefore, you need a safety deposit box, but even then recognize that the government might try and steal it from you. They did in the Depression. But owning physical gold is a straightforward way to protect yourself. You can find a local coin merchant who can provide you with any of the standard bullion coins.

ETFs (Exchange-Traded Funds)

These act just like shares and can be bought and sold through your stockbroker. There is some risk associated with buying ETFs because you are relying on the custodian to actually hold the gold that it says it has. (Full disclosure: Personally, I own shares in the biggest ETF, called GLD, mostly because it is convenient. GLD's 75-page complex description of how it holds the gold and conducts audits was not the simple explanation I was looking for in an investment that is supposed to be a protection from complex financial chicanery, but I still bought their shares.)

Central Gold Fund of Canada

The Central Gold Fund of Canada provides a closed-end fund to take advantage of gold and silver held by this fund. I found this an easy way to invest.

Perth Mint Certificate Program (PMCP)

The Perth Mint is owned by the Government of Western Australia, which makes it more credible than other forms. Perth mint certificates enable you to invest in precious metals without the inconvenience and risk of personal storage. They give you legal title to a specific precious metal, so if you have trust in the government of Perth, it is a reliable program. The Perth mint requires a $10,000 minimum investment. It charges no sales tax, and it allows you to take your gold out of the country of Australia.

Gold Futures

With futures, you are betting on whether the price will rise or fall in the future. Leverage gives you the ability to control a large position for a small amount of funds down—so you can either get rich or lose your shirt. And you should know that 90 percent of traders lose in commodity markets, so the 10 percent who win are very rich. Buying gold futures is not for unsophisticated investors. If you want to invest in as much as 100 ounces, you could take physical delivery from the COMEX (the main futures exchange) because this will have the lowest premium possible. Apparently, it is not as simple as it would seem, but it is the original intent of futures markets to provide delivery. For more information, go to the exchange web site: http://www.nymex.com/GC_spec.aspx.

Options Contracts on Futures

You can also buy these, which can limit your losses, but I recommend against them because the premiums and slippage on entry and exit are too large, in my experience.

Gold Mining Stocks

Gold mining stocks provide a leverage to outright gold because their profits and price move up more (and down more) than the bullion itself. They are discussed in the next section.

Valuing Gold Mines Based on Gold in the Ground

Comparing the rise in the price of gold to the lackluster performance of the overall stock market since the year 2000 gives a pretty dramatic indication that gold was a top investment of the decade. Figure 15.21 shows that gold was up 285 percent, whereas stocks are still down for the decade. You won't hear mainstream media touting this one.

Gold mining stocks offer an advantage over direct bullion because as the price rises and costs stay relatively stagnant, gold miners improve their profits, on a leveraged basis. So the price of gold stocks moves up more than gold. Figure 15.22 shows two indexes of gold mining shares that have done better than gold itself.

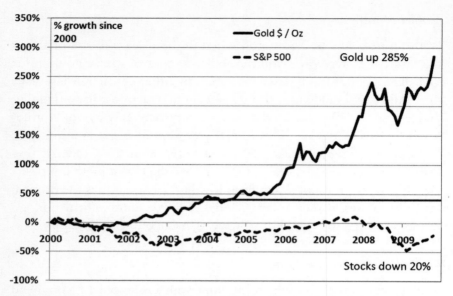

Figure 15.21   In the Last Decade, Gold is Up Almost 300% while Stocks are Down

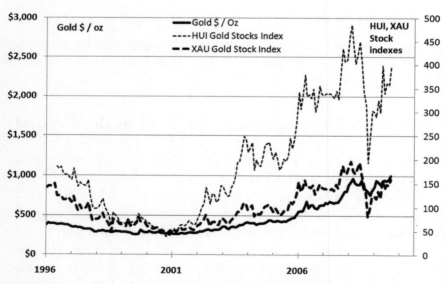

Figure 15.22   Gold Stocks Rise More than Gold But Are More Volatile

So let's look more closely at how to find the right stocks within the gold mining sector. Stocks can be in the right sector, but they can be overpriced and not worth purchasing. Traditional measures of stocks, such as P/E ratio, don't do well at assessing the true value (or the lack thereof) of a mining entity. There are other, more useful measures specific to gold mines, including ore reserves and production cost per ounce.

Although mining companies provide plenty of data, reviewing it with an eye to valuation isn't easy. Any method inevitably depends on assumptions about a company's costs, production rates, and development trends. A reasonable method applied consistently across a group of mines can extract the best stocks to own. Table 15.1 contains the basic numbers to value gold mines extracted, summarized in a fashion useful for determining the value of the gold held in the ground.

The data included in Table 15.1 refers to the following factors:

- **Proven and Probable Reserves** is what a mine is expected to eventually produce.
- **Cash Cost per Ounce** is what the company anticipates spending to extract each ounce of reserves out of the ground and get it to market.
- **Mine Asset Value** is reserves multiplied by the difference between the price of gold today, and the cash cost per ounce.
- **Debt** is borrowing by the mine. Mines aren't cheap to build, and most mining companies borrow to get things up and running.
- **Hedge Liability** is the obligation that the mine may have to deliver gold in the future at a price below the current price. It is presented in Table 15.1 as the size of the obligation at the current gold price.
- **Mine Asset Value** is Mine Asset Value minus Debt and minus Hedge Liability.
- **Market Cap** is the value the market is placing on the company (i.e., the current Share Price times the Total Outstanding Shares).
- **Valuation Ratio** is Market Cap divided by Net Asset Value.

The goal of all of this is to compare the price of the company to the assets of gold in the ground to see whether the price is low enough to be attractive. The summary number comes through in the Valuation Ratio. Table 15.1 gives you a sense of comparative value of

Table 15.1 Valuation Table

Company	Proven & Probable Reserve M oz	Cash Costs $/oz 2008E	Mine Asset Value $M	Debt M$	Hedge Liability $M	Net Asset Value $M	Share Price $	Total Outstanding Shares M	Market Cap $M	Valuation Ratio
Lihir Gold	24.8	368	15,867	−62	0	15,929	26.64	252	6,713	0.42
Barrick Gold Corp	138.5	467	74,901	2,986	4,865	67,050	37.95	874	33,168	0.49
Kinross Gold	45.6	382	28,536	103	195	28,238	22.82	695	15,860	0.56
Sino Gold	4.4	391	2,714	−53	0	2,767	5.95	292	1,737	0.63
Yamana Gold	19.4	352	12,723	367	0	12,356	11.06	733	8,107	0.66
Agnico–Eagle	18.1	326	12,341	−311	0	12,652	70.46	156	10,992	0.87
Randgold Resources	8.9	491	4,600	−237	56	4,781	71.50	77	5,506	1.15

*The Valuation Ratio is the ratio of the stock price to the Net Asset Valuation, so the lower the Valuation Ratio, the higher the ranking.

these mines where, if the price is low compared to the gold, it offers a better buy. A valuation ratio over 1.0 indicates that a company's stock may be expensive compared to its assets. A valuation ratio much below 1.0 indicates a bargain.

The price for gold per ounce will affect the value of the mine's assets. It may affect different mines differently as they have different costs. Share prices are dynamic and affect the stock market capitalization side of the ratio. Of course, the calculations change as the price of gold and the price of the stock change. When the company issues new figures for its costs and reserves, the ratio also changes. For example, a mine with a low-grade deposit that is costly to extract may have a low valuation today, but when gold rises, the benefit to the value of the asset is bigger, so its stock might rise more than other mines.

Cash positive, gold-producing gold mines that are located within democratic parts of the world, like Canada and Australia, are a good option. Remember that all shares carry some degree of risk, so you should spread this type of investment among four to six gold-producing mines.

Junior gold mines obviously carry a greater risk, and you should conduct plenty of due diligence when venturing within the junior gold share category. Junior gold miners that are producing carry less risk than exploration companies that have no revenue.

Exploration companies are the riskiest of all, because they burn a lot of cash trying to locate profitable mineral deposits, and they should represent only a tiny fraction of your overall investment strategy.

Here are five factors to considering when buying gold mining companies:

1. **Cash flow.** The company should have a strong cash flow and even have cash or gold on hand.
2. **Income generation.** The company should be generating good income by producing gold out of the earth. You also need to look at the cost of removing the gold out of the earth (i.e., the cash costs per ounce).
3. **The quantity of proven or measured reserves in the ground.** This is gold under the ground that has a 90 percent chance of recovery. Indicated and inferred reserves relate to a lower probability of extracting the metal out of the ground.

4. **Little or no hedging.** Hedging is a bad strategy for gold mining companies in a rising gold market, as described previously. Some smaller gold mines, however, engage in some hedging to raise capital.
5. **Low debt levels.**

A competent newsletter service or a broker with a focus on mining stocks can provide this type of analysis that can be used to select the best of the best in gold stocks. (For example, Table 15.1 comes from Casey Research, where I developed the methodology, and the analysis is available as part of our newsletter.)

Futures Contracts

I started this chapter with my experiences of wild success trading gold futures. But I left out a little of the heartache along the way. Futures are extremely risky—far more so than anybody realizes until they've lost their entire investment more than once. The problem is they give you too much rope, enough to hang yourself.

Another problem is that most people don't realize that their entire margin can be wiped out with only modest movements of the underlying instrument. That happens because of margin calls: You get too many contracts in place for the amount of margin dollars you have pledged, and you are asked to put up more money. Almost all traders I know strongly recommend against meeting a margin call and recommend just selling out. Halfway through my meteoric rise in precious metals in 1978, I had to take $5,000 out of savings to defend my overleveraged position. In that case, it worked out, but the lesson here is to be careful if you do consider using futures to make sure that you have several times the minimum margin required available cash to defend almost any of the positions you would take in the futures market.

For example, you typically need as little as 5 percent of the underlying value of the invested contract to make trades. If gold is priced at $1,000 and the contract is for 100 ounces, the underlying value of the contract is $100,000. However, the actual amount of cash you have to put up to buy a single contract is $5,000. But in these volatile times, if gold were to drop $50, which it does sometimes in a week, you would be wiped out.

Here's an example of how changes in conditions can create difficulties in futures markets: The explosive run in precious metals to the peaks at the beginning of 1980 included the famous attempt by the Hunt brothers to corner silver. In those days, you paid taxes only on the contracts you closed out. This left the opportunity to manage your contracts across the end-of-the-year deadline into the next year. The game I tried to play was to be both long and short silver in different months, so that I would neither make money nor lose money, but I wouldn't have to pay the taxes until the next year when the contracts were closed out. I know that sounds complicated, but normally it was just waiting for the New Year, as you would do with a stock portfolio today. There was a small hitch, however: The Hunt brothers drove the price of silver to $50! The managers of the exchanges fought back and they demanded 100 percent coverage of the contracts. They gave me almost no credit for being both long and short. There were no trades being made as I tried to figure out how to meet 100 percent margin calls. Fortunately, my broker got me out at a level that seemed pretty attractive (and I bought him a fancy watch as a thank you).

These little realities should just make you darn scared to trade futures. My Harvard Business School roommate said that most of the time trading futures is relatively boring, but that it is punctuated by periods of terror. I hope my stories give you more of a lesson than the facts of the mechanics of the market would.

Holding physical gold usually requires a gold storage facility that charges a fee. So contracts for delivery of gold in the future usually are slightly higher priced to cover the expenses that are similar to holding physical gold. Because the futures market requires only a very small margin of approximately 5 percent of the face value of the futures contract, the use of a futures contract is much like borrowing money to buy the asset. So the longer-term contracts include the equivalent of the carrying cost charge or interest rate on what would be the borrowing cost to buy and store gold.

In our current situation, the price of a futures contract delivery date for a year or two in the future is surprisingly low considering the normal storage charges and equivalent loss of return on invested capital. The conclusion here is that farther-out futures contracts are at least as good if not a better buy than the nearby futures because their price is so close to the spot market price.

So my conclusion on futures is to learn from my experience and don't trade them unless you are far more cautious than most people understand is required.

Moreover, look on the bright side: If you put up $20,000 on a futures contract and the price rises by $200, you have doubled your money. I'll leave learning the mechanics of futures trading to you and your futures broker. The warnings I have been giving are that futures trading is dangerous, but the enticement you should be aware of is that profits can be large for those who are smart and lucky.

Investing in Other Metals: Silver, Platinum, and Palladium

The stories for the other precious metals—silver, platinum, and palladium—are similarly supported in an environment of loss of trust in the dollar. Let's look at each one individually, as well as copper.

Silver is sometimes thought of as a monetary unit and sometimes as an industrial metal. There is, in fact, less silver available than gold because it is consumed in things like photographic chemicals. Traditionally, one of the biggest uses of silver has been for films and color photography, but that is all in upheaval due to the digital camera revolution.

Silver is an industrial as well as a monetary metal, but its price hasn't really reflected the monetary aspect until a few years ago. The recent shortage, although short-lived, of silver bullion coins and bars is one sign that people have realized the monetary value of silver. After all, silver is much like gold, only cheaper in today's money. Because it is less plentiful, any jump in demand will have an explosive effect on the price of silver. With the Chinese state television announcing silver bullion as an investment vehicle for the masses in 2009, there is no doubt in my mind that silver has regained recognition as money and is headed for much larger gains than gold in a precious metals bull market. The reverse is also likely true, that silver goes down more in the bear markets.

Platinum and palladium are both used in catalytic converters and therefore are supported when business is doing well so that people are buying autos. Platinum is used for jewelry in Japan (much the way gold is used in the rest of the world), so it gets some support when Japan is doing well.

Copper is not thought of as a precious metal, but it is traded often as part of the group when thinking about holding physical assets. Also, copper mining often provides other metals as byproducts, so it's important to use valuation methods that include thinking about the price of copper. Copper is used in homes for wiring and pipes, in bullet's and in autos, so it is affected by the strength of the economy more than the precious metals, which are guided by the monetary affairs.

There isn't enough space here to adequately cover these alternatives to gold, but in general, they move together and offer many of the same possibilities. All five (gold, silver, platinum, palladium, and copper) are traded in futures exchanges, where leverage is readily available for the highflying trader. The complex is in a position to continue to move higher in the decade ahead for the same reasons gold is rising: the protection from paper currency devaluation.

Predicting the Price of Gold for the Decade

This section develops a baseline scenario for where the price of gold could go under relatively normal conditions. The methodology is to look at historical price increases for gold and project that similar growth into the future. The purpose is to get a reasonable scenario of what might happen. I do believe there is a scenario for the future that is more extreme than I focus on here.

There is a key tool for looking at long-term historical charts: the use of a semi-logarithmic scale graph. Years ago, it was only engineers who thought in terms of logarithms, but today, most stock–charting systems include the option of switching the vertical access from the regular linear scale to a logarithmic scale. Now every chart analyst pretty much has this tool at his or her disposal. The effect of this calculation is to spread out the differences at the smaller price levels and compress the ones at the higher price levels so that it shows the same percentage differences as the same amount of vertical distance anywhere on the graph. What does that mean? It means the compounded growth rate, such as 10 percent a year, will appear as a straight line sloping upward to the right. In contrast, on a regular linear scale, it would be a curve sweeping increasingly higher.

Figure 15.23 shows the long-term historical price of gold since 1971, when the price started moving, on a logarithmic scale chart. The two arrows are the long-term compounded growth rates, and their extension out into the future shows where the price of gold might go, using that same growth rate. A nice thing about the logarithmic scale is that the prediction out to the future that is based on a compounded rate of growth is merely an extension of a straight line. We also get to see what would otherwise be small fluctuations at the lower prices much more easily. As you look at Figure 15.23, it is pretty easy to see how gold could move to $3,000 an ounce in just a few years.

In Figure 15.24, I've done the work of projecting a little farther out to the end of the decade, and I presented it in the traditional pattern of the linear scale that most people are used to seeing. Now a compounded growth rate, instead of being a straight line, is an exponential line increasing ever more as time goes on. On this linear scale, the projected

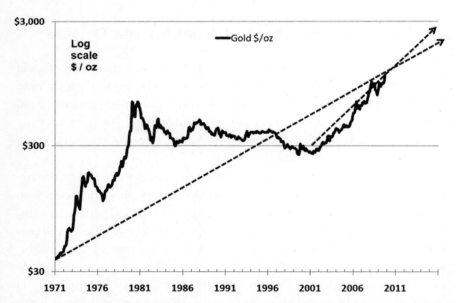

Figure 15.23 Projecting the Price of Gold to 2016 Suggests It Could Reach $3,000/oz
SOURCE: London Metals Exchange, author's projection.

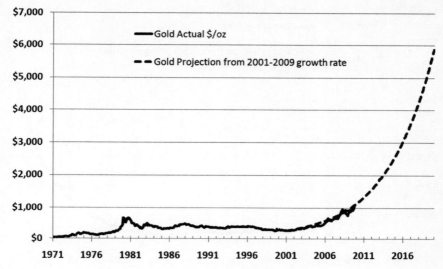

Figure 15.24   Gold Could Rise to $6,000 in the Decade

price looks like a big jump, and it's hard to calibrate based on the historical growth rate. So the logarithmic scale gives a less dramatic projection, but it provides us with an easier-to-manage graph of whether the future growth rate is consistent with the past.

It is my expectation that we are headed into a period of time where the inflation rate will be higher than it has been in the past. To get this difference, I used the consumer price index (CPI) to first eliminate inflation from the historical gold price, then to calculate its growth rate from 2001. I then projected the 2001 growth rate across the next decade, to get the real gold price. But because most of us are dealing with dollars that are not magically corrected for inflation, we need to estimate that component. I apply my estimate for the CPI to calculate what the nominal (unadjusted) price of gold would be. I estimated that the CPI will grow by 1 percent per year from basically zero at the present time. The combined calculations give a slightly higher price of $7,000 per ounce as shown in Figure 15.25. (If the CPI grew by 2 percent per year, the gold price becomes $12,000. This calculation is not shown, but it shows how important the inflation level can be for this method.)

The visual confirmation of these combined estimates is Figure 15.26, using the logarithmic scale, which makes it easy to see that the trajectory

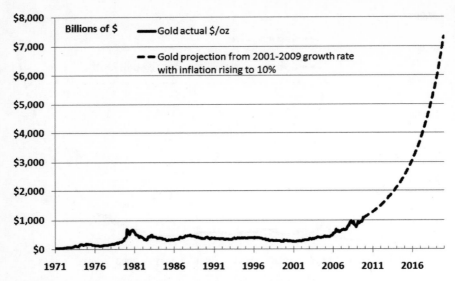

Figure 15.25   The Price of Gold Could Rise to $7,000/oz by 2016 (Linear Scale)

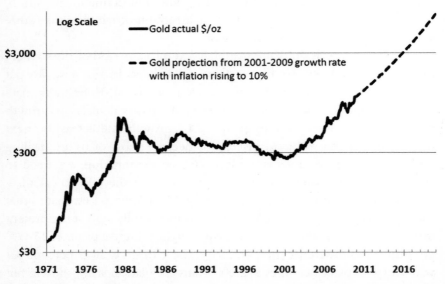

Figure 15.26   The Price of Gold Could Rise to $7,000/oz by 2016 (Log Scale)

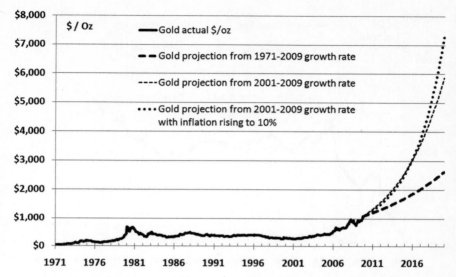

Figure 15.27 The Price of Gold Could Rise to $3,000/oz or $7,000/oz (Linear Scale)

is in line with historical growth patterns. The dotted line of the trajectory is consistent with the history from 2001 but with a little upward movement, due to my calculation for inflation.

Then, putting all three projections together, Figure 15.27—with the traditional linear scale—provides an indication of the ranges of potential prices for gold over the next decade.

For completeness, I've included the logarithmic scale chart, shown in Figure 15.28, of all three projections. I think gold will be rising more than it typically has over the previous 30 years since 1971, so I tend to think the sensible baseline should be a higher level of $7,000 per ounce by the end of the next decade.

Finally, I've added one more projection of historical growth rates that is more inclined to reflect the most bullish sentiments about where the price of gold might go. It is based on calculating the growth rate from 1971 through to the peak in 1980 and applying that growth rate to the next decade. That was a time of a bubble in gold prices that actually increased about 30 percent a year. If that were to occur in the decade ahead, the price of gold could rise to $22,000 per ounce by the end of the decade (see Figure 15.29).

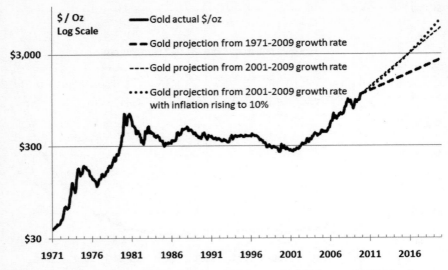

Figure 15.28 The Price of Gold Could Rise to $3,000/oz or $7,000/oz in a Decade (Log Scale)

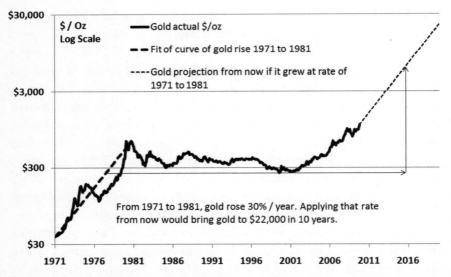

Figure 15.29 Gold Could Reach $22,000 If It Rises as Fast as It Did to 1980

The method is to fit the growth rate curve from 1970 to 1980 as the heavy dotted line in the left-hand portion of the curve, and apply it as the same growth rate to the future decade.

Despite my concerns that our financial system is heading towards convulsions that we will not be able to predict, I consider this kind of 30 percent-per-year gold price increase to be outside the normal expectations and not a likely case. But I must admit that because there is no anchor for any monetary system today, even $22,000/ounce would maybe not be high enough if confidence were lost in the overall position of the dollar. I consider that likelihood now to be below 20 percent, but conditions are set up for a change within a decade. We have to watch as the system unravels.

The $7,000 per ounce projection is based on a growth rate of about 17 percent per year, so projections of around 15 to 20 percent per year would be a good baseline. When adding in the extreme problems that seem so important about our monetary system, I look to the high end of that range. That would mean a price of around $1,350 by the end of 2010.

Conclusion

Rising demand for physical gold is a threat to the dollar because it signals a growing loss of confidence in the paper currency. It is also key to understand that gold prices aren't rising because of the changing fundamentals of gold, but because of the changing fundamentals of the *dollar*. In other words, gold isn't rallying; THE DOLLAR IS FALLING because of a loss of confidence.

Confidence is the single biggest factor in determining a currency's value, and periods of deficit expansion, such as what the United States experienced in 2009, undermine that confidence and create hyperinflation. Economic troubles, deteriorating debt ratios, and scary projections are a few of the factors resulting from an imbalanced economy that can lead investors to lose confidence in a currency.

It is not the attributes of gold and the gold market that are the reasons to buy gold; instead, it is all the reasons that are the subject of the chapters leading up to this gold chapter—the indication that the dollar is being debased—that make the case for gold. Gold is, after all, just gold: It's immutable, pretty, even romantic, but most important, it's unchanging. It is the dollar that is changing, continually and permanently, never to return to its former self.

Wrapping Up Part Four: The Investment Chapters

Looking at the investment chapters together, you can see the theme of the underlying economic problems that ties all of the investments together (with perhaps the exception of the stock market). That tie is the destruction of the dollar by the egregious government deficits and country trade deficits. One item left out is real estate. It too will have its time as an asset and anti-dollar play. Real estate, somewhat unwittingly, has been the anti-dollar play for the ordinary homeowner for two decades until the housing bubble burst. The homeowner didn't think of himself taking a hedge-fund-leveraged play in currency, but that in essence was what was going on. His mortgage provided the leverage, and the rise in house prices was an indication of the loss of currency purchasing power. He was betting on housing inflation, and for the most part won. But there are lingering difficult problems in the financing of real estate (and soon to be commercial real estate bubble) that will keep this play on the back burner for a few years.

As I look to compare the various options, gold has been the leader, and that is important because it is the most direct measure of the confidence in the dollar. Oil leapt to its peak in the summer of 2008, crashed, and has recovered. Being the world's largest commodity and most important source of industrial production and hence our wealth, oil is more important than gold. Both are political in that international tensions affect their price. Agriculture never really experienced a bubble, although it moved up to mid-2008. It could still rise if an unfavorable climate brought scarcity. Although the focus of the book has been on the collapse of the dollar, I'm not particularly excited about the competing currencies.

The situation that presents an unparalleled trade opportunity to me is that in spite of the obvious manipulation, turmoil, and publicly stated lack of confidence in the dollar, interest rates are still near 70-year lows at the short end and just barely bounced off of 50-year lows on the long end. We got these low rates because the government is manipulating rates down to revive the economy and to support weak banks. To make a trade on rising rates is playing a game against the government. That usually fails, but when it wins, profits can be colossal. Ask George Soros about betting against the Bank of England. He did, and he won—big.

I believe that gold is a safe haven and the only real money with a long trajectory of further price appreciation ahead. It has already quadrupled in the past decade, but I think it still has a long way to go. I still have my personal biggest position in gold. I think that the longer-term money would be better placed in interest rates rising, once the psychology of the deflationary pressure from this recession dissipates.

The next two chapters extend my analysis of how these very dangerous forces will affect our financial future. I give predictions for the decade and for the year ahead. Recognizing that no one actually knows the future, I give you my best interpretation of all the previous analysis as a full-time student of the markets to give you my best opinions of where all this is going.

Part Five

PUTTING IT ALL TOGETHER

In Part Five, I give my thinking about where the future of all these imbalances will lead. Many readers may be tempted to jump here rather than slog through all the many charts where I try to explain as confidently as I can how this story will unfold. I caution against taking the shortcut, because the reasons are actually more important than the conclusions. Anybody can have an opinion, and their reports are all over the Internet for free—but they are often based on nothing. On the other side of the ledger, the best economists and analysts who actually dig up the data are often reticent to step out of the comfort of analysis to make predictions. So rarely do you get both a courageous opinion and heavy economics treatise all in the same tome. These last chapters combine with the original foundation to make a sensible whole for how this plays out.

Chapter 16, "Forecast for the Future," relies on the work of others on previous crises and applies that analysis to come up with economic projections for our own situation. I try to answer the question of: "How bad could it get?"

Chapter 17, "Looking Over the Horizon to See the Best Investments," uses all that has gone before to give you my judgment of how things could move for investable items in the shorter term. I wind up with a one-year projection of these things. That's a little dangerous for a book, because of the time it takes to complete and publish all the materials during which events change things, but with that warning, I think you can benefit from my opinion in seeing the direction I suggest, even more than the specific predictions for stocks, interest rates, gold, energy, the dollar, housing; and the economic forces that drive them—GDP, inflation, budget deficit, trade deficit, and employment.

I think you'll agree that these difficult times require more understanding, but that they actually offer wonderful investment opportunities.

Chapter 16

Forecast for the Future

We are experiencing the worst financial collapse since 1929. That's no surprise today, but our government officials put off recognizing how bad it was for a year before the first shock in August 2007.

Now that it's here, I turn my attention to trying to answer the following questions: "How bad can it get?" and "How long can it last?"

Although such questions can never be answered with anything approaching absolute certainty, there are methods that can be used to assess what may lurk over the horizon. With that goal in mind, this chapter focuses on—and then expands on—the recent work of two economists who painstakingly analyzed a substantial number of previous banking and currency crises, in an attempt to derive potentially useful lessons. I have applied their data to the current circumstances to see where we are relative to those other experiences.

As you'll see, the data reveal the average depth and duration of various aspects of the crises examined (unemployment, GDP declines, stock price corrections, etc) as well as the worst case for each of those aspects. Before getting to that data, however, let me be clear that I view the current crisis as anything but average. The problems are systemic, in that they are global in nature and are negatively affecting virtually all aspects of economic activity. That said, as of this writing, I believe it is unlikely we'll match or exceed the worst case for each of the individual measures analyzed, though knowing the worst case from a historical perspective gives us a strong compass point to keep a very close eye on.

This data isn't meant to offer a prediction but rather something akin to a beacon of light to see what is reasonable and what is very extreme. The data is from a study called "The Aftermath of Financial Crises" by Carmen M. Reinhart of the University of Maryland and Kenneth S. Rogoff of Harvard University. In their study, the authors summarize the results of a broad sampling of banking crises, with between 13 and 22 crises analyzed for each of the variables.

The Reinhart/Rogoff study is itself based on data extracted from an even more comprehensive study of events in 66 countries, titled "This Time Is Different: A Panoramic View of Eight Centuries of Financial Crises," by the same authors.

I've summarized the findings from the latest study in Table 16.1.

The economic measures in the left column of Table 16.1 show how far the U.S. situation had deteriorated to late 2009. The next columns show the averaged historical deterioration and the worst case of the crisis analyzed.

Table 16.1   How Other Serious Financial Crises Affected the Economy

	U.S. to 2009	Other Crises Average	Worst
Housing	−33.5%	−35.5%	−54%
Stocks	−57.0%	−55.9%	−90%
Unemployment increase in % from bottom	6.4%	7.0%	23%
Real per capita GDP	−4.9%	−9.3%	−28%
Cum % increase in public debt (Debt)	42.5%	86.0%	175%

I then applied these data to calculate the levels that the United States could reach if it follows the path of the historical examples. The projected level is based on the measure analyzed, either from the peak prior to the downturn (e.g., the S&P 500) or from the bottom prior to the downturn (e.g., the lows in unemployment). Thus, as you can see in Table 16.2, the S&P 500 dropped from its October 2007 peak of 1,565 down to 666 in March 2009 and then recovered to over 1,150 by early 2010. If this crisis were to end up being only average, then it would drop to 690. I did the analysis the month before we reached that low, and it was calculable from the original data from Rogoff et al. much earlier. But I expect this downturn to eventually be more than average, so we may not be done if the economy weakens again.

If, however, the worst case of a 90 percent drop were to occur, as it did in Iceland in 2008, then the S&P 500 would trade down to the shocking level of 157. For further reference, if the current crisis were to cause the stock market to fall as sharply as it did during the Great Depression, the S&P would touch 469.

The analysis of previous crises also examined the duration of the various crises, calculating the number of years it took for each of the measures analyzed to reach their nadir during the event. Table 16.3 shows that it took 3.4 years, on average, for the stock market to fall from the peak to the bottom. In the worst case, it took 5 years. With the recent peak in the S&P 500 occurring in October 2007, the crisis is likely to have some time to go before reaching even an average duration.

Table 16.2   What Could Happen to the U.S. Economy If It Follows the Path of Other Historical Crises

| | Measured At | | What If Like Other Crises | |
Crisis by the Numbers	Peak or Bottom	Start 2010	Average	Worst
Case-Shiller House Price	226	158	146	104
S&P 500	1565	1115	690	157
Unemployment rate	4.4%	10.0%	11%	27%
Per capita real GDP	$44,287	$42,107	$32,330	$37,699
Public debt $ B	$4,943	$7,811	$9,300	$13,750

Table 16.3   Projecting the Time to the Bottom, from the Peak, for Various Aspects of the U.S. Economy

	Years from Peak	Average	Worst	What If Like Other Crises Average	Worst
Housing	2.7	6.0	16	2012	2022
Stocks	1.3	3.4	5	2011	2012
Unemployment	2.0	4.8	11	2012	2018
Real per capita GDP	1.3	1.9	4	2009	2011
Public debt (Debt)	1.3	3.0	3	2010	2010

More specifically, if this crisis turns out to be just average, I would not expect to see the low in the S&P before the first quarter of 2011.

The Crisis Horizon in Pictures

Historical time series charts of the summary number calculations shown in Tables 16.1 to 16.3 can provide a better visual perspective on the range of possible outcomes. With that in mind, let's look at Figures 16.1 through 16.5, along with a few observations.

The Stock Market

Figure 16.1 shows that the U.S. stock market already fell by 50 percent since 2007, to 666 in March of 2009 and so it already approached the average level of decline. We have had a 70 percent recovery from the bottom of stocks to 1,145 as of early 2010. But even the 666 bottom is still a long way from reaching the 90 percent decline Iceland's stock market experienced in 2008, or the 70 percent drop of the Great Depression here in the United States.

Where do I think the stock market is likely to head from here? With the severity of the drop so far, the bounce on the big government bailouts and funding providing hopeful news is not so surprising. Yet, given the abundance of evidence that the economic problems are far

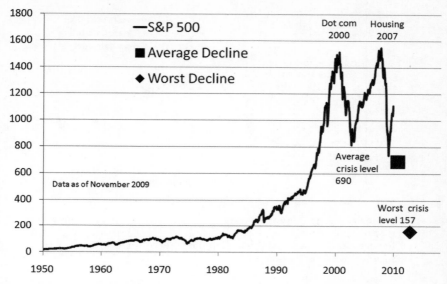

Figure 16.1   S&P 500 Has Already Collapsed to Average Crisis Level

from over, I would conclude that this rebound is likely to be fleeting, and that we still have further to go on the downside.

Housing Prices

Figure 16.2 shows that housing prices (as measured by the Case-Shiller housing price index) shot up in concert with then-Fed Chairman Greenspan's cutting of interest rates to 1 percent in 2003 to 2006. As you don't need me to tell you, those prices have fallen back, but the big inventories of unsold properties say we are not yet past a bottom. As you can see, a real estate collapse can take longer to evolve, often-times stretching out over several years. Typically, out of the five measures analyzed here, the bottom in housing comes last.

Unemployment

Unemployment has continued rising from its low in March 2007 of 4.4 percent and by the fall of 2009 hit 10.2 percent. Figure 16.3 shows how it could head higher as the unemployment rate tends to lag the other

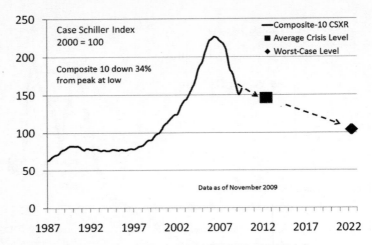

Figure 16.2 Housing Prices Can Take Years to Decline
SOURCE: Standard and Poors.

measures discussed here, and those measures are still in decidedly negative territory. It's unlikely we'll reach the worst case, which would require adding another 16.8 points to the current rate to get to 27 percent, if for no other reason than that the government would almost certainly step in with additional large public works programs before it would let things get that bad.

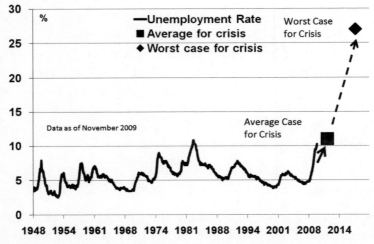

Figure 16.3 Unemployment Could Jump over the Decade

As many people know, there are measurement issues when comparing employment rates over a long period of time; the government has made numerous adjustments to the calculations used over the years. For example, if the same calculations were used today as were used in the Great Depression of 1929 (which is the worst case, as shown in Figure 16.2), then the current figures would be significantly higher than reported, as much as 11 percent. The measure quoted from the government of 10 percent unemployment does not include discouraged workers and marginally attached workers that in another measure called U-6 is now at 17.3 percent in late 2009.

Looking forward, it's hard to see where new employment is going to come from to replace the jobs now being lost; the United States has relatively little manufacturing left, its financial services sector is on its back, and real estate-related businesses—which were the powerhouse industry of recent years—are likely to be in a long-term slump. In fact, the only readily identifiable growth industry in the years just ahead appears to be in government, hardly a positive. Speaking of which . . .

U.S. Government Debt

The more easily predicted measure is the increase in government debt, the result of governments with fiat currencies printing up new debt in an attempt to counteract the economic slowing. Outstanding U.S. federal government debt has already jumped $2.2 trillion to November 2009, and, based on the various plans announced so far, another $2 trillion in new borrowings is expected in 2010.

As you'll see in Figure 16.4, the time lags from the beginning of the crisis to the average and worst-case levels are indicated as being roughly the same—about three years from the beginning of the crisis. This is because, unlike other measures analyzed, there is no finite point at which increases in government debt cease. It has almost always increased and is expected to continue to rise. The only question is how much. Thus, the data was evaluated using a fixed measuring point, and the average and worst levels were calculated at that point.

Looking over the historical record, I am not surprised to find that the United States is breaking no new ground by expanding government debt; that has been the default mode in many other crises. The surprise

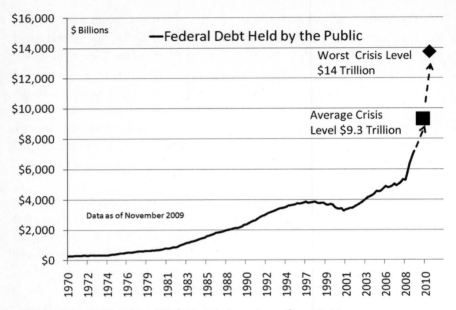

Figure 16.4   U.S. Federal Debt Is Likely to Jump from Crisis

may very well be—given the aggressive levels of stimulus in the current crisis, with promises of much more on the way—that we could see U.S. federal debt approaching the worst-case level by the end of 2012. If we add $2 trillion for each of the next three years to the $7.5 trillion, we could get there.

The implications are relatively straightforward:

- A secular trend for higher interest rates as the Treasury tries to attract buyers for its debt.
- The introduction of new and elevated tax schemes. (The new health care and stimulus spending initiatives are bringing calls for increased taxes on high-income earners to cover budget deficits.)
- A ratcheting up of the Fed's highly inflationary monetary policies.

On the latter front, as the United States is unable to pay down these debts in current dollars and is unlikely to outright default on its many obligations, the only option left is to diminish the debt over time through the hidden taxation of inflation. Expect it.

Gross Domestic Product (GDP)

GDP, the summary measure of the broader economy, is usually relatively stable, as much of the activity is not prone to sharp economic swings. To wit, although discretionary items, such as balloon rides in Napa, may see a quick fall-off in activity, nondiscretionary expenses are less sensitive; people still have to eat, clothe, and provide shelter for themselves. Figure 16.5 shows what this might look like.

Although Figure 16.5 indicates that a worst-case slowdown has not occurred for a long time, the feedback of a large number of people being thrown out of their houses and losing jobs in the current crisis provides anecdotal evidence that we are facing a worse-than-average slowdown.

In the case of the Great Depression (a worst case by any unit of measurement), GDP was nearly halved, falling from $104 billion to $56 billion. That extreme is mitigated somewhat by the deflation during the Depression, which boosted the value of the money then in circulation, the opposite of what happens in an inflation.

This time around, the government is attempting to make up for the fall-off in personal spending by engaging in a spending spree of its own.

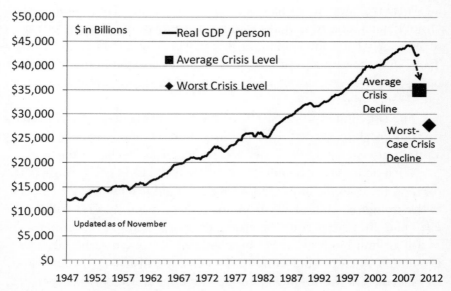

Figure 16.5   GDP Falls in Serious Crisis

To a yet-undetermined degree, that spending will help buffer the impact on GDP, but it will simultaneously debase the currency. Even so, should the downturn result in just an average-case decline of 11 percent in U.S. real per capita GDP, it would have very serious consequences. That level of decline is not at all out of the question; on an annualized basis, Japan's GDP fell by 11 percent in the quarter ending December 2008.

Combining the Average-Case and Worst-Case Scenarios of What Might Happen to the U.S. Economy

It is hard to absorb numbers developed as abstractions from historical calculations, as in the estimates I've presented so far of how bad the big economic indicators might deteriorate to. They are all interrelated, as bad things mutually affect each other. The two different cases (an average case and a worst case) leave ambiguity as to which is the right scenario. To examine the possibilities, I developed a single case by just weighing the worst case by 25 percent and the average case by 75 percent and combining that into a single scenario. My rationale is that this case is far worse than anything I have seen, at least since the Depression in the United States, and so it is likely to be worse than the average, but also to be somewhat conservative, so that it won't be as bad as the worst. Table 16.4 shows that result. It is a very bad set of economic readings, but as you will see, not at all unreasonable to expect considering the already serious decay.

The last column in Table 16.4 is the percent change to be expected from the peak to get a feel for the magnitude. Unemployment level at 15 percent is probably the easier way to get a feel for that number.

What do these levels indicate? We already got most of the way to this scenario for housing and stocks, being down 34 percent and 57 percent at the trough in 2009. Debt is estimated to expand by $1.8 trillion in 2010 and 2011, so it could be estimated to get to the scenario number of $11 trillion by 2011, ahead of schedule. The questionable items are if unemployment would jump to 15 percent and if GDP would drop 14 percent. The work force is around 150 million people, so 14 percent unemployed would be around 20 million. As of December 2009, we had 15.3 million unemployed. To get to 20 million unemployed seems

Table 16.4 Combining 75% of the Average and 25% of the Worst-Case Scenarios to Get a Single Scenario

	Measured At		What If Like Other Crises		75% Weight to Average 25% Worst	
	Peak/Bottom	Nov 2009	Average	Worst	Level	%
Case-S House Price	226	158	146	104	135	−40%
S&P 500	1565	1110	690	157	557	−64%
Unemployment rate	4.4%	10.2%	11%	27%	**15%**	250%
Per Capita Real GDP	$44,287	$42,107	$39,415	$32,330	$37,644	−14%
Public Debt $ B	$4,943	$7,712	$9,300	$13,750	$10,413	**108%**
Year					2012	

possible over three years, if the economy stays so weak and job losses were 150,000 per month.

The GDP has only dropped small amounts in the post-WWII time frame, but in the Depression it dropped about half in nominal terms, and after deflation is added back in, it dropped about 28 percent from the peak. So it would not be impossible for GDP to drop an accumulated 14 percent over the three years in the face of the worst economic downturn since then.

Given that this very bad scenario is well within reach, what are the social consequences of having double the burden of unemployed? Will they be on government short-term unemployment support, and will they be losing homes and sleeping under the bridge? Some of both will happen. Some will become squatters in the empty foreclosed homes, maybe even what used to be their own homes. Will banks be able to seize the homes? Will local squatters run the officials off the premises? What happens to the prison population? I know there are large empty prisons, but can the government afford to incarcerate people at $40,000 per year? Multiply that by 10 million, and that's another $400 billion price tag.

What happens to the tax revenue when the unemployment jumps to 15 percent? Say profits of companies also drop, perhaps more. How far down do capital gains fall as the stock market continues down? In big recessions, tax revenues drop, so say the drop is also 15 percent compared to the previous boom. That would be another $375 billion drop in the $2.5 trillion of taxes collected.

Would housing prices continue to drop in this scenario? They are down 28 percent, so dropping another 12 percent would seem to be very easy to achieve, and worse scenarios are possible if inflation stays hidden. But we could have inflation that is bigger than the decrease in real housing values, so the appearance as measured in prices might look like a recovery. Housing is the common man's inflation hedge, and inflation is inevitable in the long run from the government excess.

Who do all the banks we are bailing out lend to? Business won't be expanding with GDP down 14 percent. Consumers won't be buying houses or cars because they won't want to borrow, which will be just fine with the banks that are nursing their already bad loans on houses they have taken back in recession.

The conclusion is that this scenario may not seem likely, but should be on our radar screens, because everything could implode on itself with the related problems reinforcing each other; we need to know how bad it could get. The example is not just dreaming up bad numbers, but observing what happened. The point of this kind of analysis is not to be precise, but to use historical perspective to confirm the sensibility of how serious the current situation is and how much farther it could extend in depth and in time. It is a scenario from which we can draw further implications, and the most important one is that this is not the typical recession but a very big and serious one. We already know how bad it is around us, but the indications here are that the Great Deleveraging could extend into 2012, and that short-term spring blooms may not be evidence of a tide change in how serious this crisis actually is for another year or more.

Regardless, the question now is whether it will be just bad or a disaster.

What Should You Do

The global economic situation continues to deteriorate on many fronts.

Housing prices, a fundamental component of the current crisis, are down 30 percent in December 2009 from their bubble peak in

2006, but they still have a ways down to go to get back to their pre-bubble levels. As I have discussed, even an average downturn will mean that housing remains a problem for several more years. An increasing number of houses will come back to the market through foreclosures, so the inventory of houses for sale is still growing. Exacerbating the problems are that a great many homes were sold with adjustable rate loans that are going to reset over the next few years. Unless, of course, the government steps in to stave off those resets—a solution that carries with it a separate set of problems.

Also on the topic of housing, a fundamental new problem is that, through its directly or indirectly controlled agencies—Fannie Mae, Freddie Mac, and the FHA—the government has become the de facto sole housing lender left standing in the United States. Dismantling those structures and reinvigorating the private lending sector, a prerequisite to a housing bottom occurring, will not be simple or accomplished in a short period of time.

Making things worse, I continue to expect very serious problems in the commercial real estate sector.

The stock market reached a 50 percent decline, the average of what has been observed in past crises. For stocks to rise, corporations need customers to create sales and profits. In the current slowdown of housing prices, domestic consumers can't borrow to extend their spending. Additionally, retaliatory responses to the "Buy American" provision of the latest stimulus leaves the world with declining trade. That means that the United States will not be able to export its way out of this crisis either.

The only growth trend at this point is in government bailouts, which are in high gear, indicating we'll experience the serious growth of outstanding debt seen in other crises. The elevated levels of government borrowing required to fund that spending are absorbing all available credit from foreigners, directly competing with business in need of the new financing that will be required to expand the economy. The combination of declining business activity, coupled with declining levels of household income, will result in declining tax revenues, increasing the budget deficit beyond the size of the new bailout programs. State and municipal governments across the nation are already being confronted with large shortfalls in their budgets, shortfalls that will only widen as the crisis worsens.

The combined business slowing and jobs contraction will mean that the GDP will decline. Components of GDP having to do with necessities like food and shelter will continue to bump along regardless of the economic conditions, but the lack of growth in GDP could extend for years as it did in Japan and as it did after the 1929 stock crash.

Summarizing the History

Of the five measures defining how serious our crisis is, we have come near the average of other crises for housing and stock market drops. Unemployment and government debt are on a trajectory that suggests we could easily get quite a bit worse to line up with the scenarios of previous crises. The measure that indicates GDP dropping does not seem likely to be met in our case. It may be that much of our economy is protected during this downturn because of the government floodgates that have opened to provide bailouts. It could also be that the economy is actually worse than the government's measurements that are hidden behind their inflation measures that may be making GDP appear stronger than it actually is. My assessment is that we have more problems ahead, largely because we have not fixed the most serious of our problems that revolve around too much debt.

Inflation/Deflation

As the recession/depression will be with us for years, it's important to revisit the question of the possible role of inflation on the longer-term outcome.

I think we are just emerging from the deflationary phase, which usually occurs with the circumstances of debt deleveraging that follows a path like the Great Depression. In this circumstance it is easy to dismiss the case for inflation and many do. I think that is a mistake. We have had deflation in asset prices, but stocks and even housing have turned around. A summary tabulation of the unprecedented increases in government debt at this relatively early stage in the crisis make a compelling case for higher inflation, if for no other reason than that it shows clear intent on the part of the government to spend whatever it takes to offset the deflationary forces now stalking the land.

That is not to downplay the complexity of predicting inflation. To summarize, the current deflation is real but will be limited by the forceful actions of the government and Federal Reserve to assure availability of credit and to bail out as many participants as can be accommodated until there is an obvious loss of confidence in the dollar.

As to when that confidence will be lost, no one can forecast a precise turning date, but the persistent strength of gold and silver—arguably the only sound forms of alternative currency—suggests that the trend is now in motion against fiat currencies, including the U.S. dollar. Added anecdotal evidence comes from almost weekly announcements that major foreign holders of dollars are trading billions of those dollars for more tangible equity in mining, energy, and other companies engaged in the production of commodities.

That the current administration and the Federal Reserve Bank are committed to printing enough money to debase the dollar is not in doubt, and it has long been my expectation that this would be the path chosen. That is a fundamental reason I have consistently recommended gold, well before the excessive bailouts became policy.

What to Do Now

From the information presented in this chapter, most economists would conclude by sharing their prescription for what Obama and the Fed should do. I won't bother, because they wouldn't listen anyway. And besides, that is not the purpose of my research, which is entirely designed to help you understand and therefore properly position yourself for what is to come.

And this research paints a dismal story of years of economic stagnation. In my view, the trend is now firmly established for dollar debasement, a debasement that will eventually overwhelm the deflationary pressures from collapsing asset values.

Be extremely skeptical when you hear some pundit pronouncing that this piece of short-term good news or another is an "all clear" signal.

Keep an eye out for valid indicators of a stabilizing economy. Consumer confidence, retail sales, unemployment claims, risk spreads, and other leading indicators have already pulled back from dangerous levels, but they need to be moving strongly to confirm that a recovery is underway.

I think we are not in the recovery that the mainstream seems to like to allude to. We have not reached the worst case that so serious a crisis as this would usually experience, and we haven't resolved what to do with so much bad debt.

The next and final chapter summarizes many of the points I've been making throughout the book, and it gets closer to the shorter-term question of how far particular measures and investment items might move during the year of 2010.

Chapter 17

Looking Over the Horizon to See the Best Investments

Perhaps the most difficult challenge for all investors is to predict the future. Yet that is what we do when we allocate our resources, expecting that we will get a return on what we invest. To get big returns, it is absolutely imperative to understand the big-picture cycles and flows so that we have a background against which to make our individual investment decisions.

How Debt Affects the Currency and the Real Economy

Since about 2006, I have been forecasting that the U.S. economy is going to remain under pressure for a prolonged period, 10 years or so.

385

Nothing on the horizon has caused me to alter that big-picture forecast. The important problems have not been fixed: Debt that can't possibly be paid off has not been written down; real estate loans are still defaulting with more to come for commercial real estate; and unemployment can't be fixed easily and certainly not quickly. Overhanging the economy is an explosively growing and massive government deficit spending regime. Where others see green shoots, I see intractable problems made worse by each new bailout or government machination.

For the purpose of this analysis I have separated *Currency and Financial Problems* from those related to the growth of *The Real Economy*. Currency and Financial Problems include those involving the value of the dollar, inflation, the amount of debt, interest rates, and Federal Reserve machinations. The discussion on the real economy includes jobs, production, and competitiveness of the economy. Of course, the real economy is greatly affected by the shrinking measuring stick of the declining dollar—a 5 percent rise in stocks over the course of 2010 has a different import if, over the same period, the dollar loses 10 percent in purchasing power.

I have looked at dozens of forecasts for 2010 and found most analysts to be surprisingly unconcerned about inflation, with the general expectation that it will register at 2 percent or less for the year. The vast majority of economists also project a normal recovery with about 3 percent growth in GDP, and only nominal increases in interest rates. With the economy recovering, the consensus view is for unemployment to improve, albeit slowly.

In other words, the mainstream projections are surprisingly consistent and the range of expectations does not anticipate a continuation of any serious crisis. As you have read, my views are markedly different: The year ahead will be much more dangerous, with the potential for big surprises to the downside. Here's why.

Currency and Financial Problems

My belief is that confidence in the U.S. dollar will continue to erode in 2010, and that we'll see a corresponding fall in its purchasing power. This view is the root of my difference from the consensus. Simply, I expect we'll see both higher inflation and higher interest rates due primarily to the huge government deficits and the Fed's expansive monetary policies. The laws of money have not been repealed by the slow economy: If you print too many dollars, they become worth less.

Figure 17.1 shows the increase of Federal Government debt and the inflation as measured by the CPI.

The big picture is best seen in the long diagonal arrows on the chart, indicating the correlated trends in federal debt and CPI. In the current scenario, federal debt has exploded upward, but price inflation has lagged. I think that will change in 2010 as the CPI plays catchup. The vertical arrows point out something often ignored by those with the long-term view: The immediate reason for government stimulus is to counteract a slowdown in the economy as a result of less demand and lower prices. In the short term, we see that the movement of prices and government deficit are out of sync, or moving in opposite directions. It is occurring now, as it has in the past, but I believe we are beyond the extreme as the CPI is now rising. If the consensus view is any indicator, then rising inflation will surprise most people.

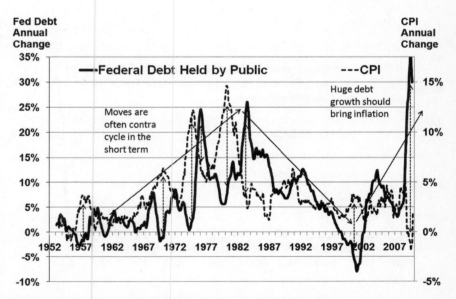

Figure 17.1   Federal Debt Growth Moves with Inflation
SOURCE: Federal Reserve.

Many analysts correctly point to weakness in the real economy—evidenced by stagnation in wages and a falloff in spending—as reasons price inflation has remained low. Yet, price inflation is obvious in commodities like gold, and other metals and stocks which rose 65 percent from the March 2009 lows. Oil, the world's most heavily-traded commodity, doubled in the year 2009. We already have price inflation, but it is not yet endemic.

The real source of inflation is not wages or even bank lending, but unsupported government spending that debases the currency. On that front, no one can deny that government deficits are out of control, as indicated by the 35 percent growth at the right of Figure 17.1. Once inflation is recognized for what it is, interest rates will have to rise in order to compensate lenders for the expected decline in the dollar's future purchasing power.

Figure 17.2 shows the increase in the debt issued by the government, added to the growth in the monetary base, to arrive at a measure of the Treasury and the Fed's combined extraordinary stimulus efforts. My rational for taking this approach is that both measures individually show the stimulus effects of the various institutions, whereas the combination is

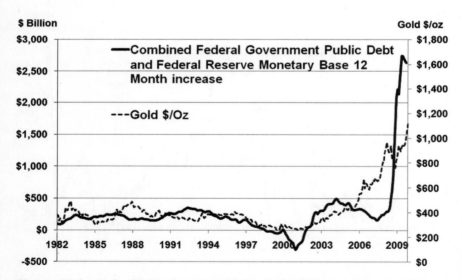

Figure 17.2 Federal Debt Growth Added to Federal Reserve Monetary Base Growth Shows the Size of Stimulation

what affects the markets. The monetary base reflects the sum of currency in circulation and the deposits by banks at the Federal Reserve. Now that the Fed is paying interest on deposits, and is asking for power to issue its own debt with interest in the latest banking legislation, we can see their efforts as parallel efforts to the Treasury's issuance of debt in order to pump money into the economy, stimulate favored industries, and eventually dilute the dollar.

I have overlaid the price of gold on Figure 17.2. As a competitive form of money, gold's rise is driven by the debasement of the dollar. Thus, as the combined stimulus grows, I expect to see the purchasing power of the dollar decline against gold, which has been the case.

Who Will Buy Our Government Debt?

Federal government debt grew by a stunning $1.885 trillion for fiscal year 2009, significantly more than the reported deficit of $1.417 trillion, thanks to accounting sleight-of-hand that uses accruals. Make no mistake, the $1.885 trillion increase in debt represents an unprecedented huge amount of new borrowing. And that raises the question, who is buying all this government debt?

This is more of a mystery than I expected. Figure 17.3 shows the categories of purchases of government debt. Foreign buyers purchased $697 billion worth of Treasuries, the Fed bought $286 billion, and a category labeled as "Households" bought another $529 billion. That latter category is where the Fed puts all the Treasuries that it can't specifically identify as being purchased by other sectors. Nobody I talk to is bragging about their Treasury holdings. I don't think it is defensible that normal households are buying that many Treasuries.

Hidden sources buying over $500 billion of Treasuries raises lots of questions. Where did the money come from? Could it be the big banks that were given great amounts of money to restimulate the economy? They are big enough to support the huge debt purchases. I don't know the details, but can point to the Household purchases of Treasuries as being of sufficient size to allow the government to kick the deficit can down the road another year, adding more spending but with little consequence so far in terms of interest rates.

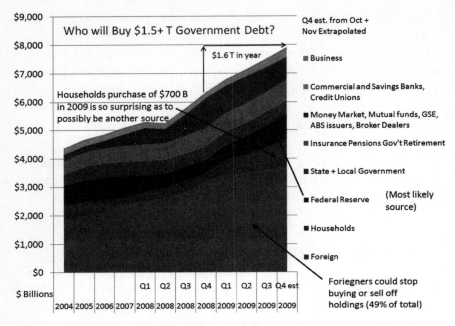

Figure 17.3   Federal Debt Holders of $8 Trillion of Treasuries Held by the Public

Will the government be able to pull another rabbit out of the hat again in 2010 when it comes back to the market for trillions in new spending?

What is important to my forecast is that the government is showing no real intention to slow its aggressive spending. On Christmas Eve 2009, when no one was watching, Treasury Secretary Geithner announced a lifting of the caps on the government's financial support for Fannie and Freddie. Until that announcement, the caps were set at $200 billion each, or $400 billion total. Going into 2010, the government's obligations to these two failed institutions becomes unlimited. That signals two things: The government policy will be to bail them out at all costs even beyond the $1.55 trillion from the Fed buying MBS, and the problems at Fannie and Freddie are worse than $400 billion.

The ability of the government to continue with this sort of open-ended deficit spending hinges in no small part on the assumed interest rate the government will pay on its many debts. As long as the carrying

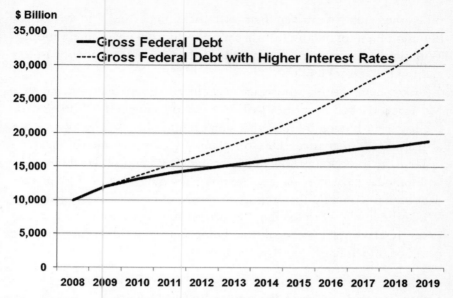

Figure 17.4 Federal Debt Could Double with Higher Rates
SOURCE: Congressional Budget Office (CBO), author's calculations.

costs of the debt are perceived to be low, and therefore manageable, some measure of confidence on the part of creditors can be maintained. However, if the interest costs on the debt are seen to be spiraling out of control, things would change, and quickly. (See related Figure 14.8.)

The Congressional Budget Office (CBO) long-term estimate for government debt anticipates interest rates staying around 5 percent. When I calculate what the deficit would be with rates rising just 1 percent per year, as I do in Figure 17.4, the deficit quickly grows to almost double the CBO estimate over the next decade.

Which brings us back to the government's favored "solution" to the economic crisis: spending like a drunken sailor to revive the private economy. But government spending is inefficient, so the positive effects are frequently less than the cost. For example, approximately $3 trillion has already been thrown at the combination of large banks and a few Detroit dinosaurs with little positive effect beyond the specific recipients. Banks are not making loans, but instead are holding $1.2 trillion in excess reserves on deposit at the Fed, where previously it was more typical for those reserves to be on the order of $10 billion. By investing in each other, the banks have driven their own stocks higher and paid themselves bonuses of tens of billions from what was originally government money. Without the government, many of the big banks would be out of business and the bankers jobless.

Elsewhere, the toxic mortgage paper held in government-guaranteed Mortgage-Backed Securities (MBS) is still on somebody's books, with the bad debt hidden by rules that don't require banks to recognize the actual value of their assets. This sort of jury-rigging is counterproductive, because the banks know how much trouble they are in, and that the piper will someday have to be paid, so are not making new loans. With private debt hard to come by, that important source of liquidity is not growing. While the low level of lending has helped keep price inflation low, the excess reserves are a potential time bomb, once confidence returns and banks begin lending.

Other Factors Leading to Worsening Budget Deficits

- **FHA**. Federal Housing Authority supported 23 percent of the new housing loans in 2009, much of it going to unqualified borrowers that are already defaulting. It is a repeat of the disastrous subprime mortgage lending fiasco, with the government as the guarantor. The agency is out of funds and will need bailouts.
- **FHLB**. Federal Home Loan Banks provide funding to banks for mortgages and are already running into problems, as evidenced by trouble at its Seattle operation. Other FHLB operations are also expected to run into problems with the next round of Option ARM resets. Together, the FHLB is about the size of Fannie or Freddie, and the story is similar—lax lending standards leading to a mountain of poorly performing loans.
- **FDIC**. Federal Deposit Insurance Corporation insures $6 trillion of bank deposits, and has exhausted its insurance fund of $60 billion on the 140 banks that they closed through the end of 2009. They have 400 more troubled banks on their list, and there are credible estimates that hundreds upon hundreds more banks will have to be closed. To fund their backing for depositors, the FDIC has asked banks to pay three years worth of insurance premiums up front, but at some point it will be necessary for the government to

step in and bail the FDIC out—probably with hundreds of billions of dollars.

- **PBGC**. The Pension Benefit Guarantee Corporation guarantees the pensions of companies if they go bankrupt. Because corporations used managed bankruptcies to shift their long-term pension obligations onto the back of the PBGC, this heavily abused entity is now effectively underwater. Expect them to join the crowd at the government trough before this crisis is over.

- **State Jobless Funds**. Around half of these state-operated funds, which are responsible for paying unemployment claims, are in trouble and are now actively borrowing from the Federal government to make up shortfalls. It has been estimated that the shortfalls in these funds are now approaching $90 billion.

- **Pension Funds for private and government workers.** Many of these funds used unrealistic projections for the returns they could earn on their investment portfolios. With stocks actually in the red over the last decade, the big returns they expected have turned to ashes. Their actuarial projections are still too rosy to be met, so we can expect that, faced with disgruntled pensioners, they'll turn to the government for support.

- **War without end.** The newest batch of 30,000 soldiers to be sent to Afghanistan will cost about $1 million each per year, adding $30 billion per year to the deficit. Private military contractors are about as big a number, so the total number of Americans in that blighted country could approach 200,000 if the war expands, all of which represents a huge ongoing cost.

As serious as all of these projected costs are, they pale compared to the $75 trillion of baby boomer bubble retirement obligations that will increasingly become due and payable.

In short, the country is already bankrupt. Adding in a new health-care program of gargantuan inefficiencies and expenditures guarantees government deficits expanding farther than can be managed. Where is the tipping point? Running a $1.5 trillion deficit to fund $3.5 trillion in government expenditures means the Federal government is now borrowing 40+ percent of the money it spends. As a highly-cautionary example: When that same ratio reached 60 percent in Weimar Germany, it lost complete control and a hyperinflation ensued. The result of these deficits will be a dollar debasement that will surprise most traditional economists and market analysts.

As I outlined in Chapter 2 on the Trade Deficit, the Achilles' heel of the United States is found in the huge international debt resulting from our accumulated trade deficit of $7 trillion. Within the next decade, and maybe even as soon as 2010, I expect one of the larger holders of U.S. debt to start heading for the exit. It could be a Middle Eastern oil state, Russia, China, or some other large holder who finds the reasons for dumping their dollars more compelling than continuing to hold them. Any significant hit to global confidence in the dollar could knock over the house of cards.

It's impossible to predict when such a widespread loss in confidence might occur, as there are vested interests that will work to prevent such a collapse. Yet, given there has never been anything close to the size of international debt that the United States has run up, a currency crisis is almost inevitable. Everyone knows that the only plausible way for the United States to meet its obligations is by debasing its currency. When a currency crisis occurs, it can happen very quickly, as the always-connected financial markets now move faster than ever, especially when a panic hits.

The Real Economy and Its Tepid Growth

As is the case with the government's fiscal problems, the root cause of the serious trouble I see ahead for the real economy is overleveraged debt, but in this case, in the private sector.

The striking increase in private debt over the last couple of decades allowed the economy to expand, even though wages didn't keep up with growth. The increase in debt was due, in large part, to the low interest rates engineered by the Fed in order to soften the blow from the bursting stock market bubble in 2000. The low rates then helped support the housing bubble. Today, even though both bubbles burst, they have not completely deflated—as we still have a lot of toxic waste mortgages hidden by banks not marking their loans to market value.

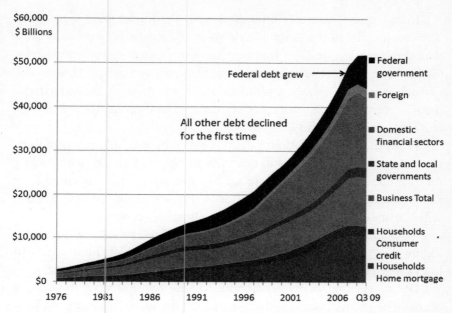

Figure 17.5 The Total of All U.S. Debt Stopped Growing Abruptly in 2009
SOURCE: Federal Reserve Z1 Report to Q3 2009.

Figure 17.5 shows the steady increase in all kinds of debt in the United States and the abrupt slowing for the private sector in 2009.

When debt is contracting, the economy slows. I do not see the floodgates of promiscuous lending opening any time soon. I do, however, see many defaults, foreclosures, and bankruptcies on the horizon. Despite the government's extreme stimulus and debt expansion, the private sector is still only moving ahead in the specific sectors where big government bailouts have made a difference.

For instance, the big banks have recovered from the brink of collapse because of a $700 billion TARP program and hundreds of billions of guarantees. The freefall in the housing market has been mitigated thanks to the $1.55 trillion intervention by the Fed in buying mortgage securities. Additional programs include those designed to provide incentives to first-time buyers, changes in regulations to allow banks to avoid writing down bad loans, and active efforts to keep interest rates low.

In the rest of the economy, however, we do not have a recovery. You can see that in the steep downturn in all categories of private sector debt shown in Figure 17.5. If it were not for the step up in Federal debt, there is no question the economy would have moved sharply downward. (Which would have been a good thing, in my view, as the sooner the misallocations of capital are recognized for what they are, the sooner the real economy can begin to recover.)

From the slowing in debt I deduce that jobs will only return slowly, meaning private spending will not increase. In the Go-Go years leading up to the crisis, consumers were willing and able to take on more debt to support spending and growth, but in the new reality private lending will continue to languish, resulting in a sluggish economy.

To confirm the relationship between GDP and private debt growth, Figure 17.6 compares annual growth rates, and shows them at record lows since 1976 with data through Q3 2009.

Before getting to my predictions for the coming year, there are a number of components that merit further discussion in order to keep things in context.

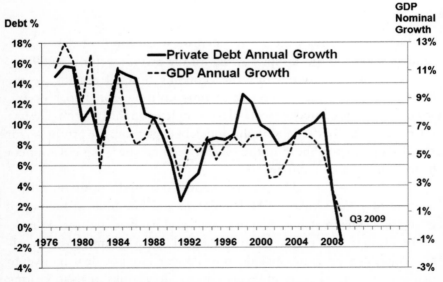

Figure 17.6 Growth in Private Debt Moves with GDP
SOURCE: Federal Reserve Z1 Report to Q3 2009.

Interest Rates

I have called rising interest rates the trade of the decade. Maybe I should be calling it the trade of the century. The basic point is that as more dollars are created and as they become less valuable, people making loans will want to charge higher interest rates to make up for the loss in purchasing power. Inflation will drive interest rates higher in the foreseeable future. The last runup in interest rates was a long one, from after World War II to the peak at 1980. I believe we hit bottom as of December 2008 with 10-year interest rates from the Treasury at 2.2 percent. In early 2010, we are already close to 4 percent, and I could easily see a 1 percent per year interest rate rise over the next decade. That would bring us only to 14 percent, which is still below the peak in 1980. I think the financial underpinnings of the dollar are far weaker now than they were when the world lost confidence in the dollar in the 1970s. This cycle is coming again and will be worse, in my opinion.

Higher interest rates are very bad for a government sitting on $12 trillion of debt, as ours is. When rates rise by 2 percent, the cost of servicing that debt rises by $240 billion a year, adding to the deficit and to the debt itself. If rates were to rise by 10 percent, as they did in the late-1970s, the additional cost would be $1.2 trillion annually, a clearly disruptive level. We aren't there yet, but just the possibility of such a scenario should be deeply concerning.

I think mortgage rates will rise above 6 percent by the end of 2010. With the Fed running out of the resources, and the political cover, to continue its extraordinary efforts in support of mortgage markets, it will be up to private lenders—and private buyers of the mortgage paper—to step in and fill the gaping hole. Simply, private lenders and purchasers of mortgage securities will demand a higher rate of return to cover their risks than was the case with the Fed, which was acting in concert with the administration to keep mortgage rates low. Private lenders and investors have no such incentive, and will only return to the market if they calculate the returns are worth the significant risk.

Figure 17.7 shows the Congressional Budget Office (CBO) estimate for interest rates. My own view is that rates will be higher still, but we agree on the direction and the history provides a useful perspective on rates: They are significantly lower today than they have been in decades.

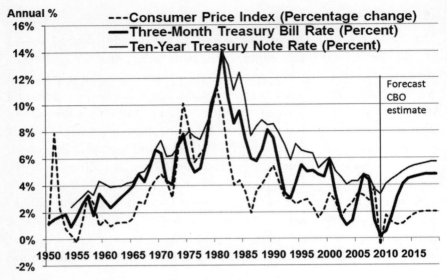

Figure 17.7   CBO Projects Interest Rates to Rise
SOURCE: Congressional Budget Office (CBO).

The absolute worst place to put money is any fixed-term investment that returns a specified number of dollars. That would be bonds, savings accounts, money markets, annuities, and being a lender in such things as mortgages.

There are investment vehicles to trade this directional change. The strongest is to use interest-rate futures to short any of the common interest-rate contracts. Be forewarned that this requires care because of the huge leverage, which creates huge profits but also huge losses for the overleveraged unsophisticated participant.

Employment

The United States labor force is not internationally competitive, so there aren't enough jobs to go around. Without incomes there isn't a source of funding to buy the products. For a while, during the housing bubble, households kept spending by extreme consumer borrowing, mostly against the rising price of their houses. But that has hit its limit.

To understand how serious the unemployment problem has become, consider that from a workforce of about 150 million, about 10 percent or 15 million people are now unemployed. To reduce that number by half would require creating 7.5 million new jobs. Just to keep up with population gains, however, the country needs to create on the order of 100,000 new jobs each month.

Let's assume that, in addition to the 100,000 new jobs needed each month to keep up with population growth, we could also create another 100,000 jobs per month—a total of 200,000 new jobs per month. In that optimistic scenario, cutting unemployment in half would still take 75 months, or $6\frac{1}{4}$ years.

It's worth noting that there has never been an extended period when the economy generated as many as 200,000 jobs per month.

The assumptions used to develop the forecasts in Figure 17.8 are a bit more complex than the preceding explanation, but reflect the same principles. The conclusion is that unemployment is likely to continue to rise and it will take years to get back to better days.

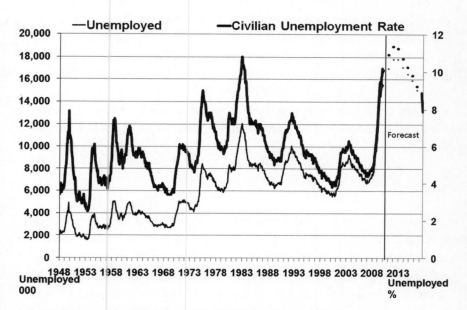

Figure 17.8   Unemployed and Unemployment Rate with Forecast
Source: Federal Reserve, author's calculations.

There are two other damaging effects of high unemployment:

1. The lack of individual income means lower taxes for the government.
2. The additional expense of paying unemployment insurance requires more government funds.

The combination makes the government deficit worse. And the losses from the lack of productive output mean that less wealth is being created, and that is lost forever. A relatively slow improvement in employment presents a serious long-term drag on the economy.

Energy Is Limited

A final input to my economic outlook has to do with the lack of sufficient new sources of oil. The world now uses 85 million barrels of oil a day, but is finding less than half of that in new fields. We are closing in on the point where we'll be unable to expand the use of oil as a source of energy. Meanwhile, the huge countries of India and China, among others, are expanding their energy consumption to levels that can't be supplied.

Relatively cheap energy has been the lifeblood of global economic growth and has supported population growth throughout the industrialization of the twentieth century. Over the decade ahead, the important economic input of energy prices will rise dramatically, causing a knock-on increase in the prices of many things, notably food, as it depends on energy.

Gold

The absolute premiere safety investment in a hyperinflationary environment is gold. Those of us who closely watch precious metals often call it the only "real money" (which is why I used that expression for the title of Chapter 15, which is devoted to gold). It isn't because gold is something so special that it merits reverence because it has some magical qualities. It's just that gold stays what it is. A relatively little amount of gold is added to the tradable supply each year from mining, and almost none is completely destroyed because it is so valuable that it is recovered and saved. It is a constant; when money systems collapse around the planet, gold will still be gold. I personally have a much higher proportion of investment in gold than I recommend to others. But this is absolutely a requirement for a portion of anyone's portfolio, and 10 percent would be small in my opinion.

Stocks

Shares in companies are the most important investment offering of all the large brokerage companies. Thus they tend to suggest which sectors to be in, and they never let you think about which ones will be collapsing or why you shouldn't be in stocks at all. For the last 10 years, the major aggregates of the stock market have remained basically unchanged. It has been a terrible investment. There have been winners, such as health care, and losers, most recently financials. But in general, in a slow economic-growth environment, stocks do not offer particularly good returns. Although the bubble has already burst, my opinion is that we are not yet at the bottom.

I'm not hugely negative, and I'm not hugely positive. There are specific sectors I like: energy because the demand to keep the population warm, fed, and mobile to get to work is continuing, even while fossil resources for energy are limited in the long term. (Peak Oil, covered in Chapter 11, is based on the idea that fossil fuels were laid down over millions of years and are being burned up in a couple of hundred years.) For the astute researcher, new green energy technologies have high-risk and high-return possibilities.

In addition, some of the best technologies in the biomedical area will eventually pay off. Some of the wonderful new communications systems and devices that now look like full computers but fit in a cell phone are a path to a wonderful new future for all of us. Agriculture is needed for us to survive, and prices are still low. And there are investments in gold mines that will do well as gold does well.

My model for valuing the stock market as a whole is to compare the earnings yield of stocks (earnings divided by price) to the 10-year Treasury note. If the return on stocks as identified by the earnings yield is higher than Treasuries, stocks are considered a good buy. When the earnings yield is lower, Treasuries are a better buy and stocks overvalued.

Figure 10.3 in Chapter 10 on stocks takes one additional step in estimating what the price of stocks should be, if their yield were the same as the 10-year Treasury. As you can see in that chart, around the year 2000 stocks were way overvalued. From 2003 to 2007 earnings were high and stocks were rising, but were still undervalued compared to earnings. The earnings crash that was worst in the fourth quarter of 2008 produced a big drop in the stock market.

Earnings have now recovered somewhat, and interest rates are still quite low, so that the current price of stocks is not overvalued. Analysts expect earnings to stay reasonably steady, but as I project interest rates to continue rising, my forecast results in a somewhat lower target price for the stock market over the next two years.

Thus, while I'm expecting a weak economy, and earnings that will probably be lower than expected by most analysts, I don't find myself projecting a particularly weak stock market.

Additionally, because I expect the dollar to drop, I also expect that the nominal price of everything will rise. It's a continuation of the paper scam the government has been running for decades. People may take comfort that the price of their stock portfolios or homes are stabilizing, in dollar terms . . . but viewed in terms of purchasing power, they'll be losing ground at an accelerating pace.

Commodities

There will be excellent returns on investments in commodities, most specifically agricultural items because the population continues to grow, and productivity per acre and per animal seems to be leveling off. In general, most agricultural commodities have lagged behind the prices of other aspects of our society because shortages were very local and abundance has kept prices low. The Green Revolution that produced much more yield per acre worked. But it seems that agricultural production may have trouble keeping up with shifts in lifestyle to higher forms of protein, as found in meat rather than rice, so that the long-term value of food should stay high and increase in price.

Industrial production that uses raw material commodities probably lags in price appreciation, but that will do well as a hedge against the dollar collapse. This becomes a trading vehicle, not a long-term invest-ment vehicle, and therefore has to be watched more closely.

Currencies

If the dollar collapses, an immediate logical reaction would be to look for another currency that might be traded against the dollar as a safer haven. Although the logic seems simple, a deeper look at other cur-rencies produces just as many gremlins as there are for the dollar. The preeminent alternative, the euro, is saddled with the political problems in that although there is a central bank that can manage the production and distribution of coins and paper, there isn't a central government that can manage the budget deficits and stimulus programs in a continent-wide coordinated way.

As my friend and great commentator Douglas Casey says, "The dollar is an IOU nothing" and the euro is a "Who owes you nothing?" It's not clear that the euro is more of a safe haven than the dollar, even though some statistics like trade-accumulated deficits of European nations make it appear to be on sounder ground.

Similarly, the Asian currencies would seem to offer an alternative. The Japanese yen is supported by the many wonderful products Japan produces. As the world buys Japanese products, the demand for Japanese yen is supported and Japan maintains a trade surplus. But that trade surplus has declined almost to zero.

The more damaging measure is that Japan's government has been trying to stimulate its economy for two decades and has run up a deficit of 180 percent of its GDP in doing so. Compare that to the U.S. deficit, which is closer to 75 percent of GDP. The United States is trying to catch up, but it's not clear that the Japanese yen is a safe haven, certainly with the spendthrift ways of the Japanese government (as reviewed extensively in Chapter 8).

The Chinese yuan will probably become a world tradable currency over the next decade, but confidence still has to be built. You would be betting on the Chinese government. About half the workers of that communist country work for the government, so it is also a gamble on the efficiency of a structure of big government. My experience is that it is easier for a country to come from behind by following the lead that has been provided by the developed countries, aided by stolen technology and using cheap labor, than it is to invent the future. I am bullish on China because I had a very positive view from my travels, but the Chinese will have their own difficulties, too. China depends on foreign exports for its prosperity. In the slowing financial economic environment, it's not clear that China's economy will be insulated from the world debacle. Being an exporter to the rest of the world, when the rest of the world collapses, China in a vulnerable position. China is taking big steps to stimulate domestic demand for its production to readjust that balance. China has a world-competitive manufacturing system and has created miracles, so it has a bright future as a nation. But China's currency may not be any safer than anybody else's. (Some data is shown in Chapter 9 on the monetary growth in China reaching 30 percent.)

World Stock Markets

If the U.S. stock market looks to be on shaky ground due to slow economic growth, the first obvious question stockbrokers ask is if there are other countries' stock markets that offer better prospects. Emerging markets did extremely well in the boom times, with the famous BRIC countries of Brazil, Russia, India, and China doing especially well.

Historical charts of world stock markets show a surprisingly similar pattern of fluctuations. It seems that the whole planet's economic system is interrelated and trends together. In a long-term view, there are no obvious immediate alternatives to the United States that could be considered safe. The additional disadvantage of foreign investment and stock markets is that the investor makes a double bet: first on the stock market of the other country, and then on the exchange rate of that currency.

Together, they can mean bigger returns, or getting one right and one wrong can mean pretty weak returns. The big picture view I have presented here is insufficient to select the particular world winners. But there are some intercontinental shifts, the most important being the ascendancy of Asia over the traditional dominance of what we have called western societies.

As the British passed the baton of world empire to the United States, the successive structural systems did not shift dramatically. But as Asia has risen as the economic power, first by the Japanese miracle and now by China and other Asian tigers, we can see well-coordinated economic plans combined with well-trained workers in a relatively compliant and productive role as excellent contributors to the productive capacity of the globe.

There is big risk that the world's manufacturing capacity has been overbuilt to such an extent that major automobile manufacturers, for example, are collapsing. The competitive edge of low-cost labor has destroyed most of the United States' traditional manufacturing strength. Going forward, it's likely to be the technological breakthroughs that give a country its important leading edge. The United States looks strong in this area and would be an area of investment for sophisticated investors who understand the technologies they're investing in.

Asia has understood the source of technological invention and focused its education toward engineering that can produce such results. The quantity of patents has grown in Asia. The United States has grown more lawyers, investment bankers, and politicians. Take Japan as an example: Its stock market, which traded to 38,000 at the peak entering 1990, is now trading at only 8,000. Certainly one of those two prices is wrong, and obviously the peak was much too high. But it may be that the current trough provides an opportunity to buy Japan "on sale." Similarly, the Chinese Shanghai stock shares grew to 6,000, then dropped below 2,000, and seem to be recovering nicely. Certainly 2,000 is a better price than 6,000 for essentially the same ownership of productive capacity. It can be expected that Asia will do well in the decade ahead. Therefore, China and Japan should both be on your radar list as opportunities.

Housing

Perhaps the most overanalyzed but misunderstood sector for investment has been housing. During the bubble that was fueled by extremely low interest rates fostered by Greenspan's cutting of the Federal Reserve rate when the rest of the economy was slowing, the common pronouncement was that real estate never falls.

Most observers at the local cocktail party would get around to how much the house down the street had just sold for, with a personal glee at how rich we now felt. Now with housing prices 40 percent off their peaks, people are no longer saying that real estate never drops. For years, the ability to buy houses with only 20 percent or 10 percent down created a leveraged play, where returns could be huge in the bull market. If the dollar decreases in value as my scenario suggests, housing will be a wonderful investment and basically be the common man's best anti-dollar play.

But the problem for housing is that we overbuilt compared to the demand, and the inventory of houses for sale is huge. Take a look at Japan, which had a real estate bubble that matched its stock market bubble up to the 1990s (as discussed in detail in Chapter 8). Japan's real estate has not even turned up over the last 19 years. Japan's experience suggests that a housing bubble burst can be with us for many years. It will be a while before speculating in housing can have a positive tailwind. My view is that it could be just a few years, say two or three, before housing turns around and becomes the anti-dollar play. It then becomes not so much an investment in housing as a *protection* against the inflation of the dollar, once it starts responding to the government bailouts.

Commercial Real Estate

Commercial real estate is waiting in the wings to follow the path already identified by housing: namely, it won't have the mortgage financial system structure to pass through new loans finding patsies to provide the funding for growth. Furthermore, in the United States, as businesses will no longer be expanding, one can be sure that the already overbuilt industrial complexes will be going on the auction block at lower and lower prices. It's simple: Beware commercial real estate and the related investment vehicle of REITs.

Reviewing the Scenario

Putting this scenario together requires information about when the current deflationary pressures will turn toward inflation. My guess is that in 2010, we will see a surprising rise in a number of traded assets, starting with interest rates, gold staying strong, and rising raw commodities like energy and food, with the more traditional investment asset classes like stocks and housing trailing behind by perhaps a couple of years. The guaranteed loser starting now and being confirmed in 2010 will be any fixed-income item such as corporate bonds or government debt. The environment of a slow economy will be with us for quite a while, particularly in the United States because manufacturing has been shipped abroad to Asia and elsewhere where labor is much cheaper. That productive capacity is not coming back.

Therefore, workers will be let go. If there are fewer workers, who will buy the goods to keep the businesses firing on all cylinders? We can expect a decline in the importance and wealth of the middle class whose major source of income came from the expanding jobs and economy. The rich, from Buffett to the million or so on top, have so much money that they could be giving it away and still not feel a change in lifestyle. The underclass, having nothing but getting caught for dealing drugs or whatever petty theft to survive, will find themselves in the revolving door of prison, welfare, and dissipation. Their incarceration is a burden on society's productivity. But we really have no place for bottom-skill rote workers. This picture does not work well for our society. It questions whether we should be changing priorities, particularly about concentration of wealth, but that would only happen if there is significant social unrest, which I think is highly unlikely in the next few years.

In summary, the trajectory ahead is bleak, with the economy either staying in the doldrums or, what I see as more probable, the financial system blowing up in an inflationary reaction to excessive debt creation. The policy of printing money to reverse the new reality of a deflated empire in which the United States has lost its status as the preeminent world competitor will fail. We have squandered our position of strength that started after World War II.

The most important lesson for individual investors is to find ways to protect themselves from the collapse of financial assets, such as holding money market funds, corporate bonds, government treasuries, retirement annuities, or plain old bank accounts. Instead, *buy gold*. Look for opportunities in energy. Identify the leading technologies of the future. And, be aware of real estate's potential recovery in future years.

International Currency Crisis

At the opening of the decade in 2010 we face a new surprise on our horizon: A potential currency crisis. The symptoms are popping up as surprises around the planet. The most prominent is the crisis in Greece related to the question of the potential weakness of the European currency, the euro. Dubai World default is rumored to potentially cost investors 40 percent. Venezuela has devalued by 50 percent. Vietnam devalued twice. Debt levels in Ireland Portugal, and Italy are discussed as dangers to the euro. Japan's new government talked of intervening to weaken its exchange rate.

All these news stories are merely symptoms. We are entering the next logical stage from a Credit Crisis to a Currency Crisis. By now we understand the steps of a banking crisis: It starts with too much debt. Banks made loans to anybody and everybody running up leverage that was dangerous, creating risk that led in some cases to their own self-destruction. It was foolishly said at the outset by our leaders that the problems were small or "contained." They obviously weren't small. The response was a firehose of government debt to bail out private banks and industries by taking on their toxic waste. It did not solve the problem. It moved to a new home. With the government taking over Fannie Mae, Freddie Mac, General Motors, and Chrysler, the problems are still with us, but now in the government's hands. The result of the stimulus was to see stocks recover and risky interest rates decline across the globe.

The problems of a credit crisis can be foreseen when we get too much debt and too much leverage in financial institutions. Too much debt eventually leads to an explosion. It was predictable, if not exactly when. It was not just a subprime crisis. It was an endemic overleveraging of all kinds of debt in our economy. The crisis eventually occurs when investors and the depositors lose confidence and we get a "run on the bank" as everybody wants their money back. Bondholders fear they will not be paid off and depositors lose confidence. Absent specific government bailout, investors are wiped out and depositors have to be made whole through a government takeover.

So what is happening now with all the symptoms mentioned above? It's a similar process for governments: when they take on too much debt, there is a loss of confidence in the government's ability to pay the debt back. That's what's happening in Greece, Dubai, and Venezuela; and is being worried about in Portugal, Spain, and Italy. The same thing happens to a government with its currency and debt as happens to a bank with its depositors and bondholders: When confidence is lost there is a run on the currency. Confidence is a result of many psychological factors, but it is the same for banks and governments: when fears arise that the debt is too big to be paid back, investors and lenders all rush to the exits together. That is when we see a crisis. A currency crisis for a country has a few more dimensions and one leading indicator that a credit crisis does not have. The leading indicator is a credit crisis as that often leads to a currency crisis. That is because government bailouts add to the deficit which adds to the loss of confidence in the currency. Trade balances that run up international debt are a serious indicator of problems for a currency. Government debt to its own citizens is not as onerous but too much debt is similar to both crises.

The importance of this is that we are not through the storm of settling world international imbalances. As the panic in the banking system has now been ameliorated by excessive government issues of new credit, the loss of confidence has been moved to the governments and central banks that have taken over the responsibility for so many private-sector risks. The opportunity for investors is then to figure out which government issues of currency and debt are more vulnerable to loss of confidence than others. The following sections fill in the news around these currency warning signs.

Greece

The financial markets awoke to the problems of a Greek tragedy when we saw the interest rate on Greek debt soar to double what it was in the strong countries of the euro currency regime. Although Greece uses the same euro as the other nations of the common currency, investors worried about the continually increasing Greek deficits and demanded higher interest rates to compensate for the growing risk. The risk is not in the purchasing power of the euro which is supported by all the member countries; It is the risk that the Greek government may not be able to pay off the debt. A precise measure is the cost of insurance against default as measured by the Credit Default Swap (CDS) that showed a crisis was brewing. As of this writing the European leaders have not articulated how or in what measure it would offer support to the Athens government to return to more normal interest rate spreads and to manage their large deficits. The stronger countries have demanded austerity programs and the Greek response has not been considered sufficient. In the recently published book *This Time is Different* by Reinhart and Rogoff, it is pointed out that Greece has been in default or rescheduling for 50 percent of the years since 1800. In other words their track record is atrocious. The problem for the stronger countries of the euro is that they see similar problems in the other peripheral countries: Portugal, Italy, Ireland, and Spain. While bailing out the economy of a country that represents only 3 percent of the Eurozone and has only 11 million people, would seem within the financial capabilities of the stronger countries, bailing out everybody who has a problem is clearly beyond their capabilities and desires.

The fundamental problem of the structure of the euro is that while there is a central bank to issue the currency, the political decisions for fiscal policy (spending and taxing) by governments are separately decided in the individual countries and do not necessarily align with the goals and desires of the single currency issued by the single European Common Bank. My conclusion is that the differences are important enough politically that the problems will not be solved except by separating out the weaker countries with either their own second-tier of currency or by their returning to their own national currency. Even if this is not done, the combined difficulties that will go back and forth over the months and few years ahead lead me to believe that the euro as a currency is damaged enough to fall in value compared to the dollar as a safer base. The United States has too much debt but it is only one government so it can coordinate fiscal and monetary policy.

Dubai

When I traveled through Dubai I was incredibly impressed at the sparkling new buildings and massive amount of construction. But I felt it was a bubble that would burst. Even with Abu Dhabi backing, the negotiations of how to handle debt that was too large are leading to the expectation of perhaps a 40 percent haircut for the value of the bonds of this country's huge construction conglomerate, Dubai World. Obviously, world slowing and oil price declines affected the prognosis for permanent growth that brought the bubble over its peak. This hubris can be seen in the world's tallest building that is now being temporarily

closed for reasons that may be as little as technical problems with eleva-
tors, or huge vacancy that can't be justified. It's hard to guess how Dubai
World debt will be resolved, but the close ties to the government add to
the perceived sovereign risk.

Japan

Japan has been a close partner with the United States and as the world's
second-largest economy and second-largest holder of U.S. government
debt is closely linked with our own economic success. Their stock
market is selling at 75 percent off their peak. They face an extremely
difficult aging population where the percentage of population over 65
will grow to almost double the United States to almost 40 percent of the
population by 2050. This burden cannot be ignored. The two decades
of no growth in GDP since their stock market and real estate bubble
peak in 1990 avoided the kind of depression that the United States took
on in the 1930s, by their government taking on debt now amounting
to 180 percent of GDP – the worst of the developed nations. The risk
from too much debt could lead to interest rate rising or yen weakening.
A weaker yen could support stock prices.

China

China is a bubble that hasn't burst. Paraphrasing a hedge fund investor,
I suggest that "Perspicacity is to avoid investing in overcapacity". The
China situation feels reminiscent of the Japanese bubble in 1989. While
many naysayers about China's growth have been proven wrong over
the last two decades, I think China is now more vulnerable than their
government statistics are telling us. With high-rise buildings, shopping
centers and industrial plants showing 20 percent vacancy, they have built
way beyond their needs and beyond the world need for more export
production. As an export oriented economy, China is dependent upon
the success of the rest of the world to buy their goods. Even though as
a $4.9 trillion economy they represent almost 10 percent of the world
economy, they are importing something like 50 percent of the traded
capacity of many raw materials like copper, cement, steel, aluminum and
have actively been buying up materials suppliers throughout the globe.

China has done what no other nation has done. With the aggressive support of government, the use of joint ventures to obtain intellectual property ideas for productivity, and using its cheap educated labor to compete in the world export markets, they have outdone what Japan did in the 1980s. China is a strong, growing and powerful nation, but the trajectory is a bit ahead of itself for now.

The investment question is what the Chinese government will do now that it has created an even bigger bailout as a percentage of GDP than the United States or any of the other countries that have been fighting economic slowdown. Chinese money supply grew by a little almost 30 percent last year. Government stimulus and banking induced loans have created 10 percent GDP growth in Q4 2009. I think there is a disconnect between the extreme growth rate of China, and the future of what I think will be a slowing world economy with more limited borrowing and spending by consumers that will slow Chinese exports.

As the world's biggest holder of U.S. government debt, the question is whether they will continue to acquire Treasuries as they have. Chinese leaders have publicly said they plan to rebalance away from the dollar. It is my belief that as the United States balks at so many Chinese imports hurting jobs in the U.S., and as China imposes restrictions on companies operating in China as it did with Google, that there will be increasing friction between our nations. The relationship will not be destroyed but it will be ratcheted down in importance in the economic slowing ahead. As the Chinese recognize that the U.S. government will be tightening its monetary policy to protect from dollar declines, China will be applying its own economic brakes through raising their bank's reserve requirements and probably letting their currency rise in world exchange markets. That will not be good for Chinese exports but it may allow for consumer expansion within China. If China slows its purchases of our government Treasuries that decreases the quantity of available funds in our credit market, and could lead to higher interest rates on our Treasuries.

Multinational Currency Analysis

Currency investment is something like a beauty contest in that it is both subjective, as well as measurable in comparative statistics of government

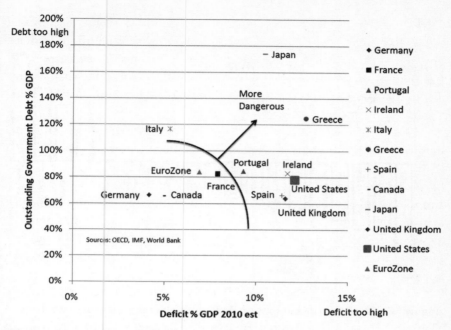

Figure 17.9   Debt and Deficits Are Too High for Many Countries

and international debt. Figure 17.9 shows the relative government debt outstanding and the growth in the deficit in the most recent year for a number of countries being discussed. If a country has too much debt, it risks a loss of confidence in its ability to pay off that debt. The vertical axis is the accumulated amount of government debt, and the horizontal axis is the deficit in the latest year where data is available, reflecting mostly 2010 estimates. Japan stands out after its two decades of extreme government spending to appear weak in this comparative analysis. In looking at the government deficit as a percent of GDP we can see that Greece at 12.7 percent of GDP is one of the worst on the scale toward the right of the chart. While the United States has not accumulated as serious a debt as either Greece or Japan, the deficit percentage of GDP is dangerously near the limit that caused other countries to lose confidence.

Another view of relative currency strength can be derived from the net international investment position of countries. Countries that accumulate trade surpluses have an inherent strength. Figure 17.10 shows

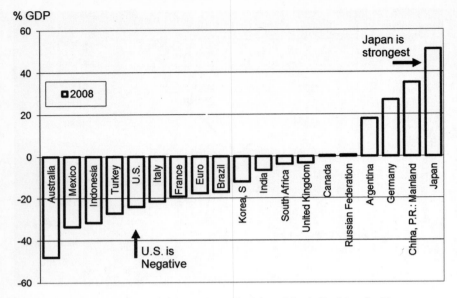

Figure 17.10   International Investment Position, Net is Positive for Exporters

how Japan, despite its very big government deficits, still maintains a very strong currency. Over the years its trade surpluses provided demand for its currency to buy Japan's products. The chart shows the net international investment position with the large exporters enjoying a cushion of strength. By contrast, the United States position as net debtor to the world is a weakness. These numbers are normalized by dividing the investment amount by GDP to give a relative comparison number that corrects for the size of the country. The United States is the world's largest debtor.

Investment Implications of these International Forces

The increases in government debt in most all countries from stimulating economies and bailing out banks will be reflected next in currency market surprises. The deficits make currencies vulnerable to downward valuation compared to hard assets. I see continuing political cracks that hurt the euro more than the dollar. In the overall shift of production to

Asia I am more optimistic about investments there than in the United States. The biggest investment opportunity I see is to expect Japanese interest rates to rise from their multi-decade lows to return to more typical world levels and to reflect the realities of their big government debt. At the same time, I think of Japanese stocks as an investment opportunity because of their 75 percent discount from the 1990 highs. I'm concerned that China, despite using its financial success to build its long-term importance in world affairs, has over invested and its over capacity will not be well managed by a government more interested in maintaining power than producing profits. I believe it is not a reliable place for investment at this time.

Governments are not limited in their ability to run their printing presses, so I believe it is better to invest in the hard assets of commodities that have been the focus of my analysis. Risk premiums will rise with defaults and weaknesses in currencies. I expect world interest rates to rise to compensate for the bigger risks.

Predictions

Before sharing my projections for 2010, I will review my 2009 projections from a talk I made on January 10, 2009, to the TradeStation User Group in Los Gatos, California. They are displayed in Figure 17.11. Many of the actual results are shown in the first column of Table 17.1 for 2010 predictions.

I'm especially proud of correctly predicting the big move in crude oil back to $80, the $1,150 on gold, the 4 percent for the 10-year Treasury, the large expansion of the government deficit, and the drop in the trade deficit. Unemployment at 9.5 percent was very close to the 10 percent actual considering we started the year at 6.5 percent. The figures are not yet completely in for GDP, but I predicted the poor performance.

I also correctly forecasted that the Fed funds rate would remain flat for the year. I didn't think the dollar would completely collapse, but that other currencies would be stronger. While I predicted stocks would fall to 800 on the S&P 500, they actually fell to a low of 666 and then rose by the end of the year, so I can't take credit for that prediction. As part

Bud Conrad's Prediction for 2009

Summary year-end est.	Actual	Bud's Est.
Prepared 10 2008	2008	2009
Stocks: S&P 500 dipping more	903	800
Crude returns higher	$45	$80
Gold rises	$884	$1150
Fed Cuts to stimulate	0-.25%	0-.25%
10 Yr treasury rises	2.2%	4%
Corn rises	4.10	4.80
Euro stays with $	130	130
Yen rises more	91	90
GDP: Slowing with consumer tapped out	-.5%	-5%
Earnings decrease in recession (operating)	-18%	-20%
Government deficit rises. slow economy, stimulus $200B	$455B	$2,000B
Trade balance (CA) Slowing economy	-$738B	-$500
Housing prices drop 15% across US	-18%	-15%
Unemployment rises	6.5%	9.5%

Economy slows. Deflation in First half is replaced by Inflation. Currency weakens as gold and oil rise. Stocks dip from weaker recession

Figure 17.11   Bud Conrad's Predictions for 2009
SOURCE: Author's calculations.

of the stock analysis, I did not expect to see the earnings hold up as well as they did, thanks to government accounting changes and direct support. Corn rose and fell but was basically flat on the year, so that was not a good call. The summary of the general direction at the bottom was right. Overall this set of predictions was more than acceptable, as these things go, with 12 out of 15 or 80 percent correct. That will be a hard act to follow for 2010.

Predictions for 2010

No sugarcoating it; 2010 worries me.

In most of my prior analysis and projections, I felt generally confident that I understood the important forces at work in the economy and key investment markets. For example, I correctly predicted the housing bubble would burst. I saw it starting with the subprime sector and knew Bernanke and Paulson were dead wrong saying that the situation was "contained." I also correctly understood that the government would apply massive bailouts to these problems. While I thought that would result in a little more price inflation in the second half of 2009 than we saw, timing the arrival of price inflation is always difficult. Even so, going into 2009 I felt I had a firm finger on the pulse of things.

Today, however, the consensus view for 2010 is so different from my own analysis that I worry I may be off base. And while not reflected in the numbers following, I worry about potential big problems that could trigger a dramatically more negative outcome for the economy. Of those outlier scenarios, the one that worries me most is a catastrophic loss of confidence in the dollar, especially by foreigners, that triggers a "run on the dollar." That would, in turn, limit the size of further government bailouts, and send interest rates ratcheting higher, causing more extreme damage to equity and housing markets.

However, one has to draw a line in the sand, and so my base case, stated in Table 17.1, assumes that we'll witness a relatively "normal" scenario over the coming year. My basic story is that we'll have mild but increasing inflation that will push interest rates higher, putting downward pressure on the price of bonds and making the government's deficits even worse. Higher rates will also not be helpful to stocks. A lot is riding on this major shift, that hardly anyone else seems to expect.

On the real economy, the consensus view is that we are already in a recovery and that things will do well in 2010. I'm afraid I'm on the fringe by suggesting that our recession is still continuing. I don't call it a W-shape, or double dip recovery; instead, I remain convinced that we are in a multiyear slump. In contrast to my views, the traditional brokerage house analysts take the conventional approach of assuming the economy will follow the usual pattern of regular four-year business cycles, experiencing a normal recovery in 2010.

I believe we could have years of lackluster economic growth ahead of us, in a fashion not unlike the decade after the 1929 crash, or Japan after the bursting of that country's financial/housing bubble (as discussed in Chapters 7 and 8). But, given the extreme government deficits and Federal Reserve monetary expansion, we also have to allow for the possibility of a dollar crisis. While that may be an extreme scenario, at the least I expect to see inflation on the rise for many years. With the government's debasement of the currency, an inflationary result should not come as a surprise to anyone—but will be.

My generally pessimistic outlook is shaped to some extent by the recognition that the dominating forces behind the current weakness were built up over decades and are intertwined with systematic challenges pertaining to a late-stage empire. Those challenges include expensive wars to maintain global status, and unsupported spending on "bread and circuses" designed to mollify the citizenry.

The numbers in Table 17.1 speak for themselves, and include five "Foundation Forces" pertaining to fundamental economic measures.

I expect the budget deficit to stay as high in 2010 as it was in 2009, because the government believes it is improving the economy by its spending. I don't believe it will be particularly helpful, and that GDP will decline. Inflation rising to 5 percent will drive many other items in the next section called "Investment Predictions."

I am not as negative on the stock market as I thought I would be, before looking at the numbers. Even so, my prediction of a stock market drop of 10 percent is decidedly less optimistic than the mainstream view. That said, I'm a little uncomfortable with that particular forecast, because if there is high inflation, stock prices could rise in nominal terms, even if in real dollars the purchasing power of stocks did not rise.

I also have concerns about my forecast for housing prices. While housing prices are now much more affordable, obtaining financing is still difficult. The biggest problem for housing is the overhang of many new delinquencies that have not yet turned into foreclosures, as banks have held back on removing people from their homes. It is called a stealth supply. And so rising prices are not likely.

While I am negative on the dollar, I am also negative on most of the currencies of the world. Most people are well aware of the egregious Federal Reserve actions in the United States, but not that similar actions have been taken by the ECB and the Bank of England. China has taken even bigger actions. So while I see the dollar declining in small amounts against other currencies, I see all fiat currencies declining against the real money, gold.

A Short-Term Snapshot

To get a picture of the short-term direction, Table 17.1 offers a view of where important components of the economy and several investment

Table 17.1   Bud Conrad's Predictions for 2010

	Dec 31, 2009	Change	1 Year Out
Foundation Forces			
GDP Q3 '09 (Real 2005 $B)	$12,973	−2.0%	$12,714
Budget Deficit (B)	$ 1,433		$ 1,500
Current Account Deficit (B)	$ 432	10%	$ 475
Unemployment %	10%	1%	11%
CPI	1.8%	3.2%	5.0%
Investment Predictions			
Gold	$ 1,097	23%	$ 1,350
10-Year Treasury	3.83%	+1.2%	5.0%
Fed Funds	0.12%	+1.1%	1.2%
Energy Crude $/bbl	$ 80	15%	$ 92
Nat Gas $/M btu	$ 5.53	15%	$ 6.30
Commodity Prices (CRB)	284	15%	325
Stock Market (S&P 500)	1,115	−10%	1000
Dollar Index	78	−10%	70
Nikkei 225	10,707	7%	11,500
Euro	1.43	−12%	1.25
Japan Gov Bond	1.25%	.75%	2%
Housing Price (Case Shiller)	156	−7%	145

SOURCE: Author's calculations.

measures may move by the end of 2010. This is not to be taken as a specific prediction so much as to provide my opinion of the direction these important economic indicators and investable items will take.

Overall, my outlook for 2010 is still pretty negative, even if it is only half as bad as I think things could get. That's why I recommend buying gold to protect against serious weakness in the dollar, energy-related investments as we are running out of cheap energy, agriculture as food will become more expensive if energy rises, and inverse interest-rate vehicles to profit from rising rates, my play of the decade.

And so we come to the end of this literary and academic odyssey. I've gone beyond the normal depth to dig up data to support my view that the current economic crisis is extremely serious and that the ramifications of currency collapse will be with us for many years. The term *singularity* is used to denote events that are entirely new. Although hyperinflationary destruction of a currency is not completely new, it will be a surprise to most Americans. So I hope that, beyond just my comparatively short-term investment recommendations, you understand enough of how the system works that you will be able to apply your own analysis to see how close we move to the cliff of major restructuring.

For the most part, I've left out political commentary except where the results become financial measures, such as in the federal budget deficit. But let me add two thoughts: I don't think we've been picking wise leaders since President Kennedy was assassinated. I have a bias to mistrust our expanding governance, so I do not have confidence that actions being taken will fix problems, but rather will make things worse. And the second point is that if economic systems do move toward collapse, often political upheaval is concomitant. That is not a prediction, and it is the opposite of my hope. Politics is an area of importance to our lives, and it should be part of your analysis for investing.

So this ends the journey. I hope I've given you some useful insights into how the world financial system will evolve. I add this minor caveat: Because I sit on the other side of the curtain offering my ideas, I also know that I have feet of clay and do not have all the answers. It's important to use your own resources to bolster my ideas and others' when you to come to your final investment decisions. But you already knew that, and if you've gotten this far reading through my story, you've taken a big step to understanding how our complicated world is put together.

List of Tables
and Figures

421

About the Author

Bud Conrad is the Chief Economist at Casey Research. He writes extensively for the thousands of subscribers to the financial newsletters of Casey Research focusing on the economy, gold, mining stocks, energy, interest rates, agriculture, and foreign investments. He has been a futures investor for twenty-five years, as well as a full-time investor for more than a decade. He holds an MBA from Harvard and an Electrical Engineering Degree from Yale. He has held positions with IBM, CDC, Amdahl, and Tandem.

Bud Conrad's comprehensive picture of the world's economy is based on a career of using long-term fundamental analysis to explain how this crisis arose and where it will evolve to. He uses insights learned from his engineering training to interpret how the investment cycles affect our economy. Mr. Conrad's predictions for 2008 were 80 percent correct. As early as 2006 he predicted the credit crisis and the massive bailouts by the government. Containing 260 figures and tables, this book reflects his devotion to looking at the data. This becomes reference material for students of the market. He has developed models that explain the dynamic feedback loops that make markets swing farther than what static economic models predict.

Bud Conrad is not just an academic but also an investor and therefore bridges both the details of economic analysis and making investment calls. The analysis is deep, but the lessons are simple. A casual reading of his predictions and recommendations will help you invest. A deeper look at the insights of long-term structural and fundamentals provide lessons for a lifetime in which to make your own investment decisions. You need to understand what he has to say to protect your wealth. The monetary systems are in disarray because they are based on a collapsing dollar which is no longer based on gold. Once you understand the basics of what this book lays out in clear detail with lots of evidence, you will be able to protect yourself from a government gone wild.

Conrad served as a local board member of the National Association for Business Economics and taught graduate courses in investing at Golden Gate University.

A popular speaker, he has delivered talks in New Zealand, Dubai, New York, Vancouver, Denver, Phoenix, Las Vegas, San Francisco, Los Angeles and Chicago. He has appeared on CNBC with Maria Bartiromo, Fox Business News with Stewart Varney, and others and has commented in many publications from the *Wall Street Journal* to *Reuters*.

Index

431